JOHN LINGARD

THE
HISTORY AND ANTIQUITIES
OF THE
ANGLO-SAXON CHURCH;
CONTAINING
AN ACCOUNT OF ITS ORIGIN,
GOVERNMENT, DOCTRINES, WORSHIP, REVENUES,
AND
CLERICAL AND MONASTIC INSTITUTIONS

VOLUME I

Elibron Classics
www.elibron.com

Elibron Classics series.

© 2005 Adamant Media Corporation.

ISBN 1-4021-7364-4 (paperback)
ISBN 1-4021-0115-5 (hardcover)

This Elibron Classics Replica Edition is an unabridged facsimile
of the edition published in 1845 by C. Dolman,
London.

THE

HISTORY AND ANTIQUITIES

OF THE

ANGLO-SAXON CHURCH.

———

VOL. I.

THE

HISTORY AND ANTIQUITIES

OF THE

ANGLO-SAXON CHURCH;

CONTAINING

AN ACCOUNT OF ITS ORIGIN,

GOVERNMENT, DOCTRINES, WORSHIP, REVENUES,

AND

CLERICAL AND MONASTIC INSTITUTIONS.

BY JOHN LINGARD, D.D.

IN TWO VOLUMES.

VOL. I.

LONDON:

C. DOLMAN, 61, NEW BOND STREET.

1845.

Printed by J. & H. COX, BROTHERS (LATE COX & SONS),
74 & 75, Great Queen-street, Lincoln's-Inn Fields.

PREFACE.

In 1806 I published, at Newcastle, a work in two volumes, with the title of "Antiquities of the Anglo-Saxon Church;" which four years later was reprinted at the same place, in one volume of a larger size. Both editions, being small, were speedily exhausted. More than thirty years have since elapsed; during which time the labours of several distinguished scholars, natives and foreigners, have done much to elucidate the Anglo-Saxon portion of our history. The treasures of our libraries have been explored; and documents, previously unknown, have been brought to light: new and improved editions of the works of our ancient writers have been given both in the Latin and the vernacular language; and the laws civil and ecclesiastical of our Anglo-Saxon ancestors, their charters, poems, homilies and correspondence, have been collected and published, some for the first time, and others in a new and more correct form. When, therefore, I lately turned my thoughts to a third edition of the "Antiquities," it immediately occurred to me, to avail myself of the additional helps offered by the present improved state of Anglo-Saxon literature; and the consequence has been, that I have enlarged the original plan, and recast the entire work: so that these volumes, while they include the substance of the former, will also contain a very large portion of new, and I trust, interesting matter. With the same view I have added to each volume a collection of notes, some of them of considerable length, appertaining to subjects, which I was unwilling on the one hand to pass by without notice, and which on the other I could not conveniently treat in the context, with that minuteness which their importance demanded.

The Anglo-Saxons, when they first landed on our shores, were hordes of ferocious pirates: by religion they were reclaimed from savage life, and taught to admire and practise the virtues of the Gospel. It is the object of these pages to exhibit that religion before the eyes of the reader; to describe to him the Anglo-Saxon church, its constitution, laws, and polity; its doctrines, sacraments, and daily service; the sources from which it derived its revenues, and the duties which it required from its prelates and working clergy; the discipline and literature of its clerical and monastic bodies, and the events which chiefly contributed to establish and confirm its influence with the people. Such subjects have always charms for an inquisitive mind; they will be doubly attractive to those, whose attention has been directed by recent circumstances to the habits of religious thought and the forms of religious worship prevalent in the mediæval ages.

In the discussion of several of these questions, it will sometimes fall to my lot to notice what I may conceive to be misstatements on the part of preceding writers; an unpleasant and ungracious task, but at the same time, in my opinion, an imperative duty, as often as matters of high importance are concerned. On most literary subjects the public mind is guided by the wisdom or prejudices of a few favourite writers, whose reputation consecrates their opinions, and whose errors are often received by the incautious reader for truths. In such cases, to be silent is criminal; for it helps to perpetuate deception; and at the same time to contradict merely without attempting to prove, may create doubt, but will not enforce conviction. Hence it becomes necessary for the writer to point out the sources from which he derives his information, to fortify his own narrative with quotations from ancient documents, and to shew that the contrary statement is not consistent with the original authorities. Controversy of this description will occasionally occur in the present volumes, but will be found chiefly in the notes at the conclusion, and will be confined entirely to historical questions. With the truth or falsehood of doctrine the following pages have no concern ; their object is to discover and to establish facts.

The records of Anglo-Saxon antiquity have come to us at the distance of so many centuries, in a very imperfect and mutilated state. Hence it will necessarily happen that, while with respect to several of the subjects which I have undertaken to treat, we possess full and satisfactory evidence, yet with respect to others, our means of information may be very scanty, and our knowledge very incomplete. When this is so, all that can be expected from the writer is, that he push his researches in every available quarter, and collect the scattered fragments to the best of his ability. So much I have endeavoured to do, but occasionally, I must own, with very little success : the industry of future inquirers will, I hope, prove more fortunate.

HORNBY,
December, 1844.

CONTENTS OF VOL. 1.

CHAPTER I.

CONVERSION OF THE BRITONS AND SAXONS.

The gospel preached in Britain—Conversion of Lucius—Persecution—Martyrdom of St. Alban—Pelagianism—Mission of
Germanus and Lupus—Gildas—State of the British church—
Conquests by the Saxons—Mission of St. Augustine—Conversion of Ethelbert of Kent—of Edwin and Oswald of Northumbria — Mission of St. Aidan — Conversion of the several
Saxon tribes—Conduct of the missionaries—Controversy
respecting the form of the tonsure—and the time of Easter
—Conference at Whitby—The withdrawal of the Scottish
monks—All the British Christians adopt the Catholic computation of Easter.

CHAPTER II.

SUCCESSION AND DUTIES OF BISHOPS.

Augustine is consecrated bishop—All the churches of the Saxons, and of the Britons, subjected to his authority—His conference with the Britons—They reject his demands—Monks of Benchor slaughtered—Theodore archbishop of Britain—Egbert archbishop of York—Archbishopric of Lichfield established —and abolished — Multiplication of bishoprics— Election of bishops—Spiritual and secular duties of bishops.

CHAPTER III.

CHURCH GOVERNMENT.

Diocesan synods—Provincial and national councils—Papal authority—Pope establishes metropolitan sees—Confirms metropolitans — Inquires into doctrine and discipline—Council at
Cloveshoe by his order—Legates prescribe laws of reform—He
receives appeals—History of Wilfrid—Wilfrid's first appeal—
His second appeal.

CHAPTER IV.

ANGLO-SAXON CLERGY.

Origin of Clergy—of monks—Union of both professions— Roman—Scottish missionaries—their progress—Origin of parish churches—Education of clergy—Duties of parish priests—Celibacy—Endowments of parish churches—Lands— Offerings—Tithes—Other church dues.

CHAPTER V.

ANGLO-SAXON MONKS.

Monks of St. Gregory—of St. Columba—of St. Benedict—
His rule—Convents of religious women—Double convents—
Monastic vows —Obedience—Chastity—Poverty—Mitigation
of rule—Adoption of secular dress—Superfluous visits, &c.—
Conversion of monks into canons.

CHAPTER VI.

DONATIONS TO THE CHURCH.

Lands bestowed on churches—Services to which lands were subject—No exemption from one class of services — Frequent
exemption from others—Additional enfranchisement by King
Ethelwulf—Causes tending to the enrichment, and others to
the depauperisation, of the church—Charges brought against
the clergy and monks—The use which they made of their

wealth—The right of sanctuary—The peace of the church—
Donations to foreign churches—Romescot.

CHAPTER VII.

RELIGIOUS WORSHIP.

The Liturgy— Celebration of the mass—General conformity of
the Roman and Scottish Ritual—The former universally
adopted—The course and canonical hours of public prayer—
Psalmody—Observance of the Sunday—of holidays—Private
prayer for morning and evening—Baptism of adults—of
infants—Confirmation—Communion—Times for communion—
Penance—Confession—Penitential canons—Commutation of
Penance—Public and private penance.

NOTES.

N.B. The day " on which Christ overcame the Devil," mentioned in p. 314, note 1, was kept on the 15th of February.

THE

HISTORY AND ANTIQUITIES

OF THE

ANGLO-SAXON CHURCH.

CHAPTER I.

CONVERSION OF THE BRITONS AND SAXONS.

THE GOSPEL PREACHED IN BRITAIN—CONVERSION OF LUCIUS—PERSE-
CUTION—MARTYRDOM OF ST. ALBAN—PELAGIANISM—MISSION OF GER-
MANUS AND LUPUS—GILDAS—STATE OF THE BRITISH CHURCH—CON-
QUESTS BY THE SAXONS—MISSION OF ST. AUGUSTINE—CONVERSION OF
ETHELBERT OF KENT—OF EDWIN AND OSWALD OF NORTHUMBRIA—MIS-
SION OF ST. AIDAN—CONVERSION OF THE SEVERAL SAXON TRIBES—
CONDUCT OF THE MISSIONARIES—CONTROVERSY RESPECTING THE FORM
OF THE TONSURE—AND THE TIME OF EASTER—CONFERENCE AT
WHITBY—THE WITHDRAWAL OF THE SCOTTISH MONKS—ALL THE
BRITISH CHRISTIANS ADOPT THE CATHOLIC COMPUTATION OF EASTER.

IT has been maintained with great parade of quotation and equal confidence of assertion that,
at a very early period, a Christian church was established by one of the apostles in Britain. But this
opinion, most improbable of itself, is totally unsup-
ported by proof, and rests on no other ground than
the forced and fanciful interpretation of a few ambiguous passages in ancient writers.

We are, indeed, told, that history has preserved
the names of two British females, Claudia and Pom-
ponia Græcina, both of them Christians, and both

living in the first century of our era. The scripture informs us that Claudia, the wife of Pudens, at Rome, was a Christian;[1] Martial, that Claudia, the wife of the senator Pudens, was a Briton;[2] and it must be confessed that the coincidence is striking, and the inference probable. The claim of Græcina is more feebly supported. She is supposed to have been a Briton, because her husband Plautus had governed Britain, and a Christian, because she was accused before the senate of practising some foreign superstition.[3] Yet if all this be granted, much will still be wanting to prove the establishment of a church in the island; because both Claudia and Græcina may have embraced Christianity in Rome, where we find them living at the time when we become acquainted with them.[4]

It was about the year 43 that the Roman power obtained a permanent footing in Britain, from which period there must have been a constant communication between the provincial government and the imperial court, and an annual influx of strangers into the island, increasing in proportion as the Romans extended their conquests. From some of these, already proselytes to the new faith, it is probable that the Christian doctrines were silently disseminated among the natives; but the earliest notice which we find of a British church, occurs in the writings of Beda, the Anglo-Saxon, by whom we are informed, that during the reign of the Emperor

---

[1] 2 Tim. iv. 21.

[2] Claudia, Rufe, meo nubit peregrina Pudenti—
Claudia cæruleis cum sit Rufina Britannis
Edita—   *Mart. Epig.* iv. 13. vi. 53.

[3] Tacit. Annal. xiii. 32.   [4] See Appendix, note (a).

Aurelius, and in the pontificate of Pope Eleutherius
—that is, between the years 177 and 181[1]—a
British king with the Latin name of Lucius—
whether he was a tributary chieftain within the province, or an independent prince beyond the vallum,
is not stated—sent messengers to the bishop of
Rome, with a request that he might be admitted
within the pale of Christianity.[2] The request was
joyfully received; missionaries were ordained and
sent to Britain; Lucius received baptism, and the
new worship was propagated without impediment
among the natives.[3]

---

[1] Though Beda copies Orosius, he has placed the accession of Marcus Aurelius in 156, whereas by the computation of Orosius it should be placed in 161. The error
is manifest, and may probably be accounted for by ascrib-
ing it to the mistake of some copyist, who wrote CLVI.
for CLXI. It has, however, perplexed many writers, who
have assigned to the conversion of Lucius a variety of
dates, though the words of the text shew that it could not
have taken place prior to the pontificate of Eleutherius,
nor later than the death of Aurelius.

[2] Bed. i. c. 5. There is a letter among the laws of
Edward the Confessor, supposed to be written by Eleutherius to Lucius (Wilkins, Leg. Sax. 201), from which it
has sometimes been suggested that Beda was mistaken,
that the Britons had long been Christians, and that the
message to the pope was for instruction in Roman jurisprudence. But the letter is manifestly spurious; and its
very text, supposing it were genuine, intimates that it is
an answer to a *second* message.

[3] The names given to the messengers and missionaries
by our chroniclers are Elvan, Fagan, Medwin, and Da-
mian. Now we learn from Mr. Rees (Welsh Saints,
84), that in the neighbourhood of Landaff are four
churches, called after the names of Llearwg or Lucius,
Dyfan, Ffagan, and Medwy. We know not the time
when they were founded, but their existence seems to
confirm the old tradition, that Lucius reigned in that
part of the country.

I shall not detain the reader to describe the manner in which this imperfect outline by Beda has been filled up by the ingenuity of later writers. The story itself is liable to suspicion, for we know not from what source Beda, at the distance of five centuries, derived his information. It seems, however, to receive corroboration from the fact, that after the time assigned to the conversion of Lucius, continental writers begin to number this island among the conquests of Christianity; and to boast that the professors of the gospel extend from the east to the west, from India to Britain.[1]

From the conversion of Lucius, we leap at once, over a chasm of more than one hundred years, to the persecution raised by the Emperors Diocletian and Maximian at the beginning of the fourth century. Britain was then governed by the Cæsar Constantius, a prince whose benevolence and humanity have been loudly extolled by his panegyrists. By some it is related to his honour, that when certain

---

[1] Thus Tertullian, about the beginning of the third century, boasts that places in Britain, where the Roman arms could never penetrate, were subject to Christ; there his name reigned, there his kingdom was established. Britannorum inaccessa Romanis loca, Christo vero subdita . . . . Christi nomen regnat . . . . Christi nomen et regnum colitur. Tert. adv. Judæos, p. 189. Origen, though he owns that the greater part of the Britons had not yet heard the word of God (Tract. 28 in Matt.), yet states that the power of the Saviour was as manifest in Britain as in Mauritania. (Hom. vi. in Luc. c. 1.) Arnobius admires the rapidity with which the word of God has reached the Indians in the east and the Britons in the west: Tam velociter currit sermo ejus, ut, cum per tot millia annorum in sola Judæa notus fuerit Deus, nunc intra paucos annos nec ipsos Indos lateat a parte orientis, nec ipsos Britannos a parte occidentis. Arn. in Ps. cxlvii.

Christians of his court offered to conform to the idolatrous worship, he dismissed them from his service, saying that men, who had been faithless to their God, could never be expected to prove faithful to their prince. But, however that might be, his conduct shews that, though he did not encourage, he dared not prevent, the execution of the imperial edicts. The consequence was, that the Christians throughout Britain were abandoned to the mercy of the pagan priests and magistrates. We are told that they were hunted into caverns and forests, where they perished of want and misery; that the churches were profaned or demolished; and that those who fell into the hands of the persecutors, had no other alternative than to abjure their religion, or to suffer death. Yet, out of the whole number, the names of three only have been preserved : of Julius and Aaron, of whom we know nothing more than that they were citizens of Caerleon, and of Alban of Verulam, the history of whose sufferings and constancy has been carefully transmitted to posterity, and who, both by natives and foreigners, has been honoured with the lofty title of the proto-martyr of Britain.[1]

Alban was a citizen of Verulam, and a worshipper of the gods of his fathers, when compassion induced him to open his door to a Christian priest fleeing from the pursuit of his enemies. The charity of the pagan met with its reward. Alban admired the virtue and piety of his guest, listened to his instructions, and received from him the sacra-

---

[1] Gildas, 16. Bed. Hist. i. c. 7. and De Sex Ætat. p. 187, inter opera minora.

ment of baptism. But the retreat of the fugitive was discovered; and Alban, to save his teacher, delivered himself to the soldiers in the attire of the priest. In presence of the governor he boldly owned the truth, acknowledged his name and belief, and refused to offer sacrifice to the gods. He was previously scourged, and then beheaded on a small eminence without the walls. (Anno 305.) When the persecution ceased, a stately church was erected over his remains by his townsmen; and, though it was afterwards destroyed by the idolatrous Saxons, the ruins were long visited by pilgrims, through a belief that miraculous cures continued to be wrought at them through his intercession. In 793, Offa, king of Mercia, founded on the same spot the princely abbey of St. Alban's.[1]

The elevation of Constantine to the empire in 313 restored peace to the church; and the subsequent conversion of his son Constantine gave to the Christians a title to the imperial favour. The history of the British church after that period may be told in a few lines. Of its communion in faith and discipline with the other Christian churches we have abundant proofs in the ecclesiastical documents of the age; and we find deputations of British bishops, sitting as the representatives of their brethren, in the councils of Arles in 314,[2] of Sardica

---

[1] Bed. ibid. Gild. pp. 17, 18; Act. SS. Jun. iv. 146—171.

[2] This deputation consisted of three bishops, who subscribed as Eborius of York, Restitutus of London, and Adelphius of Col. Lond. (Labbe, Conc. i. 1430.) The last is plainly an error of the copyist for Col. Lind. or Lincoln, which is named Lindum in the Itinerary, Lindum

in 347, and of Rimini in 359.[1] It might have
been expected that their insular situation would
have kept them aloof from the vexatious controversies which agitated the continental churches.
But we are told that the love of novelty and change
was a national habit; and that every erroneous
doctrine, from that of Arius to that of Pelagius,
found patronage in Britain.[2] There is probably
more of declamation than of truth in this language.
The prelates, indeed, who attended foreign councils,
and the pilgrims who visited the holy land,[3] must
have become acquainted with such matters; but the
orthodoxy of the Britons during the prevalence of
Arianism is attested by its most zealous oppo-

Colonia, in the Chorographia Anonymi Ravennatis, and
Lindicolinum in Beda. See Bed. ii. c. 16—18. Gale,
Anton. Iter. 96, 145.

[1] At Rimini the emperor had ordered that the prelates should be supported at his expense. Those of
Aquitaine, Gaul, and Britain refused the offer, with the
exception of three Britons, who were unable to maintain
themselves, and unwilling to be a burthen on their colleagues. Tres tantum ex Britannia, inopia proprii, pub-
lico usi sunt, sanctius putantes fiscum gravare quam singulos. Sulp. Sev. Hist. p. 401.

[2] Sic quasi via facta trans oceanum, omnes omnino
bestiæ feræ mortiferum cujuslibet hæreseos virus hor-
rendum horrido ore vibrantes, letalia dentium vulnera
patriæ, novi semper aliquid audire volenti, et nihil certi
stabiliter obtinenti infigebant. Gild. 19. The same is
repeated, but in more simple language, by Bede, l. i. c. 8.

[3] There were many such pilgrims from Britain.
Divisus ab orbe nostro Britannus, in religione proces-
serit, occiduo sole dimisso, quærit locum fama sibi et scripturarum relatione cognitum. S. Hieron. p. 44. 'Αφίκονται
δὲ πολλοὶ τὰς τῆς ἑσπέρας οἰκοῦντες ἐσχατιὰς, Σπάνοί τε
καὶ Βρεττανοὶ, καὶ Γαλάται οἱ τὸ μέσον τούτων κατέχοντες.
Theodoret, in Philotheo de Simeoue, 26.

nents;[1] and if the heresy of Pelagius afterwards
found an asylum in the island, it was not till it had
been proscribed on the continent, when some of his
disciples, Britons like himself, returning home, propagated his doctrines among their countrymen.
Their success, however, created alarm; and Pope
Celestine, at the representation of the Deacon Palladius, commissioned Germanus of Auxerre to proceed in his name to Britain,[2] while some British
bishops, at the same time, solicited theological aid
from the Gallic prelates assembled in synod at
Troyes.[3] Lupus, the bishop of that city, con-

---

[1] Ταύτῃ σύμψηφοι τυγχάνουσι πᾶσαι αἱ κατὰ τόπον
ἐκκλησίαι αἱ τε κατὰ την Σπανίαν καὶ Βρετтανίαν. κ. τ. λ.
S. Athan. 1, p. 309.

[2] Ad actionem Palladii diaconi Papa Celestinus Germanum Antisiodorensem episcopum *vice sua* mittit, ut deturbatis hæreticis, Britannos ad Catholicam fidem dirigat.
Prosper in Chron. anno 429. He states the same with
respect to Celestine in another work. Nec segniore cura
ab hoc eodem morbo Britannias liberavit, quando quosdam inimicos gratiæ, solum suæ originis occupantes, ab
illo secreto exclusit oceani; et ordinato Scotis episcopo,
dum Romanam insulam studet servare Catholicam, fecit
etiam barbaram Christianam. Prosper contra Cassian.
c. 41, p. 113. Now Prosper was contemporary with Germanus, living at the time in Gaul, where he was employed
to arrest the progress of Semipelagianism. He became
afterwards secretary to Celestine. Better authority cannot be desired.

[3] Ex Britanniis directa legatio Gallicanis episcopis
nunciavit Pelagianam perversitatem in suis locis late populos occupasse, et quamprimum fidei Catholicæ debere
succurri. Constant. Vit. S. Germani, l. 1, c. 19. The same
is stated by Beda, Erric, and the other copiers of Constantius, who was a priest of Lyons, and wrote the life of
St. Germanus fifty or sixty years after this event took
place. In the text I have endeavoured to reconcile his
testimony with that of Prosper, with which it cannot certainly compete in point of authority.

sented, or was appointed, to accompany Germanus. The Britons received the missionaries with joy: crowds followed them wherever they went: they preached in churches, streets, and fields;[1] and so great was the enthusiasm which they excited, that the teachers of the new doctrines hesitated to confront them in public. At length a general meeting—one, it appears, of the whole tribe, or perhaps of the neighbouring tribes—was held near Verulam, and the Pelagians were brought forward to defend their own tenets. The missionaries answered: their answers were received with applause by the hearers, and threats of personal violence were uttered against their opponents. The triumph of orthodoxy was complete; and Germanus, before he quitted the scene of victory, visited the tomb of St. Alban, where he deposited a small box of relics that he had brought with him from Gaul, taking in exchange a handful of dust from the grave, that he might place it in a new church at Auxerre, which he afterwards dedicated in honour of the British martyr.[2] He was not, however, allowed to remain long in peace at Auxerre. A second requisition brought him a second time to Britain, but to

---

[1] Constan. l. 1, c. 23. Did they then speak the British language?—Undoubtedly: for it appears that the Gallic clergy at that time generally understood Celtic. In the first dialogue of Sulpitius Severus, Gallus says to his hearers, " Dum cogito me hominem Gallum inter Aquitanos verba facturum, vereor, ne offendat vestras nimium urbanas aures sermo rusticior." Posthumianus replies: " Vel *Celtice*, vel, si mavis, Gallice, loquere." Dial. i. c. 20.

[2] Bed. i. c. 18. Act. SS. Julii, vii. 258.

a more easy victory.[1] In another general meeting, the chief teachers of Pelagianism—probably the same persons who had been expelled from Gaul, in conformity with an edict of the Emperor Valentinian—were condemned to banishment from Britain, and delivered into the custody of Germanus on his departure from the island. His companion in this mission was Severus of Treves, the disciple of his former colleague.[2]

The history of this mission is not calculated to impress the reader with a very high notion of the acquirements of the British clergy; but there is

[1] Constant. Vit. Germ. ii. 1—4. Erric, Vit. St. Germ. l. iv. Ussher is positive that the second visit of St. Germanus occurred at a much later period than is stated by Erric and Beda. Brit. Eccles. Antiq. c. xii. p. 435.

[2] Omnium sententia pravitatis auctores, expulsi ab insula, sacerdotibus adducuntur ad Mediterranea deferendi. Const. Vit. Germ. l. xi. c. 3, 4. On these missions of Germanus and his companions a huge mass of fable was afterwards raised by the collectors of Welsh traditions. With them Wales is the favourite spot visited by the Gallic prelates: there they reform the state of the church, introduce the division into parishes, establish two choirs of saints, or colleges of monks, at Llancarvan and Caerworgan (now Lantwit), educate, by themselves or their disciples, the chief of the Welsh saints, depose kings, appoint bishops, and work miracles of the most ridiculous description. Of all these things, Constantius, the original historian, knew nothing. He seems to have been ignorant that the missionaries ever visited Wales. According to his narrative they proceeded from the coast to Verulam (or St. Alban's), and, after the general meeting of the neighbouring British tribes, returned home. If but a small part of what has been attributed to St. Germanus were true, his memory must still have been held in veneration in Wales at the time when Gildas wrote. Gildas has not even mentioned him. On Gildas, see note (B.)

another transaction connected with it which seems to impeach their zeal in the cause of religion. While Germanus and Lupus were still in the country, an army was collected to defend a pass, through which it was expected that a numerous body of Saxon marauders would attempt to penetrate. The Gallic prelates hastened to the camp about the middle of Lent, spent the intermediate time in catechising and instructing the people, and on Easter eve administered the sacrament of baptism in a temporary church, which had been formed of branches for the occasion. It was found that the baptized on that night amounted to the majority of the whole force ;[1] whence we may reasonably conclude that, though the British hierarchy had existed above two hundred years, yet one-half of the population were still either idolaters, worshipping the gods of their fathers, or men who hesitated to be admitted into the Christian church that they might with less restraint indulge in criminal gratification.

This brief and imperfect notice is the sum of all that is known respecting the history of the British church during the first five centuries : a knowledge derived not from national and authentic documents, for no such documents are in existence,[2] but from

---

[1] Maxima exercitus multitudo undam lavacri salutaris expetiit......recens de lavacro pars major exercitus. Const. l. 1, c. 28. Beda, i. c. 20. The site of their baptism and subsequent victory is placed by Ussher at Maesgarmon (or German's field), in the parish of Mold in Flintshire. The name may answer, but not the locality ; for it is very improbable that Germanus ever travelled as far as the north of Wales, or that the Saxon adventurers should land on the western instead of the eastern or southern coast of Britain.

[2] Quippe quæ, si qua fuerint, aut ignibus hostium

isolated passages scattered here and there in the
pages of foreign historians. The case is the same
with regard to its hierarchy and discipline, and its
doctrine and worship. They are subjects on which
we can learn nothing from direct evidence : though
from the presence of British bishops in foreign
synods, and from the occasional remarks of foreign
writers, we may conclude, that the British church,
as long as the island remained under the dominion of
Rome, was in catholic communion with the other
western churches. But from the moment that the
emperors withdrew their forces from Britain, we are
left in utter darkness. Continental writers seem to
have forgotten the existence of a British church ;
and it is not till after the lapse of a hundred years
that we meet with the work and epistle of Gildas, de
Excidio Britanniæ. Gildas was a Briton; he wrote
about the year 550, the darkest period of British
history, and describes matters with which, being a
contemporary, he must have been perfectly conversant. Unfortunately his object led him to declama-

---

exusta, aut civium exilii classe longius deportata, non
compareant. Hist. Gild. § 4, p. 13. Such was the complaint of Gildas as early as in the sixth century. We
have, indeed, a work of the fifth century, which has been
supposed to be of British origin ; but is of no historical
interest, being a treatise De vita Christiana et viduitate
servanda. By Gennadius, of Marseilles, the author is said
to have been Fastidius, a Briton according to one MS.,
a bishop of the Britons according to another (Fabric.
Biblioth. Gennad. c. lvi.). Gennadius wrote about the
year 490 : and the probability is, that the Fastidius whom
he mentions, came not from this island, but was one of
the Armorican Britons. His work was published at Rome,
by Holstein, in 1663, and may also be found in the appendix to the sixth volume of the Benedictine edition of the
works of St. Augustine.

tion rather than narrative—to prove, or attempt to prove, that the evils which his countrymen suffered were sent in punishment of the immorality of the people. Yet two things may be collected from his pages : first, that the state of public morals among the Britons, owing probably to habits of incessant warfare, frequently against the Saxons, and still more frequently among themselves, was such as would have been disgraceful to a heathen people. Both laity and clergy come successively under the lash of the writer. As samples of the laity, he exhibits to us the portraits of five British princes, living at the time, whom he dignifies with the titles of kings, and describes as monsters of depravity ; charging them in detail with injustice and rapine, licentiousness and debauchery, perjury and murder.[1] Of the clergy he speaks in more general terms, but with equal severity. They are the ministers of Christ in name but not in conduct ; they are called pastors but are in reality wolves ; they are unable to correct the vices of the people because they indulge in the same vices themselves. They are defiled with simony, are unchaste, arrogant, luxurious.[2] There is, it must be owned, an appearance of bitterness in his zeal, a tone of exaggeration in his style, which should put us on our guard : yet no one who reads him can doubt that the picture which he has drawn is in general correct ; otherwise he would have defeated his own purpose, which was to hold up his countrymen to themselves, and to shame and scare them by the faithful representation of their own wickedness.

---

[1] See note (B.)   [2] Gild. 37, 72.

2. It is also clear from Gildas, that the Britons still professed the religion of their Christian ances-tors. Religion was not, indeed, the subject which he undertook to discuss ; yet he could not describe the manners of his countrymen, especially of the clergy, without occasional allusions to their doctrine and worship ; on which account the following at-tempt has been made to glean, from expressions scattered accidentally through his pages, some in-formation respecting their religious belief and the manners of their clergy. That information must of necessity be very imperfect, and confined to few particulars ; yet, as far as it goes, it is authentic, and deserving of attention.

It appears then, 1st, that the Britons believed in the oneness of the Godhead, and the trinity of the persons ; in the divine and human nature of Christ, in the redemption of mankind through his death, and in the endless duration of the bliss of heaven and of the pains of hell.

2nd. That their hierarchy consisted of bishops, priests, and other ministers ; that a particular service was employed at their ordination ; that the hands of the bishops and priests were anointed and blessed ; that they were looked upon as successors of St. Peter, the prince of the apostles, and bearer of the keys of the kingdom of heaven ; that they sate in his seat, and inherited his power of binding and loosing ; and that it was their duty to teach the people, and to offer sacrifice, to stretch out their hands at the most holy sacrifices of Christ.

3rd. That the Britons had monasteries, inhabited by monks under their abbot ; that the monks made vows of obedience, poverty, and chastity; and that widows often bound themselves by vow to a life of continence.

4th. That they built churches in honour of the martyrs; that there were several altars, the seats of the heavenly sacrifice, in the same church; that the service was chanted by the clergy in the churches, and that oaths of mutual forgiveness and peace were taken by adverse parties on the altars.

5th. That the service of their church was performed in the Latin tongue; that their translation of the scriptures was the same which is now called the Vetus Itala; that they sang the psalms from a version made from that of the Septuagint, the same still used in the Latin church; and that they quoted the books of Wisdom and Ecclesiasticus as of equal authority with the other canonical books.

6th. That according to the complaint of Gildas, there were among them clergymen who, in contempt of the third canon of the great council of Nice,[1] refused the domestic services of their mothers or sisters, and accepted those of other women, whom they seduced; and yet, while they thus lived in sin, had the presumption to aspire to the higher orders in the church; others who, to procure ecclesiastical dignities, did not hesitate to pollute themselves with the crime of simony, and to purchase churches from the tyrants that oppressed the country; and moreover some who, when they were unable to subdue the opposition of their brethren, would send messengers before them, and following with costly presents

---

[1] This canon is not mentioned in the text, but the allusion to it is manifest.

cross the sea, and traverse distant lands, till, having
obtained the object of their ambition, they returned
to Britain, took forcible possession of the altars, and
stretched their impious hands over the most holy
sacrifices of Christ.[1] All the practices to which he
here alludes, though obscurely pointed out to us by
the vehement zeal of the writer, would be well
known to his contemporaries for whom he wrote.

But it is time to leave the Britons, and to pass to
the foreign invaders, whose church and worship will
form the subject of the following pages. At the
beginning of the second century, we descry a small
and contemptible tribe, inhabiting, under the name
of Saxons, the neck of the Cimbrian Chersonesus;[2]
in the fourth, they had swelled, by the accession of
other tribes of kindred origin, into a populous and
mighty nation, whose territories progressively reached
the Elbe, the Weser, the Ems, and the Rhine.[3]
Their favourite occupation was piracy. A body of
Franks, stationed by the Emperor Probus on the
coast of Pontus, had seized a Roman fleet, and
steering unmolested through the Bosphorus and the
Mediterranean Sea, had reached in safety the shores
of Batavia. Their successful temerity awakened the
adventurous spirit of the neighbouring nations; who,
though they were ignorant of the art of navigation,

---

[1] See note (C.)

[2] Ἐπὶ τὸν αὐχένα τῆς Κιμβρικῆς χέρρονήσв. Ptol. in
quar. Europ. tab. That Ptolemy wrote before the middle
of the second century, appears from the latest of his observations, which were made in the year 139. (Encycl.
method. Physique, tom. i. p. 305.)

[3] Amm. Marcel. l. 37. Ethelwerd. l. 1, p. 474, edit.
Savile.

though they possessed neither the patience nor the skill to imitate the construction of the Roman vessels, boldly determined to try their fortune on the ocean. In light and narrow skiffs, the intrepid barbarians committed themselves to the mercy of the winds and waves ;[1] the commerce of the provincials rewarded their audacity, and increased their numbers ; and, in the midst of every storm, the Saxon squadrons issued from their ports, swept the neighbouring seas, and pillaged with impunity the unsuspecting coasts of Gaul and Britain. When the emperor Honorius recalled the legions from the defence of the island, the natives, who had often experienced the desperate valour of the Saxons, solicited their assistance against their ancient enemies, the Picts or independent Britons beyond the wall, and the Scots, the most numerous and most powerful of the tribes inhabiting Ireland. Hengist, with a small band of mercenaries, accepted the proposal ;[2] but the perfidious barbarian turned his sword against his employers, and the possession of Kent was the fruit of his treachery. The fortune of Hengist stimulated the ambition of other chieftains, who successively sought the shores of Britain ; and the natives, though they defended themselves with a courage worthy of a more prosperous issue,

---

[1] Cui pelle salum sulcare Britannum
Ludus, et assuto glaucum mare findere lembo.
Sid. Apol. carm. 7, *ad Avit.*

[2] An. 449. The reader, to avoid mistakes, should keep in mind that the Scots were originally natives of Ireland ; colonies of whom settling in the north of Britain, still retained their own name, and ultimately gave to that portion of the island the name of Scotland.

were gradually compelled to retire to the mountains
which cover the western coast.

By this memorable revolution the fairer portion
of the island, from the wall of Antoninus to the
British Channel, became unequally divided among
eight independent chieftains.[1] The other barbarous
tribes, that dismembered the Roman empire, exercised the right of victory with some degree of
moderation; and, by incorporating the natives with
themselves, insensibly learned to imitate their manners, and to adopt their worship. But the natural
ferocity of the Saxons had been sharpened by the
stubborn resistance of the Britons. For a long time

---

[1] Thus eight Anglo-Saxon kingdoms were founded in
Britain. Of these, the most ancient was that of Kent,
founded by Jutes from Jutland, who also took possession
of the Isle of Wight, and of the maritime coast of Hampshire. Then three kingdoms were established by the
Saxons: first, that of Sussex, the position of which is
still denoted by its name; second, that of Wessex, comprehending the rest of Hampshire, Wilts, Berks, Dorset,
Somerset, Devon, and great part of Cornwall; and third,
the small kingdom of Essex, containing that county,
Middlesex, and the southern portion of Hertfordshire.
Lastly came the Angles from Sleswick and its neighbourhood, who formed four kingdoms: first, East-Anglia, or
Norfolk, Suffolk, Cambridge, and some portion of Bedfordshire; second, Bernicia, from the wall of Antoninus
down to the Tyne, or more probably the Tees; third,
Deira, from the Tyne or Tees to the Humber; and
fourth, Mercia, comprising all the inland counties between the Humber and the Thames, not already mentioned as belonging to some of the other kingdoms.
Goodall, anxious for the honour of his countrymen, attempts to prove that Bernicia was bounded on the north
by the Tweed (Introd. to Fordun's Scotichronicon, p. 40):
but Beda positively contradicts him, by extending it to
the Frith—Fretum quod Anglorum terras Pictorumque
disterminat. Hist. iv. c. 26.

they spared neither the lives nor the habitations of
their enemies ; submission was seldom able to dis-
arm their fury, and the churches, towns, villages,
and all the remains of Roman civilization, were
devoured by the flames.[1] But while they thus
indulged their resentment, they dried up the more
obvious sources of civil and religious improvement.
With the race of the ancient inhabitants disappeared the refinements of society, and the knowledge of the gospel : to the worship of the true
God succeeded the impure rites of Woden ; and
the ignorance and barbarism of the north of Germany were transplanted into the most flourishing
provinces of Britain.

It was the boast, or the consolation, of the
Greeks, that, if they had been subdued by the
superior fortune of Rome, Rome in her turn had
yielded to them the empire of learning and the arts.[2]
The history of the fifth and sixth centuries presents

---

[1] Confovebatur de mari usque ad mare ignis orientali
sacrilegorum manu exaggeratus, et finitimas quasque civi-
tates agrosque populans, qui non quievit accensus, donec
cunctam pene exurens insulæ superficiem rubra occiden-
talem trucique oceanum lingua delamberet. Gild. p. 85.
Gildas was an enemy and a Briton. He may have exag-
gerated the cruelties of the invaders ; but the substance
of his narrative is corroborated by the Saxon Chronicle
(p. 15), and by Asser, from whom we learn that, when
Stuff and Wihtgar received the Isle of Wight from
Cerdic, they put to death every native in it, who had
survived the slaughter or flight of his countrymen.
Paucos Britones ejusdem insulæ accolas, quos in eâ invenire potuerunt, in loco qui dicitur Gwhitgaraburg occi-
derunt ; cæteri enim accolæ ejusdem insulæ ante aut occisi
erant, aut exules aufugerant. Asser, p. 5.

[2] Græcia capta ferum victorem cepit, et artes
    Intulit agresti Latio.   *Hor.*

c 2

an almost similar revolution. The fierce valour of
the northern barbarians annihilated the temporal
power of Rome; and the religion of Rome triumphed over the gods of the barbarians. Scarcely
had the Saxons obtained the undisputed possession
of their conquests, when a private monk conceived
the bold but benevolent design of reducing these
savage warriors under the obedience of the gospel.
Gregory, on whom the veneration of posterity has
bestowed the epithet of *the great*, had lately resigned
the dignity of Roman prefect, and buried in the
obscurity of the cloister all his prospects of worldly
greatness. While he remained in this humble station, he chanced to pass through the public market at
the moment in which some Anglo-Saxon slaves were
exposed to sale. Their beauty caught the eye of
the fervent monk; and he exclaimed with a pious
zeal, that forms so fair ought no longer to be excluded from the inheritance of Christ. Impressed
with this idea, he repaired to the pontiff, and extorted from him a reluctant permission to quit his
monastery, and announce the gospel to the barbarous conquerors of Britain. But the people of
Rome were unwilling to be deprived of a man
whose virtues they adored. Their clamours retarded his departure; and his subsequent elevation
to the papal throne compelled him to abandon the
design.[1]

Gregory, however, still kept his eyes fixed on Britain.

---

[1] This was probably a traditionary story preserved by
the clergy of Canterbury, and furnished by them to Beda.
It is told by him (Hist. l. ii. c. i.), by Paulus Diaconus
(Inter. Act. SS. Bened. tom. i. p. 391), and by the Saxon
Homilist. Elstob, Hom. in Natal. S. Greg. p. 11—18.

The absence of his personal exertions he could easily supply by those of other missionaries; and from his high station in the church, he might direct their operations, and second their endeavours. His first plan was to purchase in the slave markets Anglo-Saxon youths about the age of eighteen, and to educate them in monasteries, that they might afterwards be employed as missionaries to their countrymen.[1] But this would require a delay, which accorded not with the impatience of his zeal; and, after a short interval, he resolved to try the courage of his own monks, ignorant as they were of the language and manners of the barbarians. Having selected the most learned and virtuous of the community, he explained to them his views, elevated their hopes with the prospect of eternal rewards, and confirmed their consent with his apostolical benediction. (Ann. 596.) Animated by the exhortation of the pontiff, the missionaries traversed with speed the north of Italy, and crossed the Gallic Alps: but the enthusiasm which they had imbibed in Rome evaporated during their journey; and from Lerins, or the neighbourhood of Lerins, they despatched Augustine, their superior, to Gregory, to

---

[1] See his epistle to the presbyter Candidus (S. Greg. ep. l. v. ep. 10), administrator of the patrimony of St. Peter in Gaul, who was instructed to spend the annual income in the country whence it was derived, in clothing the poor, and in purchasing Saxon youths for the purpose specified in the text. This is generally supposed to have been written before the mission of Augustine; but it appears to me, from the letters which the missionary took with him, that the latter was accompanied by Candidus, who had only just been appointed. See S. Greg. ep. l. v. ep. 52—58.

explain their reasons for declining so unpromising
and so dangerous an enterprise. But the pontiff
was inflexible. He exhorted, conjured, commanded
them to proceed (23 July, 596) ; he solicited in their
favour the protection of the princes and prelates of
the Franks; he begged of the Gallic clergy to de-
pute some of their body to be their interpreters and
associates; and at last, after a long and tedious sus-
pense, received the welcome news, that they had
landed in safety on the Isle of Thanet, probably in
the autumn of the same year, 596.[1]

Of the Saxon kingdoms, that of Kent was the
most ancient, and the best disposed to receive the
truths of the gospel. The immediate descendants
of Hengist seem not to have inherited the mental
energy of that conqueror; and by cultivating the
arts of peace, had endeavoured to excite a spirit of
improvement among their subjects. The example
of their neighbours the Franks, who had embraced
the Christian faith, taught them to view with less
partiality the worship of their ancestors; and from
the prosperity of that apostate people they might
infer that victory was not exclusively attached to
the votaries of Woden. Bertha, daughter to Cha-
ribert, king of Paris, was married to their sovereign;
she practised the rites of the gospel in the heart of
their metropolis; and the saintly deportment of

---

[1] Can the reader divine the great object of Gregory in
the establishment of this mission ? Mr. Soames has recently discovered that it was "to extend his authority in
the West, as a counterpoise to the encroaching spirit of
his Eastern rivals," the patriarchs of Constantinople.
Hist. of Anglo-Saxon Church, p. 45. I know not from
what source this information was derived.

Liudhard, the prelate who attended her, reflected a lustre on the faith which he professed. From the epistles of St. Gregory it appears that these and similar causes had awakened a desire of religious knowledge among the inhabitants of Kent, and that application for instruction had been made to the prelates of the Franks; whose apathy and indolence are lashed with severe but merited animadversion by the pontiff.[1]

It was at this favourable period that Augustine reached the isle of Thanet, and despatched a messenger to inform the Saxon king that he was arrived from a distant country, to open to him and his subjects the gates of eternal happiness. It is strange that hitherto Bertha had made no attempt to convert her husband.[2] Whether the arrival of the missionaries awakened her zeal, we know not; but Ethelbert returned a friendly answer, and consented to receive the foreign priests, not indeed within his own residence, but in the open air, where he had been taught to believe that spells and incantations were powerless. The missionaries, elated with this faint gleam of success, approached the appointed place with the slow and solemn pomp of a religious procession: before them was borne a silver cross, and a portrait of Christ; and the air resounded with the litany which they chanted, in alternate choirs, praying for the conversion of the pagans. Ethelbert listened with attention to the discourse of Augustine: his answer was reserved

---

[1] Bed. Hist. l. i. p. 61. Malm. de reg. l. i. c. i. f. 4, edit. Savile. Greg. ep. l. v. ep. 58, 59.
[2] S. Greg. ep. l. xi. p. 29.

but favourable. Though he expressed no inclination to abandon the worship of his fathers, he acknowledged that the offers of the missionary were plausible, and praised the charity, which had prompted strangers to undertake so long a journey, for the advantage of an unknown people. He concluded with an assurance of his protection as long as they should remain in his dominions.[1]

Without the walls of Canterbury the queen had discovered the ruins of an ancient church, built by the Britons in honour of St. Martin. By her orders it had been repaired, and given to the bishop Liudhard : it was now transferred to the use of the missionaries, whose efforts she seconded with all her influence. The patronage of the sovereign ensured the respect of the subjects ; and curiosity led numbers to view the public service, and learn the religious tenets of the strangers. They admired the solemnity of their worship; the pure and sublime morality of their doctrine; their zeal, their austerity, and their virtue. Insensibly the prejudices of the idolaters wore away ; and the priests of Woden began to lament the solitude of their altars. Ethel-

---

[1] Bed. l. i. c. 25. Hom. Sax. in nat. St. Greg. pp. 33, 34. Gosceline pretends to give us the very speech of Augustine ; but it was probably composed for him by that writer. (Ang. Sac. tom. ii. p. 59.) From Beda, i. c. 25, we learn, that on this and similar occasions the priests, who accompanied him from France, served as interpreters. This was ordered by the pontiff. Quibus etiam injunximus, ut aliquos secum e vicino debeant presbyteros ducere, cum quibus possint eorum mentes agnoscere, et voluntates admonitione sua, quantum Deus donaverit, adjuvare. Ep. ad Theodric. et Theodbert. Reg. Francorum, lib. vi. ep. 58.

bert, who at first maintained a decent reserve, ventured to profess himself a Christian; and so powerful was his example, that at the feast of Christmas ten thousand Saxons followed their prince to the waters of baptism.[1]

From the natural ferocity of the Saxon character, there was reason to fear that the royal convert, in the fervour of proselytism, might employ the sword of persecution to accelerate the progress of Christianity. But his teachers were actuated by motives more congenial to the mild spirit of the gospel; and, with a moderation which is not always the associate of zeal, sedulously inculcated that the worship of man, to be grateful to the Deity, must be the spontaneous dictate of the heart; and that the obstinacy of the idolater was to be overcome, not by the sword of the magistrate, but by the labours of the missionary.[2] These lessons they had imbibed from the mouth of the pontiff; and they were frequently inculcated in his letters. In obedience to his instructions, the weakness and prejudices of the converts were respected; the deserted temples of Woden were converted into Christian churches;[3]

---

[1] Beda, l. i. c. 26. The joy of the pontiff prompted him to impart his success to Eulogius, the patriarch of Alexandria. In solemnitate Dominicæ nativitatis quæ hac prima indictione transacta est, plus quam decem millia Angli ab eodem nunciati sunt fratre et co-episcopo nostro baptisati. (Ep. Greg. l. viii. ep. 30. Smith's Bed. app. viii.) The pontifical indiction began on the 25th of December. It was therefore the year 597 according to our present calculation.

[2] Bed. l. i. c. 26. Hom. Sax. in nat. St. Greg. p. 36.

[3] This was the ancient practice. Ubi fana destruxerat, statim ibi aut ecclesias aut monasteria construebat. Sulp. Sev. in Vita B. Martini, c. 10.

and the national customs gradually adapted to the
offices of religion. Hitherto the Saxons had been
accustomed to enliven the solemnity of their worship with the merriment of the table. The victims
which had bled on the altars of the gods furnished
the principal materials of the feast; and the praises
of their warriors were mingled with the hymns
chanted in honour of their deities. Totally to have
abolished this practice might have alienated their
minds from a religion which forbade the most favourite of their amusements. By the direction of
Gregory similar entertainments were permitted on
the festivals of the Christian martyrs; tents were
erected in the vicinity of the church; and as soon
as the service was concluded, the converts were
exhorted to indulge with sobriety in their accustomed gratifications, and to return their thanks to
that Being, who showers down his blessings on the
human race.[1]

From Kent the knowledge of the gospel was
speedily transmitted to the neighbouring and dependent kingdom of Essex. Saberct, the reigning
prince, received with respect the Abbot Mellitus,
and invited him to reside in his capital.[2] But the
prospect of the missionary closed with the death of
his patron (24 Feb. 616). The three sons of Saberct, who were still attached to the worship of

[1] For this condescension, which was copied from the
practice of the first Christian missionaries (Mosh. Hist.
Eccl. sæc. ii. p. 2, c. iv. note), the pontiff has been severely
blamed by Dr. Henry (vol. iii. p. 194), who asserts, but
without proof, or attempt at proof, that it introduced the
grossest corruptions into the Christian worship.
[2] An. 604.

their ancestors, bursting into the church during the time of sacrifice, demanded a portion of the consecrated bread, which Mellitus was distributing to the people.[1] The bishop (he had been lately invested with the episcopal character) dared to refuse; and banishment was the consequence of his refusal. He joined his brethren in Kent : but they were involved in equal difficulties. After the death of Bertha, Ethelbert had married a second wife. His son, Eadbald, was captivated with her youth and beauty ; at his accession to the throne he took her to his bed ; and when the missionaries ventured to remonstrate, abandoned a religion which forbade the gratification of his passion. Disheartened by so many misfortunes, Mellitus, with Justus of Rochester, retired into Gaul.[2] Laurentius, the successor of St. Augustine, had determined to follow their example ; but spent the night before his intended departure in the church of St. Peter. At the break of day (such was the tradition in the church of Canterbury), he repaired to the palace ; discovered to the king the marks of stripes on his shoulders ; and assured him that they had been inflicted by the hands of the apostle, as the reward of his cowardice. Eadbald was astonished and confounded. He expressed his willingness to remove every cause of offence ; dismissed his father's widow from his bed ; and recalled the fugitive bishops. His subsequent conduct proved the sincerity of his conversion : and Christianity,

---

[1] Bed. l. ii. c. 5.
[2] An. 625. Both Justus and Mellitus became afterwards Archbishops of Canterbury.

supported by his influence, soon assumed an ascendency which it ever afterwards maintained.[1]

From the south the knowledge of the gospel passed to the most northern of the Saxon nations. Edwin, the powerful king of Northumbria, had asked and obtained the hand of Edilberge, the daughter of Ethelbert : but the zeal of her brother had stipulated that she should enjoy the free exercise of her religion, and had extorted from the impatient suitor a promise, that he would impartially examine the credibility of the Christian faith. Edilberge took with her to Northumbria a bishop, named Paulinus, one of the associates of St. Augustine, who for a long time laboured earnestly, but ineffectually, to bring over the king, or some of his court, to the Christian faith. It chanced that on Easter day,[2] an attempt on the life of Edwin was made by an assassin supposed to be in the pay of Cynegils, king of Wessex. The wound, though severe, was not dangerous ; and the same evening the queen was delivered of a daughter, afterwards named Eanfled. Edwin returned thanks to his gods for the safety of his wife and child ; but Paulinus interposed, saying that those thanks were due to the God of the Christians, whose blessing on them both he had implored in the service of the day. The king listened to him with attention ; he consented that his daughter should be brought up a Christian ; he even promised to become a Christian himself, if it were given to him to obtain satisfaction of the treacherous Cynegils. Before his departure with an army for that purpose, Eanfled was baptized with eleven com-

[1] Id. l. ii. c. 6.   [2] 17 Ap. 626.

panions on the eve of Whitsunday; and on his return,
crowned with victory, from Wessex, he became, according to his promise, a docile hearer of the missionary. Still he was, probably from political motives, slow to resolve; and great part of a year had
been spent in anxious deliberation, when, attended by Paulinus, he entered the great council,
requested the advice of his faithful Witan, and
exposed to them the reasons which induced him to
prefer Christianity to the worship of paganism.
Coiffi,[1] the high priest of Northumbria, was the first
to reply. It might have been expected, that prejudice and interest would have armed him with arguments against the adoption of a foreign creed: but
his attachment to paganism had been weakened by
repeated disappointments, and he had learnt to
despise the gods who had neglected to reward his
services. That the religion which he had hitherto
taught was useless, he attempted to prove from his
own misfortunes; and avowed his resolution to
listen to the reasons, and examine the doctrine of
Paulinus. He was followed by an aged thane, whose
discourse offers an interesting picture of the simplicity of the age. "When," said he, "O king, you
and your ministers are seated at table in the depth
of winter, and the cheerful fire blazes on the
hearth in the middle of the hall, a sparrow perhaps,

---

[1] It has been suggested that Coiffi, a word so like to
"Coibhi, the Celtic for helpful," may have been a British
Druid. (Jamieson, Etym. Dict. Supplem. v. Coivie, and
Palgrave, Rise and Progress of English Commonwealth,
i. 155.) But it does not seem probable that a British
Druid should be the primus pontificum of a Saxon king of
Northumberland so late as the year 627.

chased by the wind and snow, enters at one door of the apartment, and escapes by the other. During the moment of its passage, it enjoys the warmth; when it is once departed, it is seen no more. Such is the nature of man. During a few years his existence is visible: but what has preceded, or what will follow it, is concealed from the view of mortals. If the new religion offer any information on subjects so mysterious and important, it must be worthy of our attention."[1] To these reasons the other members assented. Paulinus was desired to explain the principal articles of the Christian faith; and the king expressed his determination to embrace the doctrine of the missionary. When it was asked, who would dare to profane the altars of Woden, Coiffi accepted the dangerous office. Laying aside the emblems of the priestly dignity, he assumed the dress of a warrior: and despising the prohibitions of the Saxon superstition, mounted the favourite charger of Edwin. By those who were ignorant of his motives, his conduct was attributed to temporary insanity. But disregarding their clamours, he proceeded to the nearest temple, and bidding defiance to the gods of his fathers, hurled his spear into the sacred edifice. It stuck in the opposite wall;[2] and, to the surprise of the trembling spectators, the heavens were silent, and the sacrilege was unpunished. Insensibly they recovered from their fears,

---

[1] Bed. l. ii. c. 10, 13.

[2] This circumstance is not to be found in the Latin copies of Beda; but it has been preserved in the Saxon version. Ða ꞃceaꞇ he miꝺ hiꞅ ꞅpeꞃe þ hiꞇ ꞅꞇicobe ꝼæꞃꞇe on ꝺam heaꞅ. (Bed. Hist. Sax. p. 517.) The place was Godmundham, near Wighton in Yorkshire.

and, encouraged by the exhortations of Coiffi, burnt
to the ground the temple and the surrounding
groves.[1] From so favourable a beginning, the missionary might have ventured to predict the entire
conversion of the nation : but he could not calculate
the numerous chances of war ; and all the fruits of
his labours were speedily blasted by the immature
death of the king.   Edwin was slain at Hatfield in
Yorkshire, as he bravely fought against Penda king
of Mercia, and Cædwalla king of the Britons.
(12 Oct. 633.) During more than twelve months,
the victors pillaged the kingdom of Northumbria
without opposition; Edilberg, her children, and
Paulinus, were compelled to seek an asylum in
Kent; and the converts, deprived of instruction,
relapsed into their former idolatry.

The history of the Saxon kingdoms is marked
with the most rapid vicissitudes of fortune.   Oswald
and Eanfrid were the sons of Adelfrid, the predecessor of Edwin.   In the mountains of the north
they had concealed themselves from the jealousy of
that prince ; and had spent the time of their exile
in learning from the Scottish monks of Hii,[2] the

---

[1] Alcuin has celebrated the fame of Coiffi in his poem
on the church of York :

O nimium tanti felix audacia facti !
Polluit ante alios, quas ipse sacraverat, aras.
                                        v. 186.

[2] Hii or Iona is a small island at a short distance from
the isle of Mull, and originally belonged to the Picts.
Now the southern Picts, as they are called by Beda, the
men of Galloway, had been converted to Christianity by
Nynias, a British missionary sent from Rome about the
close of the fourth century (Bed. iii. c. 3), but the
northern Picts retained their national worship till the
middle of the sixth.   Before that time several colonies

principles of the gospel. After the victory of the
confederate kings, they returned to Northumbria.
Eanfrid was treacherously slain in a parley with
Cædwalla : Oswald determined to avenge the cala-
mities of his family and country. With a small,
but resolute band of followers, he sought the army
of the enemy, and discovered it negligently en-
camped in the neighbourhood of Hexham. (Ann. 635.)
A cross of wood was hastily erected by his order,
and the Saxons, prostrate before it, earnestly implored the protection of the God of the Christians.
From prayer they rose to battle and to victory.
Cædwalla was slain ; his army was dispersed ; and
the conqueror ascended without a rival the throne
of his ancestors.[1] As he piously attributed his success to the favour of heaven, he immediately bent
his attention to the concerns of religion, and solicited
a supply of missionaries from his former instructors.
Corman was sent, a monk of a severe and unbend-

---

of Scots from Ireland had settled along the western
coast, from the present county of Kintire to that of
Braidalbin ; and soon after the year 560, the abbot
Columba came from Ulster with twelve companions, and
won to the Christian faith Bridius, king of the Picts, with
part of his people. From him, or Conan, the chief of the
Scots in Britain, or perhaps from both, he received the
donation of the isle of Iona, in which he built a monastery,
and from which he governed other monasteries of his own
foundation in Ireland, and all that were founded in Britain
among the Scots or the Picts. (Bed. ibid. Ussher, de
Primord. 703. Ann. Tigern. An. 563—574. Adomn. 1—7.)
From him the island has been named Icolmkille. Hence
the reader will understand that his monks were of Scottish,
that is, Irish origin : for it was not till after the subjection of the Picts by the Scots that the northern part of
Britain generally obtained the appellation of Scotland.
  [1] Bed. l. iii. c. 1, 2. Ann. 635.

ing temper; who, disgusted with the ignorance
and barbarism of the Saxons, speedily returned in
despair to his monastery. While he described to
the monks the difficulty and dangers of the mission,
"Brother," exclaimed a voice, "the fault is yours.
You exacted from the barbarians more than their
weakness could bear. You should first have stooped
to their ignorance, and then have raised their minds
to the sublime maxims of the gospel." This sensible rebuke turned every eye upon the speaker, a
private monk of the name of Aidan : he was selected
to be the apostle of Northumbria; and the issue of
his labours justified the wisdom of the choice. As
soon as he had received the episcopal ordination, he
repaired to the court of Oswald. His arrival was a
subject of general exultation ; and the king condescended to explain in Saxon the instructions which
the missionary delivered in his native language.
But the success of Aidan was owing no less to his
virtues than to his preaching. The severe austerity
of his life, his profound contempt of riches, and his
unwearied application to the duties of his profession,
won the esteem, while his arguments convinced the
understanding of his hearers. Each day the number
of proselytes increased ; new missionaries, mostly
monks, hastened to the aid of the bishop; and,
within a few years, the church of Northumbria was
fixed on a solid and permanent foundation.[1]

The East-Angles were indebted for their conversion to the labours of Felix, a Burgundian prelate. In the commencement of the seventh century,
their monarch Redwald had invited to his court the

---

[1] Bed. l. iii. c. 3—5.

disciples of St. Augustine, and received from them the sacrament of baptism. (Ann. 627.) Yet he abjured not the worship of his country : and the same temple was sanctified by the celebration of the Christian sacrifice, and polluted by the immolation of victims to the gods of paganism.[1] His son Eorpwald was more sincere in his belief; but the merit of firmly establishing the Christian worship was, by his death, transferred to his successor Sigebert, who, during a long exile in Gaul, had imbibed with the knowledge of the gospel a profound veneration for the monastic institute. No sooner had he ascended the throne, than Felix, commissioned by Honorius of Canterbury, requested permission to instruct his subjects. (Ann. 630.) He was received with welcome, and fixed his residence at Dunwich, the capital of the kingdom. By the united efforts of the king and the missionary, the knowledge of Christianity was rapidly diffused : and, the better to eradicate ignorance and idolatry from the higher classes of the people, a public school was instituted after the model of that at Canterbury.[2] Having

---

[1] Altare ad sacrificium Christi et arulam ad victimas dæmoniorum. (Bed. l. ii. c. 15). Hume (Hist. p. 32. Millar, 4°, 1762) inadvertently ascribes the apostasy of Redwald to his son Eorpwald.

[2] The situation and design of this school have been fiercely debated by the champions of the two universities. The partisans of Cambridge at first derived the origin of their school from Cantaber, a Spanish prince, who was supposed to have landed in Britain in the reign of Gurguntius, about four hundred years before the Christian era (see Caius De Ant. Cant. p. 20—60) ; and the Oxonians, not to yield to their opponents, claimed for their first professors, the philosophers whom Brutus had brought with him more than a thousand years before that

shared for a time the cares and splendour of royalty
with Egeric, a near relation, Sigebert retired to a
monastery to prepare himself for death. But his
repose was disturbed by the invasion of a foreign
enemy. A formidable body of Mercians had penetrated into the heart of the country; and the misfortunes of the campaign were ascribed to the want
of conduct or of valour in Egeric. The East-Angles
clamorously called for the aged monarch, who had
so often led them to victory. With reluctance he
left his cell to mix in the tumult and dangers of the
field. On the day of battle, when arms were offered
to him, he refused them as repugnant to the monastic profession, and with a wand directed the operations of the army. But the fortune of the Mercians prevailed : both the kings were slain; and the
country was abandoned to the ravages of the conquerors. Yet, under the pressure of this calamity,
the converts persevered in the profession of their
religion; and Felix, within the seventeen years of

period (Assertio Antiq. Oxon. p. 1. London, 1568). Antiquity so remote was too ridiculous to obtain credit :
both contracted their pretensions; and Sigebert was
selected for the founder of Cambridge, Alfred the Great
for that of Oxford. The war, however, was still continued,
and the most eminent scholars joined either party, as their
judgment or partiality directed. Without engaging in the
dispute, I may be allowed to observe, that there appears
no reason to believe, with the advocates for Oxford, that
the school of Sigebert was designed only to teach the rudiments of grammar, or with their opponents, that it was
established at Cambridge. Beda informs us, that it was
formed after the model of that at Canterbury, in which all
the sciences known at that period were studied ; and Smith
has made it highly probable that it was situated either at
Seaham or Dunwich. See Smith's Beda, App. p. 721.

his mission, had the merit of reclaiming the whole nation from the errors of paganism.

While Christianity was thus making a rapid progress in the kingdoms of the north and east, a new apostle appeared on the southern coast, and announced the tidings of salvation to the fierce and warlike inhabitants of Wessex. (Ann. 634.) His name was Birinus. Animated with a desire of extending the conquests of the gospel, he had obtained from Pope Honorius a commission to preach to the idolatrous tribes of the Saxons. By a fortunate concurrence of circumstances, he had scarcely opened his mission, when Oswald of Northumbria arrived at the court of Kinegils, and demanded his daughter in marriage. The arguments of the missionary were powerfully seconded by the influence of the suitor; the princess and her father embraced with docility the religion of Christ; and the men of Wessex eagerly conformed to the example of their monarch. Success expanded the views of Birinus; and from the capital he removed to Dorchester, a city on the confines of Mercia, with the expectation of adding that populous kingdom to his spiritual conquests.

But Mercia was destined to receive the faith from the zeal of the Northumbrian princes; who were eminently instrumental in the dissemination of Christianity among the numerous tribes of their countrymen. Peada, the son of Penda king of Mercia, had offered his hand to the daughter of Oswiu, the successor of Oswald (Ann. 653): but the lady spurned the addresses of a pagan; and the passion of the prince induced him to study the principles of her religion. His conversion was rewarded with the object of his affection. To those who doubted his sincerity, he replied, that no consideration, not even the refusal of Alcflede, should ever provoke him to return to the altars of Woden : but an argument more convincing than mere professions was the zeal with which he procured from Northumbria four priests to instruct the Middle-Angles, whom he governed as king during the life of his father. Even Penda himself was induced to grant his protection to the missionaries, and though he refused to yield to their exhortations, he treated with contempt such of his subjects as had enrolled themselves among the Christians, and yet retained the manners of pagans. Within a few years the fortune of war annexed the crown of Mercia to that of Northumbria, and Diuma, a Scot, and one of the missionaries, was raised to the episcopal dignity. The converts were true to the faith which they had embraced; and retained it with enthusiasm, even after they had thrown off the yoke, and replaced the sceptre in the hands of their native princes.

The zeal of Oswiu was not satisfied with one royal proselyte; and his solicitations prevailed on Sigebert, the East Saxon monarch, to receive the sacred rite of baptism. (Ann. 653.) The men of Essex supported the character of their fathers. Like them they embraced the Christian faith, and like them apostatized. A dreadful famine, which they attributed to the vengeance of Woden, induced them to rebuild the altars, and restore the worship of that deity. (Ann. 665.) Jaruman, bishop of Mercia, was alarmed : with haste he repaired to the kingdom of

Essex, and by his preaching and authority confirmed the faith of the wavering, and brought
back many of the incredulous.[1]

The inhabitants of Sussex were the most barbarous of the Saxon nations, and the last that
embraced the profession of Christianity. Unmoved
by the example of their neighbours, whom they
branded with the infamous name of apostates, they
long resisted the efforts of the missionaries; but
their obstinacy was induced to yield to the superior zeal or superior address of St. Wilfrid, a
Northumbrian prelate. Expelled from his diocese
by the intrigues of his enemies, he wandered in
honourable exile among the tribes of the south,
when Edilwalch, the king of Sussex, who had been
lately baptized, invited him to attempt the conversion of his subjects. Wilfrid had travelled through
most of the nations on the continent; to the advantages of study he had joined those of observation and experience; and while his acquirements
commanded the respect, the improvements which
he introduced conciliated the esteem of the barbarians. His first converts were two hundred and
fifty slaves, whom, together with the isle of Selsey,
he had received as a present from the munificence
of Edilwalch. (Ann. 678.) On the day of their baptism they were unexpectedly gratified with the
present of their liberty from their instructor, who
declared that they ceased to be his bondmen from
the moment in which they became the children of
Christ. The liberality of Wilfrid was felt and
applauded; numbers crowded to his sermons; and

---

[1] Bed. l. iii. c. 30.

those who were not convinced by his reasons, were silenced by the authority of the king. Within the space of five years he firmly established the Christian worship in Sussex : and after his departure the wants of the mission were supplied by the pastoral care of the bishops of Winchester.[1]

Thus in the space of about eighty years was successfully completed the conversion of the Anglo-Saxons ; an enterprise which originated in the charity of Gregory the Great, and was unremittingly continued by the industry of his disciples, with the assistance of co-operators from Gaul, Italy, and Scottish missionaries from the isle of Iona. Of the conduct which they pursued, and the arguments which they employed, a few particulars may be collected from the works of the ancient writers.[2] They were instructed most carefully to avoid every offensive and acrimonious expression ; to inform the judgment without alienating the affections, and to display on every occasion the most disinterested zeal for the welfare of their disciples.[3] The great and fundamental truth of the unity of God was the first lesson which they sought to inculcate. The statues

---

[1] Compare Beda (l. iv. c. 13, v. c. 18—24), with Eddius (Vit. Wilf. c. 40), and Huntingdon (l. iii. f. 192, int. scrip. post Bed.).

[2] Daniel bishop of Winchester, in a letter to St. Boniface, enumerates the arguments which were thought the best calculated to convince the pagans (Inter. ep. Bonif. p. 78, edit. Serrar). The letters of the pontiff to the Saxon kings (Wilk. Con. vol. i. p. 12, 30, 34), and some passages of Beda (Hist. l. ii. c. 13, l. iii. c. 22), may also be consulted.

[3] Non quasi insultando vel irritando eos, sed placide et magna moderatione. Ep. Dan. ibid.

of the gods could not, they observed, be fit objects
of adoration, since they possessed no other excellence than what they derive from the nature of the
materials, and the ingenuity of the artist :[1] and
from the successive generation of the German
deities they inferred, that none of them could be
the first great cause from whose fecundity all other
beings received their existence.[2] If *they* were the
dispensers of every blessing, why, it was asked,
were their votaries confined to the barren and
frozen climate of the north, while the warmer and
more fertile regions were divided among those who
equally despised their promises and their threats?[3]
If Woden were the god of war, why did victory
still adhere to the standards of the tribes which
had trampled on his altars, and embraced the faith
of Christ? To the incoherent tenets of paganism
they opposed the truths of revelation; the fall and
redemption of man, his future judgment, and endless existence during an eternity of happiness or
misery. For the truth of these doctrines they
adverted to the consent of the powerful and polished nations, which had preferred them to their
ancient worship; to the rapidity with which, in
defiance of every obstacle, they had been spread
over the earth; and to the stupendous events by

[1] Bed. l. ii. c. 10, l. iii. c. 22.
[2] Quoslibet ab aliis generatos concede eos asserere, ut
saltem modo hominum natos deos et deas potius homines
quam deos fuisse, et cæpisse, qui ante non erant, probes.
Ep. Dan. ibid.
[3] Cum Christiani fertiles terras, vini oleique feraces
cæterisque opibus abundantes possideant provincias, paganis frigore semper rigentes terras reliquerunt. Ibid.
See a similar argument in Bede (l. ii. c. 13).

which their diffusion was accompanied and accelerated.[1] In addition, they appealed with confidence to the testimony of God in their favour ; for it was their conviction, and that of the proselytes, that signs and wonders, similar to those which ushered in the preaching of the gospel among the Jews, had been repeated in England through their ministry. The report had even reached the ears of Gregory in Rome, who began to fear that such distinguished gifts might generate a spirit of pride in his disciple: under that impression he wrote a long letter to Augustine, exhorting him to stand upon his guard ; to close his ears against the subtle suggestions of vanity ; and to be convinced that the wonders which accompanied his preaching were wrought by God, not to reward the merit of those who were no more than humble instruments in the hands of Almighty power, but to display his mercy to the Saxons, and to attract their minds by sensible proofs to the knowledge of salvation.[2]

In one respect the missionaries ventured to deviate from the example of those who had preceded them in their sacred office. The first preachers of Christianity rapidly extended their conquests through every class of Roman subjects ; but almost three centuries elapsed before they presumed to attempt the conversion of the emperors. At the period of the Anglo-Saxon mission, circumstances were

---

[1] Inferenda quoque sæpius eis est orbis auctoritas Christiani. Ep. Dan. ibid.

[2] Quidquid de faciendis signis acceperis vel accepisti, hæc non tibi sed illis deputes donata pro quorum tibi salute collata sunt. Ep. Greg. ad Aug. apud Bed. l. i. c. 31. Wilk. Con. vol. i. p. 10.

changed. The rulers of the barbarous nations had proved themselves not insensible to the truths of the gospel; and the influence of their example had been recently demonstrated in the conversion of their subjects, the Franks, the Visigoths, and the Suevi. Hence the first object of the missionaries, Roman, Gallic, or Scottish, was invariably the same, to obtain the patronage of the prince. His favour ensured, his opposition prevented their success. The primitive Christians braved with unconquerable courage the menaces and power of the pagan world: but in the history of the Anglo-Saxon kingdoms, we shall seek in vain for a missionary who ventured to preach in opposition to the civil power. The despondency of the bishops of Kent and Essex, after the death of their patrons, proves how much they depended for success on the smile or the frown of the monarch.[1] Yet let us not on that account judge lightly of their merit. If virtue is to be estimated by the effort which it requires, they will be entitled to no ordinary degree of praise. They abandoned the dearest connections of friends and country; they exposed themselves to the caprice and cruelty of unknown barbarians; they voluntarily embraced a life of laborious and unceasing exertion without any prospect of temporal emolument, and with the sole view of civilizing the manners, and

---

[1] On this subject see the remarks of Macquer (Abrégé chronologique de l'histoire ecclesiastique, vol. i. p. 512, an. 1768), who unfortunately adduces the conduct of Cædwalla to prove that the converts were Christians only in name, and still retained all the vices of paganism. But Cædwalla was neither a Saxon nor a convert. He was a British prince, whom national animosity urged to wreak his vengeance on the vanquished Northumbrians.

correcting the vices of a distant and savage people. If they neither felt nor provoked the scourge of persecution, they may, at least, claim the merit of pure, active, and disinterested virtue : and the fortunate issue of their labours is sufficient to disprove the opinion of those, who imagine that no church can be firmly established, the foundations of which are not cemented with the blood of martyrs.[1]

[1] Mr. Soames, throughout his narrative of the conversion of the Anglo-Saxons, appears to have taken it for granted, that the Scots were the descendants of the ancient Britons, and their bishops the successors of the ancient British bishops. Aidan and his successors were, he tells us, " prelates of British origin," and brought with them " a religious system of native growth ;" that " Diuma and his three successors, under whom all our midland counties were converted, were also members of the national church ;" and that, with the exception of Norfolk and Suffolk, " every county from London to Edinburgh has the full gratification of pointing to the ancient church of Britain as its nursing mother in Christ's holy faith." Soames, 68, 69, also 101. Now the fact is, that these prelates of supposed " British origin " were bishops of Irish origin; that " their religious system " was not of " native growth," but the same which St. Patrick had taken with him to Ireland from Rome ; that the only national church of which Diuma and his successors were members, was the church of Ireland, and that not a single county " from London to Edinburgh can point to the ancient church of Britain as its nursing mother in the faith of Christ," because the British church of that age on the western coast refused, through national animosity, to communicate the doctrines of the gospel to the Saxons, and continued, as late as a century after the arrival of Aidan, to look upon the Saxon Christians, even on those who had been converted by Scottish missionaries, as no better than pagans, and treated them on all occasions as aliens from Christianity. Quippe, says Beda, cum *usque hodie* moris sit Britonum fidem religionemque Anglorum pro nihilo habere, neque in aliquo eis magis communicare quam cum paganis. Bed. ii. c. 20, also v. 23.

In the judgment of a hasty or a prejudiced observer, the faults of the disciple are frequently transferred to the master; and the facility with which the natives of Essex relapsed into idolatry after the death of Saberct, and those of Northumbria after the fall of Edwin, has encouraged a suspicion, that the missionaries were more anxious to multiply the number, than to enlighten the minds of their proselytes. It should, however, be remembered, that the teachers were few, the pupils many, and their ignorance extreme. Under such difficulties, the rapid though temporary success of Mellitus and Paulinus bears an honourable testimony to their zeal : nor should it excite surprise, if, after their unfortunate expulsion, the converts, without the aid of instruction, or the support of the civil power, gradually returned to their former idolatry. To these two instances may be successfully opposed the conduct of all the other Saxon nations, in which Christianity from its first admission maintained a decided superiority. To object, that they yielded without conviction, is to venture an assertion that certainly is not countenanced by the obstinacy with which men adhere to their religious prejudices; and is sufficiently contradicted by the reserve with which Ethelbert listened to the instructions of Augustine, by the long resistance of Edwin to the arguments of Paulinus, and by the tardy but sincere conversions of Peada, prince of Mercia, and Sigebert, king of Essex. But the claim of the missionaries to the gratitude, may be best deduced from the improvement, of their disciples; and whoever wishes justly to estimate their merit, will carefully compare the conduct of the Christian with that of the pagan Saxons.

By the ancient writers the Saxons are unanimously classed with the most barbarous of the nations that invaded and dismembered the Roman empire.[1] Their valour was disgraced by its brutality. To the services they generally preferred the blood of their captives; and the man, whose life they condescended to spare, was taught to consider perpetual servitude as a gratuitous favour.[2] Among themselves, a rude and imperfect system of legislation intrusted to private revenge the punishment of private injuries; and the ferocity of their passions continually multiplied these deadly and hereditary feuds. Avarice and the lust of sensual-enjoyment had extinguished in their breasts some of the first feelings of nature. The savages of Africa may traffic with Europeans for the negroes whom they have seized by treachery, or captured in open war; but the more savage conquerors of Britain sold without scruple to the merchants of the continent their countrymen, and even their own children.[3] Their religion was accommodated to their manners, and their manners were perpetuated by their religion. In their theology they acknowledged no sin but cowardice, and revered no virtue but courage. Their gods they appeased with the

---

[1] Julian. de laud. Constan. p. 116. Sidon. l. viii. ep. 9. Zozim. l. iii. p. 147.

[2] Altissimæ gratiæ stabat in loco. Gild. p. 87.

[3] Familiari, says Malmsbury (de reg. l. i. c. 3), ac pene ingenita consuetudine, adeo ut non dubitarent arctissimas necessitudines sub prætextu minimorum commodorum distrahere.

blood of human victims. Of a future life their notions were faint and wavering: and if the soul were fated to survive the body, to quaff ale out of the skulls of their enemies was to be the great reward of the virtuous: to lead a life of hunger and inactivity the endless punishment of the wicked.[1]

Such were the pagan Saxons. But their ferocity yielded to the exertions of the missionaries, and the harsher features of their origin were insensibly softened under the mild influence of the gospel. In the rage of victory they learned to respect the rights of humanity. Death or slavery was no longer the fate of the conquered Britons: by their submission they were incorporated with the victors; and their lives and property were protected by the equity of their Christian conquerors.[2] The acquisition of religious knowledge introduced a new spirit of legislation: the presence of the bishops and superior clergy improved the wisdom of the national councils; and laws were framed to punish the more flagrant violations of morality, and to prevent the daily broils which harassed the peace of society. The humane idea that by baptism all men became brethren, contributed to meliorate the condition of slavery, and scattered the seeds of that liberality which gradually undermined, and at length abolished, so odious an institution. By the provision of the legislature the freedom of the child was secured from the avarice of an unnatural parent; and the

---

[1] Two passages in Beda (l. ii. c. 13, l. iii. c. 30) will almost justify a doubt whether they believed in any future state at all.

[2] See the laws of Ine, 23, 24, 32, 46 (Wilk. leg. Sax. pp. 18, 20, 22).

heaviest punishment was denounced against the man who presumed to sell to a foreign master one of his countrymen, though he were a slave or a malefactor.[1] But by nothing were the converts more distinguished than by their piety. The conviction of a future and endless existence beyond the grave elevated and expanded their minds. To prepare their souls for this expected state of being was to many the first object of their solicitude: they eagerly sought every source of instruction, and with scrupulous fidelity practised every duty which they had learned.[2] Of the zeal of the more opulent among the laity, the numerous churches, hospitals, and monasteries which they founded are a sufficient proof: and the clergy could boast with equal truth of the piety displayed by the more eminent of their order, and of the nations instructed in the Christian faith by the labours of St. Boniface and his associates.[3] In the clerical and monastic establishments, the most sublime of the gospel virtues were carefully prac-

---

[1] Though this inhuman custom was severely forbidden by different legislators (Wilk. leg. Sax. pp. 17, 93, 107, 138), it was clandestinely continued long after the Norman conquest. (Ang. Sax. vol. ii. p. 258. Malm. de reg. l. i. c. 3. Girald. de expug. Hiber. l. i. c. 18.)

[2] See Beda (l. ii. c. 17, l. iii. c. 26, l. iv. c. 3. Ep. ad. Egb. ant. p. 311), and the testimony of St. Gregory. Gens Anglorum prave agere metuit ac totis desideriis ad æternitatis gloriam pervenire concupiscit. (Moral. l. xxvii. c. 8. Ep. l. ix. 58.)

[3] The Old Saxons, the Francs, the Hessians, and the Thuringians, were converted by St. Boniface; the inhabitants of Westphalia, by St. Swibert; the Frisians and the Hollanders, by St. Wilfrid and St. Willibrord; the nations north of the Elbe, by St. Willehad. See Walker's translation of Spelman's Alfred (pref. not.).

tised : even kings descended from their thrones
and exchanged the sceptre for the cowl. Their
conduct was applauded by their contemporaries : and
even those who affect to censure it, must at least
esteem the motives which inspired, and admire the
resolution which completed the sacrifice. The progress of civilization kept equal pace with the progress
of religion : not only the useful but the agreeable arts
were introduced ; every species of knowledge which
could be attained was eagerly studied ; and during
the gloom of ignorance, which overspread the rest
of Europe, learning found for a certain period an
asylum among the Saxons of Britain.[1] To this
picture an ingenious adversary may oppose a very
different description. He may collect the vices
which have been stigmatized by the zeal of their
preachers, and point to the crimes which disgraced
the characters of some of their monarchs. But the
impartial observer will acknowledge the impossi-
bility of eradicating at once the fiercer passions of a
whole nation ; nor be surprised if he behold several
of them relapse into their former manners, and on
some occasions unite the actions of savages with the
profession of Christians. To judge of the advantage
which the Saxons derived from their conversion, he
will fix his eyes on their virtues. *They* were the
offspring of the gospel; their vices were the relics of
paganism.

It was fortunate for the converts, that, during the
seventh century, the peace of the western church
was seldom disturbed by religious controversy.
Though their teachers came from different and far

---

[1] See the chapter on the Learning of the Saxons.

distant countries, they were unanimous in preaching
the same doctrine; and it was for several centuries
the boast of the Saxons, that heresy had never dared
to erect its standard within their church. In points
of discipline, national partiality would prompt each
missionary to establish the practice of his own
country; though Gregory with a laudable liberality
of sentiment exhorted his disciples to despise the
narrow prejudices of education, and to select from
the customs of different churches whatever was best
calculated to promote the general interests of virtue
and religion.[1] But all were not animated with the
spirit of the pontiff. The Scottish monks had been
taught to respect as sacred every institution which
had been sanctioned by the approbation of their
ancestors; while the Roman missionaries contended,
that the customs of an obscure and sequestered
people ought to yield to the consentient practice of
the principal Christian churches. Each party pertinaciously adhered to their own opinion; and the
controversy was conducted with a warmth which
threatened to destroy the fabric that had been
erected with so much labour and perseverance. Yet
the great objects, which called forth the zeal and
divided the harmony of these holy men, regarded
not the essentials of Christianity : they were confined,
first, to the proper time for the celebration of Easter,

---

[1] Novit fraternitas tua Romanæ Ecclesiæ consuetu-
dinem, in qua se meminit nutritam. Sed mihi placet, sive
in Romana, sive in Galliarum, seu in qualibet ecclesia
aliquid invenisti, quod plus omnipotenti Deo possit placere,
sollicite eligas, et in Anglorum ecclesia institutione
præcipua, quæ de multis ecclesiis colligere potuisti,
infundas. Bed. l. c. 27, interrog. 2.

and secondly, to the most approved method of wearing the ecclesiastical tonsure.

First. The festival of Easter, instituted in honour of the resurrection of Christ, has always been considered as the principal of the Christian solemnities. To reduce the different churches of the east and west to uniformity in the celebration of this great event, was an object which engaged the attention of the prelates assembled in the council of Nice : and as the commencement of the Paschal time depended on astronomical calculation, it was determined that the patriarch of Alexandria should annually consult the philosophers of Egypt, and communicate the result of their researches to the Roman pontiff; whose duty it was to notify the day of the festival to the more distant churches. Unfortunately, the Roman agreed not with the Alexandrian method of computation; a different cycle of years was employed; and the limits of the equinoctial lunation were affixed to different days. Hence arose an insuperable obstacle to the uniformity required by the council ; and it not unfrequently happened, that while the western Christians were celebrating the joyous event of the resurrection, those of the East had but lately commenced the penitential austerities of Lent.[1]

---

[1] The cycle of the Alexandrians contained nineteen years, that of the Romans eighty-four : according to the former the equinoctial new moon could not occur earlier than the 8th of March, nor later than the 5th of April, while the latter affixed these limits to the 5th of March and the 3rd of April. Hence it happened, in the year 417, that Easter was celebrated at Rome on the 25th of March, and at Alexandria on the 22nd of April; because the new moon which fell on the 5th of March was considered the equinoctial moon by the Romans, and that which fell

Weary of the disputes occasioned by this difference of computation, the Roman church about the middle of the sixth century adopted a new cycle, which had been lately composed by Dionysius Exiguus, and which, in every important point, agreed with the Egyptian mode of calculation.[1] But the British churches, harassed at that period by the Saxons, and almost precluded from communicating with Italy, on account of the convulsed situation of the continent, were unacquainted with this improvement,[2] and continued to use the ancient cycle, though their ignorance of its application caused them to deviate widely from the former practice of the Roman church.[3]   Hence it hap-

---

on the 4th of April the equinoctial moon by the Alexandrians.   Smith's Bed. App. No. 9, pp. 697, 698.

[1] It contained ninety-five years, or five Egyptian cycles.

[2] This is the reason which Beda assigns for their adhesion to the old method.   Utpote quibus longe extra orbem positis nemo synodalia Paschalis observantiæ decreta porrexerat. L. iii. c. 4.

[3] On this circumstance the prejudice of party has endeavoured to build a wild and extravagant system.   Because the British Christians of the seventh century disagreed from the Roman church in the time of celebrating Easter, it has been gratuitously assumed that they were Quartodecimans; that of consequence their fathers were of the same persuasion; and ultimately that the faith was planted in Britain by missionaries, who were sent not from Rome, but from some of the Asiatic churches. The truth or falsehood of the latter hypothesis is of little consequence : yet it is certain that the Britons in the time of St. Augustine were not Quartodecimans, for they observed Easter on the 14th day of the moon, only when that day happened to be a Sunday (Bed. l. iii. c. 4, 17) : and that their ancestors were not Quartodecimans is no less certain, if any credit be due to Eusebius (Hist. l. v. c. 23), to Socrates (l. v. c. 21), to Constantine in his letter to the

pened that, during the sixth and seventh centuries,
the British Christians scattered along the western
coasts of the island, and the Scots in the north of
Ireland, observed in the computation of Easter
a rule peculiar to themselves: and when it was
asked how *they*, buried in an obscure corner of the
earth, dared to oppose their customs to the unanimous voice of the Greek and Latin churches, they
boldly replied, that they had received them from
their forefathers, whose sanctity had been proved by
a multitude of miracles, and whose doctrines they
considered as their most valuable inheritance.[1]

---

bishops (Eus. l. iii. c. 14), and to the subscriptions of
the British prelates to the council of Arles (Spel. Conc.
pp. 40, 42).—I should not omit that Goodall (ad Hist. Scot.
introd. p. 66. Keith's Catal. of Scot. Bishops, pref. p. vii.)
asserts that the Scots employed the same cycle, and
observed Easter on the same day as was customary in the
Roman church previous to the council of Nice. He founds
his opinion on the ancient paschal table published by
Bucher, in which the festival is fixed on the fourteenth
day of the moon for the years 316 and 320.

[1] It should be observed that this was a question not of
doctrine, but of practice. It partook, indeed, of religious
interest, inasmuch as it regarded the time of celebrating
that, which was esteemed the chief of Christian solemnities: in other respects it was one of astronomical calculation, and depended on the proficiency of the parties
in astronomical science. The error of the British Christians arose from their adhesion to the old and incorrect
cycles and computations of their fathers, and from their
ignorance of the more correct formulæ adopted by the
rest of Christendom; and the obstinacy with which they
defended that error may be fairly attributed to the partiality with which men, particularly men secluded from
commerce with other people, cling to their national customs. Some writers have looked upon such obstinacy as
a proof of their independence on the church of Rome.
It is equally a proof of their independence on the uni-

Second. When once the spirit of controversy
has taken possession of the mind, the most trifling
objects swell into considerable magnitude, and are
pursued with an ardour and interest which cannot
fail to excite the surprise, perhaps the smile, of the
indifferent spectator. Of this description was the
dispute respecting the proper form of the ecclesiastical tonsure, which contributed to widen the separation between the Roman and Scottish missionaries.
The former shaved the crown of the head, which
was surrounded by a circle of hair supposed to
represent the wreath of thorns forced by the cruelty
of his persecutors on the temples of the Messiah :
the latter permitted the hair to grow on the back,
and shaved in the form of a crescent the front of
the head. Each party was surprised and shocked
at the uncanonical appearance of the other. The
Romans asserted that their tonsure had descended
to them from the prince of the apostles, while that
of their adversaries was the distinguishing mark of
Simon Magus and his disciples.[1] The Scots, unable

versal church ; for they disobeyed the canons of the
council of Nice as much as the decrees of the Roman
pontiffs. It is plain, however, that it was not so considered at the time. The Roman missionaries, though they
condemned it, did not look upon it as amounting to the
guilt of schism. Honorius of Canterbury, and Felix of
East-Anglia, lived in communion with Aidan, and tolerated his obstinacy on this point in consideration of his
zeal and piety. Unde ab omnibus patienter tolerabatur ...
et etiam ab his qui de pascha aliter sentiebant, merito
deligebatur, nec solum a mediocribus, verum ab ipsis quoque episcopis, Honorio Cantuariensi et Felice Orientalium
Anglorum, venerationi habitus. Bed. iii. c. 25. See also
l. iii. c. 17.
     [1] Bed. l. iii. c. 25, v. c. 21.

to refute the confident assertions of their adversaries, maintained, that their method of shaving the head, however impious in its origin, had been afterwards sanctified by the virtues of those who had adopted it.[1] The arguments of the contending parties serve only to prove their ignorance of ecclesiastical antiquity. During the first three or four hundred years of the Christian era, the clergy were not distinguished from the laity by any peculiar method of clipping the hair: such a distinction in times of persecution would have betrayed them to their enemies. Afterwards the church proscribed among them all those modes, which might be attributed to effeminacy or vanity, and of course the long locks which were worn with so much parade by the northern nations.[2] But the tonsure, properly so called, originated from the piety of the first professors of the monastic institute. To shave the head was deemed by the natives of the East a ceremony expressive of the deepest affliction; and was adopted by the monks as a distinctive token of that seclusion from worldly pleasure to which they had voluntarily condemned themselves. When in the fifth century the most illustrious of the order were drawn from their cells, and raised to the highest dignities in the church, they retained this mark of their former profession; and in consequence of the

---

[1] Numquid, says Colman, patrem nostrum Columbam, et successores ejus divinis paginis contraria sapuisse vel egisse credendum est ? quos ego sanctos esse non dubitans, semper eorum vitam, mores, et disciplinam sequi non desisto. Bed. l. ii. c. 25.

[2] Deflua cæsaries compescitur ad breves capillos. Pruden. Περὶ Στέφαν. 13.

gradual adoption of the new costume by the clergy, the tonsure began to be considered, both in the Greek and Latin church, as a necessary rite for admission into the number of ecclesiastics. It was at this period that the circular and semicircular modes of shaving the head were introduced. The names of their authors were soon lost in oblivion; and succeeding generations, ignorant of their real origin, credulously attributed them to the first age of Christianity.[1]

Such were the mighty objects which scattered the seeds of dissension in the breasts of these holy men. The merit of restoring concord was reserved for the zeal and authority of Oswiu, king of Northumbria. As that province had received the doctrine of the gospel from the Scottish missionaries, their influence was predominant with the prince and the majority of the people; but his queen Eanfled, who had been educated in Kent, and his son Alchfrid, who attended the lessons of St. Wilfrid, adhered to the practice of the Roman church. Thus Oswiu saw his own family divided into opposite factions, and the same solemnities celebrated at different times within his own residence. Desirous to procure uniformity, he summoned the champions of each party to meet him at Whitby, the monastery of the Abbess Hild, and to argue the merits of their respective customs in his presence. (Ann. 664.) On the one side stood Agilberct, a Gallic prelate,

---

[1] See Smith's Bed. App. No. ix. According to an ancient book of canons quoted by Ussher, the semicircular tonsure was first adopted in Ireland (Uss. Ant. Brit. c. 17, p. 924), the circular, if we may believe Pellicia (De Chr. Ecc. Politia, p. 30, Colon. 1829), in Gaul.

at that time bishop of Winchester, who chanced to
be on a visit to the king, with Romanus, the chaplain of Queen Eanfled, Wilfrid, the chaplain of
Prince Alchfrid, and Jacob, a deacon, who had
remained in Northumbria ever since the flight of
Paulinus. On the other were ranged Colman, the
bishop of Lindisfarne, Cedd, who had been ordained
by the Scots bishop of the East Saxons, the abbess
Hild, and the Scottish clergy. Both Agilberct and
Colman, as foreigners, were but imperfectly acquainted with the vernacular language. Agilberct,
therefore, placed the defence of his cause in the
hands of Wilfrid; but Colman would not accept the
services of a substitute, and Cedd was appointed
his interpreter, an office which he discharged to the
satisfaction of all parties.

The king, after a short preface on the benefit of
uniformity, called upon Colman to begin. He alleged in defence of the Scottish custom—first, the
example of St. John the evangelist, who was said
in books[1] to have kept Easter on the fourteenth
day of the lunar month; second, on the Paschal
canons of Anatolius, which ordered it to be kept on
the same day; third, and on the practice of Columba
and his successors in the isle of Iona, by whom he
(Colman) had been educated, and appointed bishop
of Northumbria. Wilfrid, in answer, said, that Colman was in error with respect to St. John, who, at
a time when condescension was requisite, kept the

---

[1] *Legitur* celebrasse. Bed. iii. 25. He does not rest
his assertion on tradition, derived from Columba, but on
the testimony of some book or books, probably well known,
as no name is mentioned.

pasch at the same time with the Jews, on the
fourteenth day, whether it were a Sunday or not,
whereas the Scots kept it only on that day, when it
happened to fall on a Sunday; neither could he appeal to the Paschal canons of Anatolius, for Anatolius followed a cycle of nineteen years, which the
Scots did not; and a manner of reckoning by which
he never kept the pasch till the fourteenth day was
begun, whereas the Scots often kept it before the
thirteenth day was ended. With respect to the
practice of the abbots of Iona, an obscure isle in
the Scottish sea, their authority ought not to prevail against that of the universal church, and the
decree of the great council of Nice.

Colman rejoined that these abbots were holy men,
who could not be supposed to have done wrong: to
which Wilfrid replied, that, cut off, as they were, by
their situation, from the rest of the world, they might
be excused under the plea of ignorance; but that if
Colman and his clergy, now that they knew the
decrees of the apostolic see, or rather of the universal church, refused to conform, they would undoubtedly sin. Columba might have been a great
man, but Peter was a greater, on whom our Lord
had built his church, and to whom he had given the
keys of the kingdom of heaven. At these words
Oswiu, who had hitherto been silent, exclaimed,
" Colman, is it so ?" Receiving an answer in the
affirmative, he resumed with a smile, " who then is
the greater in heaven, Columba or Peter ?" All replied " Peter :" " Then," said the king, " will I obey
the decrees of Peter; for, if he, who has the keys,
shut me out, who is there to let me in ?" The by-

standers applauded the witticism; and the conference broke up. The result was, that Hild and
Cedd, and several of the Scottish clergy, passed over
to the party of Wilfrid; and Colman, after a short
interval, taking with him his own adherents and
about thirty natives, returned to his parent monastery in the isle of Iona.[1]

The termination of this controversy has subjected
the successful party to the severe but unmerited
censures of several late historians. They affect to
consider the Scottish monks as an injured and persecuted caste, and declaim with suspicious vehemence against the haughty and intolerant spirit of
the Roman clergy.[2] But, if uniformity was desirable,
it could only be obtained by the submission or retreat of one of the contending parties : and certainly
it was unreasonable to expect that those, who observed the discipline which universally prevailed
among the Christians of the continent, should tamely
yield to the pretensions of a few obscure churches
on the remotest coast of Britain.[3] The charge of

---

[1] Bed. 1. iii. c. 25, 26. Eddius, Vit. Wilf. c. x. The
Saxon translator of Beda often passes over entire chapters
of the original. He has passed over both these chapters,
and it has been recently discovered that he omitted c. 25,
" through indignation at the victory of the Romanists over
the Scots !" Soames, p. 73. But what then was his motive
for passing over c. 26, which contains Beda's glowing
eulogium on the virtues of these very Scots? Not indignation certainly.

[2] Henry, Hist. of Brit. vol. iii. p. 204. Rapin, vol. i. p.
71.

[3] Numquid universali, quæ per orbem est ecclesiæ
Christi, eorum est paucitas uno de angulo extremæ insulæ præferenda. Wilf. apud Bed. 1. iii. c. 25. Also 1.
ii. c. 19.

persecution is not warranted by the expressions of the original writers, who give the praise of moderation almost exclusively to the Romans. Beda has recorded the high esteem in which Aidan and his associates were held by the bishops of Canterbury and Dunwich; and observes, that through respect to his merit, they were unwilling to condemn his departure from the universal discipline of the Catholic church.[1] The letters which the Roman missionaries wrote on occasion of this controversy uniformly breathe a spirit of meekness and conciliation ; and prove that the writers rather pitied the ignorance, than resented the obstinacy, of their opponents.[2] But historic truth will not permit equal praise to be given to the conduct of the Scottish prelates. When Daganus, a Scottish bishop, arrived at Canterbury in the days of Lawrence, the successor of St. Augustine, he pertinaciously refused to eat at the same table, or even in the same house, with those who observed the Roman Easter.[3] We may wonder and lament that for objects of such inferior moment men could suspend their more important labours, and engage in acrimonious controversy : but candour must admit that of the two parties, the Romans had the better cause, and by their moderation deserved that victory which they ultimately obtained.[4]

The conference at Whitby established harmony in the Anglo-Saxon church ; but many years elapsed before the question was set at rest among the Picts,

---

[1] Bed. ibid.
[2] Bed. l. ii. c. 4, 19.   Wilk. Conc. tom. i. pp. 36, 40. Ep. Bonif. 44, p. 59.
[3] Bed. l. ii. c. 4.   [4] Smith's Bed. App. viii. ix.

the Scots, and the Britons. It is not, indeed, a
subject immediately connected with the present
work, but the curiosity of the reader will probably
be gratified, if I state briefly by what means those
three nations were at last induced to conform to the
general practice of other Christians. First. The
southern Picts, or men of Galloway, had been converted by Nynias, a British missionary sent from
Rome, and had, of course, always observed the
Roman Easter; but the northern Picts, who received the rudiments of religion from the monks of
Iona, adhered to the practice of their teachers till
the year 710, when Naiton, king of the Picts,
having previously consulted Ceolfrid, abbot of Wearmouth, ordered the Roman computation to be followed in all parts of his dominions.[1] Second. In
Ireland, also, the southern tribes had conformed
some time in the first half of the seventh century,
at the admonition of the apostolic see ;[2] but the
northern tribes retained the calculation of their
fathers till 701, when they were reclaimed from
their error by Adomnan, abbot of Iona, who had
lately become a proselyte to the Roman method,

---

[1] Bed. iii. c. 3, 4, v. c. 21.

[2] Gentes Scotorum, que in Australibus Hiberniæ insulæ
partibus morabantur, jamdudum ad admonitionem apostolicæ sedis antistitis, pascha canonico ritu observare di-
dicerunt. Bed. iii. c. 3. It appears from Beda, that Pope
Honorius had written to the Irish on this subject. L. ii. c.
19. In 630, was held the synod of Leighlinn, in which
Lasrian advocated the Roman, Munic the Irish practice.
Ussher, Primord. 928. No decision followed ; but messengers were sent to Rome to consult the pontiff. Both
Honorius, and Severian, his successor, were dead, and an
answer was returned by John, the deacon, now bishop
elect. Bed. ii. c. 19.

during a visit which he paid to Aldfrid, king of Northumbria. But Adomnan could not subdue the obstinacy of his own monks, nor of the monks dependent on his own monastery; and yet a few years later, in 715, the very men who had been deaf to the voice and authority of their own abbot yielded to the arguments and exhortations of Egbert, an Anglo-Saxon missionary.[1]

Third. With the Britons there was a difficulty to be surmounted, which existed not among the Picts and Scots, that intense hatred which they cherished against the Saxons, and every thing connected with the Saxons. In their estimation, the Saxons were an accursed race, the children of robbers and murderers, possessing the fruit of their fathers' crimes, and therefore still lying under the maledictions formerly pronounced by the British bishops against the invaders. With them the Saxon was no better than a pagan, bearing the name of a Christian. They refused to return his salutation, to join in prayer with him in the church, to sit with him at the same table, to abide with him under the same roof. The remnant of his meals, and the food over which he had made the sign of the cross, they threw to their dogs or swine; the cup out of which he had drunk they scoured with sand, as if it had contracted defilement from his lips. If he came among them as a stranger and solicited an asylum, he was subjected to a course of penance during forty days, before he could be admitted to their fellowship.[2] Hence we

---

[1] Bed. iii. c. 4, v. c. 15, 21, 22.

[2] Nostram communionem magnopere abominantur, in tantum ut nec in ecclesia nobiscum orationum officia cele-

may judge that Beda was in no great error, when he
ascribed their refusal to keep the canonical time of
Easter to the influence of national hatred, as much
as to that of religious prejudice.[1] In 692, the celebrated St. Aldhelm, at that time abbot of Malmesbury, wrote by order of a synod a long letter to
Gerontius, king of Cornwall, respecting the time of
Easter, and the uncharitable dealing of the Britons
with the Saxon Christians : but it was not to be expected that they would submit to be schooled by a
Saxon teacher; his success was limited to the conformity of the tribes which acknowledged the sway
of the king of Wessex ;[2] and it was reserved for a
native prelate, Elbod of Benchor, to establish the

---

brare, nec ad mensam ciborum fercula pro charitatis gratia
pariter percipere dignentur. Quin imo fragmenta fercu-
lorum, et reliquias epularum lurconum canum ructibus,
et immundis devorandis porcis projiciunt, &c. (Epis. S.
Aldhel. ad Geront. Reg. inter Bonifacianas. Ed. Ser-
rario, p. 59). In tantum communionem nostrorum execra-
verunt ut si quispiam abbatum vel presbyterorum nostrorum, a fideli de plebe rogatus, refectionem suam ante se
positam, signo crucis benediceret, foras projiciendam et
effundendam quasi idolothytum judicabant, et vasa Dei,
quibus nostri vescebantur, lavari prius, quasi sorde pol-
luta, jubebant, antequam ab aliis contingebantur. Edd.
c. 47, p. 77.

[1] Britones maxima ex parte domestico sibi odio gentem
Anglorum, et totius ecclesiæ Catholicæ statum pascha,
minus recte moribusque improbis impugnant. Bed. v. 23.
He tells us that the Christian Briton Cædwalla was more
inhuman than the Pagan king Penda; that he sought to
extirpate the whole nation, that he paid no respect to
their Christianity, and held no more fellowship with them
than Pagans. Quippe cum usque hodie (Ann. 730), moris
sit Britonum fidem religionemque Anglorum pro nihilo
habere, neque in aliquo eis magis communicare quam
paganis. L. ii. c. 20.

[2] Bed. v. c. 18. Ep. ad Geront. Reg. p. 59.

Catholic computation, first in North Wales, soon after the middle of the eighth century, and subsequently in South Wales, about the year 777. If, as is sometimes pretended, the controversy was renewed in South Wales after the death of Elbod, it died away in silence, and was never heard of afterwards.[1]

---

[1] Ang.-Sac. ii. 648.   Archaiol. of Wales, ii. 474, 5.

CHAPTER II.

SUCCESSION AND DUTIES OF BISHOPS.

AUGUSTINE IS CONSECRATED BISHOP—ALL THE CHURCHES OF THE
SAXONS, AND OF THE BRITONS, SUBJECTED TO HIS AUTHORITY—HIS
CONFERENCE WITH THE BRITONS—THEY REJECT HIS DEMANDS—MONKS
OF BENCHOR SLAUGHTERED—THEODORE ARCHBISHOP OF BRITAIN—
EGBERT ARCHBISHOP OF YORK — ARCHBISHOPRIC OF LICHFIELD
ESTABLISHED—AND ABOLISHED—MULTIPLICATION OF BISHOPRICS—
ELECTION OF BISHOPS—SPIRITUAL AND SECULAR DUTIES OF BISHOPS.

THE existence of a national church without episcopal government is an anomaly, of which no
instance can be found in Christian antiquity. When
Augustine landed in Kent, he was only priest and
abbot ; but within a few months he recrossed the
sea, and at Arles, in virtue of a papal commission,
was consecrated bishop by Vergilius, of that city,[1]

---

[1] Here two questions may be asked; first, was not
Augustine a bishop before his arrival in England ? Wharton has attempted to prove it in Anglia Sacra. The
contrary will be shewn in note (D) at the end of the
volume. Second, if he was ordained in Gaul, was it in
consequence of Gregory's *order*, or, as it is customary to
describe it, in consequence of his *advice?* Beda says
expressly that it was in consequence of the papal *order*.
Juxta quod jussa sancti patris Gregorii acceperant (Hist.
l. i. c. 27): Gregory, that it was in consequence of the
license granted by himself—data a me licentia,—in his
epistle to Eulogius, patriarch of Alexandria, Epist. l. viii.
ep. 30. Still by modern writers we are generally told that
it was by Gregory's *advice*, as if the two were the same
thing.

vicar of the apostolic see in Gaul.[1] On his return he received from Gregory the pallium, with authority to consecrate bishops, and, in addition, a plan for the future government of the new church. By this the pontiff decreed that, in proportion as Christianity extended its conquests in the south, Augustine should ordain bishops in the most convenient places, to the number of twelve, over whom he should exercise metropolitan authority ; which authority at his death should devolve on the bishop

---

[1] Why was Augustine sent for ordination to the bishop of Arles instead of some of the metropolitans nearer to Kent ? Probably because he was the first in rank, being apostolic vicar in Gaul. Cui ecclesiæ (Arelatensi) id honoris dignitatisque collatum est, ut non tantum has provincias potestate propria gubernaret, verum omnes Gallias, sibi apostolicæ sedis vice mandatas, sub omni ecclesiastica regula contineret. (The bishops of the province of Arles to Pope Leo, Inter. Epist. D. Leonis, p. 183.) We may form a pretty correct notion of the authority belonging to the bishop of Arles as apostolic vicar from a letter of St. Leo to Anastasius, bishop of Thessalonica. From it we learn that the vicar was appointed to watch over the state of religion in all the provinces of his vicariate, to aid the metropolitans in the exercise of their authority, without at the same time encroaching on their rights, and to inform the pontiff of the most important occurrences in the churches within the limits of his jurisdiction. When the provincial bishops chose a metropolitan, the approbation of the vicar was required for his consecration ; and when the metropolitan ordained a bishop of his province, he was bound to advise the vicar. Matters which could not be determined in the provincial synod were referred to the vicar, and by him, if necessary, to the Pope. In cases of emergency the vicar had a right to assemble a council of two bishops from every province in the vicariate, but they were named by the metropolitans ; and if they differed from him in opinion, he could proceed no further, but was ordered to await the decision of the pontiff. Ep. D. Leon, p. 154.

of London, whose successors should be chosen and
ordained by the council, that is, the bishops of the
province, and receive the honour of the pallium
from Rome. He was also to send a bishop to
York, who, if the conversion of the northern tribes
would admit of it, should also ordain twelve bishops
among them, and preside over those bishops as
their metropolitan. His successors, like those of
the bishop of London, were to be ordained by the
council of the northern province; and the precedency of the two metropolitans was to be ever
afterwards determined by the date of their consecration. Augustine, in addition, was invested with a
more general authority than that of metropolitan,
an authority of superintendence over all the bishops,
not of the Saxons only, but of the Britons also, for
the correction of error in doctrine, and of abuse in
practice. "Your brotherhood," says the mandate,
"will moreover have subject to you not only the
bishops whom you or the bishop of York may
ordain, but all the bishops of Britain, by authority of
our God and Lord Jesus Christ; that from your
instruction they may learn to believe correctly, and
from your example to live religiously; and thus by
the faithful discharge of their duty obtain the
reward of the heavenly kingdom."[1] It is plain
that the authority conveyed by this instrument was

---

[1] Bed. l. i. c. 29. Gregory probably selected the two
cities of London and York for the metropolitan sees,
because they had possessed that rank under the Romans,
and till the conquests of the Saxons. We find that of
the three British prelates deputed to the council of Arles,
the first subscribes as bishop of London, and the second as
bishop of York.

personal to Augustine, and not intended to descend from him to his successors.

If the reader bear in mind the description drawn about forty years before by Gildas of the deplorable state of the British church, and of the depravity both of the clergy and people, he will readily divine the reason why the pontiff thought of placing the British bishops under the superintendence of the missionary. Gregory was not the man to invade the just rights of others. When Augustine had complained to him of uncanonical proceedings in some of the Gallic churches, he replied, " Over the bishops of Gaul we have given to you no authority. From the ancient times of our predecessors the bishop of Arles has received the pallium, and we ought not to deprive him of his authority. If you discover any thing reprehensible in the conduct of the Gallic bishops, it will be your duty to advise the bishop of Arles respecting the best manner of reforming it, and to stimulate his zeal, if he appear cold and indifferent. But authority, whenever it is to be employed, must proceed from him, that we may not subvert the order established by our fathers. But with respect to the bishops of Britain, we commit them all to your brotherhood, that the unlearned may be taught, that the weak may be strengthened by your counsel, and the obstinate be corrected by your authority."[1]

Kent, the scene of Augustine's ministry, lay at a considerable distance from the British Christians;

---

[1] Bed. l. c. 27. But were not the British bishops independent of the bishops of Rome?—Most certainly not. The reader will see that question discussed in note (E).

and many an idolatrous tribe of Saxons was to be
converted before he could reach the borders of
Wales. Mindful, however, of the charge intrusted
to him by Gregory, he availed himself of the authority of the Bretwalda Ethelbert, and, through the
influence of his patron, procured a meeting with
some of the nearest of the British clergy, at a place
afterwards called Austin's Oak, probably Austclive
in Gloucestershire, the usual ferry over the Severn.[1]
But distance was the lesser difficulty : how was he
to subdue that intense hatred with which the
Britons regarded the Saxons, and all connected
with the Saxons ; he who came to them under the
protection of the most powerful of their enemies,
and the purity of whose motives was liable to all
the suspicions which national antipathy would
excite? He requested that, joining in fellowship
with him,[2] they would grant to him their aid in the

---

[1] Beda was indebted for the history of Augustine to the
research of the abbot Albinus, who collected his information partly from written documents, and partly from the
tradition of the clergy of Canterbury (vel monimentis
literarum, vel traditione seniorum, Bed. Præf. p. 2).
That his narrative of this transaction is of the latter
description, appears from the occurrence in it of such
phrases as "ut perhibent" — "fertur" — "narratur."—
We have it, therefore, not as contained in any contemporary document, but as it was told at the distance of
more than a hundred years, with all the additions and
embellishments which it must have received in passing
from mouth to mouth during so long a period. That a
fruitless conference took place between Augustine and the
Britons can hardly be doubted : the particulars with which
that conference is said to have been attended deserve less
credit.

[2] Pace catholica secum habita. Bed. ii. c. 2.   It should
be remembered that the Britons refused to hold communion with the Saxon Christians.

conversion of the idolaters, and would conform to the usages of the universal church. They refused. He reasoned, entreated, reproved in vain. At last, according to the narrative transmitted to Beda, he concluded the dispute with a prayer that God would point out by miracle the party which defended the upright cause. This prayer, it is said, was heard: a blind man at the touch of the bishop was restored to sight; and his adversaries, confounded but not convinced, requested time to consult with their brethren preparatory to a second and more numerous meeting.

It is probable that the missionary had not anticipated so obstinate a resistance. Having re-considered the whole matter, he determined to reduce his demands to three heads—that the Britons should celebrate the feast of Easter at the same time with other Christians; that they should *complete* the administration of baptism after the Roman manner,[1] and should join with him in preaching the gospel to the Saxons. These demands are deserving of attention, because they prove that there was no dispute between him and them on any question of Christian doctrine, nor respecting the authority claimed and exercised by the bishop of Rome: for we may be assured that, if they had differed from him on either of these heads, he would never have

---

[1] Ut ministerium baptizandi, quo Deo renascimur, juxta morem sanctæ Romanæ et apostolicæ ecclesiæ *compleatis*. Bed. ii. c. 2. The complimentum baptismi was confirmation. According to the Roman ritual, when baptism was administered on the eves of the greater festivals, the baptized were led from the font to the bishop to be confirmed.

solicited them to become his assistants and fellow-missionaries.

The Britons on their part consulted a neighbouring hermit, famed among them for his wisdom and sanctity, who advised them to obey the Saxon bishop, if he were "meek and humble of heart," otherwise to reject him. But how, they asked, were they to ascertain his real disposition? " Let him," replied the hermit, " come first to the place of conference : if he do not rise to receive you, who are more in number, know that he is a man of proud and imperious spirit : despise him, as he will have despised you."

On the appointed day, the deputies, seven bishops with the most learned of the monks of Benchor,[1] returned. Augustine was seated, and did not rise. This, according to the doctrine of the hermit, they

---

[1] Here two questions may be asked : 1. Whence did the seven bishops come at a time when there were no fixed bishoprics in Wales? To which it may be answered, that there were chorepiscopi in the neighbourhood: for it is believed that the successors of St. David were in the habit of ordaining a great number of such suffragan bishops.

As the place of conference, whether it was Austclive or not, was situated in the south, on the confines of the Huiccii and the West Saxons (Bed. ii. c. 2), how came the monks of Benchor in Flintshire, which lay at the northern extremity of Wales, to be present? I think it is probable that this was an addition to the original story. There were sixteen Benchors in Wales, most of them much nearer in situation than Benchor Iscoed in Flintshire (Rees, Welsh SS. p. 181). But the clergy of Kent, having heard of the slaughter of the monks of this last Benchor by the king of Northumbria, might easily confound them with the monks at the conference; because both belonged to a monastery with the same name.

took for an insult : they disputed his statements, rejected his three proposals, and refused to own his authority : " for," said they, " if we once yield, he will trample us under foot." " Know then," exclaimed the archbishop in the anguish of disappointment,— " know that if you will not assist me in pointing out to the idolaters the way of life, they, by the just judgment of God, will prove to you the ministers of death." The menace was received with derision, and the parties separated.[1]

Augustine did not long survive this unsuccessful attempt, and his prediction was supposed to have been verified within eight years after his death.[2] Edilfrid, the warlike and pagan king of Northumbria, had entered the British territories, and discovered the army of his opponents near the city of Chester. Diffident of their own courage, they had recourse to spiritual weapons : and a detachment of more than twelve hundred monks from the monastery of Benchor occupied a neighbouring eminence, whence,

---

[1] Bed. ii. c. 2. According to the narrative in Beda, Dinoot was abbot of Benchor. He is called by the Welsh authorities Denawd, the son of Pablo, which presents some chronological difficulty. However, a supposed answer by him to Augustine has been honoured with a place in the English councils by Spelman and Wilkins, though it betrays its real origin by the modernism of its language, that of the fifteenth century, and by its anachronism respecting the see of Caerlion. The forgery was detected by Turberville (Manual, p. 460), and, notwithstanding the advocacy of Stillingfleet (Orig. Brit. 360), and of Bingham (i. 348), is now generally admitted.

[2] There can be little doubt that the death of Augustine should be fixed to the year 605, and the battle of Chester to 613. See Langhorn, pp. 145, 149. Smith's Bed. p. 81, n. 29.

like the Jewish legislator, they were expected to
regulate by their prayers the fate of the contending
armies. As soon as they were descried, "If they
pray," exclaimed the king, "they also fight against
us." He led his troops to the foot of the hill; Brocmail, who had been intrusted with its defence,
fled at the approach of the Saxons; the monks were
slaughtered without mercy; and of the whole
number no more than fifty were able to save themselves by flight.[1]

---

[1] Bed. p. 81. About five hundred years after this event
the fabulous Geoffrey of Monmouth, anxious perhaps to
exalt the character of his forefathers at the expense of their
conquerors, attributed the massacre of the monks to the
intrigues of St. Augustine and King Ethelbert; and his
account was adopted by the credulity of two obscure historians, Gray and Trivet (Langhorn, p. 159). But religious
are more powerful than national prejudices. The story
was improved by the reformed writers, and the archbishop
was represented as departing in sullen discontent from the
conference, and exhorting the Saxon princes to efface with
the blood of his adversaries the insult which had been
offered to his authority. (See Bale, cent. 13, c. 1;
Parker, p. 48; God. p. 33, and a crowd of more modern
writers, who have re-echoed the calumny.) But this
heavy accusation is supported by no proof whatsoever:
it is most improbable; for Edilfrid was not a Christian
but a pagan, not a prince subject to Ethelbert, but king
of Northumbria, independent of the Bretwalda, whose
power was confined to the south of the Humber (Bed. i.
c. 25): and it is fully refuted by the testimony of Beda,
who refers the massacre of the monks to its true cause,
their appearance in the field of battle; and expressly
declares that it occurred long after the death of Augustine
(ipso Augustino jam multo ante tempore ad coelestia regna
sublato. Bed. p. 81). To elude the force of this passage,
Bishop Godwin has boldly asserted that it was added to
the original text of Beda by the solicitude of some
admirer of the missionary, resting his opinion principally
on the absence of the passage from the Saxon version

II. Events subsequent to the death of Augustine rendered it impossible to carry into execution the decree of Gregory respecting the metropolitans of London and York. Mellitus was expelled from London by the apostacy of the citizens ; and, returning to Canterbury, assumed the government of that church after the death of Lawrence, the colleague and successor of St. Augustine : and Paulinus, compelled to abandon York after the fall of Edwin, sought an asylum in Kent, and spent the remainder of his days in the church of Rochester. Hence it happened that neither of the metropolitan sees was permanently established. The bishops of Canterbury continued to receive the pallium from Rome ; and their authority was acknowledged in all the Saxon churches founded by missionaries from the continent, whilst the churches founded by the Scottish monks after the retirement of Paulinus, obeyed a succession of bishops sent from Iona by order of the abbot of the monastery established in that island. The inconveniences growing out of this state of things have been described in the preceding chapter : the remedy that was adopted was to place all the bishops of the Saxon nations under the authority of the archbishop of Canterbury.

The four immediate successors of St. Augustine

---

attributed to king Alfred (God. p. 33). But such reason is nought : for the royal translator frequently abridged the original, and omitted entire lines, when they were not necessary to complete the sense. Thus, for example, in the sentence preceding the controverted passage, he has not translated the account of Brocmail's flight, nor in the sentence which follows it, the date of the ordination of Justus and Mellitus. See Smith's edition of Alfred's version, p. 504.

had been his fellow-labourers, and joint founders
with him of the mission. They were of course
Italians: nor can it be thought extraordinary if the
native clergy, in the choice of their bishops, preferred to all others the men who had been their
teachers, and had brought them to the knowledge
of the gospel.[1] The sixth bishop was a native, of
the name, it is said, of Frithona, but called in Latin
Deudedit.[2] At his death in 665, the presbyter

---

[1] Yet this fact has supplied Mr. Churton with a pretext for taunting the Romans " as unwilling to turn the
Roman plantation into an English church, whilst the
Scottish churchmen, on the contrary, being less anxious
to prolong their own mission than to make Christians of
the Saxons, began very soon to associate natives of the
country with them in their labours." Churton, p. 33.
Now let us test this insinuation by the facts. Aidan, the
first bishop of Northumbria, was a Scottish monk sent
from Iona by the abbot of that monastery: on the death
of Aidan, Finan, another Scottish monk, was sent from
Iona by the abbot ; on the death of Finan, Colman,
a third Scottish monk, was sent from Iona by the abbot.
It would appear as if the monks of Iona looked upon the
bishopric as their exclusive property, so long as they retained their influence with the kings of Northumbria.
What was there like this in the conduct of the Italian
clergy at Canterbury?

[2] The Saxon name of Deudedit is said to have been
Frithona : when or why he took the Latin name is not
noticed. Two other disciples of the Romans are mentioned, whose names were Thamar and Berctgils. Thamar
kept his name without change or addition; Berctgils
acquired the surname of Bonifice. (Bed. l. iii. c. 20.)
Yet from these facts the imagination of Mr. Churton has
deduced the inference, that the Romans changed the
names of their disciples for some interested purpose,
whereas "the Scots did not make a point of turning
their converts into Scotsmen. (Churt. 63, 64.) If it were
worth the while it would be easy to shew that such
change of names was not unusual in the Western churches
both centuries before, and centuries after, this period.

Wighard was appointed to succeed him, with the
election and consent of the holy church of the
Angles. It was about the time when the Scottish
monks, after the conference at Whitby, abandoned
Northumbria, and Oswiu, in conjunction with Egbert,
king of Kent, embraced the opportunity of apply-
ing to the Roman pontiff. Wighard proceeded to
Rome for consecration, carrying with him presents
from the two kings, and a letter of request, the
object of which was, if we may judge from the
result, that all the bishops of the Anglo-Saxons
might be placed under the authority of the successor
of St. Augustine.

Wighard, however, as well as most of the companions of his journey, fell a victim to the plague
soon after his arrival in Rome : and the task of
providing an archbishop in his place devolved upon
Pope Vitalian, according to the request of the two
kings conveyed in their joint letter.[1] It was not

---

[1] That such was their request is certain. Beda calls
Theodore, who was selected by Vitalian, the " archbishop *asked for* by the king "—episcopum quem petierant
a Romano pontifice (Bed. iv. c. 1), and " the bishop whom
the country had anxiously sought "—doctorem veritatis,
quem patria sedula quæsierat. Id. Oper. Min. p. 142.
Vitalian, in his answer to the two kings, reminds them
that their letter requested him to choose a bishop for them
in the case of Wighard's death—secundum vestrorum
scriptorum tenorem. Bed. iii. c.29. Certainly these passages must have escaped the eye of Mr. Soames, who
boldly, and without an atom of authority for his statement, ascribes the choice of a bishop by Vitalian to
Italian subtlety. " The death of Wighard," he tells us,
" was not lost on Italian subtlety. For Vitalian, then
pope, determined upon trying whether the Anglo-Saxons
would receive an archbishop nominated by himself."
Soames' Hist. p. 78.

till after several refusals on the part of those who
objected the distance of the place, and the barbarism of the people, that the office was accepted by
a Greek monk, Theodore of Cilicia, who, to great
severity of morals, was believed to add a perfect
knowledge of ecclesiastical discipline. After his
consecration the new prelate left Rome in the
company of the abbot Adrian, an African, and of
Bennet Biscop, a Northumbrian, both experienced
travellers: for the first had twice visited Gaul, the
other was now on his second pilgrimage to the
tombs of the Apostles. Adrian was one of those
who had refused the office, but had consented to
furnish a competent escort for the new archbishop,
and to remain with him for some time as his coun-
sellor at Canterbury:[1] and from the good offices of
Bennet, who was well acquainted with several of
the Saxon princes, much benefit was expected by
the new archbishop. They landed at Marseilles,
and proceeded as far as Arles, where their progress
was arrested by order of Ebroin, mayor of the palace, who had persuaded himself that some political
intrigue, hostile to his interests, was concealed
under this religious mission. Before winter they
obtained permission to leave the roof of the apostolic vicar;[2] and to separate, that they might not,
accompanied as they were with a numerous retinue,

---

[1] The Pope had some fears that Theodore, a Grecian,
might introduce novelties into the Anglo-Saxon church—
ut Adrianus ei doctrinæ co-operator assistens, diligenter
attenderet, ne quid ille contrarium fidei, Græcorum more
in ecclesiam, cui præesset, introduceret. Bed. iv. c. 1.

[2] Coegerat enim eos imminens hyems, ut ubicumque
potuissent, quieti manerent. Ibid.

prove too great a burthen to those whose hospitality they solicited. Theodore proceeded to Paris, where he was entertained by the bishop Agilberct; and Adrian was received with equal kindness, first by the archbishop of Sens, and afterwards by the bishop of Meaux. The arrival of Theodore at Paris was soon made known to Egbert, who despatched the caldoman Raedferth to Ebroin, and obtained his consent to the departure of the archbishop, but not to that of Adrian. In the spring, Theodore came under the care of Raedferth to Estaples, where he was detained by a very severe illness, and at last reached the archiepiscopal city, to the great joy both of the king and the people. He appointed Bennet abbot of the monastery of Peter, which was governed by him during two years, and then resigned into the hands of Adrian, who, having at last succeeded in allaying the jealousy or the vengeance of Ebroin, rejoined the companions of his journey at Canterbury.[1]

The arrival of Theodore forms a new era in the ecclesiastical history of the Anglo-Saxons. Adrian remained at home in his monastery. To him was assigned the important office of educating the natives for the duties of the ministry, and the school

---

[1] Ibid., and Oper. Min. p. 142. I have entered into this detail that the reader may notice the real cause of Theodore's long stay in France. Mr. Soames, shutting his eyes to the pages of Beda, and drawing, as before, from his own imagination, hints that it was owing to prudential considerations; for, "as former nominations to Anglo-Saxon sees had been domestic, some doubt would naturally arise as to his reception." Soames, p. 78.

which he opened was frequented by students from
every part of the south. Theodore, with the lofty
title of archbishop of Britain, made a progress
through the Anglo-Saxon territory, and was everywhere received by the princes, the clergy, and the
people with testimonies of the most profound respect.
For a time his will was the law. He deposed
bishops, established new bishoprics, and convoked
national councils. Occasionally he ventured to
transgress the letter of the canons; conceiving himself justified perhaps by the wants of the people and
the anomalous state of the church. Even in his
dispute with St. Wilfrid, Pope Agatho appears to
have approved his policy, though he condemned his
treatment of that prelate. The same pontiff confirmed to him and his successors the authority
which he possessed, by a decree published in
a council at Rome (anno 697) fixing the number
of Anglo-Saxon bishops at twelve, of whom the
bishop of Canterbury should be the metropolitan,
and the other eleven his suffragans.[1] For some
years no attempt was made to disturb this
arrangement, but the successors of Theodore were
not long permitted to retain his authority with-

---

[1] Unde ex auctoritate beati Petri Apostolorum principis.
...definimus atque statuimus ut unumquodque regnum
in Britannia insula institutum habeat secundum modera-
minis mensuram episcopos ita statutos, ut simul omnes
cum archiepiscopo duodecim ecclesiarum principes nume-
rentur, quos archiepiscopus, qui pro tempore ab hac
Apostolica sede pallii honore decoratur, provehat atque
sacerdotali gradu canonice ordinet.   Labbe, Tom. vii.
601. Venetiis, 1728.   Spelman Con. 159.   The word
Sacerdos in the language of the time generally meant a
bishop.

out a struggle. The first who succeeded in assert-
ing his independence was Egbert, bishop of
York. Founding his pretension on the original
scheme which had been devised by St. Gregory, and
supported by the influence of his near relative Ceolwulf, king of Northumbria, he claimed the title and
rights of a metropolitan ; and appealed in support of
that claim to the justice of the pontiff. It was now
more than one hundred years since Paulinus had
abandoned the church of York; and during that
interval the regulation of St. Gregory had been
superseded by the subsequent decrees of Vitalian
and Agatho. But Egbert persisted, and his efforts,
after much opposition and discussion, were crowned
with success. By a decree of Gregory III. the Anglo-
Saxon bishoprics north of the Humber were subjected to the authority of the bishop of York, and
to Egbert was sent the pallium, the badge and confirmation of the metropolitan dignity.[1]

Still the churches south of the Humber looked

---

[1] Chron. Sax. Anno 735.   Malm. de Pont. l. iii. f. 153.
From the narrative of Mr. Soames, it would appear, not
that Egbert sought the pallium, but that the Pope forced
it upon him, and that he only consented to accept it as
a compliment, and at the prayer of the king. "He was
chosen to the see of York, and Ceolwulf, who yet filled
the throne, desired him to accept the complimentary pall
—a mark of deference to Rome paid by no one of his
predecessors since Paulinus." Soames, History, p. 104.
Of course no authority is given for this statement, which,
if Malmbury's account is true, must certainly be fabulous.
He tells us that Egbert was very ambitious of the honour,
and, being a man of spirit, animosioris ingenii homo,
succeeded by dint of importunity and perseverance—pallium multa throni apostolici interpellatione reparavit.
De Pont. ibid.

up to the archbishop of Canterbury as their metropolitan. But the success of Egbert awakened the hopes of other parties. If the Northumbrians were exempted from the jurisdiction of the Kentish bishop, why should not the Mercians? Such, we may suppose, was the reasoning of Offa, the powerful king of Mercia,[1] who, in addition to the suggestions of pride, had personal causes of displeasure against Jaenbyrct, the metropolitan of Kent, whom he suspected of being secretly leagued with Charlemagne in opposition to his interest. A council was held at Calcuith in 785. Offa advanced several charges against Jaenbyrct, took forcible possession of the lands belonging to that prelate in Mercia, and obtained the assent of his bishops to the erection of an archiepiscopal see at Lichfield.[2] Whether this was preparatory to, or consequent on, an application to the pontiff, is unknown: but he succeeded in procuring from Pope Adrian (Ann. 787) a decree, which severed from the jurisdiction of the Kentish metropolitan all the churches of Mercia and East-Anglia, and subjected them to the authority of

---

[1] The testimony of Alcuin is, that Offa acted not from any rationabili consideratione, sed quadam potestatis cupiditate, Alc. Oper. i. p. 80 : that of Cœnulf, the successor of Offa, that the king acted thus propter inimicitiam cum venerabili Lamberto et gente Cantuariorum susceptam. Apud. Malm. de Reg. i. p. 123.

[2] "It was a quarrelsome synod," says the Saxon Chronicle, " and the archbishop lost a portion of his bishopric." Chron. Sax. p. 60. Accusatus est archiepiscopus accusationibus pervalidis, quarum una fuit quod promiserat Carolo, quod si hostiliter ingressurus Britanniam adveniret, liberum in archiepiscopatum suum introitum inveniret, favorem et adjutorium. Vit. Off. Wilk. i. 153.

Higebert, and his successors, the bishops of Lichfield.[1] Jaenbyrct was compelled to submit; but in
the course of a few years, not only he, but all the
principal parties in this transaction, Offa, Higebert,
and Adrian, died. To Offa, after the short reign of
his son Egferth, succeeded Cœnulf, the fifth in descent from a brother of Penda, and one who had no
reason to respect the memory of Offa: to Adrian,
Leo III., to whom Cœnulf sent a present of one
hundred and twenty mancuses,[2] with letters expressive of his obedience, and requesting from the pontiff,
in his own name and that of his bishops, ealdormen
and thanes, the solution of two questions often
mooted among the Anglo-Saxon prelates: 1st,
whether Pope Adrian had motives which could justify
the division of the province of Canterbury in opposition to the decree of St. Gregory; and 2nd, whether
the metropolitan authority ought not, in conformity

---

[1] In the Codex Diplomaticus (i. 184—190) are two
charters, of undisputed authenticity, for the year 788, and
three for 789, in all which Higebert subscribes as archbishop, but only in the second place. The first place is
given to Jaenbyrct, as his senior. But after the death of
Jaenbyrct Higebert's signature occupies the first place,
and that of Æthelheard, the successor of Jaenbyrct, the
second, because Æthelheard, though of Canterbury, was
the junior bishop.
[2] In 787, at the council of Calcuith, Offa had promised
a benefaction of 365 mancuses, one for every day in the
year, from himself and his successors, to the church of
St. Peter in Rome, towards the support of the poor, and
of the lights burnt in the church. This promise was fulfilled, as far as regarded Offa, but Cœnulf did not understand that the successors of Offa were bound by it. He
sent only one-third of the amount, and that as a personal
donation. See the epistle of the king in Malm. i. 124,
and that of Leo, ibid. and in Ang. Sac. i. 461.

with the same decree, to be canonically transferred
to the church of London.[1] From these questions it
will perhaps be inferred, that Cœnulf had no objection to the re-union of the two provinces under one
metropolitan, if that metropolitan were a Mercian
bishop : for London was within the kingdom of
Mercia. But, if that were the object of the monarch,
it was defeated by the answer of Leo, that the reason,
which had induced Adrian to send the pallium to the
bishop of Lichfield, was the representation of Offa
that the province of Canterbury was too extensive to
be properly governed by any single prelate : and that
with respect to the decree of St. Gregory, he dared
not now deprive the church of Canterbury of the
metropolitan dignity, after the prescription of so
many centuries, and the repeated sanction of the
apostolic see in its favour.[2]

On this occasion, Æthelheard of Canterbury was
not wanting to himself. He cultivated the friendship of Cœnulf, sought and obtained a personal conference with Eanbald, the northern metropolitan,

---

[1] The letters of Cœnulf are described by Mr. Soames as
an application to the Pope to learn " whether, in his
opinion, and that of his wise men, the Saxon canonists had
taken a correct view of the question." (Bampt. Lectures,
174.) Yet the cases are proposed on the part of the king
with a promise of obedience, a declaration that no man can
dare to oppose the judgment of the pontiff, and an assurance that, whatever the answer may be, it shall be carried
into execution. Tuis sanctis jussionibus aurem obedientiæ
nostræ humiliter inclinari—Quicquid vobis videatur, nobis
postea servandum rescribere dignemini—Apostolicis sanc-
tionibus nullus Christianus contraire præsumit. Malm.
de Reg. i. 120—126. Ang. Sac. l. 460. And accordingly,
Leo, in his answer, assumes the language, not of a counsel,
but of a judge. See note 2 in the next page.
[2] Ibid.

and then, having secured support at home, set out to plead his cause in Rome, attended by two bishops, and two noblemen as representatives of the kingdoms of Mercia, Wessex, and Northumbria[1] (Anno 799). He was successful. Leo avowed his conviction that the suggestions of Offa to Adrian had been founded in falsehood; and issued a decree by which he restored the province of Canterbury to its former extent, and granted to the bishops of Canterbury the privilege of confirming the elections of all bishops within that province.[2] With this instrument Æthelheard returned to England, repaired to the residence of Cœnulf, and imparted and ex-

---

[1] We learn these particulars from Alcuin, who sent to St. Josse, a small monastery not far from Estaples, a horse with his own saddle for the use of the archbishop. He was greatly afraid that the richness of dress and magnificent equipage of the archbishop's retinue would scandalize the French, and advised them particularly to appear in plain attire before Charlemagne—cum sella, qua ego caballicare solitus sum, sic parata sicut solent ecclesiarum pastores in hac patria habere—Admone socios tuos, ut honorifice se observent in omni religione sancta—prohibe eos auro vel sericis uti vestimentis in conspectu Domni regis, sed humili habitu incedant. Op. Alc. l. 86.—Also 234.

[2] Unde nos, *veritate ipsa reperta,* ordinatione seu confirmatione nostra, apostolica auctoritate, eas illi *in integro,* sicut antiquitus fuerint, constituentes, reddidimus, et *privilegium* confirmationis, secundum sacrorum canonum censuram ecclesiæ suæ observandum tradidimus. Leonis ep. apud Malm. l. 127. Æthelheard himself states the same. Ipse apostolicus Papa, ut cognovit quod *injuste fuisset factum,* statim sui *privilegii* auctoritatis præceptum posuit, et in Britanniam misit, et præcepit ut honor Sti. Augustini sedis cum omnibus suis parohhiis *integerrime redintegraretur.* Cod. Dipl. l. 225. (The words in italics in this statement seem to refer to those in italics in the letter of Leo.)

plained to him and his witan the whole transaction.
They heard him with joy, and promised their adhesion and concurrence.   He then summoned the
twelve bishops subject to the see of St. Augustine
to meet him in synod at Cloveshoe, in obedience to
the precept of Pope Leo : " where he, and his fellow-
bishops and all the dignitaries of the council, with
the aid of God, and of the Pope, decreed that the
archiepiscopal see should never after be fixed in the
minster of Lichfield, nor in any other place but in
Christ-church in Canterbury ; and in addition, with
respect to the grant of the pallium and archiepiscopal seat by Pope Adrian to the minster of Lichfield,
they forbade, with the consent and permission of
Pope Leo, that it be of any force, because it had been
fraudulently and surreptitiously obtained" (12 Oct.
1803).[1]   We do not read that Adulf of Lichfield
made any opposition : he yielded, apparently without
a murmur, to his lot, but was permitted, according
to the request of Alcuin, to wear the pallium, and to
take precedence of his colleagues.[2]   Such was the

---

[1] Ego Adelheardus archiepiscopus cum omnibus xii episcopis sanctæ sedi beati Augustini subjectis per apostolica
præcepta Domni papæ Leonis ...... et cartam a Romana
sede missam per Hadrianum Papam de pallio et archiepiscopatus sede in Licedfeldensi monasterio, cum consensu et
licentia Domni Apostolici Leonis Papæ præscribimus
aliquid valere, quia per subreptionem et male blandam
suggestiorem adipiscebatur.   Cod. Dipl. i. 226.   (This
passage was omitted in Spelman's councils, but restored
by Smith (Bed. App. 787), Wilkins (Con. l. 167), and Mr.
Kemble (Cod. Dipl. i. 224).

[2] Ita tamen ut pater pius in diebus suis pallio non
exuatur, licet ordinatio episcoporum ad primam ac sanctam
sedem recurrat.   Alcuin's letter to Æthelheard, Oper.
i. 80.

result of this important contest—a result which so firmly established the authority of the see of Canterbury, that it has since borne without material injury the revolutions of ten centuries.[1]

III. The first Saxon dioceses were of enormous

[1] From the original grants, it is plain that the extensive authority conferred on Augustine was meant to expire at his death. Yet his successors often exercised the metropolitan authority beyond the limits of their own province, perhaps in virtue of their office of Apostolic Vicar, which seems to have been constantly granted to them together with the pallium. Thus I understand the words in the letter of Gregory II. to the bishops of England respecting Tatwine, the second from Theodore—cui vices nostras per omnia gerendas in illa regione commissimus; in that of Formosus to the English bishops respecting Plegmund—ei vices apostolicas per omnia gerere mandamus; and of John to St. Dunstan—Tibi ex more antecessorum tuorum vices apostolicæ sedis exercere convenit. Malm. de Gest. Pont. f. 116—6. Hence we find the archbishops of Canterbury consecrating occasionally the bishops of foreign churches. The Danes settled in Ireland were converted soon after the middle of the tenth century, and several of their bishops are known to have repaired to Canterbury for consecration (Ussher, Sylloge, epist. 68, 118, 119, 195. Ang. Sac. i. 80, 81. Chron. Sax. 1070), a fact which, coupled with the coins struck in Dublin bearing the name of king Ethelred, gives some appearance of truth to the assertion in the disputed charter in Heming (Chart. Eccl. Wigorn. p. 571), that Edgar had made conquests, or at least established his dominion in Ireland. In Wales, though the majority of the prelates continued to profess obedience to the bishop of St. David's, yet those of Landaff, who disputed the archiepiscopal dignity with the possessors of that see, rather than submit to their adversaries, sought episcopal consecration from the English metropolitan. Their celebrated bishop Oudoceus, with the approbation of Mouric, king of Glamorgan, is said to have been ordained by St. Augustine; and his successors were careful to observe a practice which had been sanctioned by his example. Langhorn, p. 137. Ussher de Prim. p. 85. Ang. Sac. vol. ii. p. 673, and Liber Landavensis.

extent, and generally commensurate with the kingdoms in which they were established. The jurisdiction of the see of Winchester stretched from the
frontiers of Kent to those of the Cornwall Britons :
a single bishopric comprised the populous and extensive province of Mercia, and the prelate who resided
sometimes at York, and sometimes in Lindisfarne,
watched over the spiritual interests of all the tribes
of Saxons and Picts, who dwelt between the Humber
and the friths of Forth and Clyde. No powers of
any individual were adequate to the government
of dioceses so extensive ; and Theodore, from the
moment of his arrival in England, had formed the
design of breaking them into smaller and more proportionate districts. But few men can behold with
pleasure the diminution of their authority or profit :
and the duty of transmitting unimpaired to future
ages the dignity which they enjoyed would furnish
the reluctant prelates with a specious objection
against the measures of the primate. Theodore,
when he first proposed the measure in the council at
Hertford, met with a resistance which compelled
him to postpone it for subsequent consideration.[1]
Secure, however, of the protection of the holy see,
he pursued his design with prudence and firmness.
The contumacy of Winfrid, the Mercian bishop, he
chastised by deposing him from his dignity, and suc-

---

[1] In commune tractatum est, ut plures episcopi, crescente
numero fidelium, augerentur; sed de hac re ad præsens
siluimus. Bed. l. iv. c. 5. Notwithstanding the contrary
authority of Mr. Soames (p. 81, note) and of the British
Magazine (Ap. 1839, p. 371), I think that the expression
siluimus justifies my former statement that the canon was
not passed, but left for subsequent consideration.

cessively consecrated five other prelates for the
administration of his extensive diocese :[1] and when
Wilfrid of York had incurred the resentment of his
sovereign, the king of Northumbria, he improved the
opportunity, to divide into four bishoprics the several
provinces of that kingdom. The conduct of Theodore was imitated by Brithwald, his immediate successor, who, though he was compelled to enforce
obedience by the sentence of excommunication
against the king and witan of Wessex, succeeded in
dividing that kingdom into the two bishoprics of
Winchester and Sherborne, and in establishing
an independent bishopric at Selsey, for the tributary
people of Sussex.[2] By these means the number of
Saxon bishops before the death of Beda had been
increased from seven to fourteen : Canterbury and
Rochester for the kingdom of Kent ; Dunwich and
Helmham for that of East-Anglia ; Winchester and
Sherborne for that of Wessex ; Lichfield, Worcester,
Hereford, and Dorchester for Mercia ; and York,
Hexham, Lindisfarne, and Witherne for Northumbria.[3] This augmentation was not, however, sufficient to satisfy the spiritual wants of the people ; and
the Venerable Bede laments that, in the great and
populous diocese of York, there were many districts
which had never been visited by their bishop, and

---

[1] Bed. iv. c. 6. Anglia Sac. i. 423, note.
[2] Bed. v. c. 18. Ang. Sac. ii. 20. Memor sum quomodo
in præteriti anni synodo statutum est, illis non communi-
candum, si non tuum judicium in ordinatione episcoporum
implere festinarent, quod adhuc neglectui habent. Letter
of Waldhare, bishop of London, to Brithwald. Smith's
Beda, 784.
[3] Bed. v. 23.

thousands of Christians, whose souls had not received
the Holy Spirit by the imposition of his hands. To
remove so alarming an evil, this enlightened monk
earnestly proposed that the original plan of Gregory
the Great should be completed; that the church of
Northumbria should be intrusted to the separate
administration of twelve prelates; and that the new
episcopal sees should be fixed in some of the rich but
nominal monasteries, which covered and impoverished
that kingdom.[1] But not only did his advice remain
unheeded; even one of the four northern bishoprics,
that of Hexham, was suffered to become extinct
before the end of the century. In the province of
Canterbury, if we except the suppression, but for a
time only, of the see of Leicester, no very important
change took place before the reign of Edward. It
had often been complained that two bishoprics, one
of them spreading over six whole counties, comprised the extensive and populous kingdom of
Wessex; and Plegmund, the Kentish metropolitan,
had been reprehended by the Pope on account of his
remissness in allowing bishoprics to remain vacant
after the death of the last possessor. About 909,
the two bishops of Winchester and Sherborne died:
the archbishop availed himself of the opportunity to
propose a multiplication of bishoprics; and in a

---

[1] Habito majore concilio et consensu pontificali simul et
regali, prospiciatur locus aliquis monasteriorum ubi sedes
episcopalis fiat . . . . Quod enim turpe est dicere, tot sub
monasteriorum nomine hi, qui monachicæ vitæ prorsus
sunt immunes, in suam ditionem acceperunt, ut omnino
desit locus ubi filii nobilium aut emeritorum militum possessionem accipere possint. Bed. ibid. p. 309. The
nature of these nominal or lay monasteries will be explained in one of the following chapters.

national council it was resolved that three more episcopal sees should be established. Plegmund consecrated on the same day seven prelates, two for
vacant churches in Mercia, two for Winchester and
Sherborne, and three for the new bishoprics, of which
one was fixed at Wells for Somersetshire, another at
Crediton for Devonshire, and the third at Wilton
for Wiltshire.[1]

IV. The election of bishops has frequently been
the subject of controversy between the civil and
ecclesiastical authorities. As long as the professors
of the Gospel formed a proscribed but increasing
party in the heart of the Roman empire, each private

[1] The reader, who is no stranger to the chronological
difficulties with which this event has tortured the ingenuity of antiquaries, will have observed that I admit the
authenticity of the letter of Pope Formosus, but reject as
fabulous much of the narrative in Malmesbury (De Reg.
i. 203). I admit the letter on the authority of Eadmer,
who assures us that he found it among the ancient records
of the church of Canterbury, many of which had been rendered illegible through age and damp (Eadm. p. 128,
129): and of Malmesbury, who transcribed it in his work
de Gestis Pont. p. 116. The narrative in Malmesbury, which
he copied verbis eisdem, is found in a MS. given by Leofric
to the church of Exeter in the middle of the eleventh century, which is now in the Bodleian Library, No. 579 (Mr.
Hardy's note to Malm. ibid.). But that narrative cannot
be correct. It states that Wessex was seven years without a bishop; that Formosus on that account excommunicated King Edward and his subjects; that Plegmund
hastened to Rome, appeased the Pope, and on his return
consecrated seven bishops. Now Forsomus died in 896,
and the two bishops of Wessex lived till 909. It appears
to me, therefore, that some one, who had heard of the
letter from Formosus and of the consecration of the
bishops, but was ignorant of the date of either, had with
the aid of his imagination connected them together in the
manner stated in the MSS. See note (F).

church observed without interruption the method
established by its founder. But after the conversion
of Constantine, when riches and influence were
generally attached to the episcopal dignity, the emperors began to view with jealousy the freedom of
canonical election; they assumed the right of nominating to the vacant sees, and the clergy deemed it
expedient to submit to a less, rather than to provoke
by resistance a more dangerous evil. However, the
exercise of the imperial prerogative was chiefly confined to the four great patriarchal churches of
Antioch, Alexandria, Constantinople, and Rome:
and of the eighteen hundred dioceses which the
empire comprised, the greater part enjoyed, till the
irruption of the barbarians, the undisturbed possession of their religious liberties. But the Saxon
church in its infancy was divided among seven
independent sovereigns, ignorant of ecclesiastical
discipline and impatient of control. Their impetuosity was not easily induced to bend to the authority of the canons, and their caprice frequently displayed itself in the choice and expulsion of their
bishops. Of this, a remarkable instance is furnished
by the conduct of Coinwalch, king of Wessex.
Agilberct, a Gallic prelate, whom his industry and
talents had recommended to the notice of the king,
was appointed by him to succeed Birinus, the apostle
of that nation. But the influence of the stranger
was secretly undermined by the intrigues of Wini,
a Saxon ecclesiastic, who possessed the advantage
of conversing with the king in his native tongue;
and after a decent delay, the foreign bishop received
from Coinwalch an order to surrender to the favou-

rite one-half of his extensive province. Opposition was fruitless : and Agilberct, rather than subscribe to his own disgrace by retaining a mutilated diocese, retired from the kingdom of Wessex, and left his more fortunate antagonist in possession of the whole. But Wini in his turn experienced the caprice of his patron. On some motive of disgust he was also compelled to abdicate his see, and an embassy was sent to Agilberct to solicit him to return. Agilberct refused, for he was now bishop of Paris, and Wini purchased from the king of Mercia the bishopric of London.[1] This and similar instances which occur during the first eighty years of the Saxon church shew the inconstant humour and despotic rule of these petty sovereigns : and the submission of the prelates proves that they were either too irresolute to despise the orders, or too prudent to provoke the vengeance of princes, whose power might easily have crushed the fabric which they had reared with so much labour and difficulty.[2]

By Theodore the discipline of the Saxon church was reduced to a more perfect form. Under him and his immediate successors the appointment of bishops was generally made in the national synods, in which the primate presided, and at which the deputies of the vacant church attended to give their consent.[3] In Northumbria it appears that the right of canonical election was recognized in the

---

[1] Beda, l. iii. c. 7.
[2] Wilk. p. 46. Bed. iv. c. 28, v. c. 8—18.
[3] Malmesbury writes—Electio olim præsulum et abbatum tempore Anglorum penes clericos et monachos erat. De Pont. l. iii. f. 157 b. But this assertion must be taken with many qualifications, before it can be correct.

clergy of each church ; and that its exercise was,
in some instances at least, permitted to take place
without any undue interference on the part of the
secular authorities. Thus, when Eanbald, the
northern metropolitan, died in 796, Alcuin, though
domiciled in France, was invited, as a member of
the church of York, to take his part in the election
of a new archbishop. He declined on account of
the state of his health, and of the absence in Germany of his patron, Charlemagne : but the letters
which he wrote on the occasion assure us, that up
to that day the clergy of York had exercised the
right of election, pure from the stain of simony
and free from external control.[1] But at the same
time, his extreme anxiety that they should continue
to maintain that purity and freedom authorizes us
to suspect, that there were many churches which
would lay no claim to the same praise.[2] In effect,
that system was rapidly growing up in England
which began to prevail on the continent. On the
one hand, the rank, the wealth, and the importance
which accompanied the episcopal office, rendered it
an object of pursuit to many, who spared not cost,
nor promises, nor services to gratify their ambi-

---

[1] Iterum, iterumque obtestor vos per nomen Domini
nostri Jesu Christi ut nullatenus aliquem sinatis per
simoniacam hæresim episcopatum adquirere...Hucusque
sancta Eboracensis Ecclesia in electione sua inviolata
permansit. Videte ne in diebus vestris maculetur. (Alcuini epistola ad dilectissimos amicos Eboracenses. Oper. i.
62.) Nullam violentiam super Ecclesiam Christi fieri
ullatenus permittas : sed fratres libera electione in timore
Dei summi optimum, Deo donante, eligant. Epist.
Domino omnium dilectissimo, p. 63.
[2] Ibid.

tion; on the other, the kings had learned to look
upon bishoprics as benefices, of which the disposal
belonged to themselves, because such benefices had
been founded by their predecessors. Under this
pretence they claimed a right to sway the election,
urging in justification of their conduct the necessity of providing that offices so important to them
might not be suffered to devolve on their enemies.
In historical records of the ninth and tenth centuries we meet with frequent mention of the succession to bishoprics: but the vague and doubtful
language of the authorities throws but little light
on the subject, sometimes describing the appointment as made by the unfettered choice of the clergy
and people, and sometimes as proceeding solely
from the absolute will of the sovereign.[1] The probability is that both were conjoined : that the
recommendation of the prince operated as a command ; while the choice of the clergy and people
was a mere form preliminary to the confirmation
and consecration of the prelate elect. Thus it was
certainly under our native kings, the descendants of
Egbert ; who, however, appear to have disposed of
the most important sees in national councils, and
with the consent of the bishops and ealdormen :[2]

---

[1] Favente rege et populo acclamante—voto totius cleri
et populi cum favore regio consonante.—In Adnothum
uniformi omnes sententia convenerunt, quem rege annu-
ente in Abbatem ordinavit—libera omnium electione præ-
ficitur—Rege tam cleri quam populi votis consentiente—
Jubente rege Edgaro—jubente rege Adelthredo—tam
rege Cnutone præcipiente, quam toto conventu petente—
Cnutus sacrari præcepit. Hist. Ram. et Elien. pp. 392,
429, 432, 434, 447, 492, 503, 504.
[2] Even Edgar, the great patron of the monastic order,

but under Canute and his successors the will of the
king was notified in a more imperious manner,[1] and
by them the practice of investiture with the ring
and crosier seems to have been introduced.[2] From
that period the mitre frequently became the reward of intrigue and influence: the new bishops
were generally selected from the twelve chaplains of the king, or the clerical favourites of
some powerful earl; and the nomination of the
monarch was often made to fall on the most
ambitious or the least worthy of the applicants.
In this respect the simplicity of Edward the
Confessor appears to have been frequently deceived.
Ulf, to whom he gave the bishopric of Lincoln,
proved a disgrace to the episcopal body, and was
driven into exile; Sparhavoc, whom he appointed

---

when he granted to the monks in cathedrals and abbeys
the liberty of electing their bishops and abbots according
to their rule, was careful to add that the election should
be made with the consent and advice of the king—mib
cýnᵹeꝛ ᵹeþeaᴄe ꝺ mýb þæbe. Seldeni ad Eadm. Spicil.
p. 149.

[1] The following letter of Wulfstan of York, on the
consecration of Ethelnoth of Canterbury, shews that it
had been ordered by the king:—"Wulstan, archbishop,
humbly greeteth king Canute his lord, and Elfgive
(Emma) the lady. And I inform you, beloved, that we
have done to bishop Ethelnoth as came to us in the *order*
from you; that we have consecrated him." He then prays
that the new metropolitan may equal his predecessors,
"Dunstan the good, and many others," and that his promotion may answer the expectation of the king and
queen "both before God and the world." Mores. Comment. de Ælf. p. 204.

[2] Ingulf, f. 497—509. Hist. Elien. 512. In some MS.
copies of Malmesbury mention is made of the delivery of
the crosier by Edgar, but the passage does not appear
deserving of credit. See it in Malm. l. ii. p. 241, not.
Edit. of Historical Society.

to the see of London, though he repaired twice to
Canterbury for consecration with the royal mandate
in hand, was as often rejected by the archbishop ;[1]
Egilric, nominated by him to the metropolitan
church of York, was ignominiously refused by the
canons ;[2] and Eadsig, the southern metropolitan,
when he wished to retire from the cares of his high
station, procured permission from Edward and Earl
Godwin to consecrate Seward his coadjutor in
private, " because he thought that, if many knew of
his purpose, some one might buy or beg the office,
who was less truthful and less learned."[3]   Through
such intrigues it occasionally happened that men, in
no wise qualified for the episcopal office, wormed
their way to the episcopal bench.   They were, however, the exception : for the very writers who lament
their promotion bear willing testimony to the virtues
of their colleagues.   But in the reign of Edward, the
prevalence of the abuse attracted the notice, and
provoked the severity of Pope Nicholas II.[4]   His
legates arrived in England, and conferred with the
king; but the death first of Nicholas, then of
Edward, occurred shortly afterwards; and within a

[1] Chron. Sax. 161, 2, 7.   Chron. Lambardi ad ann.
1050.
[2] Hist. Cœnob. Burg. 45.
[3] Chron. Sax. 157.   I call him coadjutor; because
Siward never bore the title of Archbishop, and, after his
death three years later, Eadsig resumed his former duties.
Chron. Sax. 158.   According to Malmesbury, Siward took
upon himself all the authority, and behaved so ungrate-
fully to Eadsig, that he was removed to Rochester, a
church reduced to such poverty that it was served by four
canons only, who lived on the alms of the people.   De
Pont. f. 132 b.
[4] In 1060 Aldred, bishop of Worcester had obtained

year the battle of Hastings transferred the English sceptre into the hands of the Norman conqueror.

IV. It will be superfluous to describe the official duties of the bishop—they are the same in all places —but his private life must of necessity be variously modified by the prevailing habits and notions of the age. Of his daily occupations, and the manner in which he was expected to spend his time when he was not employed in his public duties, we may form a correct idea from an Anglo-Saxon treatise on the obligations attached to different ranks and professions. The following chapter, taken from it, is entitled " the daily work of a bishop ;" which it

---

the archbishopric of York, with permission from the king to keep also his former see. He proceeded to Rome with Tostig, earl of Northumberland, and Giso, bishop-elect of Wells, and Walter, bishop-elect of Hereford. Pope Nicholas, in a synod which he had assembled against simoniacal promotions, placed Tostig by his side, but examined the three prelates. The two bishops-elect gave satisfaction, and were consecrated by the pontiff. Aldred was convicted of simony on his own confession, and deposed. On their departure from Rome, the four Englishmen fell into the hands of banditti, who despoiled them of every thing but the clothes on their persons. They returned to Rome ; Tostig stormed.—The Pope could not control robbers at his very gates; could he expect that people in England would fear him ? King Edward should forbid the payment of the Peter-pence till all that had been taken away should be restored. The Romans took his part, and his anger was appeased with presents. The promotion of Aldred was reconsidered, and he was at last permitted to retain York, on the condition of surrendering Worcester. Two cardinals immediately followed them ; of whose proceedings we know nothing more than that they approved of the choice of Wulstan as successor to Aldred at Worcester, and assisted at his consecration ; nor should we even know so much, had it not been connected with Wulstan's history. Malm. de Pontif. f. 154, 159, 163.

defines thus—" In the first place, of right, his
prayers ; and then his book-work, that is, reading
or writing, teaching or learning; and his church
hours at the right times, always in the manner that
thereto belongeth; and the washing of the feet of
the poor; and the dealing out of his alms ; and the
ordering of work where it may be needful. Also good
handy-crafts befit him, that men in his family may
practise crafts, at least that no one may dwell there
idle. Moreover, wisdom and wariness always befit
bishops, and that those have worthy ways who follow
them; and that they know some separate craft.
Nothing that is needless becometh bishops, nor
deceit, nor folly, nor excess in drink, nor childishness
in talk, nor idle buffoonery in any wise, neither at
home nor on the road, nor in any place : but wisdom
and wariness becometh their station, and good behaviour is the duty of them that follow them."[1]

1. The reader will, perhaps, be surprised at some
of these particulars. Why should handicraft become
a bishop ? Because, it was answered, idleness is the
hot-bed of vice, and industry the antidote to idleness. Hence every man educated for the church
was taught to practise some kind of manual labour,
that it might furnish him with employment in his
leisure hours, and with relaxation from graver studies.
This was expected from the priest, while he watched
over his parish, and from the bishop, while he governed his diocese : nor could they consider such
labour beneath their station, since it had been the
daily employment of the great apostle St. Paul.[2]

---

[1] Thorpe, 11. 314.   [2] Acts xviii. 3. 1 Cor. iv. 12.

Many were content with the more humble crafts; but several practised the valued and costly arts of painting, of correcting or illuminating manuscripts, of binding books, and of embroidery and working in gold and silver. The result of their labour was generally given to the library or the altar, and there was scarcely a church that could not boast the possession of valuable ornaments wrought by the hands of its most celebrated prelates or abbots.

2. Teaching was an employment of still higher repute, and sanctified in the estimation of the clergy by the example of Theodore and Adrian. With men of learning it became a favourite occupation. Thus it was with Egbert, brother to the king of Northumbria, and archbishop of York, when his time was not demanded by more important concerns. As soon as he was at leisure in the morning, he sent for some of the young clerks, and sitting on his couch taught them successively till noon, at which time he retired to his private chapel and celebrated mass.[1] After dinner, at which he ate sparingly, he amused himself with hearing his pupils discuss literary questions in his presence. In the evening he recited with them the service of complin, and then calling them in order, he gave his blessing to each, as they knelt in succession at his feet.[2] Thus also we read of St. Ethelwold, bishop of Winchester, that it was his delight to teach boys and youths; to explain to them Latin books in the English tongue; to instruct them in the rules of grammar and prosody, and to

---

[1] ' Offering for all the body and blood of Christ.' Sanctificabat eos offerens corpus Christi et sanguinem pro omnibus. Vit. Alcuini, in Act. SS. Bened. sec. iv. Tom. 1. p. 149.   [2] Ibid.

allure them by cheerful language to study and improvement.[1]

3. A daily distribution of alms was expected from bishops and the superiors of the greater monasterial establishments : and occasionally the feet of the paupers were washed by the distributor himself, in imitation of the example, and in obedience to the command, of our blessed Lord, who on the evening before his death washed the feet of his apostles and said—" I have given to you a command that ye should do as I have done unto you."[2] On the Thursday before Easter this washing of feet formed a part of the public service of the day.[3] At other times it was repeated by priests and bishops through private devotion ; and their example often induced laymen and lay-women of the highest rank to perform in a spirit of penitence the same humbling service to the objects of their bounty.[4]

---

[1] Dulce erat ei adolescentes et juvenes semper docere, et Latinos libros Anglice eis solvere, et regulas grammaticæ artis et metricæ rationis tradere, et jocundis alloquiis ad meliora trahere.   Wolstan, in Vit. Ethelw. p. 617.

[2] John xiii. 15.

[3] During the ceremony was sung the anthem—" A new command I give to you, that ye love one another," whence, as it began with the Latin word *mandatum,* the day was called Maunday-Thursday.

[4] The following is the manner in which St. Oswald performed this ceremony. Yearly, on Ash-Wednesday, twelve paupers were chosen out of the great number of those who usually partook of his charity. The archbishop washed, dried, and kissed their feet, then poured water on their hands before dinner, waited on them at table, and dismissed them with the present of a silver penny to each. This he repeated every day in Lent. On Easter Sunday he gave to each a new suit of clothes, and detained them during the holidays as honoured guests (honorifice) at the

In addition to the rank and rights which the bishop held in the church, he also derived high authority and important privileges from the state. He was by office one of the chief advisers of the king, was summoned to the national councils, and was listened to with deference on account of his character and influence. In some respects the archbishop enjoyed privileges in common with the monarch: for his word, like that of the king, was received in courts of justice as equivalent to his oath: and he possessed the right of granting nine days' grace to the offender whose life was sought by the family of an injured or murdered man. In all other respects he was placed on the same footing with the etheling, or princes of the blood.[1] Other bishops ranked as ealdormen above the king's thanes, and exercised all those rights and enjoyed all those emoluments to which the ealdormen were entitled.[2] To travellers from all other nations, and

---

palace. No indisposition could induce him to dispense with this practice. The weaker he grew, the more anxious was he to perform it. Nulla eum infirmitas corporalis ab istis retardabat, sed quo se corpore sentiebat debiliorem, eo sibi ad serviendum eis ingessit vim validiorem. Ang. Sac. ii. 208. In fact, he died in the performance of this ceremony, as he bent the knee at the 'Gloria Patri,' which terminated the service. Malm. de Pont. fol. 154. Hoved. f. 245—6. We read something similar of St. Wulstan, when he was prior of Worcester. Singulis diebus (in Quadragesima) tres pauperes affectuose coluit, quibus, Dominici sequax mandati, et victum quotidianum et pedum exhibebat lavacrum. Ang. Sac. ii. p. 250. Birnstan bishop of Winchester performed the same office in private every day, after which he waited on the paupers at table without any assistant. Malm. ibid. f. 138.

[1] Thorpe, i. 40, 330, 408.
[2] Ibid. 62, 330, 408.

ecclesiastics who were injured, they were appointed
by law "kinsmen and protectors" in conjunction
with the sovereign.[1] Each bishop was invested with
the right of inquiring into the grievances of the
poor, and of shielding the friendless from oppression;
and, in compliance with a custom coeval with the
introduction of Christianity among the Saxons, attended, either personally or by his archdeacon, the
chief courts of justice within his diocese, particularly the shiremotes, which were regularly held
twice in the year. There he presided in company
with the ealdorman, " that they might expound
God's law and the world's law."[2] Many benefits
were derived from his presence : for his education enabled him to instruct the ignorance of the
domesmen, his authority to control their passions
and prejudices, and his station in the church to
prevent the re-introduction of the charms and
pagan practices of their forefathers. In these
courts ecclesiastical pleas were taken first, in which
the proceedings were in a great measure directed by
him : next came the pleas of the crown, then the
plaints of individuals against one another, in both
of which he was ordered to keep a watchful eye
over all cases requiring the oaths of compurgators,
or the trial by ordeal ; and lastly followed those
disputes in which it seemed possible to reconcile
the contending parties by compromise or arbitra-
tion, a matter particularly recommended to his
care, as the only effectual mode of putting an end
to feuds between adverse and powerful families.[3]

---

[1] Ibid. 174, 192.   [2] Thorpe, i. 268, 386.
[3] Thorpe, i. 514, §§ 2, 3 ; ii. 312, 550.

It was no easy matter to shew that this judicial interference in secular concerns was consistent with the prohibitions of the canons;[1] but it was justified in the eyes of the prelates in consideration of the benefits which sprung from it, and perhaps through a natural attachment to national usages. It continued in full practice till the conquest; after which the foreign divines, whom the king had placed by degrees in the English bishoprics, protested against a custom which they considered a desecration of the episcopal office, and obtained from the first William a law for the separation of the civil from the ecclesiastical courts. In it the conqueror states that hitherto the episcopal laws have not been canonically observed in England; and, therefore, to put an end to the abuse, he decrees, with the common consent and advice of the archbishops, bishops, abbots, and all the great men of the kingdom, that no bishop nor archdeacon shall hold episcopal pleas in the courts of the hundred, or suffer any cause appertaining to the government of souls to be brought before secular judges: that the episcopal court shall sit in the episcopal city, unless the bishop appoint some other place; that every man who, after he has been thrice summoned, shall refuse to answer, shall be excommunicated, and then be compelled to obey

---

[1] The papal legates, Gregory and Theophylact, in 787, had noticed and condemned this practice of the Anglo-Saxon prelates. Vidimus etiam ibi episcopos in conciliis suis secularia judicare, prohibuimusque eos voce apostolica (2 Tim. ii. 4)—nemo militans Deo implicet se negotiis sæcularibus, ut ei militet cui se probavit. Spelm. Con. p. 295.

by secular authority; and that no sheriff or officer
of the king, nor any layman, shall interfere in
matters which ought to be determined according
to the laws of the church.[1] Thus courts Christian
were established under the sole authority of the
bishops, and from that day to the present ecclesiastical judges have been withdrawn from the civil
courts.

The great evil springing out of the influence
and consideration which the state attached to the
episcopal office was, that it tended to engender and
nourish a worldly and dissipated spirit, especially in
the possessors of the more opulent sees. The private clerk or monk was suddenly drawn from the
retirement of the cloister, and transformed into a
secular lord. He became at once the possessor of
extensive estates: his residence was crowded with
dependents; wherever he moved he was accompanied by a numerous escort. Thus he found himself
placed in a situation most foreign to his previous
habits: the management of his property, the necessity of defending the rights of his church against
adverse claims, the applications to him for patronage and aid, and the controversies among the
principal families in his diocese, involved him in a
vortex of secular cares and disputes: nor ought we
to be surprised if, in such circumstances, some of
these prelates, acting in their twofold capacity as
temporal and spiritual lords, adopted the manners
of ealdormen and thanes, seeking to add to their
possessions, multiplying, by the "læn or loan" of
lands, the number of their military retainers, and

---

[1] See it in Thorpe, i. 495.

employing, for the protection of themselves and their friends, secular as well as spiritual arms. The reader has seen that Jaenbyrct, the southern metropolitan, had excited by his power and proceedings the jealousy of Offa, king of Mercia; a few years later, Eanbald, the northern metropolitan, ventured to place himself openly in opposition to Eardulf, king of Northumbria;[1] and about a century and a half later we find Wolstan, a successor of Eanbald, holding the balance between king Edmund and the Danish kings Anlaf and Reginald, and afterwards braving, though in vain,

---

[1] We learn from two letters written by Alcuin on this occasion, that Eanbald had granted an asylum to the king's enemies, and undertaken to protect their lands; that he lost no opportunity of augmenting his own possessions; that he maintained a much greater number of thanes or military men than his predecessors; that, whereas they did not allow more than one follower to each thane, when the latter attended the archbishops, Eanbald permitted his thanes to have as many followers as they pleased, to the intolerable burthen of all the monasteries where he called. Eanbald had been the beloved disciple of Alcuin, who wrote to him on the subject in respectful terms, but blamed him more openly in a letter to two of Eanbald's friends. The archbishop's excuse was, that he acted thus through charity, for the relief of certain distressed and persecuted men:—" A singular kind of charity," replied his preceptor, " which provides for the relief of a few, and probably guilty, persons at the expense of many, and those too innocent of crime."—Quid ei in comitatu suo cum tanta militum copia? De misericordiæ causa eos habere videtur. Nocet monasterialibus qui eum cum suis suscipiunt. Plures, sicut audio, multo habet, quam antecessores sui habuerunt ..... imprudens est misericordia paucis prodesse, et illis forte reis, et multis nocuisse et illis etiam bonis. Non me accuset talia suggerentem, sed se emendet talia facientem. Ep. clxxv. p. 236. See also the preceding letter to Eanbald himself, p. 234.

the enmity of king Edred.[1] We meet also with numerous instances of the presence of bishops in military expeditions, whether they led their own retainers to the field, or accompanied the quota of armed men furnished from their respective dioceses. We are however assured, that they never mingled in the fray of battle; that they attended the camp as the king's chaplains to pray and not to fight, and that those who fell on one occasion by the swords of the enemy were employed in a tent offering the sacrifice of the mass for the success of their countrymen.[2]

---

[1] Flor. 603, 604. Hant. 203. Mail. 148. West. 189.

[2] In the battle of Charmouth in 833 duo episcopi, scilicet Herefridus et Wilfridus, perierunt. Hoved. f. 236. Chron. Sax. 72. In eodem certamine (the battle of Assington in 1016) occubuerunt Ædnothus episcopus Dorcastriæ et Wulfsius abbas Ramesiæ qui cum multis aliis religiosis personis, juxta morem Anglorum veterem, ibidem convenerant, non armis sed orationum suppetiis pugnantem exercitum juvaturi. Hist. Ram. 433. Ædnothus apud Assandune, dum missam cantaret, a Danis interfectus est cum Abbate Wulfsio. Hist. Elien. p. 497.

CHAPTER III.

CHURCH GOVERNMENT.

THE national church of the Anglo-Saxons was
not an isolated body, unconnected with, and independent of, the rest of Christendom : it formed
from its establishment an integral part of the
Catholic or universal church, governed by the same
laws, and acknowledging the same gradation of rank
and authority from the parish priest to the prelate
who sate in the chair of St. Peter. The present
chapter will, therefore, have for its object to
describe the manner in which such authority was
chiefly exercised—1st, by each individual bishop in his
diocesan synod ; 2nd, by the episcopal college in
provincial or national councils ; 3rd, by the Pope, the
successor of the prince of the apostles, as head of
the universal church.

I. The Anglo-Saxon bishops, in their respective
dioceses, exercised episcopal jurisdiction according to
the ecclesiastical canons ; and few instances are
recorded in history of either clerk or laymen who

dared to refuse obedience to their legitimate authority. It was enjoined that twice in the year, on the calends of May and November, they should summon their clergy to meet them in the diocesan synod. Every priest, whether secular or regular, to whose administration any district had been intrusted, was commanded to attend : and his disobedience was punished by a pecuniary fine, or by suspension from his office during a specified term.[1] As the subjects of their future discussion involved the interests of religion, and the welfare of the clergy, each member was exhorted to implore by his prayers, and deserve by his conduct, the assistance of the Holy Spirit. With this view, they were commanded to meet together, and travel in company to the episcopal residence ; to be attended by the most discreet of their clerks, and carefully to exclude from their retinue every person of light or disedifying deportment.[2] Three days were allotted for the duration of the synod ; and each day was observed as a fast till the conclusion of the session. At the appointed hour they entered the church in order and silence ; the priests were ranged according to their seniority ; below them were the principal among the deacons ; and behind was placed a select number of laymen, distinguished by their piety and wisdom. After an appropriate prayer, the bishop opened the synod with his charge, in which he promulgated the decrees of the last national council ;[3] explained the

---

[1] Wilk. Con. i. 220, xliv. Tom. iv. p. 784.
[2] Id. vol. i. p. 225; iv. 266, iv.
[3] Id. p. 98, xxv. Of the discourses spoken by the bishops on these occasions, a few are still preserved ;

regulations which he deemed expedient for the reformation of his diocese, and exhorted the members to receive with reverence the mandates of their father and instructor. He did not, however, prohibit the freedom of debate.[1] Each individual was requested to speak his sentiments without restraint; to offer the objections or amendments which his prudence and experience might suggest ; to expose the difficulties, against which he had to struggle in the government of his parish ; and to denounce the names and crimes of the public sinners, whose contumacy refused to yield to the zeal of their pastor, and defied the censures of the church.[2]

In conformity with the wish of St. Paul, that his converts would prefer, for the decision of their disputes, the assembly of the saints to the tribunal of a pagan magistrate, the ancient fathers, the inheritors of his spirit, had advised, that the controversies of the clergy should be withdrawn from the cognisance of the secular judges, and committed to the wisdom and authority of their ecclesiastical superiors.[3] The synod, therefore, as soon as the plan of reform had been adjusted, resolved itself into a court of judicature ; every clerk, who conceived himself aggrieved by any of his brethren, was admitted

---

two of which were composed by Ælfric, probably the same who wrote the Saxon homilies.   See them in Thorpe, ii. 342, 364.   Wilkins imagines that they were collected from the rule of St. Benedict : but a diligent comparison will shew, that they were formed after the admonitio synodalis of the Roman pontifical, which has been accurately published by Georgi.   De Liturg. Rom. Pont. vol. iii. p. 425.
[1] Wilk. vol. iv. p. 785.   [2] Id. vol. i. p. 225, v. vi.
[3] Id. vol. iv. p. 785, 786.

to prefer his complaint, and justice was administered according to the decisions of the canons and the notions of natural equity. But, as the testimony and recriminations of the contending parties might have scandalized their weaker brethren, during these trials, the laymen were excluded from the debates. On their re-admission, they were publicly invited to accuse, before the assembly of his peers, the clergyman who had notoriously neglected the duties of his profession, or dared to violate the rights of his fellow-citizens: and if a prosecutor appeared, the parties were heard with patience, and judgment was pronounced. The business of the meeting was then terminated: the bishop arose, made a short exhortation, gave his benediction, and dissolved the assembly.[1]

II. The many and important advantages which must have been derived from diocesan synods, thus organized and conducted, were felt and duly appreciated by the Anglo-Saxon prelates: but the superior dignity and superior authority of the national councils have chiefly claimed the notice of historians. The right of convoking these assemblies was vested in the archbishop of Canterbury; but in the exercise of this privilege he was directed, not only by the dictates of his own prudence, but sometimes by the commands of the Pope, more frequently by the decrees of the preceding council.[2] At his summons the bishops repaired to the appointed place, accom-

_____

[1] Ibid.
[2] After York became an archbishopric, each of the metropolitans convoked, on certain occasions, the bishops of their respective provinces.

panied by the abbots and the principal ecclesiastics
of their dioceses ; who, though they pretended to no
judicial authority, assisted at the deliberations and
subscribed to the decrees.[1]   Of these assemblies the
great objects were, to watch over the purity of faith
and the severity of discipline ; to point out to the
prelates and the parochial clergy the duties of their
respective stations ; to reform the abuses, which the
weakness of human nature insensibly introduces into
the most edifying communities ; and to regulate
whatever concerned the propriety and splendour of
the public worship.   The selection of the subjects of
discussion appears to have been intrusted to the wisdom of the metropolitan, who composed a competent
number of canons, and submitted them to the judgment of his brethren.[2]   Their approbation imparted

---

[1] See Wilkins, Con. pp. 51, 94, 167, 169. Respecting
the council of Calcuith, Henry informs us (and he affects
to consider the information as highly important, Hen. vol.
iii. p. 241), that in the preamble to the canons, it is said to
have been " called in the name, and by the authority of
Jesus Christ, the supreme head of the Church." Were
the assertion true, I know not what inference he could
justly deduce from it : but unfortunately the passage is
not to be found in any edition of the acts of the council.
See Spelman (p. 327), and Wilkins (p. 169).

[2] Among the constitutions of the Anglo-Saxon metropolitans, is preserved a code of laws, which St. Odo appears to have selected from the canons of preceding
synods (Wilk. p. 212).   It has been particularly noticed
by Henry, as characteristic of the haughty spirit which he
is pleased to ascribe to that prelate (Hen. Hist. vol. iii. p.
264).   But from what lexicographer had the historian
learned that *ammonemus* regem et principes, means, " I
command the king and the princes ?"   It is a singular
fact, that Henry's short version of ten lines is disgraced by
four mistakes, each of which is calculated to enforce the
charge of arrogance against the archbishop.

to them the sanction of laws, which bound the whole
Saxon church, and were enforced with the accustomed threat of excommunication against the transgressors.   Thus far the proceedings were strictly
ecclesiastical, without any interference of the king
or the witan;[1] but it was soon discovered, that the
dread of spiritual punishment operates most powerfully on those, who from previous habits of virtue
are less disposed to rebel; and that it is necessary,
among men of strong passions and untutored minds,
to oppose to the impulse of present desire the restraint of present and sensible chastisement.   With
this view, the bishops frequently solicited and obtained the aid of the civil power.   As the council
of bishops was generally held at the same time and
place with the witena-gemot, or council of the sages,
they were careful to improve the favourable opportunity;   to call the public attention to the more
flagrant violations of ecclesiastical discipline, and to
demand that future transgressors might be amenable
to the secular tribunals.   To the success of these
applications the statutes of the Saxon councils bear
ample testimony.   So early as the reign of Ethelbert,
the laws of Kent had guarded the property of the
church with the heaviest penalties;[2] and the zeal of
his grandson Earconbert prompted him to enforce
with similar severity the observance of the canonical
fast of Lent.[3] Persuaded of the necessity of baptism
by the instructions of his teachers, the legislator of

---

[1] See the councils of Hertford and Hatfield, Bed. iv.
c. 5,17 ; of Cloveshoe, Spel. p. 245; and of Calcuith, ibid.
p. 327.
[2] Thorpe, i. 2.
[3] Bed. l. iii. c. 8.   An. 640.

Wessex placed the new-born infant under the protection of the law, and by the fear of punishment stimulated the diligence of the parents. The delay of a month subjected them to the penalty of thirty shillings : and if, after that period, the child died without having received the sacred rite, nothing less than the forfeiture of their property could expiate the offence.[1] To relapse into the errors of paganism provoked a still more rigorous punishment. The sincerity of the convert was watched with a suspicious eye ; and the man that presumed to offer sacrifice to the gods, whom he had previously abjured, besides the loss of his estate, was condemned to the disgrace of the healsfang, unless he was redeemed by the contributions of his friends.[2]   By degrees, these penal statutes were multiplied, till there scarcely remained a precept of the decalogue, the overt transgression of which was not punishable by the civil law.   But of nothing were the Saxons more jealous than of the honour of their women.   Every species of insult, which could be offered to female chastity, was carefully enumerated ; the degrees of guilt were discriminated ; and the chastisement was proportioned to the nature of the offence and the dignity of the injured person.[3]   The fines arising from these

---

[1] Thorpe, i. 102.
[2] Ibid. p. 45. Healʃʃanʒe meant the pillory, but generally a legal compensation instead of the punishment.
[3] Ibid. pp. 6, 10, 24, 68, et passim. If the clergy were assisted by the power of the civil magistrate, the civil magistrate in return was much indebted to the superior knowledge of the clergy. It was by the persuasion and with the assistance of the missionaries that the first code of Saxon law was published by Ethelbert, "juxta morem Romanorum." Bed. l. ii. c. v. From the time of their

ecclesiastical crimes were paid into the treasury of the bishop under the denomination of ' bots,' and to his prudence was intrusted the administration of the money: but he was strictly commanded to devote it to charitable and religious purposes, to the relief of the poor, the repairs of decayed churches, the purchase of books, and the clothing and education of those, who were designed for the ministry of the altar.

III. There was still another authority acknowledged in the Anglo-Saxon church, higher even than that of the national council, the authority of the bishop of Rome, as the successor of St. Peter. Of that apostle our ancestors had been taught to believe,

---

conversion, the study of the Roman jurisprudence appears to have been a favourite pursuit with the clergy. St. Aldhelm visited the school at Canterbury, that he might learn "legum Romanorum jura, et cuncta jurisconsultorum secreta" (Ep. Aldhel. apud Gale, p. 341); and Beda speaks of the code of Justinian as of a work well known to his countrymen (Bed. Chron. p. 28, anno 567). To this study was necessarily added that of the ecclesiastical canons; and the knowledge of each must have given to the clergy a great superiority, both as legislators in the witena-gemot, and as magistrates in different courts. Alfred the Great, in his laws, seems to ascribe the substitution of pecuniary compensation in the place of corporal punishment to the advice of the clergy, who taught that mercy rather than revenge should distinguish the penal code of a Christian people (Thorpe, i. p. 58). It is, however, difficult to reconcile this assertion with the testimony of Tacitus, who observed, several centuries before, that such compensations were common among the nations of Germany. Levioribus delictis, pro modo, pœna : equorum pecorumque numero convicti multantur : pars multæ regi, vel civitati, pars ipsi qui vindicatur, vel propinquis ejus exsolvitur—Luitur enim etiam homicidium certo armentorum ac pecorum numero, recipitque satisfactionem universa domus. Tac. German. c. 12, 21.

that 'he was the first pastor of the church,' the prince
of the apostolic college;[1] 'the shepherd of the Lord's
flock;'[2] 'the man whom the Lord Jesus Christ had
appointed the pastor of all pastors, the head of his
chosen flock;'[3] 'the teacher and shepherd of all believing nations;'[4] 'whose happy lot it had been to
receive by a peculiar privilege the power of binding
and the monarchy of loosing both in heaven and on
earth.'[5] Nor did they conceive that the distinguished
office which he had enjoyed became extinct at his
death. The same reasons to which was owing its
original establishment, pleaded for its continuance;

[1] Primi pastoris ecclesiæ, principis apostolorum. Bed.
l. ii. c. 4. Primo pastori ecclesiæ. Oper. Min. p. 143.

[2] Pastor gregis Dominici. St. Aldhelm. de Virg. p. 361.

[3] Quem Dominus Jesus Christus caput electi sibi gregis
statuit—omnium pastorum pastor. Alc. Oper. l. 65,134.
Dedicat ecclesiæ quem caput alta fides. Ceolfrid, abbot
of Wearmouth, apud Bed. Op. Min. ii. p.332.

[4] Eallum geleaꝼullum leodum lareop and hyrde. Hom.
apud Whelock, 395.

[5] Ipse potestatem ligandi et monarchiam solvendi in
cœlo et in terra felici sorte et peculiari privilegio accipere
promeruit. St. Aldhel. ep. Geron. inter Bonif. p. 61.
It were easy to cover the page with similar testimonies.
yet several writers (Hickes, Gram. 20; Whelock, p. 237;
Elstob. pref. p. xl.; and Mr. Soames, Bampt. Lect. p. 160),
pretend that the Saxons looked upon St. Paul as the equal
of St. Peter. But where do they find St. Paul called
"the head of the church, the prince of the apostles?"
Even the very text of the Saxon homilist, on which they
chiefly found their opinion, cannot, if translated faithfully, afford them any support. "Paul is the thirteenth
of this company. He was not bodily with Christ during
the life of Christ; but he was chosen afterwards from
heaven, and is reckoned along with Peter on account of his
many deservings and labours." The word "ȝeenꝺebýnꝺ"
does not mean "made equal," as they translate it, but
reckoned in the same number, or of the same order—that
is, he is reckoned an apostle.

and the high prerogatives of Peter were believed to
descend to the most remote of his successors, who
was still his representative, sitting in his chair, and
inheriting his wonderful authority.[1] Hence the
church of Rome was pronounced 'the head of the
churches,' the distinguished head of the whole
church ;[2] and the bishop of Rome was said to ' hold
the first episcopal office in the whole world,' 'to be
set over the churches converted to Christ,'[3] ' to be
intrusted with the government of the whole church,'[4]
' to be the bishop of the world.'[5]

Impressed with these notions, the Anglo-Saxons
looked up to the pontiff with awe and reverence ;
consulted him respecting the administration of
their church, and bowed in respectful silence to
his decisions. His benediction they courted as the
choicest of blessings ;[6] and to obtain it was one of
the principal motives which drew so many pilgrims
to the threshold of the Vatican. No less than

---

[1] Petri te, ut vicarium sanctissimæ sedis agnosco, ita et
mirificæ potestatis heredem confiteor. Alcuin, ad Adrian.
Pap. Oper. 1. 25.
[2] Sancta Romana ecclesia quæ est caput ecclesiarum.
Id. 1. 792. Totius ecclesiæ caput eminet eximium. Bed.
Op. Min. ii. 336.
[3] Cum primum in toto orbe pontificatum gereret, et
conversis ad fidem veritatis prælatus esset ecclesiis. Bed.
Hist. ii. c. 1.
[4] Gratias agere non cesso, quod te nostris temporibus
regimini totius ecclesiæ præficere dignatus est. Huæt-
bert, abbot of Wearmouth, to Pope Gregory, apud Bed.
Op.Min.159,329. The Pope is summus pastor—omnium
pastorum pastor. Alc. i. ep. xcii. p. 134.
[5] Audire sapientiam præsulum mundi Romam venit.
Eddius, Vit. Wilf. c. v. p. 45.
[6] See the Epistles of Alcuin to the Popes Adrian and
Leo. Alc. Op. i. 25.

eight Saxon kings,[1] besides crowds of noblemen
and prelates, are recorded to have paid their
homage in person to the representative of Saint
Peter: and those who were deterred by reasons of
policy or the dangers of the journey, were yet careful to solicit by their ambassadors, and to deserve
by their presents, the papal benediction.[2] Highly as
they prized his friendship, so they feared his enmity.
The dread of his resentment struck terror into the
breasts of the most impious; and the threat of his
malediction was the last and strongest rampart
which weakness could oppose to the rapacity of
power. The clergy of each church, the monks of
each convent, sought to shelter themselves under his
protection; and the most potent monarchs, sensible
that their authority was confined within the narrow
limits of their own lives, solicited, in favour of their
religious foundations, the interference of a power
whose influence was believed to extend to the most
distant ages. Papal charters, said to have been
issued at the prayer of kings, bishops, and abbots, in
confirmation of grants and concessions made by the
civil power, are to be found in the collections of
Anglo-Saxon councils. The authenticity of many
of them may be questioned; but there cannot be
a doubt of the actual existence of such instruments
as early as the middle of the seventh century.

---

[1] Cæadwalla, Ine, Offa, Cœnred, Offa, Siric, Ethelwulf,
and Canute.

[2] Hanc benedictionem omnes qui ante me sceptro præficere Merciorum, meruerunt ab antercessoribus tuis adi-
pisci. Hanc ipse humilis peto, et a vobis, o beatissime,
impetrare cupio. Ep. Cœnulphi Regis Leoni Pap. Wilk.
164. See also pp. 40, 165. Chron. Sax. 86, 89, 90.

For this we have the testimony of Beda and
Eddius, two contemporaries. When Bennet Biscop
had built the monastery of St. Peter at Wearmouth on the land given to him by king Egfrid, he
proceeded to Rome, with the permission, consent,
desire, and exhortation of that monarch, to procure
a letter of privilege from Pope Agatho, which
might protect the monastery from all external vio-
lation of its rights. Ceolfrid, who succeeded Bennet
in the government of the abbey of St. Peter, having
added to it the new monastery of St. Paul, was careful to procure from Sergius, the successor of Agatho,
a new charter of the same tenour with that granted
to Bennet. Both instruments were confirmed in
national councils, the first with the subscriptions of
king Egfrid and his bishops, and the second with
those of king Alfred and the bishops of his day.[1]

But the confirmation of royal grants and monastic
privileges was the least important part in the exer-

---

[1] Epistolam privilegii a venerabili papa Agathone cum
licentia, consensu, desiderio, et hortatu Egfridi Regis
acceptam, qua monasterium ab omni prorsus extrinsica
irruptione tutum perpetuo redderetur ac liberum. Bed.
Op. Min. p. 145. Pro tuitione sui monasterii instar illius
quod Agatho Papa Benedicto dederat: quod Brittanias
perlatum, et coram synodo patefactum, præsentium episcoporum simul et magnifici Regis Aldfridi subscriptione
confirmatum est, quomodo etiam prius illud sui temporis
regem et episcopos in synodo publice confirmasse non
latet. Ibid. 156, 338. Bed. Hist. iv. c. 18. St. Wilfrid
about the same time obtained a similar charter of confirmation from Pope Agatho for his monasteries at Ripon
and Hexham—Duo monasteria quod primum dicitur
Hrypis, et alterum quod Hagulstaldense vocatur, a sancto
Agathone Papa sub uno privilegio adscripta sunt. Eddius,
Vit. Wilf. p. 79. See also the synod of Calcuith, Wilk.
Con. 147.

cise of the papal prerogative. By his authority the
pontiff—1, established, extended, or restricted the
jurisdiction of the archiepiscopal sees; 2, confirmed
the election of the metropolitans; 3, enforced the
observance of canonical discipline; 4, and revised
the decisions of the national councils.

1. While the division of old, or the erection of
new, bishoprics was intrusted to the metropolitan in
his provincial council with the consent of the king
and the witan, no establishment, or alteration of
metropolitan sees, could take place without the authority of the pontiff. Of this the reader has already
met with numerous proofs in the preceding chapter.
Gregory the Great divided the Anglo-Saxon territory
into two provinces; Vitalian placed all the Anglo-
Saxon churches under the jurisdiction of Theodore;
Agatho limited the number of bishops to one metropolitan and eleven suffragans; Leo I. established
a second metropolitan at York; Adrian a third at
Lichfield; and Leo III. revoked the grant to Lichfield, and confirmed to the church of Canterbury
that precedence of rank and authority which it has
since possessed down to the present day.

2. According to the discipline of the age, the
archbishop formed the connecting link between the
bishops of the province and the bishop of Rome.
Their election was confirmed by him, his by the
Pope. The new metropolitan might receive episcopal consecration from the bishops of the province,
or some neighbouring archbishop, according to pre-
cedent or necessity,[1] but he could not enter on the

---

[1] We have instances of both in Bed. i. c. 29, and ii. c.
17, 18.

exercise of his office as metropolitan—that is, claim
the ordination of the bishops of the province, or
call them to his synod, or sit on the archiepiscopal
throne till he had obtained the papal confirmation ;[1]
which was granted at his petition by the delivery to
him of the pallium, the badge of the metropolitan
dignity, to be worn by him only during the celebration
of mass, and in the discharge of his duties as metropolitan.[2]   Regularly it was expected that he should

---

[1] This is fully explained in the letter of Pope Nicholas
to the Bulgarians on the erection of an archiepiscopal see
among them.—Qui archiepiscopatus privilegia per nos
accipiat, et ita demum episcopos sibi constituat, qui ei
decedenti successorem eligant ; et propter longitudinem
itineris non jam huc consecrandus veniat, sed hunc episcopi qui ab obeunte archiepiscopo consecrati sunt, simul
congregati constituant, sane interim in throno non seden-
tem, et præter corpus Christi non consecrantem, prius-
quam pallium a sede Romana percipiat, sicuti Galliarum
omnes, et Germaniæ et aliarum regionum archiepiscopi
agere comprobantur.   Labbe, Com. viii. 542.

[2] There are many proofs that this practice was observed
in the Anglo-Saxon church.   Eanbald had been ordained
coadjutor bishop, with the right of succession in the
church of York, by archbishop Ælbert.   On the death
of Ælbert in 780, Alcuin hastened to Rome to obtain the
pallium for Eanbald (Vit. Alc. c. vi. f. lvi.), who, on the
receipt of it, was solemnly confirmed archbishop—qui
eo accepto in episcopatum solemniter est confirmatus.
Hoved. f. 152.   In 796 he died, on August 6, and Eanbald
the younger was immediately elected, and was consecrated by the bishops of his province ; but a year passed
before he received the pallium, when he was solemnly
confirmed archbishop on the 8th September, 797.—In
archiepiscopatum genti Northanhymbrorum solemniter
confirmatus est.   Id. f. 153.   On the death of Archbishop
Odo, Ælfsy, of Winchester, was elected and installed as
his successor; but Ælfsy never sat on the archiepiscopal
throne, because he died among the Alps before he could
receive the pallium.   Ang. Sax. ii. 56.

receive it in person from the hands of the pontiff;
but, if any legitimate impediment intervened, he
solicited it by messengers specially deputed for that
purpose.[1] Thus by his reception of the pallium when
he first entered on the office of metropolitan, and
the obligation of wearing it as often as he exercised
that office, he was constantly reminded of his subor-
dination in dignity and authority to him from whom
he had received it.[2]

By Gregory the Great it was decided, that in the
Anglo-Saxon church, on account of the distance
from Rome, the new archbishop should be consecrated
by the bishops of his province; by Honorius, that
he should receive consecration from the other metropolitan.   Both, for the same reason, were willing to

---

[1] The pallium consisted of a long strip of fine woollen cloth
ornamented with crosses, the middle of which was formed
into a loose collar resting on the shoulders, while the
extremities before and behind hung down nearly to the
feet.   Alcuin calls it the pallium, or superhumerale sanctitatis, and thus exhorts the metropolitan when he puts
it on:—Cogita semper, dum pallio sanctitatis vestieris, et
videas sanctæ crucis signum, sive ante sive retro, in eo
fixum, te sequi debere illum qui crucem suam portavit, in
qua redemptionis nostræ tropheum paravit.   Dum videas
osculare illud, et venerare sicut decet hujus signi sancti-
tatem, et te sequi debere memento illum, qui ait, *qui vult
post me venire, tollat crucem suam, et sequatur me.*   Alc. i.
ep. lxxxii. p. 121.

[2] On this account Berctwald or Brihtwald, though
elected by the church of Canterbury, is called by his own
agents the envoy of the holy see—Sancti Brihtwaldi Cantuariorum archiepiscopi et totius Britanniæ archiepiscopi
ab hac apostolica sede emissi.   Eddius, Vit. Wilf. c. 51,
p. 80.   On the same account Pope John says that Brihtwald had been confirmed by him — quem auctoritate
principis apostolorum ibidem confirmavimus.   Ep. Joan.
ibid. c. 52, p. 82.

spare him the fatigue of a journey to Rome for the
pallium, and consented that it should be forwarded
to him by his own messengers.[1] Thus it was
for more than two centuries: but later pontiffs
were less indulgent; and at some time, probably
about the end of the ninth century, it began to be
exacted that the new metropolitan should receive
the pallium in person from the Pope.[2] This was
considered a grievance; and to this another was now
added. According to the received notions of the
northern nations no Anglo-Saxon would venture to
ask a favour of a superior without the offer of a present: such offers were always made with the request
for the pallium; but the sums, which at first had
been received as gratuitous donations, were in time
exacted as a debt; and the increasing demand was
followed by loud and repeated complaints. During
the pontificate of Leo III. the Saxon prelates, in
a firm but respectful memorial, urged the indults of
former popes to their predecessors, and requested
that the pallium might be granted to their primates
without the fatigue of a journey or the expense of
a present.[3] The petition was unsuccessful; repeated
precedents had given a sanction to the obnoxious

---

[1] Bed. i. c. 29; ii. 17, 18. Ne sit necesse ad Romanam
usque civitatem per tam prolixa terrarum et maris spatia
pro ordinando archiepiscopo semper fatigari — ut hæc
vobis concederemus, longa terrarum marisque intervalla,
quæ inter nos et vos obsistunt, nos condescendere coege-
runt. Bed. ibid.

[2] In the ninth century the longa intervalla seem to
have formed no obstacle, because every year crowds of
Anglo-Saxons were attracted by devotion or curiosity to
Rome.

[3] Wilk. Con. p. 166. Ann. 801.

custom; and the bishops at last desisted from a fruitless opposition. After the lapse of two centuries the hopes of their successors were awakened by the pilgrimage of Canute the Great to the tombs of the apostles. The king pleaded with warmth the cause of his prelates; the reluctance of the Romans yielded to the arguments of a royal advocate, and the pontiff contracted his claims to the personal attendance of future metropolitans.[1]

3. To preserve the purity of the Christian worship, and enforce the observance of canonical discipline, were always considered by the popes as the most important of their duties. With this view they frequently demanded from the Saxon prelates an exposition of their belief, and admonished them to reform the abuses which disfigured the beauty of their church. As early as the year 680, when the rapid progress of Monothelitism alarmed the zeal of the orthodox pastors, Agatho had summoned the archbishop of Canterbury and his suffragans to attend a council at Rome;[2] but the length of the journey, and the necessities of their dioceses, were

---

[1] Conquestus sum iterum coram Domno Papa, et mihi vade displicere dixi, quod mei archiepiscopi tantum angariabantur immensitate pecuniarum, quæ ab eis expetebantur, dum pro pallio accipiendo secundum morem apostolicam sedem expeterent : decretumque est ne id deinceps fiat. Malm. de Reg. l. 310. Wilk. Con. p. 298.

[2] Sperabamus de Britannia Theodorum confamulum et coepiscopum nostrum, magnæ insulæ Britanniæ archiepiscopum et philosophum, cum aliis qui ibidem hactenus demorantur : et hac de causa concilium huc usque distulimus. Ep. Agath. ad Imp. apud Bar. ann. 680. Malm. de Pont. l. i. f. 112. Spelman conjectures this council to have been that of Constantinople, but his mistake is corrected by Alford. Tom. ii. p. 368.

probably admitted as a legitimate excuse; and in lieu of their presence in the synod, the pontiff consented to accept a public profession of their faith. John, abbot of St. Martin's, was selected as the papal deputy on this occasion; and shortly after his arrival, Theodore and his suffragans assembled at Hatfield, and declared their adhesion to the decrees of the five first general councils, and to the condemnation of Monothelitism by Martin the First. The deputy subscribed with the bishops, and received a copy of the acts, which he forwarded to Rome.[1]

From the faith, the inquiries of the popes were soon directed to the manners of the Saxons. While Theodore lived, the vigilance of his administration supported the vigour of ecclesiastical discipline : but under his more indulgent, or less active, successors, it was insensibly relaxed, till the loud report of Saxon immorality aroused the patriotism of St. Boniface, and provoked the animadversions of Zachary, the Roman pontiff. The missionary, from the heart of Germany, the theatre of his zeal, wrote in terms of the most earnest expostulation to the principal of the Saxon kings and

---

[1] Intererat huic synodo, pariterque Catholicæ fidei decreta firmabat vir venerabilis Joannes...Volens Agatho Papa, sicut in aliis provinciis, ita etiam in Britannia, qualis esset status ecclesiæ ediscere, hoc negotium reverentissimo Abbati Joanni injunxit. Quamobrem collecta ob hoc synodo, inventa est in omnibus fides inviolata Catholica, datumque illi exemplar ejus Romam perferendum. Bed. l. iv. c. 18. It is probable that John was instructed to recommend the holding of the council, if Theodore objected to a journey to Rome.

prelates: and the pontiff commanded archbishop
Cuthbert and his suffragans, by authority of the
holy see, to oppose the severity of the canons to the
corrupt practices of the times. His injunctions were
obeyed. Cuthbert convened the bishops of his
province at Cloveshoe, and, according to "the apostolic mandate," laid before them the letters of
Zachary, both in the original Latin and in an
English translation. These documents have perished : but we learn from the acts that in them
the Pope addressed himself to all the natives of
Britain ; that he warned, and expostulated, and
entreated ; and that at last he threatened to strike
with the curse of excommunication all whose contumacy should despise his commands.[1] The prelates
listened with attention and awe : they exhorted
each other to discharge at least their own duty;
and, having consulted the decrees of the councils,
and the homilies of their holy father St. Gregory,
they enacted thirty-two canons of discipline for the
reform of the clerical and monastic bodies, the
greater uniformity and regularity of the public wor-

---

[1] The letter of Zachary is thus described in the procœ-
mium to the acts of the council :—Scripta toto orbe
venerandi pontificis, Domni Apostoli papæ Zachariæ, in
duabus chartis in medium prolata sunt, et cum magna
diligentia, juxta quod ipse apostolica sua auctoritate præcepit, et manifeste recitata, et in nostra quoque lingua
apertius interpretata sunt. Quibus namque scriptis Britanniæ hujus insulæ nostri generis accolas familiariter
præmonebat, et veraciter conveniebat, et postremo amabiliter exorabat, et hæc omnia contemnentibus, et in sua
pertinaci malitia permanentibus, anathematis sententiam
procul dubio proferendum insinuabat. Wilk. Con. 94.
Spelm. 245. Ann. 747.

ship, and the general encouragement of piety and devotion.[1]

Whether the result of the council of Cloveshoe answered the expectations of Zachary we are ignorant: but about forty years later, Gregory, bishop of Ostia, and Theophylact, of Todi, accompanied by Wighode, the envoy of Charlemagne, landed in Kent, and were received with due reverence by Jaenbyrct, archbishop of Canterbury. They came as legates from Pope Adrian, and brought with them a code of laws to improve the discipline of the Anglo-Saxon church. From Canterbury they proceeded to the court of Offa, of Mercia, where they found also Cynewulf, of Wessex, and received from both kings every demonstration of respect, and the strongest assurance of obedience to the papal admonitions. Here they separated, Gregory hastening to Northumbria, that he might visit the province of the northern metropolitan, Theophylact remaining in Mercia to regulate the concerns of the southern province. Gregory found archbishop Eanbald at York; but the king, Alfwold, was on the borders of the kingdom ; from which cause it happened that much time elapsed before the monarch and his witan, with the metropolitan and the heads of the clergy, could meet in a national council. From his inquiries, Gregory discovered the existence among the inhabitants of customs which he pronounced disgraceful to a Christian people; and on that account made

---

- Ibid. This council has been selected by Henry as furnishing proofs that the Anglo-Saxon prelates considered themselves totally independent of the bishop of Rome. Mr. Soames (Hist. p. 113, note 2) has undertaken to prove the same doctrine in the face of the most unanswerable evidence to the contrary. See note (G).

several additions to those canons which he had brought originally from Rome.[1] The amended code was read before the council, and all the members present unanimously declared that they would observe it to the utmost of their power. The chiefs then personally affirmed this promise before the legate, as representative of the pontiff, by the sign of the cross in his hand, and afterwards "subscribed the same sacred sign before their names on the written copy of the canons."[2]

Hence Gregory, accompanied by messengers from Alfwold and Eanbald, repaired to a council at Calcuith, where "the glorious king Offa, with his witan, and the archbishop with his colleagues," waited to receive him. Before them were read the canons passed in the northern council, both in Latin and in Teutonic, as he calls the English language: similar assurances of obedience were given : similar affirmations by the sign of the cross were made; and similar subscriptions added in the same manner. These particulars we derive from the report of the legates to the Pope : our own historians merely relate that " legates came to renew the faith and

---

[1] Probably the legate meant the following customs, which he calls remains of paganism :—1. That of marking the body with the infusion of colouring matter into wounds or punctures made in the skin. 2. Of wearing clothes after the manner of pagans. 3. Of deciding litigation by the drawing of lots. 4. Of cruelty to horses, by fastening their ears together, slitting their nostrils, and depriving them of their tails and of the sense of hearing. 5. Of using horse-flesh as animal food. Spelm. 300.

[2] What is meant by "the sign of the cross in his hand?" I cannot explain it. It occurs twice in the original—signo sanctæ crucis, vice vestra in manu nostra. P. 300. In manu nostra in vice dominii vestri, signum sanctæ crucis formaverunt. P. 301.

peace that St. Gregory sent to us through Augustine the bishop."[1]

These several instances occurred during the time when it was customary for the new archbishop to procure the pallium through the agency of a messenger : but later, when it became obligatory on him to solicit it at Rome in person, an opportunity was furnished to the pontiff of interrogating him respecting the state of the Anglo-Saxon church, of issuing instructions to him and his bishops for their future conduct, and of exacting from him a solemn promise to put down the more flagrant abuses. It arises probably from this cause that we read no more of the presence of legates in England before the last years of the Saxon period. In 1060 Kynsey, of York, died, and Aldred, of Worcester, was promoted to the archbishopric, with permission to retain his own more wealthy see of Worcester. The next year he proceeded to Rome to receive the pallium. But Robert, archbishop of Canterbury, who had been ejected by force from his church, and died at the abbey of Jumieges on his way back from Rome, had already acquainted the pontiff with the abuses prevalent in the English church. Nicholas returned a positive refusal unless Aldred would relinquish

---

[1] Chron. Sax. p. 64. From this expression it has been pretended by Carte, that these legates were not invested with any authority, but came to renew the correspondence between the two churches, which somehow or other had been interrupted. (Carte, l. 270.) But the notion is fully refuted by their despatches to the pontiff. Scripsimus capitulare de singulis rebus, et per ordinem cuncta disserentes auribus illorum pertulimus, qui cum omni humilitatis subjectione, clara voluntate, tam admonitionem vestram, quam parvitatem nostram amplexantes spoponderunt se in omnibus obedire. Wilk. Con. 148.

the see of Worcester. With the result, as far as
Aldred was concerned, the reader is already
acquainted.[1] He was followed immediately to
England by Ermanfroi, bishop of Sion, and another
cardinal, as legates to the king from Nicholas, or
more probably Alexander II., who succeeded to
Nicholas in the month of September of the same
year. They had in charge to watch the conduct of
Aldred, and to confer with Edward on several questions respecting the English church; questions
which are not specified, but one of which undoubtedly would regard the pretensions of Stigand to the
see of Canterbury. We know nothing more of their
proceedings than that they remained with the king
a great part of the summer, and returned to Rome
in 1663. Three years later England had passed
under the dominion of the Normans.[2]

4. There remains another branch of the papal
prerogative, which the bishops of Rome were occasionally called upon to exercise among our ancestors,
that of receiving and determining appeals from the
partial or unsatisfactory judgments of provincial or
national councils. The first of the Saxon prelates,
who invoked in this manner the protection of the
holy see, was Wilfrid, the celebrated bishop of York;
and by this proceeding he has earned the enmity of
the modern writers, who make the notions prevalent
in their own age and locality the standard by which

---

[1] P. 96, note.
[2] Hoved. f. 255. Malm. Vit. Wulst. in Ang. Sax. ii. 250.
The dissector of the Saxon Chronicle looks upon Malmesbury's life of Wulstan as unworthy of credit, and proceeding
from a conspiracy to falsify the history of that period.
(See Dissection, pp. 79, 133.) I do not, however, see that
he produces any thing like proof of the assertion.

they judge of ancient times and transactions. In their pages Wilfrid stands forth a proud, ambitious man, who, to preserve his own power, scrupled not to sacrifice the religious liberties of his countrymen; but if we look into the writings of those who knew him personally, and were actually acquainted with the particulars of his case, we shall find him a much-injured prelate, seeking redress according to the laws universally recognized by his contemporaries. In relating, therefore, the proceedings on his appeals, I shall make it my endeavour to clear away that mass of fiction which modern prejudice has spread over his story, taking for my vouchers Eddius, the constant companion of his fortunes, and Beda, the personal acquaintance both of him and of several of his opponents, and trusting that the importance of the matter will fully atone for the length of the narrative.

Wilfrid was of noble parentage in Northumbria. He lost his mother in his childhood; and was sent at the age of fourteen, with his father's consent, to the monks at Lindisfarne by Queen Eanfled. A few years later he expressed a wish to travel to Rome for improvement: the monks assented; and his patroness recommended him to the notice of Earconbert, king of Kent. From Canterbury he proceeded on his road as far as Lyons; where Anemund, the Dolphin bishop of that city, captivated with the manners and conduct of the young Saxon, proposed to adopt him for his son, to give to him his niece in marriage, and to transfer to him the government of a considerable district. But Wilfrid was proof against this tempting offer; and Anemund, respect-

ing his motives, dismissed him with a guide and a
suitable retinue.   At Rome he studied under the
archdeacon Boniface;[1] then, returning to Lyons, he
received the ecclesiastical tonsure from the bishop,
and became his favourite attendant.   But Anemund
had incurred the displeasure of Ebroin, who
governed under the nominal authority of Queen
Bathild; and by his orders, a body of soldiers surprised and murdered the bishop.   It was in vain
that Wilfrid begged to die with his benefactor.   He
was dismissed, and returning to Northumbria, was
admitted into the family of Alchfrid, the son of
Oswiu (An. 658).[2]   He was subsequently raised to
the priesthood, and, having distinguished himself in
the conference at Whitby, was, after the death of
Tuda, the successor of Colman, chosen unanimously,
in 664, bishop of Northumbria.   As the see of Canterbury was vacant, he repaired to Gaul with a letter
of recommendation from Alchfrid to Clotaire, king
of Neustria, and was consecrated in a synod of
bishops, at Compeigne, a royal villa, by his former
friend, Agilberct, now bishop of Paris.[3]

Whilst Wilfrid was yet in Gaul, Oswiu appears to
have repented of his choice, and at the instigation,
it is said, of the party favourable to the Scottish
monks, named the presbyter Chad for his bishop.
Chad hastened to Canterbury for consecration, supposing probably that Wighard would by that time

---

[1] From Boniface he learned the four gospels, perfecte,
according to Eddius (c. 5), ex ordine, according to Beda,
l. v. 19.   What does this mean? That he learned them by
heart?   Or that he learned to expound them?
[2] Bed. v. 19.   Eddius, Vit. Wilf. c. 2—8.
[3] Bed. iii. c. 28.

have returned from Rome. But Wighard, as the reader is aware, had died in that city: and the Northumbrian repaired to Wini of Winchester, the only bishop then alive among the Anglo-Saxons, who performed the ceremony with the aid of two British prelates. Wilfrid, on his return, found Chad already in possession of the northern bishopric, and retired to his monastery at Ripon, whence he issued occasionally to perform the episcopal office in the kingdoms of Kent and Mercia. At the end of three years Theodore arrived. He visited Northumbria, condemned the intrusion of Chad, and established Wilfrid in possession of the bishopric to which he had been ordained. The deprived prelate withdrew to his beloved monastery of Læstingham: but Wilfrid bore a willing testimony to his piety and virtue, and he was re-ordained in 669 to the bishopric of Mercia.[1]

---

[1] Beda in different places relates these events in a very summary manner (iii. 28, iv. 3, v. 19): the particulars are supplied from Eddius. The dioceses of both bishops were very extensive: that of Wilfrid contained episcopatum Eboracensis ecclesiæ et omnium Northanhymbrorum, sed et Pictorum, quousque Rex Oswiu imperium protendere potuit (Bed. l. iv. c. 3): that of Chad, episcopatum gentis Merciorum simul et Lindisfarorum (Ibid.) According to Eddius, Chad was deprived because prædonis more alterius episcopi sedem præripere ausus sit (Eddius, c. 15, 59). Of his re-ordination Beda says that the defects were supplied—Ordinationem ejus denuo catholica ratione consummavit (Bed. l. iv. c. 2); Eddius, that he was fully ordained through every step—per omnes gradus ecclesiasticos plene eum ordinaverunt (Eddius, c. 15, p. 59). Did they look on his ordination by Wini as void, or only incomplete, on account of some omission? He confessed that it was sinful, because the two assistant bishops were quartodecimans (Edd. ibid.), but the objection against

What became of Alchfrid is unknown. Oswiu died in 670, and was succeeded by another son, of the name of Egfrid. For some years Wilfrid enjoyed the favour and the confidence of the new monarch. No objection could be made to his private or public conduct. In private he led an abstemious and mortified life; in public he was indefatigable in the performance of his episcopal duties; but his power and wealth provoked animadversion: his power, because he alone governed all the churches of Deira and Bernicia; and his wealth, because in addition to the episcopal income, he possessed as his own property the great monasteries of Hexham and Ripon, with their many dependencies. We are told that he had offended Ermenburge, the wife of Egfrid, and that the queen, in revenge, sought to instil these notions into the mind of her husband. However that may be, the conquest of the province of the Lindissi, or of Lincolnshire, by Egfrid, in 677, afforded a pretext to invite Theodore of Canterbury to the Northumbrian court. What passed there between the archbishop and the king, or the archbishop and Wilfrid, is unknown: but it was the declared object of Theodore to break into smaller districts the extensive dioceses of the Anglo-Saxon bishops, and in pursuit of this object he seems occasionally to have acted in a very arbitrary manner. Unexpectedly, without the participation or the knowledge of Wilfrid, and even without the co-operation of any other bishop in the ceremony, he consecrated at York three new prelates, Eadhead

---

him by Theodore was, that he had not been *rite* consecratus, which appears to refer to the form.

for the province of the Lindissi, Bosa for York and
the kingdom of Deira, and Eata for Hexham and the
kingdom of Bernicia.[1] Wilfrid received the news
with surprise. By this partition he was ejected, not
from a part only, but from the whole of his bishopric
and his monastery of Hexham, and that too without any legal process or charge against him. He
hastened to court, complained of the injustice which
had been done to him, and reclaimed in his favour the
aid of the canons. But his remonstrances were
received with contempt; the courtiers congratulated
each other on his disgrace ; and the injured prelate,
with the advice of some bishops who were present,
appealed from the judgment of the metropolitan to
the superior authority of the pontiff.[2]

At first the enemies of Wilfrid attempted to prevent him from prosecuting his appeal, by despatch-
ing a royal messenger to Thierry, king of Neustria,

---

[1] Inordinate *solus* ordinavit. Eddius, c. xxiv. p. 63. Had
Theodore then obtained from Vitalian the same permission which Augustine had from Gregory, of dispensing,
when it appeared necessary, with the co-operation of other
bishops, in episcopal consecrations ? Bed. i. c. xxvii.
Wharton (Ang. Sac. 1. 693), and Carte (Hist. i. 248), state
that Lindisfarne was kept open for the acceptance of
Wilfrid. But the contrary is plain from Eddius (c. 24),
compared with Beda, Hist. iv. c. 12. Whether, in case
of his submission, he would have been permitted to retain
Ripon, does not appear.

[2] Cum consilio coepiscoporum suorum. Edd. c. 24.
By some modern writers it is said that Theodore merely
carried into execution the ninth canon of the council of
Hertford respecting the division of larger dioceses, and that
Wilfrid justly deserved deposition for the obstinacy with
which he opposed it. But all this is fiction. The very
canon to which they allude, proves that it was proposed by
Theodore, but withdrawn. In commune tractatum est,
sed de hac re ad præsens *siluimus*. Bed. iv. c. 5.

with a request that he would intercept that prelate
on his way through Gaul, and order him to be kept
in close custody. Now it happened that Wynfrid,[1]
a name very like to that of Wilfrid—the bishop of
Mercia, had also been deposed by Theodore, and had
also appealed to the holy see. Unsuspicious of
danger, he landed at the usual port, Quentavic or
Estaples, and was taken for Wilfrid, seized by the
emissaries of Ebroin, mayor of the palace to
Thierry, despoiled of all his property, and, after
many indignities, permitted or compelled to return
to England. But the Northumbrian, aware perhaps
of the design, taking advantage of a favourable wind,
directed his course to Friesland, where he was gra-
ciously received by the king, Aldgils, and spent the
winter in preaching to the pagans. In the spring
of 679, he sought the protection of Dagobert, who
reigned in Alsace, and who, in return for the good
offices which he formerly, an exile himself, had
received from Wilfrid, forwarded him in safety to
Rome in the company of Deodatus, one of his own
bishops.[2] There Wilfrid found that Theodore,
anxious to preoccupy the ear of the pontiff, had
already sent the monk Cœnwald with instructions to
justify his conduct.[3] Agatho summoned a council to

---

[1] By Beda the deposed bishop of Mercia is called Wyn-
fred (l. iv. c. 6), by Eddius, Wulfred of Lichfield (c. 24,
p. 64). Both plainly mean the same individual.

[2] Edd. c. 25—8. Bed. lv. c. 19.

[3] Not only Cœnwald, but several others were present.
Præsentibus ejus contrariis, qui a Theodoro venerandæ
memoriæ archiepiscopo ex hac apostolica sede mandato,
et Hilda religiosæ memoriæ abbatissa ad eum accusandum
huc prius convenerant. Ep. Joan. Papæ apud Eddium,
c. 52, p. 81.

his assistance; and the bishops of the suburbicane churches, with the priests and deacons of Rome, to the number of fifty, assembled to judge the cause of the Anglo-Saxon prelates. Before this court Wilfrid appeared, with the dignity of conscious innocence. He called on the members to do justice to an injured and persecuted bishop, who, from the extremities of the earth, had been compelled to invoke the equity of the successor of St. Peter. Could his adversaries impeach his moral conduct? Could they point out in his administration a single instance, in which he had violated the holy canons? Yet had he been expelled from his diocese, and had seen it parcelled out, and bestowed on two intruded prelates. Of the motives which had induced the metropolitan to treat him with such harshness, it was not for him to judge. Theodore was the envoy of the holy see : he respected his character; and did not presume to condemn his conduct. As for himself, his great anxiety had been to secure the peace of the Anglo-Saxon church : he had not raised a clamorous opposition, but had withdrawn in silence from the violence of his enemies, and thrown himself with confidence on the justice of the Roman church. The judgment of that church he now implored : and in its decision, favourable or unfavourable, he should willingly and respectfully acquiesce.[1]

With the answer and recriminations of Coenwald we are not acquainted. The cause was patiently and impartially discussed; and the judgment of the synod condemned the irregularity of his expulsion, though it seemed to approve the policy of the par-

---

[1] Edd. c. 29.

tition. It was ordered that Wilfrid should be restored to the diocese of which he had been unjustly deprived, and that the bishops intruded in his place should be expelled; but that he should, in conjunction with the other bishops, select from his own clergy a certain number of prelates, to assist him in the government of so extensive a diocese. To this decision was annexed the sentence of suspension against the clergyman, of excommunication against the layman, that should presume to oppose its execution.[1] A copy was delivered to Wilfrid, who remained some months in Rome, assisted, in 680, with one hundred and twenty-five bishops, at a second council, subscribed to the decrees, and bore testimony to the catholic belief of the Britons, Saxons, Picts, and Scots, who inhabited the northern provinces of the two British islands.[2]

But the enmity of Egfrid and Ermenburge was too violent to listen to the dictates of justice, or to be subdued by the terrors of a papal mandate. In his journey to Rome, Wilfrid had with difficulty escaped the many snares which, by their direction, had been

---

[1] Eddius, c. 31. Inett (Hist. p. 101), tells us that the reason why judgment was given in favour of Wilfrid was the absence of his accusers; with what truth may be seen in the preceding note. Mr. Soames does not believe that there was any judgment at all. It was merely the opinion of the Roman canonists, which bound nobody. Bampt. Lect. 167. Yet he quotes these lines from Fridegode—

"Theodoro Regique *jubet sancita* notari,
Ni pietate pari conservent *jussa* magistri,
Judicio Domini cunctos anathemate plecti."
Act. SS. Ben. iii. 169.

Do canonists, when they are consulted, excommunicate those who do not adopt their opinion?

[2] Edd. c. 51. Bed. l. v. c. 19, Anno 679.

laid for his life: at his return, he was apprehended by their order, and committed to prison. During a confinement of nine months, the influence of threats and promises was alternately employed to extort a confession, that the decision of the pontiff was a fabrication, or had been purchased with presents.[1] But his constancy defeated every artifice; and his liberation was at last granted to the earnest prayer of the abbess Ebba, provided he would promise never more to set his foot within the territories of Egfrid. Wilfrid subscribed the condition; and retiring from Northumbria, solicited the protection of Brithwald, nephew to the king of Mercia. That nobleman granted to him a small property, on which he built a monastery for himself and the faithful companions of his exile. But the emissaries of Egfrid discovered his retreat; their menaces excited the fears of the Mercian; and Wilfrid, rather than endanger the safety of his friend, fled into the kingdom of Wessex. At this distance he might have hoped to elude the notice of his enemies : but Irmenigild, the queen of Wessex, was the sister of Ermenburge; she had imbibed the sentiments of the Northumbrian princess; and the fugitive bishop having sought in vain an asylum among his Christian countrymen, was compelled to intrust his safety to the honour and compassion of a pagan people. Edilwalch, king of Sussex, received him with welcome; pitied his misfortunes; and swore that he would protect him against the open violence or the secret intrigues of the court of Northumbria.[2] Wilfrid soon repaid the hospitality of his royal patron. By

---

[1] Edd. c. 33, 35. [2] Ibid. c. 39, 40.

his preaching he converted numbers of the idolaters
to the faith of Christ; by his superior knowledge he
instructed them in the arts of civilized life. A continued drought for three years had exhausted the
sources of vegetation, and the horrors of famine frequently urged the barbarians to put an end to their
existence. From Beda we learn, that in bodies of
forty or fifty persons, they would proceed to the
nearest cliff, and there, linked in each other's arms,
precipitate themselves into the waves. Their distress excited the compassion of the stranger, who,
observing that the sea and the rivers abounded with
fish, taught them the art of making nets, and of
drawing from the waters a plentiful supply of food.[1]
For these services, Edilwalch bestowed on him
Selsey, the Isle of Seals, where he was often visited
by Cædwalla, an exile of the royal race of Cerdic.
The similarity of their fortunes endeared him to
the prince; who, when he had ascended the throne
of his fathers, invited Wilfrid to his court, granted
to him a fourth part of the Isle of Wight, and raised
him to a distinguished place in his councils.[2] But
here a new prospect at length opened before him.
Theodore, as he had been the first to inflict, was also
the first to repair the injury. Before his death he
condemned the injustice of his former conduct,
solicited a reconciliation, and wrote in favour of the
exiled bishop to the kings of Mercia and Northumbria. Of these letters, one is still extant. In it the
primate urges the obedience due to the pontiff;
bears testimon tyo the merit of Wilfrid, his inno-

---

[1] Edd. c. 40.   Bed. l. iv. c. 13.
[2] Edd. c. 41.   Bed. l. iv. c. 16.

cence, his patience, and his zeal; and entreats the king to grant this last request to his friend and father, ready to sink into the grave.[1]

Theodore did not live to witness the effect of his exhortations, and his death was speedily followed by that of Egfrid. In 685, the Northumbrian prince fell in battle, and with him expired the influence of Ermenburge. Aldfrid, the new king, cheerfully consented to receive the exile under his protection, gave him immediate possession of the church of Hexham, and shortly after restored to him the see of York and the monastery of Ripon. During five years he possessed his former episcopal authority: but they were years of toil and conflict. Of all his churches, he valued mostly that of Ripon. It had been a present from Alchfrid, the friend and patron of his youth: its revenues had been greatly increased by his industry; the magnificence of its buildings was the result of his genius and liberality; and the monks, the first in the north who professed the rule of St. Benedict, revered him as their father and benefactor. The monastery itself had been restored to him; but when he sought to recover the manors, which had been torn from it during his exile, he met with a most obstinate resistance. The clamour against his rapacity and ambition was revived; he was called upon to comply with the decrees of Theodore respecting the episcopal partition of the kingdom; and at last received from Aldfrid an order to resign the possession of Ripon, that it might be converted into the seat of a bishop-

---

[1] Eddius, c. 42.

ric.[1] Wilfrid returned a refusal : the monarch
threatened vengeance ; and the bishop, alarmed for
his life, placed himself under the friendly protection
of Ethelred, king of Mercia. There he remained
for the space of nine years, during which he received
a letter favourable to his cause from Pope Sergius,
who had been an exile from Rome for the space of
seven years.[2] About 702, Brithwald, the successor
of Theodore in the see of Canterbury, summoned
a council, which Wilfrid was invited to attend.[3]

---

[1] Eddius, c. 44. It is difficult to discover what is here
meant by the decrees of Theodore. By the death of St.
Cuthbert of Lindisfarne, and the retirement of Bosa from
York, and of John from Hexham, Wilfrid had recovered
the whole of his diocese, and the first part of the judgment pronounced by Pope Agatho had been carried into
execution. There still remained the second part, that
Wilfrid should consent to the partition of his diocese, but
should choose the new prelates out of his own clergy,
with   the   approbation   of a council.   Now of this
nothing   was   done,   with the exception of the tardy
appointment of a successor to St. Cuthbert at Lindisfarne (Bed. l. iv. c. 39). We find from the sequel that
Bosa and John, the two bishops who had retired in obedience to the papal judgment, became, ostensibly at least,
the chief opponents of Wilfrid. Might they not maintain
that Theodore's partition was tacitly approved by the
rescript of Agatho, and that Wilfrid was bound to allow
of it, instead of keeping almost the whole of the kingdom
under his own jurisdiction ?

[2] We have not this letter, but he repeatedly refers to it
in the pleadings before the Pope. Edd. c. 49—52.

[3] It has been supposed that this council was held soon after
Wilfrid's retreat into Mercia in 692 : whence it has been
inferred that the narrative of Eddius is contradicted by
Beda (l. v. c. 11), who says that Brithwald was then
beyond the sea, where he had gone to be consecrated. See
Mr. Wright, Biograph. Brit. p. 180, note. Now Beda,
indeed, says that the archbishop was absent when Wilfrid
retired into Mercia, but it is plain from Wilfrid's own speech,

On his arrival, he was met with a requisition to promise, upon oath, that he would abide by the decree of the metropolitan. He saw the object of his opponents: they hoped to wrest from his hand that powerful weapon with which he had formerly defeated them, to deprive him of the right of appeal. He therefore replied mildly, but warily, that it was his wish and his duty to abide by the decision of his metropolitan, provided that decision were conformable to the canons and the previous decrees of the apostolic see. Neither argument nor threatening could remove him from this answer: noise and confusion ensued. The voice of Wilfrid was drowned in the clamours of his adversaries; his contumacy was pronounced worthy of the severest punishment; and as a last, and unmerited favour, he was offered the monastery of Ripon, provided he would engage to confine himself within its precincts, and to resign, from that day, the exercise of the episcopal authority. This harsh resolve roused the spirit of the injured prelate. " What !" he indignantly exclaimed, " shall I, who have spent my whole life in the service of religion ; I, to whom my country is indebted for the knowledge and practice of the canonical observances, tamely subscribe to my own degradation, and, though unconscious of guilt, confess myself a criminal ? No, if justice be denied me here, I appeal to a higher tribunal; and let the man, who presumes to depose me from the episcopal

---

that the council was held ten years later ; for he says that it was then twenty-two years since the decree of Pope Agatho had been made known to his opponents, which could not have happened before 680 ; per viginti et duos annos, c. 45.

dignity, accompany me to Rome, and prove his
charge before the sovereign pontiff." This bold
reply exasperated Aldfrid, who threatened to commit him to the custody of his guard: but the
bishops interposed, observing, that to violate the
safe conduct which had been granted would fix an
indelible stigma on their proceedings.[1]

The controversy was now transferred from Northumbria to Rome. The first who arrived was an
Anglo-Saxon deacon, whose name has not tran-
spired, the representative of the archbishop, with
several advisers and a huge mass of papers, and he
was soon followed by Wilfrid, with a deputation of
his monks. Every charge against him was successively debated in several sittings during four
months : the pleadings were conducted on both
sides with spirit and freedom ; and the judgment
delivered by the pontiff, John VI., was most honourable to the exiled prelate, inasmuch as it
acquitted him of every accusation which had been
brought against him.[2] Yet no definitive sentence

---

[1] Eddius, c. 45. After this council the monks who still
adhered to the cause of Wilfrid were treated as excommunicated persons, by those who obtained possession of his
monasteries (id. c. 47), whence some writers have inferred
that Wilfrid himself had been excommunicated for his
contumacy. But of that there is not so much as a hint in
Eddius ; nor is it probable that Brithwald would venture
to excommunicate a bishop for appealing to Rome, at the
same time that he was preparing to oppose the appeal in
the papal court.

[2] The only charge specified by Eddius is, that Wilfrid
had refused to submit to the judgment of the archbishop
(Edd. c. 51). But Henry has supplied the deficiency, on
the authority, as he pretends, of Eddius himself. He tells
us that Wilfrid was charged with refusing to subscribe to

was pronounced, but the archbishop received an order to convoke a council, and then leave it to the option of Bosa, of York, and John, of Hexham, either to end the controversy amicably by accepting such terms from Wilfrid as to the synod should seem reasonable, or to repair to Rome and plead their cause personally before a more numerous council.

With this answer Wilfrid returned to England. Brithwald promised his best services for the restoration of peace: Ethelred, of Mercia, received him with his accustomed kindness, and recommended him to Cœnred, to whom he had resigned the sceptre : but Aldfrid was inflexible. "My brothers," he replied to Wilfrid's messengers, whose friendship he had formerly prized, and whose character he still respected, "ask for yourselves, and you will not meet with a refusal. But ask not for Wilfrid. His cause has been judged already by

---

the synods of Hertford and Hatfield, and of appealing to a foreign judge, which by the laws of England was a capital crime. He has also thought proper to compose an answer for Wilfrid to the first of these charges ; "that he was willing to subscribe to these synods as far as they were agreeable to the canons of the church of Rome and the will of the Pope:" but to the second he appears to have been unable or unwilling to form any reply (Henry, vol. iii. p. 219). Such fables have no pretension to truth or probability. That Wilfrid should refuse to subscribe to the synod of Hertford, to which he had already subscribed by his legates (Bed. Hist. l. iv. c. 6), or to that of Hatfield, which only published a profession of faith (id. l. iv. c. 17), will not be readily believed; but that Aldfrid and his bishops should send deputies to Rome, to accuse a prelate of the capital crime of appealing to Rome, is an idea which outrages probability.

Ficta . . . . . . sint proxima veris,
Nec quodcumque volet, poscat sibi fabula credi.

myself, by the archbishop, the envoy of the apostolic see, and by almost all the bishops of Britain.
That judgment I will not alter for writings, as you
call them, of the apostolic see." He lived but a
few weeks after this answer; and, before his death,
requested the abbesses Ælflede and Ædelburge to
bear testimony of his wish to be reconciled with
Wilfrid. After an interregnum of two months, he
was succeeded by his son Osred, under the tutelage
of the ealdorman Berectfrid; and the archbishop
made use of the opportunity to hold a council at Nid
in Yorkshire. Every thing now concurred to produce peace between the two parties. Wilfrid had
long ago consented to the establishment of a separate bishopric at Lindisfarne, and had declared at
Rome his willingness to resign his pretensions to
that of York; and on the other hand, the death, or
the approaching death, of Bosa,[1] offered to John an
indemnity for the surrender of the see of Hexham.
The arrangement was soon made, that Eadfrid should
remain without molestation at Lindisfarne, that
John should succeed Bosa at York, and that Wilfrid should recover the bishopric of Hexham, with
his beloved abbey of Ripon. The three prelates
promised to forget all past causes of dissension, and,
in token of their perfect reconciliation, received
together the communion at mass.[2]

---

[1] It is certain that Bosa died about this time, but not
whether it was before or after the council that John succeeded him. Bed. l. v. c. iii.

[2] Eddius, 56—58. Mr. Wright tells us that Wilfrid
"was not restored to his *bishopric*" (p. 183); but the
contrary is plain from Beda and Eddius.—Cunctis faven-
tibus in præsulatum est suæ receptus ecclesiæ. Bed. l. v.

Thus ended this long and tedious controversy. It has been often said that the great object of Wilfrid was to establish in Northumbria the authority of Rome : but it must be evident to every reader that he found the authority of Rome already established, and had recourse to it only to protect himself from oppression. The result proved the utility of this supreme jurisdiction claimed by the pontiff: for we read no more, from the time of Wilfrid till the reign of Edward the Confessor, of any arbitrary deposition of bishops at the will either of the king or of the metropolitan.[1]

---

c. 19. Post longum exilium in episcopatum est Hagustaldensis ecclesiæ receptus, et Joannes, defuncto Bosa, episcopus pro eo Eburaci substitutus. Id. v. c. iii. After Wilfrid's death suscepit pro Wilfrido episcopatum Hagustaldensis ecclesiæ Acca presbyter ejus. Id. v. c. 20. Accan presbytero qui post eum erat gratia Dei episcopus. Edd. c. 62.

[1] See note (H).

CHAPTER IV.

ANGLO-SAXON CLERGY.

ORIGIN OF CLERGY — OF MONKS — UNION OF BOTH PROFESSIONS — ROMAN — SCOTTISH MISSIONARIES — THEIR PROGRESS — ORIGIN OF PARISH CHURCHES — EDUCATION OF CLERGY — DUTIES OF PARISH PRIESTS — CELIBACY — ENDOWMENT OF PARISH CHURCHES — LANDS — OFFERINGS — TITHES — OTHER CHURCH DUES.

IN the ancient church, the ministers of religion formed a distinct body, under the name of 'the clergy;' a name derived from the Greek language, and supposed to denote, either that they had taken the Lord for *their* κλῆρος or portion, or that they had devoted themselves to him for *his*.[1] These ministers were at first confined to the three orders of bishops, priests, and deacons : but in proportion as the number of proselytes increased, the services of additional but subordinate officers were required: and we soon meet, in the more celebrated churches, with subdeacons, lectors or cantors, exorcists, acolythists, and ostiarii or door-keepers, whose respective duties are sufficiently indicated by their very names. All these were ordained, with appropriate forms, by the bishop : all were numbered among the clergy

---

[1] Si enim κλῆρος Græce, sors Latine appellatur, propterea vocantur clerici, vel quia de sorte sunt Domini, vel quia ipse Dominus sors, id est pars, clericorum est. S. Hieron. ad Nepot. de Vita Cleric. tom. i. 258.

both in the ecclesiastical canons, and in the imperial laws. Care was moreover taken to define the age at which the postulant might be admitted, and the time which he ought to serve in each office ; and at last it became a rule that no one should be ordained deacon, till he had passed through all the subordinate classes, and had proved by his conduct in a lower, his fitness to be promoted to a higher and holier order. Such was the constitution of the clergy when Augustine preached the gospel to our ancestors ; but it should be remembered that the Saxon word preost, whether they now borrowed it from the Latin presbyter, or had used it in their national worship before their conversion, was employed by them to denote any, even the lowest, member of the clerical body: he who had received the order of priesthood was distinguished by the prefix mæsse : he was the mæsse-preost, because it was his peculiar office to consecrate and offer the sacrifice of the mass.[1]

The monastic institute had a different origin.

---

[1] Pneɼbɪcen ɪɼ mæɼɼe-pɼeoɼc· ɼe halȝað Loðeɼ huɼel ɼpa ɼpa ɼe Pælenð bebeað. Ælfric's canons, 17. apud Thorpe, ii. 348. Preost is used for a clerk not yet in holy orders. Clerici extra sacros ordines constituti (Bed. i. c. 27) is translated by Alfred—pneoɼcaɼ bucan halȝum habum— priests without, or not in, holy orders. When Wilfrid was admitted among the clergy by receiving the tonsure, but not any holy order, Beda says simply, attonsus est; which Alfred translates, pæɼ co pneoɼca beɼcoɼen—he was shorn to priest. Bed. v. c. 19. Many mistakes have been caused by inattention to this distinction between the meaning of the two Anglo-Saxon words. Priest is a generic term including all clergymen from the lowest rank; mass-priest specifies one who has received the order of priesthood. The simple clerk is the mass-priest's priest —mæɼɼe-pɼeoɼceɼ pneoɼc. Thorpe, ii. 412. No. 15.

Its first professors were laymen, who, condemning the lax morality of their contemporaries, sought to practise in the solitude of a desert the severe and unfashionable virtues of their fathers. As long as the Christians lived in the constant fear of persecution, the very knowledge that they were a proscribed people, contributed to maintain among them that fervour of piety and strictness of discipline which they had derived from their first teachers: but when this pressure was removed by the transfer of the sceptre into the hands of princes of their own faith, the austerity of the Christian character began to relax, and the influx of crowds of proselytes introduced a spirit of dissipation and worldliness which many contemplated with sorrow and aversion. The more zealous resolved to withdraw from a scene so hateful to their feelings, and dangerous to their virtue: the Egyptians Anthony and Pachomius set the example; and in a short time the sandy deserts of the Thebais were peopled with anachorets, who sought by utter seclusion to preserve themselves from the contamination of worldly society.[1] Hence they obtained the name of monks—that is, solitaries; and from that name the huts which they raised, or the cells which they excavated for their habitations, were denominated monasteries, or the mansions of the solitaries.[2] But they did not long remain inde-

---

[1] Commanent per eremum dispersi et separati cellulis. Ob hoc autem dirimuntur habitaculis, ut in silentii quiete, et intentione mentis divina sectantes, nec vox aliqua, nec occursus ullus, aut sermo aliquis otiosus obturbet. Rufin. Vit. Pat. l. ii.

[2] From μοναχὸς and μοναστὴς, a solitary, came μοναστήριον, the mansion of the solitary.

pendent of each other. Wherever there dwelt a monk of superior reputation for sanctity, the desire of profiting by his advice and example induced others to fix their habitations in his neighbourhood: he became their Abbas or spiritual father, they his voluntary subjects: and the group of separate cells which they formed around him was known to others by the name of his monastery.[1] To obtain admission into these societies no other qualification was required in the postulant than a spirit of penitence and a desire of Christian perfection. As long as this spirit continued to animate his conduct, he was exercised in the several duties of the monastic profession: if he repented of his choice, the road was open, and he was at liberty to depart. But the number of apostates was small: the virtue of the majority secured their perseverance; and it was not till a much later period, and after the decline of the original fervour, that irrevocable vows were enjoined by the policy of subsequent legislators.[2]

From Egypt the institute rapidly spread over the neighbouring provinces; and the Western eagerly imitated the example of the Eastern church. In every corner of the empire, into which the gospel had penetrated, we soon discover monks; some leading solitary lives in wilds and among mountains, some in the midst of cities testifying by their mien and garb their contempt of worldly pursuits and

---

[1] The reader will observe that thus the word which originally signified the single mansion of one solitary, now denoted a collection of such mansions.

[2] See Bingham i. 243. Fleury, Hist. l. vi. c. 20. Droit Eccles. c. xxi.

pleasures; and others in great numbers living in
monasteries under the sway of their respective
abbots. Gradually the distance which separated
them from the clergy was contracted. St. Atha-
nasius, the patriarch of Alexandria, admitted some
of them to holy orders, that the brethren might
have among them ministers of religious worship ;[1]
and shortly afterwards Pope Siricius decreed that
monks might be aggregated to the clergy; provided
that, in the choice of subjects, due attention were
paid to their morals and to their fitness for the
clerical office.[2] At Vercelli the bishop Eusebius
formed the plan of engrafting one institute on the
other, by compelling the clergy of his church to live
in common, and subjecting them to the monastic
discipline, when they were not employed in the
exercise of their appropriate duties. The reform
was admired and imitated ; and from that time the
name of monastery was applied indifferently to
clerical and monastic establishments.[3]

---

[1] Sandini, Vit. Pont. p. 108, not. 7.

[2] Quos tamen morum gravitas, et vitæ ac fidei insti-
tutio sancta commendat. Ep. Siric. ad Himer. Terrac.
c. 13.

[3] Monasterium, in quo erat non parva congregatio
clericorum. Hist. Elien. p. 481. Alford, the learned
annalist, has adopted the common error that the word
monastery implies of course a house belonging to monks.
(Tom iii. 182.) But the distinction of clerical and monastic
monasteries continually occurs in our ancient documents,
and was equally known to other nations. See the epistle
of St. Ambrose to the church of Vercelli (l. iii.), the life of
St. Augustine by Possidius (c. xi.), the sermons of the
same holy bishop (De diversis, 49, 50), the council of
Mentz (c. 20), and historia de los seminarios clericales
(En Salamanca, 1778, p. 6—14.) The word itself was

Among the founders of monasteries, a distinguished place is due to Gregory the Great, whose piety prompted him to exchange the dignity of Prefect of Rome for the cowl of a private monk, and whose merit drew him from the obscurity of his cell to seat him on the throne of St. Peter. In Sicily his ample patrimony supported six separate families of monks : and the remainder of his fortune was devoted to the endowment of the great monastery of St. Andrew's in Rome. After such important services, he might with propriety assume the office of legislating for those who owed their bread to his liberality : and from the scattered hints of ancient writers we may safely collect, that the regulations which he imposed on his monks were widely different from the statutes of most religious orders.[1] The time which *they* dedicated to manual labour, *he* commanded to be employed in study ; and while they claimed the merit of conducting their lay disciples through the narrow path of monastic perfection, he

---

destined gradually to assume two other significations. It was soon applied to country churches with buildings dependent on them, and lastly to churches exclusively of their buildings. We have still retained it in this sense, in York minster, Westminster, &c. It will be used in its more extended signification in the following pages.

[1] See Broughton, Memorial, p. 231. Reyner (Apost. p. 167) and Mabillon (Anal. vet. p. 499) have claimed this pontiff as a member of the Benedictine order : but I am compelled to think with Baronius (Ann. 581, viii.), Broughton (Mem. p. 244), Smith (Flores Hist. p. 81), Henschenius and Papebroche (Act. SS. tom. 2, Mart. p. 123), Thomassin (De vet. et nov. discip. l. iii. c. 24), Basnage (Annal. anno 581), and Gibbon (vol. iv. p. 457), that their claim is unfounded. See also Sandini, Vit. Pontif. vol. i. p. 203.

aspired to the higher praise of forming men, who by
their abilities might defend the doctrines, and by
their zeal extend the conquests, of the church. Of
these, the most eminent were honoured with his
friendship, and enjoyed a distinguished place near
his person. They attended him in his embassy to
the capital of the East : they were admitted into his
council at his elevation to the pontificate ; and they
supplied him with missionaries, when he meditated
the conversion of the Saxons. It was to Augustine,
one of their number, that he intrusted the execution
of this important enterprise; and the success which
attended it bears testimony to the merit of the missionary, and the judgment of his patron.

When Augustine landed on the Isle of Thanet
he had brought with him more than thirty of his
brethren, selected from the monasteries of St. Gregory, and an additional supply of Gallic clergymen,
whose duty it would be to interpret between him
and the Anglo-Saxons. All these, it is probable,
lived at first in one community, under the eye of
their abbot. But the munificence of Ethelbert
soon enabled the missionary to found two monasteries, one in Canterbury itself, where he repaired
a ruined church that had formerly been built by the
Britons, and dedicated it again in honour of " the
holy Saviour Jesus Christ ;" the other at some distance without the walls, in which Lawrence, his
successor, dedicated a new church in honour of the
apostles, the Saints Peter and Paul.[1] In this, Augustine placed one portion of his monks under the
abbot Peter, that there in privacy they might devote

---

[1] Bed. l. i. c. 23, 25, 33.

themselves to the practice of the monastic profession: the other portion, consisting of clerks, he retained at Christchurch, that they might perform divine service in his cathedral, and be employed by him in the instruction of the people. With them he fixed his own residence, an arrangement which had already been recommended by the pontiff.[1]

It was not till eight-and-forty years after the arrival of Augustine on the coast of Kent that Oswald, of Northumbria, solicited a supply of missionaries for his people from the monks of Iona. The reader is already aware that Columba, of the royal race of the O'Neils in Ireland, had converted a part of the barbarous inhabitants of Caledonia, who, in recompense of his labours, had made, or confirmed to him, a donation of the isle of Iona, one of the smallest of the Hebrides.[2] The memory of Columba was long cherished with veneration by the northern nations. They maintained with obstinacy every custom which had been sanctioned with his approbation: the monastery which he had founded in his island, and had peopled with his countrymen, was selected for their sepulchre by many kings of Ireland, of Norway, and of the Picts and Scots in the north of Britain;[3] and the neighbouring bishops, though in their episcopal duties they preserved the superiority of their order, submitted

---

[1] Tua fraternitas, monasterii regulis erudita, seorsim non debet fieri a clericis suis. Bed. Hist. i. c. 27.

[2] Bed. l. iii. c. 3. The isle contained about five hides of land, Anglo-Saxon measure.—Chron. Sax. p. 21.

[3] See Buchanan, Rer. Scot. l. i. p. 28. A chart of the island may be seen in Pinkerton's Collection of the Lives of the Ancient Saints in Scotland.

on other points to the mandates of the abbot as the legitimate successor of Columba; a singular institution, of which scarcely another example is recorded in history, and for which Beda appears to find it difficult to frame an apology.[1]

From this monastery came Aidan, the successful apostle of the northern Saxons. During his labours the missionary kept his eyes fixed on his patron Columba: to imitate him was his highest ambition; and after his example he obtained from the king the donation of a small and lonely island, called Lindisfarne, lying at no great distance from the coast of Northumbria. There he built a monastery after the model of the parent establishment in Iona; peopled it with a colony of monks from the same place; and, making it his residence when he was not actually employed in preaching to the people, submitted with his clergy to the observance of the monastic rule under the government of the abbot.[2]

---

[1] Bed. l. iii. c. 4. The life of Columba by Adomnan shews that the abbot, notwithstanding his superiority as owner of the monastery, acknowledged his inferiority to a bishop in the offices of religion. Pinkerton, Vit. SS. Scotiæ, 93; Adomnan, l. i. c. 45.

[2] Neque aliquis miretur...revera enim ita est ... ab Aidano omnes loci ipsius antistites usque hodie sic episcopale exercent officium, ut regente monasterium abbate, quem ipsi cum concilio fratrum elegerint, omnes presbyteri, diaconi, cantores, lectores, cæterique gradus ecclesiastici, monachicam per omnia cum ipso episcopo regulam servent. Bed. Vit. Cuthb. c. xvi. As Northumbria was principally converted by the Scottish missionaries, the clergy were there known by the Scottish name of Culdees (Colidei or Keledei, from Keile servus, and Dia Deus, Goodall, Introd. ad Hist. Scot. p. 68. But why not from the Latin cultores Dei?). In the cathedral church of York they retained this appellation as late as the eleventh century.

Neither the Italian nor the Scottish monks were acquainted with the language of the people whom they came to evangelize. Augustine was supplied with interpreters from Gaul: Aidan occasionally employed the services of Oswald himself, who was pleased to explain to his ealdormen and thanes the lessons delivered by the bishop.[1] Both, in their missionary excursions, appear to have pursued the same method. They proceeded from home accompanied by their clergy and servants;[2] stayed at appointed stations a competent time to preach, administer baptism, and celebrate their accustomed worship; and, when they had completed the circuit, withdrew again to the retirement of their monasteries. Perhaps, in their circumstances, no better plan could be devised: but it must have been evident that, to produce general and permanent benefit, instead of this desultory method, more frequent opportunities should be offered to the distant inhabitants of hearing the doctrines, and practising the rites, of their religion. Hence the establishment of monasteries became an object of the first import-

---

(Monast. Ang. vol. ii. p. 368.) This circumstance alone is sufficient to refute the strange notion of some modern Scottish writers, that the Culdees were a kind of presbyterian ministers, who rejected the authority of bishops, and differed in religious principles from the monks. Goodall has demonstrated from original records that they were the clergy of the cathedral churches who chose the bishop, and whose disputes with the monks regarded contested property, not religious opinions. See preface to Keith's Catalogue of Bishops, p. viii.

[1] Bed. iii. c. 3.

[2] Omnes, qui cum eo incedebant, sive attonsi, seu *laici*, aut legendis scripturis aut psalmis discendis, operam dare debebant. Bed. iii. c. 5.

ance with all the apostles of the Saxons. Through the influence and liberality of Ethelbert, Augustine was able to erect one at Rochester, and a second in London, in which he placed bishops as heads of their respective missions :[1] and Birinus, who first preached the gospel in Wessex, is particularly praised for his zeal in "founding and dedicating churches ;"[2] nor can we doubt that Aidan acted in a similar manner, since we find several monasteries existing in Northumbria shortly after his death. These establishments were so many centres round which the knowledge of the gospel was spread by the labours of their inmates: and history has preserved the names of several among these missionaries celebrated for the success which attended their preaching. Thus Aldhelm, the abbot of Malmsbury, availed himself of his skill on the harp to attract crowds on bridges and at the crossings of roads, that he might thus have an opportunity of addressing them on religious subjects ;[3] and Boisil and Cuthbert, successively provosts of Melrose, were accustomed, the latter especially, to spend weeks together in the instruction of the peasantry in the wildest districts of Northumbria.[4]

In this respect it was fortunate that the feelings of the kings corresponded with the views of the missionaries. These princes, after their conversion, were naturally wishful to possess the means of attending at the public worship ; and for that purpose established churches in those villas where they chiefly resided :[5] and we are warranted in the sup-

---

[1] Bed. i. c. 32.   [2] Bed. iii. c. 7.   [3] Aug. Sac. ii. 4.
[4] Bed. iv. 27.   [5] Bed. i. c. 33; ii. 14, 16; iii. 7.

position that their example was frequently copied
by the ealdormen and principal thanes, from the
casual mention by Beda of the dedication of a
church at South Burton in Yorkshire, built by the
ealdorman Puch, and of another at North Burton,
built by the ealdorman Addi.[1] Still such erections
proved but an inadequate resource compared with
the wants of the people; and we find the same
writer, at the distance of one hundred years from
the arrival of Aidan, lamenting the spiritual destitu-
tion of his countrymen in the less populous districts,
and exhorting Archbishop Egbert to ordain a competent number of priests, to be his assistants in the
discharge of his duty, whose office it should be
"to visit every village, preaching the word of God,
consecrating the heavenly mysteries, and administering the sacrament of baptism as often as opportunity might serve."[2] If this advice, as is probable,
was adopted, there can be little doubt that the
services of these itinerants would be gradually
exchanged for those of resident ministers.

In many parts of the south the establishment
of such ministers had already been accomplished.
From the enactments of a provincial council, held
at Calcuith, under Archbishop Cuthbert, in 747, two
things are plain :—1. That the collegiate and conventual bodies had been induced to erect on their

---

[1] Bed. Hist. v. c. 4, 5.

[2] Necessarium satis est, ut plures tibi sacri operis adju-
tores adsciscas, presbyteros scilicet ordinando, atque insti-
tuendo doctores, qui in singulis viculis prædicando Dei
verbo, et consecrandis cœlestibus mysteriis, ac maxime
peragendis sacri baptismatis officiis, ubi opportunitas in-
gruerit, insistant. Ep. ad Egbert. tom. ii. 210.

lands churches, which were served by priests under the superiors of those bodies;[1] and that moreover the lands of the lay proprietors had been divided into districts by the bishops, and committed by them to the pastoral care of certain priests.[2] It is impossible not to recognize in these enactments the establishment of parishes, as they first grew out of that state of things which has been already described.

There have, indeed, been writers who have sent us to the laws of the Christian emperors for the origin of this institution. They pretend that Theodore of Canterbury, being a Greek by birth, could not have been ignorant of the Novellæ of Justinian; and that, in conformity with the provision in that collection, to encourage the building of churches, he held out the right of patronage as an inducement to the founders.[3] But this is nothing better than conjecture, founded on no authority whatsoever. Had the Anglo-Saxon been the only church

---

[1] That such priests were resident in their districts will follow from their being ordered oratorii domum, et cuncta ad cultum ipsius pertinentia sub sua cura conservare, missarum celebrationi, psalmisque canendis invigilare, &c. Can. 8; Spelm. 247.

[2] Ut presbyteri per loca et regiones laicorum, quæ sibi ab episcopis provinciæ insinuata et juncta sunt, evangelicæ et apostolicæ prædicationis officium diligenti cura studeant implere. Can. 9, p. 248. These districts allotted to priests were called priestshires, shriftshires, and kirkshires, from the Anglo-Saxon word scire, a division or district. The word parish denoted at that time the more extensive diocese of the bishop; though in the following pages it is used, in accordance with modern practice, for the district intrusted to the priest.

[3] Soames, Anglo-Saxon Church, 2, 4, 85.

in which parishes existed, it might have been allow-
able to frame a fanciful theory in order to explain
a singular phenomenon: but in every missionary
country, both in the east and the west, the bishop,
in proportion as Christianity penetrated to a distance from the city, considered it his duty to provide the means of instruction and worship for the
rural population : and this of necessity led everywhere to the division of the country into small
ecclesiastical districts, in each of which, as circumstances would permit, a church has been built and
a resident minister appointed.[1]   In England it was
so before the council of Calcuith, and continued to
be so afterwards.   Each year added to the number
of these sacred edifices : and worldly as well as religious motives concurred to their erection, till at last
the existence of a church on the lands of a proprietor became a necessary qualification for elevation
to the rank of thane.[2]

As the first district churches were built on the

---

[1] This is expressly stated by Alcuin in his narrative of
the conversions made by St. Willibrord —Cœperunt plu-
rimi fidei fervore incitati, patrimonia sua viro Dei offerre.
Quibus ille acceptis, mox ecclesias in illis ædificari jussit,
statuitque per eas singulos presbyteros, et verbi Dei sibi
cooperatores, quatenus novus Dei populus haberet, quo
se diebus festis congregaret, vel salutares audiret admoni-
tiones, vel a quibus sacri baptismatis munera acciperet, et
Christianæ religionis regulas edisceret.   Alc. Oper. ii. 188.
He distinguishes these churches from monasteries : Ecclesias per singula loca construxerat, Deo famulantium con-
gregationes aliquibus adunavit in locis. Id. 186.
[2] Thorpe, Ancient Laws and Institutes, i. 190.   The
authority also mentions a bell-house, which has been
taken to mean a belfry, annexed to the church ; but, as it
comes after the kitchen, I take it to have meant part of
the thane's secular establishment.

domains of the great cathedral and monastic establishments, there cannot be a doubt that they were
served by clergymen from the same bodies. Each
colony would consist of a mass-priest with his deacon—for he was forbidden to officiate without the
ministry of a deacon[1]—and the clerks necessary for
the performance of the service at mass and the
daily hours of prayer. For their accommodation
a mansion would be raised in the vicinity of the
church, with an additional building for the reception of strangers and travellers. Thus the example
was set, and then copied by subsequent founders of
district churches : each parochial establishment became a sort of minor monastery on the lands of an
ecclesiastical or lay proprietor: and the priest's
minster or monastery was the name by which it was
distinguished throughout the old English church.[2]
Rectories, vicarages, and curacies are institutions of
later date: among the minsters of this period the
only distinction which was acknowledged appears
to have grown out of the ecclesiastical rank of
him who officiated, and of the manner in which
provision had been made for the celebration of
divine worship. "Though all churches," says the

---

[1] Thorpe, ii. 348.
[2] Id. 246, 352, 386. They were sometimes called mo-
nasteriuncula. Offa confirms to the church of St. Peter,
prince of the apostles, whatever had been granted to it
by its founders, the viceroy Frithwald and the abbot
Erkenwald, in omnibus monasteriunculis, terris, campis,&c.
Cod. Dipl. i. 182. From several instances, I am inclined
to think that occasionally, because the house was called
a monastery, the mass-priest was denominated abbot, and
his clerks monks, though they had no real connection with
the monastic order.

law, " have the same godly consecration, they are
not entitled to the same degree of worldly respect.
The breach of the privileges granted to a *chief
minster*, when compensation is due, shall be compensated with five pounds, or two hundred and forty
shillings; of a minster of lower rank, with one hundred and twenty shillings; of one yet lower, in
which there is *little service*, but at the same time a
burial-place, with sixty shillings; and of a field
church, without a burial-place, with thirty shillings."[1]
The chief minster was the cathedral or mother-church
of the diocese: the next in rank appear to have
been the churches of ancient date, with a full complement of clergy and extensive jurisdiction; the
third, the ordinary parish churches of long standing;
and field churches without a burial-place, will be
chapels of ease of more recent foundation.

It is plain that, for many years after the arrival
of the missionaries, the supply of priests would be
inadequate to the wants of the people, whence it
happened that many individuals were advanced to
holy orders who, whatever may have been their
qualifications in other respects, could have little

---

[1] Thorpe, i. 340, 360. In the translation of this enactment, entered among the laws of Henry I., lytel þeopþoin
(little service) is rendered parva parochia. Matris et
capitalis ecclesiæ grithbrece est ad minus V. lib. in Anglorum lege, medie L. sol. (shillings of twelve pennies), et
adhuc minoris, ubi parva *parochia* est, et atrium cum sit,
xxv. sol. et campestris capellæ, ubi non sit atrium, xii. sol.
et vi. den. I may add here, that the number of churches
and chapels in England at the time of the conquest was
very great. In Domesday they are entered only occasionally : yet about 250 are mentioned in Lincolnshire,
about the same number in the county of Norfolk, and
above 350 in that of Suffolk. See note (I).

pretensions to learning, and are called by Beda
sacerdotes idiotæ,[1] because they were acquainted
with no other than the vernacular tongue. In proportion as Christianity extended its sway, and as
district churches were multiplied, a more regular
supply was afforded, and that, as far as we may collect from the imperfect records of the time, from
three sources:—1. The parish minsters themselves
appear to have furnished many candidates for
the priesthood: for the clerks belonging to these
minsters were compelled to apply to learning, and
the mass-priests were enjoined to superintend their
religious studies. 2. We meet with many instances
of clergymen who had been educated from their
childhood in the schools of the monasterial establishments, and were afterwards drawn thence to undertake the care of parochial churches.[2] 3. But the
chief resource of the bishop lay in the cathedral

---

[1] Bed. Oper. Min. ii. 211.

[2] I may mention one instance, because it is instructive
on another account. Headda, who calls himself mass-
priest and abbot, by a testamentary paper, about the year
790, disposes of his patrimonial inheritance, which consisted of two large parcels of land, with a minster on one
of them; limiting the succession to such clergymen of
his family as may be thought capable of governing a
minster according to ecclesiastical law, and totally ex-
cluding all his lay relatives, so that, in default of clergymen properly qualified, the property should go to the
cathedral of Worcester, because *he was a pupil of that
house, and bred and schooled at its threshold.*—Quia alumnus sum illius familiæ, et juxta liminibus ecclesiæ disciplinatus et nutritus fui. Cod. Dipl. i. 206. Yet that
church was at the time served by persons sometimes
called monks and sometimes canons, or, as was often
the case, by a community consisting of both at the same
time.

monastery, where the clergy were carefully instructed in the duties, and trained in the exercise of their holy profession. They were distinguished by the name of Canons, because the rule, which they observed, had been framed in accordance with the canons enacted in different councils.[1] To all were allotted the same hours for prayer, and study, and recreation : all ate at one common table, all slept in the same dormitory; and all lived continually under the eye of the bishop, or in his absence, of the superior appointed by him.[2] Their number was

[1] Canones dicimus regulas, quas sancti patres constituerunt, in quibus scriptum est, quomodo *canonici*, id est, clerici regulares vivere debeant. Excerp. Egb. apud Wilk. tom. i. 101; also 147, 286; iv. 754. St. Boniface addresses a letter to all the Saxon bishops, priests, deacons, *canons*, clerks, abbots, monks, &c. (S. Bonif. ep. 6, edit. Serarii); Eugenius IV. ascribes the institution of canons in England to the order of St. Gregory.—Beatissimus Gregorius Augustino Anglorum episcopo velut plantationem sacram in commisso sibi populo præcepit institui. Bul. Eug. iv.

[2] Bed. l. i. c. 27; Wilk. 147, 293. There is a curious but authentic grant by Archbishop Wulfred in 813, which affords much information on this subject. He had rebuilt the monastery of Christchurch, in Canterbury. Now, in monasteries, besides the buildings intended for common use, there was a long range of separate, but probably contiguous, buildings for the private accommodation of the members of the community. These the canons had rebuilt at their own cost. Wherefore the archbishop grants to the "priests, deacons, and the whole body of clergy serving the Lord God in the monastery, the houses which they had built for their own use, to have and enjoy the said houses in perpetual inheritance, so that the possessor shall have full right to give the same, or bequeath the same at his death, to any other person whom he may select, provided that person be not a stranger, but a member of the community." In return, he requests that they will carefully observe the canonical hours in the church, praying for themselves and for others, and will

M 2

continually supplied from the children who were
educated under their care, and the proselytes, who,
disgusted with the pleasures or the troubles of the
world, requested to be admitted into their society.
Among them were to be found the descendants of
the noblest families, and thanes, who had governed
provinces, and commanded armies.[1] A severe probation preceded their admittance: nor did they
receive the clerical tonsure from the hands of the
bishop, till their conduct had been nicely investi-
gated, and the stability of their vocation satisfac-
torily proved.[2]

These communities formed the principal semi-
naries for the education of the clergy ; it was from
them that the bishop selected the most learned and
valuable portion of his clergy.   With the assistance
of the best masters, the young ecclesiastics were
initiated in the different sciences which were studied
at that period : while the restraint of a wise and
vigilant discipline withheld them from the seduc-
sions of vice, and inured them to the labours and
the duties of their profession.   According to their

---

repair constantly to the common refectory for their meals,
and to the common dormitory to sleep, according "to the
rule of monasterial discipline." In conclusion, he declares,
that if any among them infringe this constitution, by
entertaining guests in his cell, or sleeping in the same, he,
be he who he may, shall forfeit the possession of his house
to the archbishop for the time being, who shall dispose of
it as he pleases, in conformity with the preceding regulation.   It is subscribed by Wulfred archbishop, Wernoth
priest and abbot, seven other priests, and three, who were
probably deacons.   Cod. Dipl. 1. 251.
    [1] Hoved. an. 794, 796 ; Wilk. p. 226, xiii.
    [2] Wilk. p. 98.

years and merit, they were admitted to the lower
orders of the hierarchy; and might, with the approbation of their superior, aspire, at the age of five-and-
twenty, to the order of deacon, at thirty, to that of
priest;[1] but not unless their services were actually
required for the performance of some office to which
they had been appointed. At his ordination it was
incumbent on the candidate to prove that no
canonical impediment forbade his promotion; that
he was not of spurious or servile birth; that he had
not been guilty of any public and infamous crime;
and if he had formerly lived in the state of wedlock,
that neither he nor his wife had been married more
than once. From that moment he was bound to
obey the commands of his bishop; to reside within
the diocese; to limit the exercise of his functions
according to the directions of his superior; and to
serve with fidelity the church in which he might be
placed.[2] But, though he was rendered dependent
on the nod of his diocesan, that prelate was admonished to temper the exercise of his authority with
mildness and discretion, and to recollect that if in
the discharge of the episcopal office he was the
superior, on other occasions he was the colleague of
his priests.[3]

By ecclesiastical law, no mass-priest could be
instituted, by both ecclesiastical and national law,
none could be removed, without the consent of the
bishop. In the language of the time, he was wedded,
to his church, and could not be divorced from it, but

---

[1] Thorpe, ii. 110, 111.
[2] Wilkins, 43, 83, 102, 105, 127, 171.   [3] Id. 103.

for a reasonable cause and by his own judge.[1] Hence he was instructed to devote to it the whole of his attention without interfering with the minster, the shriftshire or the gildship of any other priest.[2] Much less was he allowed to seek by prayer, or service, or contract, to exchange his own for a more wealthy benefice.[2]

The duties of the mass-priest were accurately defined, and the infraction of them subjected the offender to proportionate punishment. Once at least, often twice in the year, he was obliged to attend the episcopal synod, taking with him one or two of his clerks, and one or two orderly laymen as servants; bringing at the same time the sacerdotal vestments, and whatever was necessary for the celebration of mass, that his manner of performing the service might be approved; and being furnished with ink and vellum, that he might commit to writing the regulations which should be published by the bishop in the synod. He was, moreover, to lay before his diocesan the true state of his shrift-shire, to detail the injuries which had been done to his church in its rights, or to himself in the discharge of his duties, and to claim the aid of the bishop in his endeavours to coerce powerful sinners, who bade defiance to his authority.[3]

---

[1] Thorpe, i. 306, 318; ii. 73, 78, 100.—Lᵹþıce ıſ mıð þuhte ſaceᵹðeſ æpe. "Rightfully the church is the priest's wife." Id. ii. 246, 340.

[2] Id. 73. Quod vitium late diffusum summo studio emendandum est. Ibid. See the penalties for buying another priest out of his church. Ibid. 290; also 352, 410, 412.

[3] Ib. ii. 244, 318.

Among the duties incumbent on the parish priest the first was to instruct his flock in the doctrines and duties of Christianity, and to extirpate from among them the lurking remains of paganism ; such as their reverence for the fountains, oaks, and rocks at which their ancestors had worshipped, their belief in the supernatural effects of spells and incantations, and their recourse in cases of difficulty to the aid of men who pretended to practise the art of magic.[1] He was ordered to explain to his parishioners the ten commandments, to take care that all could repeat and understand the Lord's Prayer and the Creed ; to expound in English on Sundays the portion of scripture proper to the mass of the day, and to preach, or if he were unable to preach, to read at least from a book some lesson of instruction.[2]

To him was committed the charge of repairing his church, and of furnishing it with every necessary for religious worship. He was to remember that it was

[1] Ib. i. 378, ii. 33, 34, 84, 191. Con. Calc. apud Spelman, p. 300. In a canon enacted in the time of King Edgar they are thus described—" We forbid well-worshippings, and necromancies, and divinations, and enchantments, and tree-worshippings, and stone-worshippings, and that devil's craft whereby children are drawn through the earth, and the merriments that men make on the night of the year." Thorpe, ii. 248. In explanation of the last superstition we learn from the Penitentiary of Theodore, that on the night which ushers in the new year, they were accustomed to dress themselves in the skins of sheep, calves, and deer, with heads of the same animals, and pass the night in merriment. It is also noticed that women would place their children for the recovery of their health in an oven or on the roof of the house, or pass through an opening in the ground, and fill it with thorns behind them. Ibid. 33, 34.

[2] Ib. ii. 98, 254, 350, 384, 424.

a house of prayer, and not to be employed for any worldly purpose. Whatever was profane or unbecoming was to be removed out of it, and the altar, the sacerdotal garments, and the vessels employed in the sacrifice were to be kept in a state of the utmost cleanness.[1] It was there, in his church, that he ought to be daily found at the seven canonical hours, to sing the praises of God, and to pray for himself, for his flock, and for all Christian people.[2]

In the discharge of the priestly office he could demand no fee, unless it were at burials.[3] The baptism of infants was particularly recommended to his care. He was to be ready to administer that sacrament at all hours; to see that it was not delayed beyond a certain time after the birth; and to compel the parents to offer the child soon afterwards to the bishop for confirmation.[4] Attention to the sick was another important branch of his duty. He was to visit them frequently, to hear their confessions, to carry and administer to them the eucharist, and then to anoint them with the last unction.[5] In the tribunal of penance, an institution which formed the most difficult of his duties, he was advised to weigh with discretion every alleviating or aggravating circumstance, that he might apportion the penance to the offence; and, in aid of his own judgment, he was advised to consult and follow the directions of the Penitential.[6]

In addition to these duties the parish priest was charged with the obligation of instructing his clerks in

---

[1] Thorpe, ii. 111, 250, 350, 380.   [2] Ib. 98, 254, 350.
[3] Ib. 98, 352.   [4] Ib. i. 102, ii. 103, 246, 292, 352.
[5] Ib. 100, 258, 354, 384.   [6] Ib. 100, 172, 258, 352.

the Latin language, and in ecclesiastical learning; and not only them, but generally the children also of his parishioners. " Mass-priests," says the authority, " shall always have at their houses a school of learners; and, if any good man will trust his little ones to them for lore, they shall right gladly receive, and kindly teach them. Ye shall remember that it is written : *They that be learned, shall shine as heaven's brightness; and they that draw and instruct many to righteousness, shall shine as stars for ever.* They shall not, however, for such lore, demand any thing of the parents, besides that which the latter may do of their own will."[1]

It may be supposed that with so many duties to discharge, the parish priest would have few idle hours. Yet he was advised to learn and to practise, as far as regarded himself, and also to teach to his clerks, some mechanical art, or handicraft, that both he and they might possess the means of useful employment or relaxation at their leisure hours, and might from the produce of their industry add to the fund for the relief of the indigent.[2] With respect to men in distressed circumstances, the parish priest was to look upon himself as their father and protector. Charity to them he was to inculcate by word, and recommend by example. He was to devote to their relief whatever he could spare from his own wants, and in distributing the alms of the people, to keep in view the good pleasure of God, and the intention of the donors.[3] Besides the indigent of his own dis-

---

[1] Ibid. ii. 414.   [2] Ib. 246, 254, 404.
[3] Id. 30, 98, 256.

trict, he had also to provide for the stranger and wayfarer, for whose accommodation a building was erected near to the parish church. There they were supplied with board and lodging for one day, or for more, if necessity should require it: but he was not permitted to demand any remuneration, though he might accept such presents as were spontaneously offered.[1]

He was moreover enjoined to confine himself to the duties of his profession. Every species of traffic, all secular offices were forbidden. He was to shun the company of gamesters; to abstain from the field sports of hawking and hunting; never to enter the wine-house or ale-house; to keep aloof from all parties assembled for the purpose of singing and carousing, and above all to preserve himself from the habit of drunkenness, the besetting sin of his countrymen.[2] His dress was to be plain but decent, without unnecessary ornament, and conformable to the severity of the canons. To bear arms was strictly forbidden: but arms were worn by the Saxon in token of his freedom: and the number of canons by which they were forbidden to the clergy

---

[1] Thorpe, 30, 101, 429.

[2] Id. 99, 199, 256, 410.—" The mass-priest," says a bishop, " ought neither to eat nor to drink at ale-houses, nor should he visit strange men's ' tunes' or houses, through eagerness for sights, nor have convivial meetings with women or impure persons : but if any respectable father of a family invite him, who with his wife and children desire to be glad in spiritual joy, and to receive from him the refection of spiritual lore, and to give to him through true love bodily refection, then is it natural that you humbly visit him, and feed with spiritual refection him who feeds you with his worldly goods."—Ibid. 410.

is a proof of the diffusion and obstinacy of this national prejudice.[1]

In return for these privations the laws raised the mass-priest to an equality of rank with the secular thane. His oath was of the same value; his were-gild amounted to the same sum. He was entitled to all the rights of a thane, during his life, and his body was committed with the same ceremony to the grave.[2] The consideration which this rank imparted aided him to discharge the most difficult perhaps of the duties imposed on him, the duty of seeing that right was done to every inhabitant, even the lowliest, in his parish. With him were deposited the standard weights and measures; with his rod were decided all disputes respecting the measurement of field-labour: he was ordered to shield the lower from oppression by the higher classes, the tenant from oppression by his lord, and the slave or thrall from oppression by the man that owned him. He was to admonish the latter that he ought for his own sake to be just to his thrall. " For," continues the document, " the thrall and the free are equally dear to God, bought by him at the same price: and he will so judge us, as we may judge here the men who are subject to our judgment. Hence it is necessary for us to be a protection to those who obey us; then we may look for more protection at the judgment-seat of God."[3]

---

[1] Ib. 99, 124, 354, 386.

[2] Id. i. 182, 186, 306, 316, 346, 365. When the priest took his oath, he put on his sacerdotal vestment, and placing his hand on the altar, said, Veritatem dico, in Christo non mentior. Ib. 41.—What particular ceremony accompanied the burial of a thane, I know not.   [3] Ib. ii. 215.

It added to the estimation in which he was held, that he was strictly obliged to a life of continency; a regulation equally practised and enforced by the Roman and the Scottish missionaries. This discipline was based on the doctrine of Christ in the gospel, that his disciples must be ready to renounce the gratifications of sense, to forsake parents, wife, and children through love of him; and on the reasoning of the apostle, that while the married man is necessarily solicitous for the concerns of this world, the unmarried is at liberty to turn his whole attention to the service of God.[1] Hence it was inferred that the embarrassments of wedlock were hostile to the profession of a clergyman. His parishioners, it was said, were his family : and to watch over their spiritual welfare, to instruct their ignorance, to console them in their afflictions, and to relieve them in their indigence, were to be his constant and favourite occupations.[2] But the first teachers of Christianity, though accustomed to extol the advantages, did not impose the obligation of clerical celibacy. And the reason is plain. Of those who had embraced the doctrine of the gospel, the majority were married previously to their conversion. Had they been excluded from the priesthood, the clergy would have lost many of its brightest ornaments : had they been compelled to separate from their wives, they might justly have accused the severity and impolicy of the measure. They were, however,

---

[1] Mat. xix. 10; Luke xvi. 26 ; 1 Cor. vii. 32, 33.
[2] The validity of this inference is maintained in the very act of parliament which licenses the marriages of the clergy. 2 Ed. 6, c. 21.

taught to consider a life of continency, even in the married state, as demanded by the sacredness of their functions:[1] and no sooner had the succession of Christian princes secured the peace of the church, than laws were made to enforce that discipline, which fervour had formerly introduced and upheld.[2] The regulations of the canons were supported by the authority of the emperors : by Theodosius, the priest who presumed to marry, was deprived of the clerical privileges; by Justinian, his children were declared illegitimate.[3] Insensibly, however, the Greek and Latin churches adopted a diversity of discipline, which was finally established by the council in Trullo. Both indulged the inferior clerks with permission to marry : though that marriage, until it was dissolved by the natural death of the wife, or interrupted by her voluntary assumption of the veil, was an effectual bar to their future promotion. But by the Greeks they were only forbidden to aspire to the episcopal dignity ; by the severity of the Latins they were excluded from the inferior orders of deacon and priest.

The reader who is more conversant with modern than with ancient historians may not, perhaps, be disposed to believe that the discipline of the Latins was ever introduced into the Saxon church. He

---

[1] Orig. Hom. 23 in lib. num. Euseb. Dem. Evan. l. i. c. 9.

[2] See the councils of Elvira (can. 33), of Neocæsarea (can. 1), of Ancyra (can. 10), of Carthage (con. 2, can. 2), and of Toledo (con. 1, can. 1).

[3] Ne legitimos quidem et proprios esse eos, qui ex hujusmodi inordinata constupratione nascuntur, aut nati sunt. Leg. 45, cap. de epis. et cler.

has, probably, been taught, that "the celibacy of
the clergy was first enjoined by the popes in the
tenth century, and not adopted by our ancestors till
five hundred years after their conversion : that the
Saxon bishops and parochial clergy, like those of
the present church of England, added to the care of
their flocks that of their wives and children : and
that even the monasteries of monks were in reality
colleges of secular priests, who retained the choice,
without quitting the convent, either of a married or
a single life."[1] This language, if it be meant to
apply to the first ages of the Anglo-Saxon church,
is contradicted by every monument of that period
which has descended to us. Of the discipline established by the Roman missionaries, every doubt
must be removed by the answer of St. Gregory to
St. Augustine ; according to which only the clerks
who had not been raised to the higher orders, and
who professed themselves unable to lead a life of

---

[1] See Tindall's Rapin (tom. i. p. 80); Burton's Monasticon Eboracense (p. 30); Hume (Hist. c. ii. p. 28);
and Henry (Hist. vol. iii. p. 215). Of the writers
who contend that the Saxon clergy were permitted to
marry, I am acquainted with no one besides Inett, who
has ventured to appeal to any contemporary authority.
He refers his reader to Theodore's Penitentiary (Inett,
vol. i. p. 124). The words are these :—" Non licet viris
fœminas habere monachas, neque fœminis viros : tamen
non destruamus illud quod consuetudo est in hac terra."
(Thorpe, ii. 64.) But this passage, if genuine, speaks not
of the clergy nor of marriage : it probably alludes to the
secular monasteries, which will be afterwards described,
and in which it sometimes happened that communities of
monks or nuns were established on the lands, and subjected to the government of persons of a different sex.
This custom the canon disapproves, though it dares not
abolish it.

continency, were permitted to marry;[1] and the consentient practice of the northern Saxons is forcibly expressed by Ceolfrid, the learned abbot of Wearmouth,[2] by Beda in different passages of his writings,[3] and by Egbert, the celebrated archbishop of York in his Excerpta.[4] In many of the canons which are acknowledged to have been observed by their successors, the same is either evidently supposed[5] or openly commanded.[6] The sentence of degradation is pronounced against the priest or deacon who shall presume to marry:[7] and the ecclesiastic who had

---

[1] Si qui sint clerici *extra sacros ordines* constituti, qui se continere non possunt, sortiri uxores debent. Bed. Hist. l. i. c. 27.

[2] Carnem suam cum vitiis et concupiscentiis crucifigere oportet eos, qui . . . gradum clericatus habentes arctioribus se necesse habent pro domino continentiæ frænis astringere. Ep. Ceolf. ad Naiton reg. apud Bed. l. v. c. 21.

[3] Sine illa castimoniæ portione, quæ ab appetitu copulæ conjugalis cohibet, nemo vel sacerdotium suscipere vel ad altaris potest ministerium consecrari; id est, si non aut virgo permanserit, aut contra uxoriæ conjunctionis fœdera solverit. Bed. de Taber. l. iii. c. 9; see also his Commentary on St. Luke, c. 1.

[4] Clerici extra sacros ordines constituti, id est, nec presbyteri nec diaconi sortiri uxores debent; sacerdotes autem nequaquam uxores ducant. Exc. Egb. apud Thorpe, ii. 125.   [5] Ibid. 99, 101.

[6] Lober racenðar. ꝺ ꝺiaconar. ꝺ oðꝛe Lober þeopar þe on Lober temple Lobe þeniȝan ꝛcýlon. ꝺ haliȝðom. ꝺ haliȝ bec hanðliȝan. þa ꝛcýlon ꝛýmble hýꝛa clænnýꝛꝛe healban. "God's priests and deacons, and God's other servants, that should serve in God's temple, and touch the sacrament and the holy books, they shall always observe their chastity." Pœnit. Eg. Ibid. ii. 196; iv.

[7] Liꝛ mæꝛꝛe ꝛꝛeoꝛt oððe ꝺiacon ꝛiꝛiȝe þoliȝon hýꝛa haber. "If priest or deacon marry, let them lose their orders." Ibid. p. 196. But the marriage was not annulled. It was only in the twelfth century that holy orders were

separated from his wife to receive the sacred rite of
ordination, and had returned to her again, was condemned to a penitential course of ten or seven
years.[1] An improvement was made on the severity
of the fathers assembled in the great council of
Nice, and even female relations were forbidden to
dwell in the same house with a priest.[2] During
more than two hundred and fifty years from the
death of Augustine, these laws respecting clerical
celibacy, so galling to the natural propensities of
man, but so calculated to enforce an elevated idea
of the sanctity which becomes the priesthood, were
enforced with the strictest rigour: but during part
of the ninth, and most of the tenth century, when
the repeated and sanguinary devastations of the
Danes threatened the destruction of the hierarchy

---

declared to incapacitate a person for marriage.   Pothier,
Traité du Contrat de Mar. p. 135.

[1] Ᵹiƿ hpýlc ᵹehaboð man. birceop oððe mæᵹᵹe preoᵹt
oððe munuc oððe ðiacon hir ᵹemæccan hæᵹbe æn he
ᵹehaboð pæᵹie. ⁊ þa ᵹon Ᵹobeᵹ luᵹon hiᵹ ᵹoᵹileᵹ. ⁊ to
habe ᵹenᵹ. ⁊ hiᵹ þonne eᵹt ᵹýþþan toᵹæðene hpýnᵹbon
þuᵹih hæmeð ðinᵹ. ᵹæᵹte ælc be hiᵹ enðebýᵹiðnýᵹᵹe ᵹpa
hit buᵹan apᵹiiten ýᵹ be manᵹilte. " If any man in
orders, bishop, priest, monk, or deacon, had his wife ere
he were ordained, and forsook her for God's sake, and received ordination, and they afterwards return together
again through lust, let each fast according to his order,
as is written above with respect to murder." Ibid. p. 272.

[2] . . . Ælcon Ᵹobeᵹ þeope þe on clænnýᵹᵹe Ᵹobe
þeopiᵹan ᵹcýle. ýᵹ ᵹonboðen ꝥ he naþon ne hiᵹ maᵹan
ne oðenne piᵹman ᵹon naneᵹ peonceᵹ þinᵹon inne mið
him næbbe. þilæᵹ he þuᵹih beoᵹleᵹ coᵹnunᵹe þæn on
ᵹeᵹinᵹiᵹe. " To every servant of God, who should serve
God in chastity, it is forbidden that he have in the house
with him any relation or other woman for any kind of work,
lest he through temptation of the devil sin therein."
Ibid. p. 198, vi. ; also Egb. Excerp. xv. ; Ibid. p. 99.

no less than of the government, the ancient canons opposed but a feeble barrier to the impulse of the passions: and of the clergy who escaped the swords of the invaders, several scrupled not to violate the chastity which at their ordination they had vowed to observe. Yet even then the marriage of priests was never approved by the Saxon prelates: and as often as a transient gleam of tranquillity invited them to turn their attention to the restoration of discipline, the prohibitions of former synods were revived, and the celibacy of the clergy was recommended by paternal exhortations, and enforced with the severest penalties.[1]

---

[1] " To no altar-thane (mass-priest) is it allowed to marry—it is forbidden to them all. Men in orders are some so deceived by the devil that they marry unrighteously, and foredo themselves by the adultery in which they continue: but I earnestly pray that this deadly sin may henceforth be carefully abstained from. The church is the mass-priest's wife." (From an Episcopal Charge, probably of the tenth century. Thorpe, ii. 334; see also 336, 345, 411.) The celebrated Ælfric is also very severe against the marriages of priests, though he acknowledges the inability to put them down: for he concludes with these words—" Beloved, we cannot now force you of necessity to chastity, but we admonish you nevertheless that ye live chastely as God's ministers ought." Ibid. 373.

By the laws of Edmund (an. 943) the punishment ordered by the canons was enforced, that all offenders, who had vowed chastity by their orders, should forfeit their property, and the right of Christian burial, unless they did penance before death. (Thorpe, i. 246.) The severity of the law probably prevented its execution. When Ethelred renewed it as to mass-priests, he was content to enact in general terms that the honour of the offender "should wane both before God and before the world." (Ib. 306.) Canute commanded mass-priests to observe chastity, but did not add any penalty. Ib. 411.

From the parish clergy we now proceed to the parish churches, to inquire in what manner they were endowed and supported.

1. We may presume that in the foundation of such churches the missionaries would proceed on the same principles, which are known to have prevailed among the Franks and the other northern tribes already converted to Christianity. Now we learn from a synod held at Orleans before the arrival of St. Augustine in England, that, if a lord wished to have an ecclesiastical district established on his property, he must previously make a competent provision in land for the maintenance of the church, and of the clerks who are to serve it.[1] To the same purpose we find the following canon in the compilation under the name of Archbishop Egbert:—
" Let an entire manse without other (that is secular) service be assigned to each church ; and let not the mass-priests appointed in churches render any other than church-service from the tithes, or the oblations of the faithful, or the buildings, courts, and orchards adjacent to the church, or the aforesaid manse ; but if they hold any thing more than these, let them render to their lords the service due by the custom of the country."[2]

---

[1] Si quis in agro suo aut habet, aut postulat habere diocesim, primum ei terras deputet sufficientes, et clericos qui ibidem sua officia impleant. Con. Auris. can. 33 ; p.1370, tom. v. Concil. anno 541.

[2] Thorpe, ii. 100. A manse in different charters is made to contain a hide of land.—Bis denas mansas, quod Anglice dicitur twentig hida. (Cod. Dipl. 247, 271.) As, however, mansa is distinguished in the canon from the buildings, courts, and orchards contiguous to the church, I conceive it to mean here only a dwelling-house with every requisite appurtenance.

It may be fairly presumed that these canons
represent to us the state of the ecclesiastical law
with respect to the foundation of district churches
at that period. It was strictly in unison with the
habits of the Anglo-Saxons that, if they made any
provision at all, they should make it also in land.
It was thus that they were accustomed to found the
larger monasteries, and it was natural that they
should found the lesser on their own estates, in like
manner. The quantity of land, and the conditions
annexed to it, whether it should be held in free and
pure alms, or subject to the accustomed services
of the township or hundred, depended probably on
the bounty of the founder : but there can be little
doubt that originally each of these churches had a
certain portion of land annexed to it for its endowment. We know, indeed, that their rights were in
many cases invaded by the avarice of succeeding
lords, who by force, or with the connivance of the
incumbents themselves, resumed the lands, or abolished the privileges which had been granted; and
it must have been that, during the revolutions of
three centuries, amidst domestic turbulence, the devastations of the sea-kings, and the successive conquest of the kingdom by two foreign nations, these
obscure country churches would suffer in their property as well as the richer establishments. Yet we
find in the authentic document of Domesday a considerable number of them still in possession of land,
though in very different proportions, some holding
to the amount of several hides, many a single hide,
and others not more than a few acres. Of two or

three only is it entered that they were churches
without land.[1]

2. But besides the produce of their lands there
were other sources of income possessed by the parish
priests. Of these the most ancient was the custom of voluntary offerings made by the people at
the mass. It was upon these that during the first
three centuries the church depended, to enable her
to support her ministers, to relieve the wants of the
indigent, and to maintain the decency of religious
worship. Every Sunday collections were made for
this purpose, and deposited in the hands of the
bishop, or of the presiding minister, whose duty it
was to apply them according to the best of his judgment.[2] Afterwards, though the church became
possessed of landed property through the piety of
the Christian emperors, and of the more wealthy of
her children, the custom of voluntary offerings was
not abolished. Those who could afford it, continued to offer the bread and wine for the sacrifice
at the chancel, and money, provisions, and any
article that might be of service, at the treasury of
the church. This was a practice which harmonized
with the previous notions of the Anglo-Saxons.
They never presented a petition to a superior without its accompanying present : how then could they
presume to pray to God for mercy without making
to him an offering? Hence, as late as the close of
the tenth century, we find Ælfric reckoning among
the duties of the Sunday, that "every Christian man,

---

[1] See note (I) at the end of the volume.
[2] Justin Martyr, Apol. 2a, p. 100.

that has it in his power, should come in the morning with his *offering* to the celebration of the mass, and intercede there for himself, and all God's people, both with his prayers and his *alms*."[1]

3. To these must be added tithes, which, though at first like them a voluntary, became afterwards a compulsory payment. Under the law of Moses the Israelite was bound to set apart the tenth portion of his annual produce for the relief of the suffering poor, and the maintenance of the priests and the Levites. It was a national institution, which obliged no other people: and the first Christians commuted it for the hebdomadal oblations, which have just been mentioned. These oblations were based on the same principle of charity, were devoted to the same purposes, and were sometimes improperly designated by the same name. In defence of them we find preachers and commentators appealing to the very passages in scriptures, in compliance with which tithes had been originally established. It was argued that the spirit of the law affected all men in the same manner; that the obligation of the Jew could not be less than that of the Christian; and that if the man, who lived under a religious system,—— ' the mere shadow of the good things to come,'—was bound to consecrate a tenth part of his income to God, the Christian, under a more holy and more perfect dispensation, must not be content with giving less, but should be careful to exceed in that respect the righteousness of the Jew. But this doctrine, though occasionally conveyed in language the most

---

[1] Thorpe, ii. 420.

positive,[1] expressed only the sentiments of individual teachers: it is plain from the comparison of numerous passages that there existed not any general or compulsory law, but that it was still left to each individual to determine, according to his judgment and his circumstances, the quantity and quality of his offerings.[2] Subsequently, however, these exhortations of the fathers were more strictly interpreted; and we discover towards the close of the sixth century, what is thought to have been, the first attempt to enforce the payment of tithes in a provincial council at Macon in Gaul.[3] The missions of St. Augustine and of St. Aidan followed; but they were too prudent to imitate this example,[4] nor

---

[1] See Orig. in c. xviii. Num. and St. Ambrose Serm. in fer. 2a post Dom. prim. Quadrag.

[2] Thus St. Chrysostome, having urged the example of the Jews, adds that he does not mean to lay down any law, or to prevent his hearers from giving more, but thinks it fit that they should not give less. Ταῦτα δέ οὐ νομοθέτων, οὐδὲ κωλύων τὸ πλέον, λέγω, ἀλλ᾽ ἀξίων μὴ ἔλαττον τῆς δεκάτης μοίρας καταθεῖναι. (Hom. 43, in ep. 1 ad Cor. c. xvi.) So also St. Jerome concludes, if we will not sell all and give to the poor, saltem pauperibus partem demus ex toto, et sacerdotibus et levitis honorem debitum deferamus. (Tom. vi. p. 978. in cap. iii. Malachiæ.) To the same sense St. Augustine says, Præcidite aliquid et deputate aliquid fixum vel ex annuis fructibus vel ex quotidianis quæstibus vestris. Exime aliquam partem redituum tuorum. Decimas vis? Exime decimas, quanquam parum sit. Pharisæi decimas dabant; et quid ait Dominus? Nisi abundaverit justitia vestra plus quam scribarum et phariseorum, non intrabitis in regnum cœlorum. Enarratio in Ps. cxlvi.

[3] Con. Matisc. ii. anno 585, can. v. tom. vi. 675.

[4] Cuncta hujus mundi velut aliena spernendo, et ea tantum, quæ victui necessaria videbantur ab eis quos docebant, recipiendo. Bed. i. c. 26.

do we find any trace of such institution in the history of Beda, though he has recorded the principal events in the English church from its foundation to the time of his death, a space of one hundred and thirty years. It was in the eighth century that tithes were established by civil and ecclesiastical authority in Gaul and the neighbouring provinces: and it is in the same century that we meet with what appears an allusion to them in England, in the remark made by Beda in one of his last letters, written about the year 730, "that there was not a village in the remotest parts of Northumbria, which could escape the payment of tribute to the bishop."[1] In 745, Archbishop Boniface, writing to Archbishop Cuthbert, couples the tithes with the oblations, and denominates them " the milk and the wool which the flock yields to the shepherd ";[2] and about forty years

---

[1] Quorum tamen nec unus quidem a tributis antistiti reddendis esse possit immunis. (Ep. ad Egb. Antist. ii. p. 213.) There is also mention of tithe in Eddius, who wrote before Beda, and tells us that Tatbercht, abbot of Ripon, ordered, as long as he lived, all the tithes of sheep and cattle to be divided among the poor, on the anniversary of Wilfrid—Anniversaria die obitus sui universas decimarum partes de armentis et de gregibus pauperibus populi sui dividere constituit. (Eddius, c. 62, p. 88.) But the expression is ambiguous, and perhaps means the tithe of the cattle and sheep belonging to the monastery, not any tithe which was paid to it.

[2] Lac et lanam ovium Christi oblationibus quotidianis et decimis fidelium suscipiunt. (Spel. Con. p. 240.) I am aware that tithes are mentioned in the collection of canons, which goes under the name of Egbert, the archbishop of York at this period. But we cannot be certain that this mention was made by him. Copies of such collections were made for the private use of particular monasteries; whence the transcriber often introduced among them without scruple such other canons as were in force at the time.

later the papal legates inform Pope Adrian that they
had laboured in the council of Calcuith both by
prayer and precept to promote the faithful payment
of tithes.[1] It would perhaps be rash to infer from
such data that this imposition was already enforced
throughout the Anglo-Saxon kingdoms : and it most
vexatiously happens that after the council of Calcuith every vestige of its existence disappears. Not
a single notice of tithe is to be found in the history
of the next one hundred and twenty years, till after
the death of Alfred ; when it presents itself to us as
a national institution long since recognized by law,
sanctioned with pains and penalties, and evaded or
resisted by many, when evasion or resistance could
be attempted with the prospect of impunity.[2] This
appears from the laws, which were passed at that
period. Edward, the son of Alfred, placed his
Danish, on the same footing as his English
subjects, with respect to the payment of tithe,
ordaining that the defaulter, if a Dane, should be
fined in the ' lah-slite,' if an Englishman, in the
' wite ' to the king.[3] Æthelstan, his successor, sent
to his officers the following circular : " I Æthelstan king, with the counsel of Wulfhelm, archbishop, and my other bishops, make known to my

---

[1] Spelm. Con. p. 298.
[2] The same was the case on the continent, as appears
from several councils, and the letters of Alcuin, who draws
from it an argument to dissuade Charlemagne from impos-
ing tithes on the lately converted Saxons : Nos in fide
catholica nati, enutriti et edocti, vix consentimus substantiam nostram pleniter decimare ; quanto magis tenera fides,
et infantilis animus, et avara mens illarum largitati non
consentit. Alc. Op. i. 38.   [3] Thorpe, i. 170.

reeves at each 'burh,' and beseech you in God's
name, and by all his saints, and also by my friendship,
that ye, in the first place, of mine own goods render
the tithes both of live stock and of the year's early
fruits, so that they may most rightly be meted, or
told, or weighed out : and then let the bishops do
the like from their own goods, and my ealdormen
and my reeves the same. And I will that the
bishop and the reeves command it to all those that
ought to obey them, that it may be done at the right
term."[1]

From the tenor of this circular it seems probable
that numerous pleas of exemption had been set up
both in favour of the lands belonging to the crown,
the bishops, and the ealdormen, and also of lands
held under them by others. A subsequent enactment by king Edgar discloses to us an additional
source of disquietude and contention. Originally
the tithes of each district had been assigned to the
chief minster of the district : but in the course of
time places formerly without inhabitants had become peopled ; and thanes had erected churches on
their estates for their own convenience, and that of

---

[1] Ibid. 194. To this letter we have the answer returned
by a meeting of the bishops, thanes, and householders of
Kent, who thank the king humbly for his admonition, and
declare themselves ready and very desirous to obey—
Primum est de decima nostra, ad quam multum cupidi
sumus et voluntarii, et tibi suppliciter gratias agimus
admonitionis tuæ. (Ibid.) The meaning is evident; in
consequence of the king's admonition they promise to pay
the tithe; but the compiler of the index to Mr. Thorpe's
Laws and Institutes, has understood it to mean that they
were very desirous of (getting) the tithes. See Index, art.
Tithe.

their tenants. The consequence was, that they claimed a right to their own tithes, on the ground that they maintained a church establishment for their people. It was to put an end to this question and to secure the full payment of the tithe at the proper season that Edgar published the following law.[1] " Let men give every tithe to the old minster,[2] that the district is subject to : and then let it be so paid, whether it be of the thane's inland, or of the husbandman's outland, as the plough traverses it."

" But if there be a thane who hath on his bocland a church to which there is a burial-place, let him give the third part of his own tithe to his church. If any one hath a church to which there is no burial-place, then out of the nine parts let him give to his priest what he will."[3]

" And let the tithe of younglings be paid by Pentecost, and of the fruits of the earth by the equinox, under peril of the full 'wite,' that the doom-book directs ; and if any one then will not pay the tithe,

---

[1] Thorpe, i. 262.

[2] This was in conformity with the law on the continent, which continually assigns the tithe to the old minsters (ecclesiis antiquitus constitutis).

[3] The churches of more recent foundation were divided into two classes ; of those with, and those without a burial-ground. To the first, probably because they must have been considered of greater necessity by the bishop, a part of the tithe, amounting to one-third, was allotted, and in Domesday we find several churches in possession of that portion of the tithe from the manor or township. The others were looked upon as merely private chapels belonging to the founders, who might assign to them what portion they pleased out of the nine parts which remained after the payment of the tenth to the old minster.

as we have ordained, let the king's reeve go thither, and the bishop's (reeve), and the mass-priest of the minster, and take by force the tenth part for the minster to which it is due ; and let them assign to him (the defaulter) the ninth part : and let the (remaining) eight parts be divided into two, and let the lord of the land take possession of half, and the bishop of half, whether he be a king's man, or a thane's man."[1] It was probably thought that a law so precise and so severe would at once extinguish all disputes concerning the rights of churches, and insure for the future the exact payment of the tithe : but its subsequent re-enactment in the reign of Ethelred, and again in the reign of Canute, will justify a suspicion, that in many places its provisions were set at defiance, and in many but very imperfectly enforced.[2]

Tithe, while it was only a matter of counsel, was looked upon as an alms intrusted for distribution to the good faith of the clergy : the change, by which it was converted into a compulsory payment, did not alter its destination. It was still considered as the alms of the faithful, and could be legitimately

---

[1] That is, let them divide the whole produce into ten equal parts, give the one which is due to the minster, leave one for the defaulter, and divide the other eight between the landlord and the bishop, in punishment of the owner.

[2] See Thorpe, i. 342 and 366, and another law by Ethelred—Omnis consuetudo reddatur super amicitiam Dei et nostram ad matrem ecclesiam cui adjacet ; et nemo auferat Deo, quod ad Deum pertinet, et prædecessores nostri *concesserunt*. (Ib. 388.) There are many proofs in Domesday that these provisions, both with respect to the old minsters and the field churches, had been carried into execution.

employed in two ways only; in the maintenance of
divine service, and in works of Christian charity.
The first council, by which it was enjoined as an
obligation, ordered it to be devoted to the use of the
poor, or the ransom of captives :[1] succeeding councils,
to the use of the church and of the poor :[2] to which
was added that, where the church was amply
endowed, the poor should be entitled to two-thirds
of the tithe ; where it was not, to one-half.[3]   The
doctrine of the Anglo-Saxon church was substantially the same as that of the churches on the continent : and not a single national document relative
to the subject has come down to us, in which the
right of the poor to a considerable portion of the
tithe is not distinctly recognized.   In the compilation, which goes under the name of Archbishop
Egbert, we meet with the following canon.   " Let
the mass-priests themselves receive the tithes from
the people, and keep a written list of the names of
all who have given, and divide, in presence of men
fearing God, the tithe according to the authority of
the canons ; and choose the first portion for the
adornment of the church, and let them distribute
humbly and mercifully with their own hands the
second portion for the benefit of poor and wayfaring

---

[1] Quas sacerdotes aut in pauperum usum, aut in capti-
vorum redemptionem prærogantes, suis orationibus pacem
populo ac salutem impetrent.   Con. Matisc. ii. can. v.
tom. vi. p. 675.

[2] Ut decimæ quæ singulis dabuntur ecclesiis per con-
sulta episcoporum a presbyteris ad usum ecclesiæ et
pauperum summa diligentia dispensentur.   Con. Turon. iii.
cn. 16, tom. ix. 537.

[3] Capit. Ludov. Pii, cap. v.   Ibid. 569.

men; and then may they retain the third portion for themselves."[1] To the same effect it is enjoined in a canon passed during the reign of Edgar, that priests dispense the people's alms, so as to please God, and accustom them to alms : " and right it is that one portion be set apart for the clergy, the second for the need of the church, and the third for the need of the poor.[2] Nor let it be supposed that this distribution was commanded by ecclesiastical authority only : in 1013 it was confirmed by the legislature. " And respecting tithe, the king and his witan have chosen and decreed, as is right, that one-third part of the tithe go to the reparation of the church, and a second part to the servants of God (the ministers), and the third to God's poor, and to needy ones in thraldom."[3] It has, indeed, been pretended that this division concerned the larger monastic establishments only ; but the contrary is evident from the following passage in the charge of Bishop Wulfsine, which was delivered to the parish priests of his diocese, and regarded the tithes of their churches:— " The holy fathers have appointed that men pay their

---

[1] Thorpe, ii. 98.   [2] Id. ii. 256.
[3] Id. i. 342.   It is probable that after the Danish invasion, which at last transferred the crown to the head of Canute, many churches were found in a very ruinous condition, while the payment of tithes had considerably decreased. For that prince, in one of his laws, declares that " all ought to give assistance to the repair of the church with (or according to) right."· (Id. 410, No. 66.) But here he appears to me to speak not of any legal, but of a moral duty ; for in the same law he imposes a penalty of one hundred and twenty shillings on those who eluded the obligation of repairing the burgh or the bridge, to which they were bound by law, but no penalty whatever on those who refused to aid in the repair of the church.

tithe unto God's church : and let the mass-priest go
to, and divide it into three; one part for the repair of
the church, and another for the poor, and the third
for God's servants who have the care of the church."[1]
Besides the tenth portion of his produce, the
Israelite was commanded to offer to God the first-
fruits of his harvest. There cannot be a doubt that,
as the Christians borrowed the first of these institutions from the Jewish scriptures, so they also borrowed the other; and that, by a similar process of
reasoning, that which was at first a voluntary offering,
was at length commuted into a compulsory payment.[2]
It was known in the Anglo-Saxon language by the
term ciricsceat, or kirk-shot, and was declared by law
to be payable, like the tithes, to the old minster.[3]
It was calculated at the rate of one seame (or horse-
load) of winnowed grain for every hide of land occupied by a free tenant ;[4] and was ordered to be paid

[1] Thorpe, ii. 352. This charge was composed for Wulfsine
by the celebrated Alfric. Ibid. See note (I).
[2] I make this remark, because there have been antiquaries, who have derived it from some imaginary payment
by the pagan Saxons to their priests, which at their conversion was transferred to the Christian priesthood. Of
the existence of such original payment there is no satisfactory proof; and the first-fruits are associated with the
tenths, the primitiæ with the decimæ, in documents more
ancient than the conversion of the pagan tribes.
[3] Edgar's Domas, Thorpe, i. 262. That the first-fruits
were meant by kirk-shot, is plain from the letter of Canute :
—In festivitate S. Martini primitiæ seminum ad ecclesiam
sub cujus parochia quisque degit, quæ Anglice cyricsceat
nominatur. Apud Malm. de Reg. i. 312.
[4] The kirk-shot for Bentley, two hides of land, was two
modii of winnowed grain. (Cod. Dipl. ii. 386.) It is frequently mentioned in Domesday, as being a suma of grain
for every hide, and still payable under the same penalty to
the church as by the law of Ine. Domesd. i. 174, 175.

annually at Martinmas by him who held 'the hearth and the haulm' at the preceding Christmas. It was the first of the church dues, which, as far as existing documents can be trusted, obtained the protection of the legislature ; and in the laws of Ine (anno 680), we find it enjoined under the penalty of a fine of sixty shillings to the king, and of twelve times the amount of the shot to the church.[1] Subsequent legislators doubled the fine, but the penalty to the church remained the same till the conquest.[2]

To the kirk-shot must be added three other payments, to which the legislature had given to the church a legal claim : 1st, the payment of plough-alms, a penny from every plough-land, which was

---

[1] Thorpe, i. 140, 244, 262,342, 366. "Let church-scot be given in at Martinmas; if any one do not do it, let him forfeit lx shillings, and give the church-scot twelve-fold." p.104. On this law Mr. Soames makes the following comment : " Ina's legislature wisely commuted voluntary offerings for a regular assessment upon houses. . . . This pious care of divine ministrations may be considered as the legal origin of *church-rates*." (Soames, p. 92.) Now this commutation is plainly imaginary. There is no mention of it in the law, nor were the voluntary offerings abolished. Neither is it easy to understand how this could be the legal origin of church-rates. Church-rates and kirk-shot have scarcely a single feature in common. Church-rates are contingent, and levied only when they are wanted ; kirk-shot was a certain and annual payment : the amount of the church-rate varies according to circumstances; that of the kirk-shot was always the same : the church-rate is voted by the parishioners; the kirk-shot was imposed by the legislature : the church-rate is paid in money; the kirk-shot was delivered in grain. Mr. Churton, like Mr. Soames, is positive that kirk-shot was applied to the building and repairing of churches, and that it is the same with what are now called church-rates (Churton, p. 78); but where is the proof ?   [2] Thorpe, 342, 366.

yearly offered to God during the fortnight after
Easter, to beg his blessing on the labours of the
husbandman during the spring ;[1] 2nd, of leot-shot,
that is, of a certain quantity of wax, of the value of
half a silver penny, furnished from every hide of
land, thrice in the year, at Candlemas, on Easter eve,
and on the feast of All Hallows,[2] of which the principal object was to provide lights for the altar, because it was ordered that "there be always lights
burning in the church while mass is singing ;"[3] and
3rd, that of soul-shot, the mortuary ordered to be
paid for the dead, while the grave was yet open, or
to be reserved for the church to which the deceased
belonged, if his body were buried in any place out of
the 'shrift-shire.'[4]

Here, however, it should be observed that, though
the church by consecration was devoted, with its
lands and its income from all these sources, to religious purposes, yet the ownership was not necessarily
severed from the founder.   It was still, according to
the national jurisprudence, *his* church.   He might,
indeed, and often did, divest himself of his right in
favour of some bishopric or abbey; but, if he did
not, the ownership still remained in him, and he disposed of the church and its profit to the incumbent,
as a lœn, or benefice for life.   Hence two very im-

---

[1] Thorpe, i. 170, 244, 306, 342, 366.
[2] Ib. 170, 308, 366.   [3] Id. ii. 252.
[4] Id. i. 264, 308, 342, 368. Hence it will follow that the
soul-shot was a fixed sum due to a particular church, and
very different from the money left by will for the benefit
of the testator's soul. Both these have sometimes been
confounded by writers, who have termed such legacies the
soul-shot.

portant consequences followed. 1st, He appointed
to his church, whenever it became vacant. By ecclesiastical law no person so appointed could take possession without the consent of the bishop ; and, as
long as clerks were not promoted to priests' orders
until they had been appointed to a cure or office, that
law could not often be evaded ; but, in the latter
part of the Anglo-Saxon period, when the rule for
ordination was less strictly observed, priests might
be found elsewhere than in the episcopal monastery ;
and the lords of vacant churches began to negotiate
with such priests for the sale of the ecclesiastical
benefice, as they would for that of a secular lœn.
The abuse made a rapid progress. Covenants were
entered into between the lord and his nominee, by
which the latter consented to purchase the benefice
by the payment of a gross sum, or of a yearly rent,
or by the surrender of a portion of the annual oblations, tithes, or dues, and, in some cases, of the whole
of the church income, in lieu of a yearly stipend.
The incumbent thus became the vassal of his lord ;
the clerical establishment of which he was the head
was reduced to poverty, and the property itself became frequently subject to litigation in the courts of
law.

Another consequence, intimately connected with
the above, was that when the ownership was retained
by the founder, it passed from him to other parties,
according to the laws regulating the transfer of
landed property, by sale, or gift, or bequest, or inheritance.[1] Hence we find churches in the posses-

---

[1] I may here be allowed to add a few instances of the
manner in which churches passed from the possession of

sion of individuals of every rank and profession; of clergymen, who, though they sometimes are, frequently are not, the incumbents ; of lay proprietors, both men and women; and of associated bodies, as guilds, burghers, and religious communities. Frequently several churches belong to a single individual; frequently a single church belongs to several coparceners, who divide the profits among them, accord-

---

one party to that of another. 1st, Wilgils built a small church and monastery near the Spurn-head, in Holderness, and left them to his heirs, so that they came at last by legitimate succession to Alcuin, though he lived in Gaul, and principally at Tours. Alcuin says : Posteri ejus usque hodie ex sanctitatis ejus traditione possident, quorum ego meritis et ordine postremus eandem cellulam per legitimas successiones suscepi gubernandam. (Alc. Oper. ii. 184.)

We have already seen that, a little before the close of the eighth century, Headda, who styles himself mass-priest and abbot, and appears to have possessed a monastery or district church on his own lands, limits the succession to descendants of his family in holy orders, as long as one may be found among them fit to govern according to ecclesiastical rule ; and, in default of any such, gives the whole inheritance to the episcopal see of Worcester, adding this reason for the gift—Quia alumnus sum illius familiæ, et juxta liminibus ecclesiæ disciplinatus et nutritus fui.   Cod. Dipl. i. 205.

In 850, King Ethelwulf gave to his beloved thane Ealhere the half-acre of land without the walls of Rochester, on which was the church of St. Mary, with every thing thereunto belonging (consequently the church itself), to possess it during life, and leave it qualicunque homini voluerit in sempiternum. Ibid. ii. 36.

In 880, King Alfred gave to Asser, of Wales, in reward of his services, the two monasteries of Ambresbury and Barnwell, with a schedule of all things belonging to each. Now these monasteries must have been district churches ; for there were at that time no monasteries of monks in Wessex, as Asser himself assures us. (Asser, 50, 61.) For additional examples of the gift and sale of churches, see Hist. Rames. 402, 3, 13, 18, and note (I).

ing to the number of shares held separately by each. On all occasions these churches are considered private property, in the same manner as the mills, and mines, and fisheries of their owners.[1]

The evils arising out of this state of things were deeply felt by the bishops, by those among them, at least, in whom the sense of duty was not deadened by views of personal interest. They complained in the assemblies of the witan; they published canons against the men who made merchandize of God's houses;[2] they threatened with divine judgment the enslavers of churches. " Now," says one of them, " churches far and wide are weakly protected, evilly enslaved, and cleanly bereft of their ancient rights, and stripped of in-door decencies. Woe to the man who is the cause of this, though he wene not so; for he, who is the foe of God's church, is the foe of God himself."[3] Nor was it in England alone that these abuses existed. They grew out of the same causes among every Christian people of northern origin.[4] The local and national churches everywhere found themselves powerless against the lay lords, who with obstinacy maintained as their undoubted right, what had been at first surrendered to them through weakness, or extorted by them through injustice. It required the authority of the universal pastor to stem the torrent which threatened to overwhelm Christianity. Nicholas II. distinguished himself by the

---

[1] See note (4) infra; and note (I) at end of the volume.
[2] Thorpe, ii. 292, 294, xx. xxi.
[3] Ibid. 341.
[4] See the canons of the sixth council of Arles, and of that of Chalons sur Saône, in 813. Con. ix. 323, 365; also Con. Brac..ii. c. 6.

zeal with which he stepped forward to check the usurpations of the feudal aristocracy in every part of the west; and it is probable that it was partly with a view to this object, that he sent the two legates, already mentioned, to Edward the Confessor, on the departure of Archbishop Aelred.[1] But Nicholas only began the contest: the lay appropriation of church revenues, simonial appointments, and the consequences of the practice of investiture, were questions too intimately connected with the worldly interests of a martial nobility, and too injurious to the spiritual rights of the church, to be terminated on a sudden; and the quarrel continued under the successors of Nicholas to a period long beyond the scope of the present work. I shall, therefore, be content with adding that their efforts were ultimately successful. The independence of the church in spiritual matters was recognized, and laws were enacted to restrain the encroachments of the lay powers on the exercise of her office and jurisdiction.

At the conclusion of this chapter, I may be allowed to notice the appeals which have often been made to the enactments of the Anglo-Saxon legislature in favour of the church dues already enumerated, as if they were the prototypes, and furnished a sufficient justification of the present system of legislation, which imposes upon all persons, without distinction of creed, certain payments in support of the established church. In such reasoning, one, and that too a most important, consideration is overlooked. Among the Anglo-Saxons there was no diversity of

---

[1] See end of last chapter.

religious sects. But one religion was known. The church of each parishioner was the church of all his neighbours. All professed the same creed; all practised the same worship ; and the law was based on this just principle, that, where all shared in the benefit, all ought to bear a share in the burthen. But at the present day it is otherwise. Different religious creeds and different forms of worship are, with the sanction of the legislature, intermingled in every part of the country; and, consequently, to tax all in support of one favoured system, is to reverse the principle established by our ancestors, and to make those bear a share of the burthen, who do not, and cannot conscientiously, enjoy any share of the benefit.

CHAPTER V.

ANGLO-SAXON MONKS.

MONKS OF ST. GREGORY—OF ST. COLUMBA—OF ST. BENEDICT—HIS RULE—CONVENTS OF RELIGIOUS WOMEN—DOUBLE CONVENTS — MONASTIC VOWS — OBEDIENCE — CHASTITY—POVERTY—MITIGATION OF RULE—ADOPTION OF SECULAR DRESS—SUPERFLUOUS VISITS, ETC.— CONVERSION OF MONKS INTO CANONS.

IN the last chapter have been briefly noticed the origin of the monastic institute in Egypt, its subsequent diffusion throughout Christendom, and the innovations gradually wrought in its constitution by the wants of religion and the spirit of the times. When Augustine brought the light of the Gospel to the Anglo-Saxons, the solitary of the desert had become the inmate of a numerous establishment, and the lay recluse, earning a scanty subsistence with the labour of his hands, had been transformed into a clerk actually discharging, or preparing himself to discharge, the duties of the priesthood. This change was productive of numerous benefits. The monk, though still withdrawn from secular pursuits, no longer existed for himself alone : his virtues were made serviceable to others : he was become an active minister of religion, and was able, not only to edify the worldling by his example, but also to instruct the ignorant by his preaching, and to labour with the zeal of an apostle in the conversion of pagan nations.

I. The reader is aware that the first of these apostolic labourers in England, came from the monastery founded by St. Gregory in Rome. He was "their teacher and their head;" under his eye they had been educated in the duties of their profession; and the same code of domestic discipline or, in monastic language, the same rule, to which they had been habituated at home, they were careful to establish in the houses of their foundation among their converts.[1] But there exist no documents from which we may learn what were the peculiar enactments of this code, the points in which it differed from other monastic rules, and the length of time during which it was retained without innovation. Christchurch, in Canterbury, was for some hundred years served by a body of canons, who were displaced by a colony of Benedictine monks in the reign of Ethelred, about four centuries after the original foundation.[2]

II. With regard to the rule followed by the Scottish monks, who subsequently established themselves in Northumbria, Mercia, and East Anglia, we are equally ignorant. There have, indeed, been writers who, founding their opinion on some fancied resemblance between them and the monks of St. Basil, have boldly assigned to them an oriental

---

[1] Vestram dilectionem sectantem magistri et capitis sui Sancti Gregorii regulam. Ep. Honorii Papæ apud Bed. Hist. ii. c. 18.

[2] Wilk. 282, 284. Mores, Comment. de Ælfrico, 84, 88.

origin. But the premiss will not bear out the conclusion. The codes of the several monastic legislators are modified by diversity of judgment and
variety of circumstances : but as all are primarily
directed to the attainment of the same object, they
must of course present many points of resemblance.
These monks of St. Columba came from Ireland :
they were a branch of the order as it had been
established there by St. Patrick : and it is unreasonable to suppose, without some cogent proof, that he
would prefer the rule of certain Asiatic monks, of
whose existence he was probably ignorant, instead of
borrowing from the discipline of the western monasteries, which he had personally visited both in Italy
and Gaul.[1]

But, though we know nothing of the rule, we are
well acquainted with the virtues of these Scottish
monks. For this information we are indebted to
Beda, who, though he belonged to a different section
of the monastic body, has portrayed in glowing
colours their patience, their chastity, their frequent
meditation on the sacred writings, and their indefatigable efforts to attain the summit of Christian
perfection. They chose for their habitation the
most dreary situations : no motives but those of
charity could draw them from their cells ; and, if
they appeared in public, their object was to instruct
the ignorant, to discourage vice, to reconcile enemies,
and to plead the cause of the unfortunate. The
little property which they enjoyed was common to
all : poverty they esteemed as the surest guardian of
virtue : and the benefactions of the opulent they

---

[1] See Lanigan on the Scottish monks, iv. p. 348.

respectfully declined, or instantly employed in relieving the necessities of the indigent. One only stain
did he discover in their character, an immoderate
esteem for their forefathers, which prompted them to
prefer their own customs to the consent of all other
Christian churches : but this he piously trusted would
disappear in the bright effulgence of their virtues.[1]

III. To these two forms of monachism, which
came in with the foreign missionaries, we have to
add a third, subsequently introduced by native
Christians, who, in their travels to the apostolic see,
had become acquainted with the rule of St. Benedict,
and, aware of its superior excellence, were desirous
to establish it in their own country. Benedict was
a native of Norcia, who about the close of the fifth
century, to avoid the contagious example of the
Roman youth, buried himself at the age of fifteen in
a deep and lonely cavern, amid the mountains of
Subiaco. Six and thirty months the young hermit
passed in this voluntary prison, unknown to any but
his spiritual director, a monk of an adjacent monastery : but an accident betrayed him to the notice of
the public ; his example diffused a similar ardour
around him ; and his desert was quickly inhabited
by twelve confraternities of monks, who acknowledged and revered him as their parent and legislator. But the fame of Benedict awakened the
jealousy of his neighbours. Their calumnies compelled him to quit his solitude, and he withdrew to
the summit of mount Cassino, in the ancient territory of the Volsci. There he spent the remainder
of his years in the practice of every monastic virtue,

----
[1] Bed. Hist. l. iii. c. 17, 26.

and the possession of those honours which that age was accustomed to render to superior sanctity. To his care the patricians of Rome intrusted the education of their children ; his cell was visited by the most distinguished personages, who solicited his benediction ; and Totila, the haughty conqueror of Italy, condescended to ask the advice, and trembled at the stern reproof, of the holy abbot.

That austerity of life, which distinguished the first professors of monachism had in the course of two centuries admitted of considerable mitigation ; and Benedict composed *his* rule, not so much to restore the vigour, as to prevent the total extinction of the ancient dicipline. " The precepts of monastic perfection," says the humble and fervent legislator, " are contained in the inspired writings : the examples abound in the works of the holy fathers. But mine is a more lowly attempt to teach the rudiments of a Christian life, that, when we are acquainted with them, we may aspire to the practice of the sublimer virtues."[1] But the admirers of the institute were not slow to appreciate his labours : from Gregory the Great his rule obtained the praise of superior wisdom ;[2] and the opinion of the pontiff was afterwards adopted or confirmed by the general consent of the Latin church.

In distributing the various duties of the day, Benedict was careful that every moment should be diligently employed. Six hours were allotted to sleep. Soon after midnight the monks rose to chant the nocturnal service; during the day they were sum-

---

[1] Reg. St. Ben. c. 73.   [2] St. Greg. Dial. l. ii. c. 36.

moned seven times to the church, to perform the
other parts of the canonical office: seven hours were
employed in manual labour ; two in study ; and the
small remainder was devoted to the necessary
refection of the body.[1] Their diet was simple but
sufficient : twelve, perhaps eighteen, ounces of bread,
a hemina of wine,[2] and two dishes of vegetables
composed their daily allowance. The flesh of
quadrupeds was strictly prohibited : but the rigour
of the law was relaxed in favour of the children, the
aged, and the infirm.[3] To the colour, the form, and
the quality of their dress, he was wisely indifferent ;
and only recommended that it should be adapted to
the climate, and similar to that of the labouring
poor. Each monk slept in a separate bed ; but all
lay in their habits, that they might be ready to repair,
at the first summons, to the church.[4] Every thing
was possessed in common : not only articles of convenience, but even of necessity, were received and
resigned at the discretion of the abbot.[5] No brother
was allowed to cross the threshold of the monastery without the permission of his superior : at his
departure he requested the prayers of the community: at his return he lay prostrate in the church,
to atone for the dissipation of his thoughts during
his absence. Whatever he might have seen or heard
without the walls of the convent, he was commanded
to bury in eternal silence.[6]

---

[1] Reg. St. Ben. c. 8, 16, 48.
[2] The exact measure of the hemina is unknown. It has
been the subject of many learned dissertations by the
Benedictine writers. See Nat. Alex. tom. v. p. 468.
[3] Reg. 39, 40.   [4] Ibid. c. 22.
[5] Ibid. c. 33.   [6] Ibid. c. 67.

The favour of admission was purchased with a severe probation. On his knees, at the gate, the postulant requested to be received among the servants of God : but his desires were treated with contempt, and his pride was humbled by reproaches. After four days his perseverance subdued the apparent reluctance of the monks ; he was successively transferred to the apartments of the strangers and of the novices ; and an aged brother was commissioned to observe his conduct, and to instruct him in the duties of his profession. Before the expiration of the year, the rule was read thrice in his presence ; and each reading was accompanied with the admonition, that he was still at liberty to depart. At last, on the anniversary of his admission, he entered the church, and avowed before God and the community, his determination to spend his days in the monastic profession, to reform his conduct, and to obey his superiors. The solemn engagement he subscribed with his name, and deposited on the altar.[1]

The legislator who wishes to enforce the observance, must punish the transgression, of his laws. But in apportioning the degree of punishment, Benedict advised the superior to weigh not only the nature of the offence, but the contumacy of the offender. There were minds, he observed, which might be guided by a gentle reprimand, while others refused to bend to the severest chastisement. In his penal code he gradually proceeded from more lenient to coercive measures. The inefficacy of private admonition was succeeded by the disgrace

---

[1] Reg. c. 58.

of public reproof: if the delinquent proved insensible to shame, he was separated from the society of his brethren ;[1] and the continuance of his obstinacy was rewarded with the infliction of corporal punishment. As a last resource, the confraternity assembled in the church by order of the superior, and recommended, with fervent prayer, their rebellious brother to the mercy and grace of the Almighty. He was then expelled : but the gates of the convent were not shut to repentance. Thrice the returning sinner might expect to be received with kindness in the arms of an indulgent father; but the fourth relapse filled up his measure of iniquity, and he was ejected for ever.[2]

From mount Cassino and the desert of Subiaco, the Benedictine order gradually diffused itself to the utmost boundaries of the Latin church. The merit of introducing it to the knowledge of the Saxons, was claimed by St. Wilfrid.[3] That prelate, in his pilgrimage to the tombs of the apostles, had conversed with the disciples of St. Benedict, and though he had been educated in the Scottish discipline at Lindisfarne, he bore a willing testimony to the superior excellence of their institute. Having

---

[1] This was termed excommunication ; but the culprit during his confinement was often visited and consoled by the senipetæ, id est, seniores sapientes. (Ben. Reg. c. 27.) Does not this passage unfold the mystery which antiquaries have discovered in the Sempectæ of Croyland ? Sempectæ has been substituted for senipetæ by the mistake of the copyist.

[2] St. Ben. Reg. c. 23—29.

[3] Nonne ego curavi, quomodo vitam monachorum secundum regulam St. Benedicti patris, quam nullus ibi prior invexit, constituerem. Wilfrid apud Edd. c. 45.

afterwards obtained a copy of the Benedictine rule,
he recommended its adoption to the different
monastic bodies in the kingdoms of Northumbria
and Mercia. Of the success of his labours we may
form an estimate from the thousands of monks, who,
at the time of his disgrace, are said to have lamented
the loss of their guide and benefactor.[1] Yet the
zeal of Wilfrid was tempered with prudence. If he
preferred the foreign institute, he was not blind to
the merit of the discipline previously adopted by his
countrymen : many customs which experience had
shewn to be useful, and antiquity had rendered
venerable, he carefully retained ; and by amalga-
mating them with the rule of St. Benedict, greatly
improved the state of monastic discipline.[2]

Contemporary with Wilfrid, and the companion
of his youth, was Bennet Biscop, the celebrated
abbot of Wearmouth. At the age of five-and-
twenty he quitted the court of his friend and patron
Oswiu, king of Northumbria, and directed his steps
to the capital of the Christian world (anno 663).
His intention was to embrace the monastic profession ; but he wished previously to visit the places

---

[1] Multa millia. Edd. c. 21.

[2] Revertens cum regula Benedicti instituta ecclesiarum
Dei melioravit. (Edd. c. 14.) In the regulations drawn
up by St. Dunstan (Apost. Bened. App. par. 3, p. 80),
and the letter of St. Ethelwold to the monks of Egnesham
(Wanley's MSS. p. 110), may be seen several of the
customs peculiar to the ancient Saxon monks. St. Wilfrid,
instead of leaving to his disciples the choice of their
future abbot, as was ordered by the Benedictine rule, made
the choice himself, and ordered the monks to obey him.
Edd. Vit. Wilf. c. 60, 61. See also Butler's SS. Lives,
March 21.

in which it was practised in the highest perfection.
With pious curiosity he perused the rules, and
observed the manners, of seventeen among the most
celebrated foreign monasteries ; thrice he venerated
the sacred remains of the apostles at Rome ; and
two years he spent among the cloistered inhabitants
of the small isle of Lerins (now St. Honorat near
Marseilles), who gave to him the religious habit, and
received from him the monastic vow. At the command of Pope Vitalian, he accompanied Archbishop
Theodore to England, as his guide and interpreter ;
and was intrusted by that prelate with the government of the monks of Canterbury. On his resig-
nation of that office, devotion led him again to the
Vatican, and the labour of his pilgrimage was
amply repaid with what he considered a valuable
collection of books, paintings, and relics. At his
return, he was received with joy and veneration by
Egfrid, king of Northumbria, and obtained from the
munificence of that prince a spacious domain near
the mouth of the river Wear, on which he built his
first monastery, dedicated in honour of St. Peter.
The reputation of Bennet quickly multiplied the
number of his disciples ; another donation from the
king enabled him to erect a second convent at Jarrow,
on the southern bank of the Tyne ; and so prolific
were these two establishments, that, within a few
years after the death of the founder, they contained
no less than six hundred monks.[1] Of the discipline
to which he subjected his disciples, the rule observed
at Lerins probably formed the groundwork : but he
added improvements, derived partly from the code of

---

[1] Bed. Vit. Abbat. Wircm. p. 293.

St. Benedict, and partly from the practice of the several monasteries which he had visited in the course of his travels.[1] From his labours, the most valuable benefits were derived to his countrymen. By the workmen, whom he procured from Gaul, they were taught the arts of making glass, and of building with stone : the foreign paintings with which he decorated his churches, excited attempts at imitation : and the many volumes which he deposited in the library of his monastery, invited the industry, and nourished the improvement, of his monks. Bennet contributed more to the civilization of his countrymen than any person since the preaching of the Roman missionaries : and his memory has been gratefully transmitted to posterity by the venerable Beda, in the most pleasing of his works, the Lives of the Abbots of Wearmouth.

While the Benedictine order was thus partially established in the kingdom of Northumbria, its in-

---

[1] That he adopted the regulation of St. Benedict with respect to the election of the abbot, is certain from Beda (ibid. p. 298); and in the next century, Alcuin recommended to the monks, the frequent study of the rule of St. Benedict. (Alc. ep. 49.) Hence Mabillon contends, that the monks of Wearmouth were Benedictines. (Anal. Vet. p. 506.) But Bennet himself seems to ascribe the discipline which he established, to his own observations : Ex decem quippe et septem monasteriis, quæ inter longos meæ crebræ peregrinationis discursus optima comperi, hæc universa didici, et vobis salubriter observanda contradidi. (Bed. ibid. p. 297.) Non pro captu decreta nobis statuens, sed antiquorum statuta certissima monasteriorum, quæ in peregrinatione didicerat, sibi suisque observanda proponens. (Hom. in Nat. S. Ben. Abbatis. Bed. Op. Min. p. 336.) Alcuin also recommends to them the observance of the regulations prescribed by their founder Bennet, and the Abbot Ceolfrid. Alc. i. 21. ep. xiii.

terests were espoused with equal or greater zeal in the more southern provinces by Aldhelm, bishop of Sherborne, and Egwin, bishop of Worcester. The former introduced it into his three monasteries of Malmesbury, Frome, and Bradanford :[1] the latter erected a magnificent abbey at Evesham, in which, by the order of Pope Constantine, if we may believe a very suspicious document, he placed Benedictine monks, whose institute was scarcely known in that province.[2] Their example was imitated by many of their brethren, who, according to their fancy or their judgment, adopted in a greater or less proportion the foreign discipline. There was, however, in the rule of St. Benedict, one regulation, which could not fail to claim the suffrages of the whole monastic body. Formerly the right of nominating to the vacant abbeys had been vested in the bishops of each diocese :[3] but the legislator of Subiaco saw, or thought that he saw, in this practice, the source of the most grievous abuses ; and made it essential to his rule, that the superior of each monastery should be chosen by the suffrages of its inhabitants.[4] This regulation,

---

[1] Anno 675.   Malm. de pont. 1, v. pp. 344, 353, 356. Aldhelm says of St. Benedict,

> Primo qui statuit nostræ certamina vitæ
> Qualiter optatam teneant cœnobia formam.
>
> *De Laud. Virg. in Biblioth. Pat. vol. viii.*

[2] Quæ minus in illis partibus habetur.   Bulla Cons. apud Wilk. p. 71, an. 709.

[3] Thus St. Aldhelm was appointed by the bishop of Winchester, pro jure tunc episcoporum.   Malm. de. reg. 1, i. c. 2, f. 6.   Gale 344.   Apost. Ben. p. 20.   Wilk. pp. 57, 86.

[4] Ben. reg. c. 64.   This, with the other monastic exemptions, were successively granted by the pontiffs, to

so flattering to their independence, was eagerly accepted by the monks of every institute, and was opposed with equal warmth by several of the bishops, who considered it an infringement of their ancient rights. But the episcopal order contained within its bosom the avowed protectors of the monastic claim; and the contested privilege was soon confirmed by the decrees of popes, and the charters of princes.[1]

IV. But monasteries were not inhabited exclusively by men: the retirement of the cloister appears to have possessed peculiar attractions in the eyes of the Saxon ladies. The weaker frame, and more volatile disposition of the sex, seemed, indeed, less adapted to the rigour of perpetual confinement, and the ever recurring circle of vigils, fasts, and prayers: but the difficulty of the enterprise increased the ardour of their zeal: they refused to await the erection of convents in their native country; crowds of females resorted to the foreign establishments of Faremoutier, Chelles, and Andeli; and the former of these houses was successively governed by abbesses of the royal race of Hengist.[2] But before the close of the seventh century, the southern Saxons could boast of several fervent communities of nuns under the guidance of Eanswide, Mildrede, and Ethelburge, princesses no less illustrious for their piety than for their birth. In Northumbria, at the same period,

---

secure the monks from the oppressive conduct of certain bishops. Yet there were many, who considered the remedy more pernicious than the disease. See St. Bernard (De consid. 1, iii. c. 4), and Richard, archbishop of Canterbury (Ep. Pet. Blessen. ep. 68): also Fleury (Discours viii. c. 13).

[1] Wilk. con. pp. 44, 49, 71, 74. Gale, 311, 345, 353.
[2] Anno 640. Bed. l. iii. c. 8.

the abbess Heiu, the first lady among the northern tribes who put on the monastic veil, governed, under the patronage of the bishop Aidan, a small and obscure convent at Hereteu, or the isle of the hart.[1] She was succeeded by Hild, whose family, virtue, and abilities, reflected a brighter lustre on the institute. Hild was allied to the East-Anglian and Northumbrian princes; her advice was respectfully asked and followed by kings and prelates; and to her care Oswiu commended his infant daughter Ælfled, with a dower of one hundred and twenty hides of land.[2] Enriched by the donations of her friends, she built at Whitby a double monastery, in one part of which a sisterhood of nuns, in the other a confraternity of monks, obeyed her maternal authority. Among her disciples she established that community of goods, which distinguished the first Christians at Jerusalem: riches and poverty were equally banished from the convent; and whatever they possessed, was the common property of all. Their virtue has been attested by the venerable Beda: and no less than five of the monks of Whitby were raised to the episcopal dignity, during the life of their foundress.[3] From Northumbria the institute was rapidly diffused over the kingdom of Mercia.

---

[1] Hartlepool. Bed. l. iv. c. 23.

[2] Oswiu had vowed to consecrate his daughter to the service of God, if he were successful in his war against Penda. Bed. l. iii. c. 24. The Terræ centum et viginti familiarum, are translated by Alfred, hunð ꞇƿelꝼꞇiᵹ hiða. (Ælf. vers. p. 556.) The hide contained sometimes 120 acres, but the amount varied with the nature of the soil, and its capability of maintaining what was called an entire family. Hist. Elien. pp. 472, 481.

[3] Bed. l. iii. c. 24; l. iv. c. 23.

The reader will perhaps have been surprised, that a society of religious men should be placed under the government of a woman. Yet this scheme of monasterial policy, singular as it may now appear, was once common among the northern nations, and grew out of their habits, and the institutions of the age. The first care of the founder or foundress of one of these establishments was to provide for the religious wants, not only of the sisterhood, but also of the tenants and labourers located on the domain. With this view a church was erected, frequently on a large and magnificent scale :[1] and contiguous to the church a range of buildings for the accommodation of the priests, deacons, and inferior clerks, whose ministry would be required in the daily and solemn performance of the service, and in the office of imparting religious instruction and spiritual aid to the neighbouring inhabitants. The discipline adopted in this second monastery, was the same as in similar episcopal and abbatial establishments; its inmates were subject to the same regulations, and bound to perform the same duties. But they still looked up to the abbess as their head : for her religious profession had not deprived her of her secular rights. She was the " lady," they were her " men," living on her property, and supported by her bounty. Their immediate superior was of her appointment, and through him they received her commands.

It may, perhaps, be thought that the proximity of the two monasteries might prove an occasion of danger to the virtue of their inhabitants; but it was

---

[1] See the description of one of these churches in Alcuin's works, ii. p. 549.

hoped that the mortified life to which they had bound themselves by the most solemn vows, would render them superior to temptation; and to eschew even the suspicion of evil, the strictest precautions were enforced, to confine the sisters within the spacious precincts of their convent, and to prevent any man from entering within their inclosure, except it were on some particular occasion, with the permission of the abbess, and in the presence of witnesses. Of this discipline, as it was observed in the double monastery at Wimborne, we have the following minute account by a contemporary—Ralph of Fulda, the writer of the life of St. Lioba, who, at the invitation of St. Boniface, repaired from Wimborne to Bischofsheim, and propagated the institute among the females in Germany :—" There were two monasteries at Wimborne formerly erected by the kings of the country, surrounded with strong and lofty walls, and endowed with competent revenues. Of these, one was designed for clerks, the other for females; but neither (for such was the law of their foundation) was ever entered by any individual of the other sex. No woman could obtain permission to come into the monastery of the men; none of the men to come into the convent of the women, with the exception of the priests who entered to celebrate mass, and withdrew the moment the service was over. If a female, desirous of quitting the world, asked to be admitted among the sisterhood, she could obtain her request, be she who she might, on this condition only, that she should never seek to go out, unless it were on some extraordinary occasion, which might seem to justify such indulgence. Even the abbess

herself, if it were necessary that she should receive
advice, or give orders, spoke to men through a win-
dow; and so desirous was she to remove all opportunity of conversation between the sisters and persons
of the other sex, that she refused entrance into the
convent not only to laymen and clergymen, but even
to the bishops themselves."[1]

It is easy to account for the existence of such communities in England. The first Anglo-Saxon ladies,
who sought the retirement of the cloister, found this
form established in the convents, to which they resorted in France: whence it happened that the same
plan was adopted by those who afterwards erected convents in England. By our ancestors these establishments were held in the highest estimation: the most
distinguished of the Saxon female saints, and many of
the most eminent prelates, were educated in them:
and so edifying was the deportment of the greatest
part of these communities, that the breath of slander

---

[1] Vit. S. Liobæ in Act. SS. Bened. Sær. iii. p. 246, in
beginning of the eighth century. Thus also Beda, speaking of the monastery at Barking, in Essex, mentions the
plague in that part of the monastery qua viri tenebantur,
before it reached that other part, qua ancillarum Dei
caterva a virorum erat secreta contubernio. Lib. iv. c. 7.

[2] That the monasteries of Faremoutier, Chelles, and
Andeli, were double, appears from Bede (l. iii. c. 8,) and is
proved by Broughton (Mem. p. 343.) Among the Saxons,
the principal at least were of the same institute : Whitby
(Bed. l. iv. c. 23, Vit. Cuth. c. 24,) Berking (Id. c. 7,)
Coldingham (Id. c. 25,) Ely (Id. c. 19,) Wenlock (Bonif.
ep. 21, p. 29,) Repandun (Gale, p. 243 ; Wigor, p. 568,)
and Wimborn (Mab. Sæc. 3, Vit. St. Liob. p. 246.) See
also Leland's Collectanea (vol. iii. p. 117.) At Beverley,
a monastery of monks, a college of canons, and a convent
of nuns, obeyed the same abbot. Mon. Ang. vol. i. p. 170;
Lel. Coll. vol. iii. p. 100.

never presumed to tarnish their character. The
monastery of Coldingham alone forms an exception.
The virtue of some among its inhabitants was more
ambiguous : and an accidental fire, which was ascribed to the vengeance of heaven, confirmed the
suspicions of their contemporaries, whose indignant
piety has transmitted to posterity the knowledge of
their misconduct.[1] The account was received with
the deepest sorrow by St. Cuthbert, the pious bishop
of Lindisfarne : and in the anguish of his zeal, he
commanded his disciples to exclude every female
from the threshold of his cathedral. His will was
religiously obeyed, and for several centuries no
woman entered with impunity any of the churches,
in which the body of the saint had reposed.[2] But
notwithstanding the misfortune at Coldingham, and
the disapprobation of Cuthbert, the institute continued to flourish, till the ravages of the pagan Danes
levelled most of the double monasteries with the
ground, and a new system grew up with the revival
of the order by archbishop Dunstan.[3]

---

[1] Bed. l. iv. c. 25.

[2] Sim. Dunel. Hist. Ecc. Dun. p. 102. For the accommodation of the women, a new church was built, and
called the green kirk. Ibid. A similar regulation was observed in several of the monasteries of St. Columban, in
France. See Butler's SS. Lives, Sept. 5. Mab. præf. 1,
Sæc. 3, cxxxvii.

[3] Another, but imaginary order of religious women, was
descried by one of our most learned antiquaries. Spelman
had observed that the Saxons always made a distinction
between Nonna and Monialis in Latin, and Nunna and
Mynekin in their own language : whence he inferred, that
the latter must have been the wives of married clergymen,
by whose enemies they had been branded with the name
of mynekin from minne, a Gothic word of no very decent

V. Here it should be observed that the different
gradations of authority in the monastic hierarchy, as
they exist at present—its provincials, generals, chapters, and congregations—were then unknown. Each
founder of a monastery legislated for his subjects,
uncontrolled by the opinion or the commands of a
superior; and each succeeding abbot assumed the
right of modifying by addition or retrenchment the
discipline established by the founder, sometimes borrowing from the rules of other monasteries, and
sometimes framing new constitutions of his own.
Of this practice the reader has already met with instances in the foundations made by St. Wilfred and
Bennet Biscop. In the same manner St. Botulf is
said to have established at Ikanho (anno 650), a rule
taken from that of St. Benedict and the customs of
the ancient monks, to which he added improvements

---

signification. (Spel. Con. p. 529; Wilk. Con. p. 294.) It
would be difficult to err more egregiously. From the excerpta of Egbert of York we learn, that the mynekins were
women, "who had consecrated themselves to God, who
had vowed their virginity to God, and who were the spouses
of Christ." Ꝺe Loƀe ꞃýlꝼum beoꝺ ᵹehalᵹoeꝺ. ⁊ hýꝺa
ᵹehat Loƀe ᵹehatan habbaꝺ. Wilk. p. 134, xi. Ꝺe Loƀe
ꞃýlꝼum bepeꝺꝺoꝺ biꝺ to bꝛýꝺe. Ibid. p. 136. Ꝺe Loꝺeꝛ
bꝛýꝺ biꝺ ᵹehaten. Ibid. p. 131, xviii. The truth is, that
the mynekins were so called from the Saxon ' munuc,' because they observed the rule of the monks, while the nuns
observed the rule of the canons. This distinction is clearly
marked in the Codex Constitutionum, in the Bodleian
library, in which the mynekins are classed with the monks,
and ordered to practise the same duties : and the nuns are
classed with the priests, and commanded like them to observe chastity, and live according to their rule. Ꞃiht iꞃ
þ mýnecena mýnꞃteꝑlice macian. eꝑne ꞃꝑa ꝑe cꝑæꝺon
æꝑoꝑ be munecan.—Ꞃiht iꞃ þ ꝑꝛeoꞃtaꞃ ⁊ eꝑen ꝑel nunnan
neᵹollice liƀƀan ⁊ clæanýꞃꞃe healꝺan. Cod. Jun. 121.

suggested by his own judgment.[1] Thus also, after
the secession of the Scottish monks from Lindisfarne,
St. Cuthbert, by order of the abbot Eata, composed
a rule to be observed by the Anglo-Saxons who
supplied their place; and to this new rule was
shortly afterwards added the rule of the Italian St.
Benedict.[2] Hence it happened that in the distribution of time, the arrangement of feasts and fasts,
and the minor points of domestic discipline, these
several establishments differed from one another :
yet they all looked upon themselves as members of
the same great family, because in all every individual bound himself, at his admission, to the observance of the three obligations which are still considered essential to the monastic institute : 1st, an
unlimited obedience to the lawful commands of his
abbot ; 2nd, a life of perpetual continency ; and, 3rd,
the practice of voluntary poverty.

1. In the language of monastic discipline, the most
important of the virtues, which are not absolutely
imposed on every Christian, is obedience.[3] The

---

[1] Quod transmarinis partibus didicerat de monachorum
districtiori vita et regulari consuetudine memoriter repe-
tendo quotidianis inculcationibus subditos consuescit so-
lita mansuetudine.   Præcepta salutis secundum B. patris
Benedicti documentum, vetera novis, nova veteribus mis-
cens, nunc antiquorum instituta, nunc per se intellecta
discipulos edocuit.   Vit. S. Botulphi, Auctore Felice, in
Act. SS. Bened. iii. p. 2.

[2] Nobis regularem vitam primum componens constituit, quam usque hodie cum regula Benedicti observa-
mus.   Vit. S. Cuthb. auct. anonymo, in Oper. Min. Bed.
p. 271.

[3] Tota monachorum vita in simplicitate consistit obedientiæ, Alcuin, i. ep. xlvii. p. 61, in caritate, humilitate,
et obedientia, ep. ccxxiv. p. 289.

natural perversity of the human will is considered
as the source of every moral disorder; and to prevent it from seeking forbidden gratifications, it
should resign the right of deciding for itself, and be
taught to submit on all occasions to the determination of another. He, who aspires to the praise of a
true religious, ought, according to the patriarch of
the western monks, to place at the disposal of his
superior, all the faculties of his mind, and all the
powers of his body.[1] In the rule which St. Dunstan
promulgated for the observance of the Anglo-Saxon
monasteries, may be seen the extent to which this
maxim was carried. It regulates not only the
more important points, but descends to the minutest
particulars; requires the permission of the superior
for the most ordinary actions of life; and severely
condemns the brother, who on any occasion should
presume to determine for himself, without having
asked and obtained the advice, or rather command
of his abbot.[2] The obedience which is required,
must be prompt and cheerful;[3] it comprises the decision of the judgment no less than the resolve of the
will:[4] but admits of one exception. When the commands of the superior are contrary to the law of
God, the monk is exhorted to throw off the shackles
of obedience, and boldly to hazard the frowns and

---

[1] Quibus nec corpora sua nec voluntates licet habere in
propria potestate. Reg. S. Bened. c. 33.

[2] Nullus quippiam quamvis parum sua et quasi propria
adinventione agere præsumat. Apost. Bened. app. par. 3,
p. 92.

[3] Reg. St. Columb. c. 1; Reg. St. Bened. c. 5.

[4] Ibid. c. 5, 7.

vengeance of his abbot, rather than incur the displeasure of the Almighty.[1]

2. To obedience was added the strictest attention to chastity. The high commendations with which this virtue is mentioned in the inspired writings, had given it a distinguished place in the esteem of the first Christians. As early as the commencement of the second century, we discover numbers of both sexes, who had devoted themselves to a life of perpetual celibacy;[2] and their example was eagerly followed by the founders of the monastic institute whose successors, to the present day, bind themselves in the most solemn manner to observe it with scrupulous exactitude. To the Saxons, in whom, during the tide of conquest, the opportunity of gratification had strengthened the impulse of the passions, a life of chastity appeared the most arduous effort of human virtue : they revered its professors as beings of a nature in this respect superior to their own; and learned to esteem a religion, which could elevate a man so much above the influence of his inclinations. As they became acquainted with the maxims of the gospel, their veneration for this virtue increased : and whoever compares the dissolute manners of the pagan Saxons with the severe celibacy of the monastic orders, will be astonished at the number of male and female recluses, who, within a century after

---

[1] Admonendi sunt subditi, ne plus quam expedit, sint subjecti. St. Greg. apud Grat. 2, q. 7, can. 57.

[2] St. Just. Apol. 1, c. 10; Athenag. leg. c. 3. Yet Mosheim has discovered, that this practice owed its origin not to the doctrine of the gospel, but to the influence of the climate of Egypt! (Mos. Sæc. ii. p. 2, c. 3, xl.; Sæc. iii. p. 2, c. 3.)

the arrival of St. Augustine, had voluntarily embraced a life of perpetual continency. Nor was the pious enthusiasm confined within the walls of convents : there were many, who in the midst of courts, and in the bonds of marriage, emulated the strictest chastity of the cloister. Of this, Edilthryde exhibited to the world a remarkable example. She was the daughter of Anna, the king of the East-Angles, and at an early period of life, had bound herself by a vow of virginity. But her secret wish was opposed by the policy of her friends, and she was compelled to marry Tondberct, Ealdorman of the Girvii. Her entreaties, however, moved the breast of her husband; and compassion, perhaps religion, prompted him to respect her chastity. At his death she retired to a solitary mansion in the unfrequented Isle of Ely ; but her relations invaded the tranquillity of her retreat, and offered her in marriage to Egfrid, the son of the king of Northumbria, a prince who had scarcely reached his fourteenth year. Notwithstanding her tears, she was delivered to the care of his messengers, and conducted a reluctant victim to the Northumbrian court. Her constancy, however, triumphed over his passion : and after preserving her virginity during the space of twelve years, amid the pleasures of the palace and the solicitations of her husband, she obtained his permission to take the veil in the monastery of Coldingham. Absence revived the affection of Egfrid : he repented of his consent ; and was preparing to take her by force from her convent, when she escaped to her former residence in Ely. After a certain period, her reputation attracted round her a sisterhood of nuns, among whom she spent the remainder of her days in the practice of every monastic duty, and distinguished by her superior fervour and superior humility.[1]

To secure the chastity of their disciples, the legislators of the monks had adopted the most effectual precautions which human ingenuity could devise. The necessity of mortifying every irregular inclination was inculcated both by precept and example. The sobriety of their meals, and the meanness of their dress, perpetually recalled to their minds, that they had renounced the world and its concupiscence, and had dedicated their souls and bodies to the service of God. They were commanded to sleep in the same room : and a lamp, which was kept burning during the darkness of the night, exposed the conduct of each individual to the eye of the superior. The gates of the convent were shut against the intrusion of strangers : visits of pleasure and even of business were forbidden : and the monk, whom the necessities of the community forced from his cell, was constantly attended, during his absence, by two companions.[2] To the precautions of prudence, were added the motives of religion. The

---

[1] Ibid. Hist. Eliensis, p. 597. Hume observes (Hist. c. 1, p. 31), that Egfrid died without children, because his wife refused to violate her vow of chastity. He should, however, have added, that the king, at the time of their separation, was only twenty-six years of age, that he married a second wife, and that he lived with her fourteen years. Egfrid came to the throne in 670, separated from Edilthryde in 671, and was killed in battle in 685. Compare Beda (l. iv. c. 19, 26) with the Saxon Chronicle, an. 670, 673, 679.

[2] Wilk. Conc. pp. 97, 100; Apost. Bened. App. par. 3, pp. 78, 79.

praises of chastity were sung by the poets, and ex_
tolled by the preachers: its votaries were taught to
consider themselves as the immaculate "spouses of
the Lamb;" and to them was promised the trans-
cendent reward, which the book of the Apocalypse
describes as reserved for those, "who have not been
defiled with women." But where thousands unite
in the same pursuit, it is impossible that all should
be animated with the same spirit, or persevere with
equal resolution. Of these recluses there undoubtedly must have been some, whom passion or seduc-
tion prompted to violate their solemn engagement :
but the unsullied reputation of an immense majority
contributed to cast a veil over the shame of their
weaker brethren, and bore an honourable testimony
to the constancy of their own virtue, and the vigilance of their superiors.

3. The practice of voluntary poverty was the
third condition required from the proselyte to the
monastic state. The Saviour of mankind had
denounced the severest woes against the worldly
rich : and to his approbation of a life of poverty was
originally owing the establishment of monachism.
Anthony, a young Egyptian, who had lately succeeded to a valuable estate, was prompted, by
curiosity or devotion, to enter a church during the
celebration of the divine worship. "Go, sell that
thou hast, and give to the poor, and thou shalt have
treasure in heaven," were the first words which met
his ear. He considered them as a voice from heaven
addressed to himself; sold all his property; distributed the money to the poor; and retired into the
desert of Thebais. His reputation soon attracted a

considerable number of disciples ; and the profession of poverty was sanctified in their eyes by the conduct of their teacher. With the monastic institute this spirit was diffused through the western empire : and the same contempt of riches which distinguished the anachorets of Egypt, was displayed by the first monks of Britain. Wealth they considered as the bane of a religious life : the donations of their friends, and the patrimony of their members, were equally refused: and the labours of husbandry formed their daily occupation, and provided for their support.[1] The same discipline was anxiously inculcated by each succeeding legislator. St. Benedict informed his followers, that " they would then be truly monks, when, like their fathers, they lived by the work of their hands:"[2] and St. Columban exhorted his disciples "to fix their eyes on the treasure reserved for them in heaven, and to believe it a crime not only to have, but even to desire, more than was absolutely necessary upon earth."[3]

---

[1] Ang. Sac. Tom. ii. pp. 645, 646.

[2] Tunc vere Monachi sunt, si labore manuum vivunt sicut patres nostri. St. Ben. Reg. c. 48.

[3] Non solum superflua eos habere damnabile est, sed etiam velle. Dum in cœlis multum sint habituri, parvo extremæ necessitatis censu in terris debent esse contenti. St. Colum. Reg. c. 4. He also composed a poem in praise of poverty, of which I shall transcribe an extract, as a specimen of his poetic abilities.

> O nimium felix parcus, cui sufficit usus,
> Corporis ut curam moderamine temperet æquo.
> Non misera capitur cæcaque cupidine rerum ;
> Non majora cupit quam quæ natura reposcit;
> Non lucri cupidus nummis marsupia replet ;
> Nec molles cumulat tinearum ad pabula vestes.

The ancient discipline was long observed in the east : but the western monks gradually departed from its severity, and the departure was justified by the prospect of greater benefit. The reader has already seen that, when the irruptions of the barbarians had in several provinces swept away the principal part of the clergy, the duty of public instruction devolved on the monks, whose good fortune had preserved them from the general devastation. To perform their new functions with decency and advantage, a certain fund of knowledge was necessary: and, from the moment when the pursuit of learning was numbered among the duties of the cloister, the drudgery of manual labour began to be exchanged by a great portion of the brotherhood for the more honourable and more useful occupation of study. Monasteries were now endowed with extensive estates, adequate to the support of their inhabitants : and their revenues were constantly augmented by the liberality of their admirers. Yet the profession of poverty was not resigned. With the aid of an ingenious distinction, it was discovered, that it might still subsist in the bosom of riches ; that each individual might be destitute of property, though the wealth of the community was equal to that of its

---

Pascere non pingui procurat fruge caballos ;
Nec trepido doluit tales sub pectore curas;
Ne subitis pereat collecta pecunia flammis,
Aut fracta nummos rapiat fur improbus arca.
Vivitur argento sine, jam sine vivitur auro.
Nudi nascuntur, nudos quos terra receptat.
Divitibus nigri reserantur limina Ditis :
Pauperibusque piis cœlestia regna patescunt.
    Ep. Hunaldo discip. apud Massingham, p. 411.

most opulent neighbours. Monastic poverty was defined to consist in the abdication of *private* property : whatever the convent possessed was common to all its members : no individual could advance a claim in preference to his brethren : and every article both of convenience and necessity, was received from the hands, and surrendered at the command, of the abbot.[1] Hence it happened that, wherever the original rule was faithfully observed, this influx of property made no alteration in the habits or comforts of individuals : their clothing and diet were still the same; their hours of prayer and study, and labour and recreation, followed each other in the same course: and the additional wealth of the community was employed for the general benefit, in repairing, renewing, or beautifying the buildings, or supporting a greater number of inmates, or providing ornaments for the church, or manuscripts for the library.

VI. Yet the acquisition of estates in perpetuity by religious establishments was productive of several evils. 1st, It gave occasion to a species of fraud which cast a temporary but unmerited stain on the fair fame of the order. Men of rank and influence, under the pretence of founding monasteries, obtained from the king charters of bocland of the same tenour with those which had been granted to different abbots for that purpose. To insure the permanence of the grant, it was necessary to comply with the

---

[1] Nullus ex vobis avaritiæ studeat, nec caducas congregare divitias quærat : nec unum habeat absque patris sui licentia nummum : sufficiat unicuique communis vitæ jucunditas, seu in vestimentis, seu in cibi potusque religiositate. Alc. i. 291. ep. ccxxv.

condition; and therefore they were careful to erect certain buildings which they called the monastery, and to place in them a certain number of inmates who assumed the name of monks. They themselves were the abbots, though they did not quit their secular offices or pursuits, retaining the property in their own hands, and at their death bequeathing both monastery and lands to their heirs and posterity.[1] The success of the first adventurers encouraged others to follow their example : and this fraudulent plan of converting folcland into estates of inheritance grew up into a system, by which similar grants were purchased of the king at a competent price, and subscribed by the witan.[2] In addition, it occasionally happened, that on the death of the legitimate abbot of a real monastic establishment, his heirs took forcible possession, on the pretence that they had a right to his property, and were chargeable only with the burthen of supporting the monks. It cannot be supposed that monasteries, existing in this manner, under the government of seculars, would be a soil favourable to the development of monastic virtue ; and yet it is from the description which has been left of such monasteries, that some writers have borrowed the distinguishing traits of the portrait, which they have drawn of the Anglo-Saxon cœnobites.[3] By the real

---

[1] See note (K) on Bocland and Folcland.

[2] Bed. Oper. Min. 218—220.

[3] Inett, Orig. Sax. i. 127; Biog. Brit. art. Bede; Henry, Hist. iii. 209. Inett (ibid.) tells us, on the pretended authority of Beda, that on account of the known depravity of the English monks, people sent their children for education to the continent. He refers to Beda in his letter to Egbert : but neither in that letter nor in any other part of Beda's works is there any such statement.

monks they were disowned as having no connection with the institute : by the council of Cloveshoe it was declared a species of profaneness to give to them the name of monasteries. The same council, lamenting that in these cases the power of the holders was more than a match for the authority of the church, requires the bishop to visit such establishments occasionally, to admonish the inmates of the spiritual danger in which they live, and to provide that individuals during sickness many have the ministry of a priest, with the consent and aid of their lords.[1] After that council, we lose sight of the secular monasteries entirely : the probability is, that in process of time they settled down into parochial churches, whilst the lands remained in the undisturbed possession of the family.

2. To return to the real monks : it is generally at the commencement of religious societies that their fervour is the most active. The Anglo-Saxon cœnobites of the seventh century were, many of them, men who had abandoned the world from the purest motives, and whose chief solicitude was to practise the duties of their profession. They had embraced a life, which to the votaries of pleasure must have been most irksome and uninviting. Their devotions were long ; their fasts frequent, their diet coarse and scanty. For more than a century, wine and beer were excluded from the beverage of the monks at Lindisfarne, and the first mitigation of this severity

---

[1] Monasteria, si tamen est fas ea ita nominare, quæ temporibus istis propter vim tyrannicæ quandam avaritiæ ad religionis Christianæ statum nullatenus immutari possunt. Con. Clov. Spelm. 247. No. v.

was introduced in favour of a royal novice, Ceolwulf, the king of Northumbria.[1] The discipline which St. Boniface prescribed to his disciples at Fulda had been brought by him from England ; and from it we may conclude that the Saxon monks, whose institute was less austere than that of the Scottish cœnobites, were men of the strictest abstinence. They refrained from the use of flesh, wine, and beer, refused the labour of slaves, and cultivated with their own hands the deserts in which they had built their monastery.[2] But experience shewed how difficult it was in the midst of riches to retain that ascetic fervour which had flourished under the influence of poverty. Mitigations of the rule were occasionally allowed by the indulgence of the abbots —nor is there any reason to suppose that they were not at first justified by circumstances—but concession followed concession ; and the love of ease so natural to man, joined with national tastes and predilections, made continual encroachments on the primitive severity of the order. Of this the alterations in the monastic habit will furnish a striking instance. It is well known from contemporary writers that the Anglo-Saxons of the higher classes were passionately fond of finery of dress. Colours of the richest and most gaudy hues were held by them in the highest estimation : so much so, that by Archbishop Lullus flammea puella is used as synonymous with a lady of fashion.[3] The attire of a female

---

[1] Hoved. anno 742.

[2] Viros strictæ abstinentiæ absque carne et vino, absque sisera, et servis, proprio manuum suarum labore contentos. Ep. Bonif. p. 211.

[3] Ep. inter Bonifacianas, xlv. p. 63.

of rank is thus described by St. Aldhelm. She wore an undervest of fine linen of a violet colour, and over it a scarlet tunic with full skirts, and with wide sleeves and hood, both striped or faced with silk. The hair was curled with irons over the forehead and temples: ornaments of gold in the form of crescents encircled the neck : bracelets were worn on the arms, and rings with precious stones on the fingers, the nails of which were pared to a point to resemble the talons of the falcon. The shoes were of red leather, and stibium was employed to paint the face.[1] The dress of the men was not unlike to that of the females ; only they wore the tunic shorter, and bound the legs with fillets of various colours. Both sexes on occasions of ceremony wore mantles of blue cloth, with facings of crimson silk, ornamented with stripes or vermicular figures.[2] Now to the founders of the monastic order all such parade was an object of sovereign contempt. They had chosen for themselves and their disciples, the meanest dress of the labouring classes, that it might remind the wearer that he had bidden farewell to the vanities of the world, and looked for his reward in a future life.[3] This dress, at the time when our ancestors were converted, was made up of a coarse woollen tunic

---

[1] S. Aldhelm de Laud. Virg. 307. 364.

[2] Clavatæ—vermium imaginibus clavata. (Ep. S. Bon. p. 149.) Vestitus crurum per fasciolas. (Spel. Con. 254.) Longus fasciarum nexus. (Alc. 203.) Circumdatio capitis per coculas in modum pallii. (Spel. ibid.) This must refer to some style of wearing the cowl or hood.

[3] Non vestibus pictis superbi, sed horrentibus cilicibus humiles. (Paulin. ad. Sever. ep. vii.) Vilis tunica contemptum sæculi probet. S. Hieron. ad Rustic. ep. iv.

reaching to the feet, over which was worn a looser
garment of the same material, with a cowl and long
sleeves; no very tempting object to the admirers of
fine clothing and gaudy colours. How far it was
introduced at first among the converts, is not mentioned, but of the reluctance with which it was
accepted, we may judge, when we are told that it
required all the patience and perseverance of St.
Cuthbert to induce the Anglo-Saxons, the successors
of the Scottish monks at Lindisfarne, to adopt the
same sort of habit, which he, their instructor, was
accustomed to wear.[1] If it were ever universally
established, yet it is clear that it was superseded by
the secular dress in many monasteries, before the
end of the seventh, and probably in all, by the end
of the eighth century. This was the fact not only
with respect to monks, but also to nuns. The latter
were often of noble and princely families : and we
learn from St. Aldhelm that in his time their attire
in the cloister resembled that which they had worn
in the world, with the addition of the veil, fastened
with ribands to the head, crossing over the chest,
and falling to the feet behind.[2] It was not that

---

[1] Vestimentis utebatur communibus, ita temperanter
agens, ut horum neque munditiis neque sordibus esset
notabilis. Unde usque hodie in eodem monasterio ex-
emplo ejus observatur, nequis varii aut pretiosi coloris
habeat indumentum, şed ea maxime vestium specie sint
contenti, quam naturalis ovium lana ministrat. (Vit. S.
Cuth. int. Oper. Min. p. 82.) Yet seventy years had not
elapsed before Alcuin admonished both the bishop and
the monks at Lindisfarne to beware of the luxus vestium.
Alc. Op. i. p. 12.

[2] St. Ald. de Laud. Virg. 364. It is stated by Beda of
St. Ædilthryde that, ex quo monasterium petiit, nunquam
lineis sed solum laneis vestimentis uti voluerit, raroque in

such innovation was suffered to pass without censure and condemnation. In one of the canons passed in the council of Cloveshoe (anno 747) is was ordered that both monks and nuns should lay aside the pomp of dress, the badge of a vain and worldly spirit, and wear the habit appropriated to their manner of life, such as had been worn by those before them :[1] and in another the nuns were reminded of the poor and simple habit in which they made their vows at their profession, and informed that it was no longer lawful for them to be seen in the rich and splendid dress of women who had never renounced the world.[2] In addition, about forty years later, among the decrees of reformation issued by the legates Gregory and Theophylact, it was enacted that canons should be distinguished from monks and nuns, and these from laics, by their dress, and that such dress should be like to that which was worn by persons of the same orders in other Christian countries.[3] But the authority of bishops and the decrees of councils were no match for national taste and national vanity; the obnoxious attire seems still to have retained the ascendency : and we find Alcuin, at the beginning of the ninth century, in his letters to the inmates of

---

calidis balneis, præter imminentibus solemniis majoribus lavari voluerit, et tunc novissima omnium, lotis prius suo suarumque ministrarum obsequio, cæteris, quæ ibi essent, famulis Christi. Bed. iv. c. 19.

[1] Spelm. Con. p. 250.

[2] Non debent iterum habere indumenta sæcularia, et ornatis et nitidis vestibus incedere, quibus laicæ puellæ uti solent. Ibid. 254.

[3] Ibid. p. 294, No. iv. In the canon these other countries are called oriental, because Gaul, Germany, &c. lay to the east of England.

several monasteries, imploring them to sacrifice this empty gratification to the sense of duty,[1] and to prefer the virtues of their profession to the display of hoods of silk, of bands round the waist, of rings on the finger, and of fillets round the feet. This is the last notice which we find on the subject.[2] Probably the abuse was so deeply rooted, that the hope of extirpating it was entirely abandoned.

There was another point in which the Anglo-Saxon cœnobites had widely departed from the austerity of the more ancient discipline. In most monasteries, probably in all, the cells of the brotherhood formed a long range of small and separate buildings, which were allotted to the senior members for the purposes of study and meditation. It was in one of these that Beda was accustomed to teach, and in the same that he spent the last days of his life. Now it often happened that, where the superior was not vigilant and resolute, these small mansions were diverted from their original destination to the reception of company both of friends and strangers, to meetings of parties for recreation and amusement, and, according to Alcuin, to "secret junketings and

---

[1] See in particular his letters to the monks of Lindisfarne, Wearmouth, and Jarrow: Nolite gloriari in vanitate vestium. Hæc non est gloria sacerdotum et servorum Dei, sed contumelia. Vestimentorum cultus in clericis et maxime in monachis, reprehensio esse cognoscitur. Quid servis Dei, qui monachicæ vitæ voto se obstrinxerunt, inanis vestimentorum pompa. Vanitas est, et superbia et perditio vitæ regularis (pp. 12, 23, 281, 283).

[2] Ib. p. 203. The reader is already acquainted with his anxiety that the court of Charlemagne should not be shocked at the pomp and dress of the retinue of Archbishop Æthelheard. See Chap. ii. p. 83, note I.

furtive compotations."[1]   Allowance ought certainly
to be made for the usual exaggeration of zeal, but to
drink immoderately was the besetting sin of the
Anglo-Saxons; and there is reason to believe that
this vice occasionally introduced itself into the
cloister.   In many documents this is expressly
asserted : and Alcuin, in his correspondence with
monastic bodies, declaims with as much vehemence
against inebriety, as against vanity of apparel.[2]   By
the council of Cloveshoe all inhabitants of monasteries, both clergy and monks, are forbidden to drink
to excess themselves, or to encourage such excess in
others : they are to be content with homely food
and sober cheer; to exclude from their entertainments delicate viands, and coarse unseemly amusements; to devote their cells to silence, study, and
prayer, and never to allow them to become the
resort of gleemen, harpers, and buffoons.   With
respect to convents of nuns, it is enacted that, where
the original rule is not enforced, more attention shall
be paid to study and prayer, and less to the wearing and embroidering of works of vanity ; and that
the cells of the sisters shall be closed against lay
society, superfluous visits, and private feasting ;
practices which, if they lead to nothing worse, provoke suspicions highly dishonourable to the monastic
profession.[3]

But it is not merely to the decay of ascetic fervour
that we are to attribute the temporary extinction
of the order in the latter half of the ninth century.

---

[1] Absconditæ commessationes et furtivæ ebrietates.
Alc. i. 22.
[2] Ibid. xii. 22, 80.   [3] Spelm. Con. i. 250, 251.

There was another cause which gradually led to this result, the same which had formerly proved so beneficial in the conversion of the Northern nations—the admission of monks to holy orders. By it each community was divided into two classes; one the smaller, of clerks,[1] who looked upon themselves as masters, and who considered the others in the light of servants. "There are," says Alcuin, "monasteries of canons and monks, orders recognized in the church: in addition there are other communities without any legitimate name, in which the members of a higher grade assume the privileges of canons, and those of the lower are left in the situation of monks. These, however, must not escape the vigilance of the bishops, for they form the more numerous body in the temple of God."[2] Thus it was at the time of Alcuin, and in the very abbey which had been committed to his care. After his death, the spirit of innovation proceeded still more rapidly: in some places the conversion of the clerical members into a college of canons was silently effected, whilst in others the monastic rule was renounced and that of the canons

---

[1] At Winchecomb, the proportion was about one-sixth. In illo magno religiosorum numero vix fortassis quadraginta aut circiter in sacerdotes aut clericos ordinari cerneres: reliqua vero multitudo, heremitarum et laicorum more, diversis artificiis et aliis manuum laboribus operam dantes, pro his, quæ in necessariis defuerunt, prout ab antiquo boni fecere monachi, diligenter prospiciebant. Monast. Angl. i. 190.

[2] In his instructions to Bishop Arno, he tells him to consider quid cuique conveniat personæ, quid canonicis, quid monachis, quid tertio gradui, qui inter hos duos variatur, superiori gradui canonicis, inferiori monachis stantes. Nec tales spernendi sunt, quia tales maxime in domo Dei inveniuntur. Ep. ad Arnon. p. 168.

substituted by a formal act and with the general consent.[1] Of this there are many instances in the records of monastic establishments on the continent: and there can be no doubt that the same took place in England, as is plain from the language of several contemporary charters, and from the positive testimony of Asser in the reign of King Alfred. From him we learn that Alfred could not find in his dominions a Saxon of free or gentle birth, who would condescend to become a monk : not that there were no monasteries in Wessex, for they were numerous, but in none of them was any monastic rule observed ; and the time was gone by in England, as well as in other countries, when men sought the retirement of the cloister. He knew not how to account for it. It might perhaps arise from the devastations of the Northmen ; perhaps, and more probably, from the wealth of the people ; which made them look down with contempt on the poor

---

[1] Thus, before the appointment of Alcuin to the abbey of St. Martin's at Tours, the monks of that monastery had made so many innovations in their rule, that they assumed the name of monks or canons, as was best suited to their interests. Aliquando monachos, aliquando canonicos, aliquando neutrum vos esse, dicebatis. (Ep. Carol. Mag. apud Alc. i. 174.) Under Fridugise, the successor of Alcuin, they assembled before the tomb of St. Martin, and, laying aside the monastic, put on the canonical habit. Monachi S. Martini Turonis nemine cogente, ante corpus ejusdem, abjecto monachi schemate, schema induunt canonicale. (Ademar, in Chron. apud Frob. Op. Alcuini, i. xxx. See also a similar instance at St. Bertin's, ibid. No. xxxiv.) In the third council of Tours, in 813, we read : Aliqua sunt monasteria, in quibus jam pauci sunt monachi qui prædicti patris regulam suis abbatibus professam habeant, quippe cum ipsi abbates magis canonice quam monachice inter eos conversari videntur. Labbe, ix. 352, can. 25.

and laborious profession of monachism.[1] But whatever may have been the real cause, it is a certain fact that the monastic institute had ceased to exist in England at the beginning of the ninth century ; the manner in which it was resuscitated at a later period by Alfred and his successors, will be detailed in a subsequent chapter.

---

[1] Nullum de sua propria gente nobilem et liberum hominem, qui monasticam voluntarie vellet subire vitam, habebat. Per multa retroacta annorum curricula monasticæ vitæ desiderium ab illa tota gente necnon a multis aliis gentibus funditus desierat, quamvis perplurima adhuc monasteria in illa regione constructa permaneant, nullo tamen regulam illius vitæ ordinabiliter tenente. Nescio quare—aut pro alienigenarum infestationibus, aut etiam pro nimia illius gentis in omni genere divitiarum abundantia, propter quam multo magis id genus despectæ monasticæ vitæ fieri existimo. (Asser, p. 61.) The truth of his assertion as to other countries is proved by many local councils, which allow the name of monks to a few houses only in which the rule of St. Benedict was observed. See Council of Aix la Chapelle, in 801.

CHAPTER VI.

DONATIONS TO THE CHURCH.

WE have already seen that every band of missionaries, from whatever country they came, or whatever Anglo-Saxon tribe they visited, were received with kindness and hospitality by the sovereign. He protected the strangers from insult; he provided for their subsistence; and, as soon as he became a Christian, made to them, after the custom of his people, donations of land, either from his own property or from the common property of the nation. Ethelbert of Kent, as he was the first of the royal proselytes, stands the foremost in the list of royal benefactors. He withdrew from Canterbury to Reculver, and bestowed the former city with its dependencies on the missionaries: with proportionate munificence he founded the episcopal see of Rochester; and, as soon as Saberct, the tributary king of Essex, had received the sacred rite of baptism, assigned in that country an ample territory for the

support of the bishop Mellitus and his clergy.[1]   The
other Saxon monarchs strove to equal the merit of
Ethelbert, and the fame of their liberality has been
gratefully transmitted to posterity by the ecclesiastical historians.   Kinegils of Wessex gave the city of
Dorchester to his teacher Birinus, and from his son
and successor Coinwalch, the church of Winchester
received a grant of all the lands within the distance
of seven miles from that capital:[2] the isle of Selsey,
containing eighty-seven hides, together with two
hundred and fifty slaves, was bestowed by Edilwalch
of Sussex, on the missionary St. Wilfrid;[3] that of
Lindisfarne by King Oswald, on the Scottish bishop
St. Aidan;[4] and the munificence of Oswald's successors is sufficiently attested by the great wealth
of the Northumbrian bishops.   The motives which
actuated these princes, and the manner in which they
proceeded, may be learned from an interesting document of the early date of the 6th of November, 676,
one of the charters issued by Osric, the first of the
Christian kings or viceroys of the Hwiccas, the inhabitants of Worcestershire:—" After we had received," says that prince, " the sacrament of baptism,
when the doctrine of the gospel was, by the grace of
God, preached in our country, and the senseless idols
of paganism had been levelled with the ground, we
made it our first object, for the increase of the orthodox faith, to establish an episcopal see in conformity
with the canons: and now, that the grace of God
displays itself far and near, we have resolved to found,

---

[1] Bed. l. i. c. 33, l. ii. c. 3;   Monast. Ang. i. p. 18;
Ang. Sac. i. p. 333.   [2] Ibid. pp. 190, 288.
[3] Bed. l. iv. c. 13.   [4] Ib. l. iii. c. 3.

in separate places, monasteries both of men and women devoted to the service of God; that, where the devil formerly deceived mankind with the doctrines of error, the clerical orders may chant the praises of the Lord;—wherefore I, Osric the king, for the benefit of my soul and the pardon of my sins, have resolved to make this donation to the honour of the Lord: that is, I give to thee, the abbess Bertane, who through devotion to Christ, and the hope of everlasting happiness, hast consecrated thyself a handmaid of God, one hundred folclands lying near to the city of Bath, that therein thou mayest found a convent of holy virgins," &c.[1] Thus, in proportion as Christianity pushed its conquests, new churches and monasteries were founded; to the grants from princes were added donations from wealthy individuals; and the heads of the clerical and monastic establishments found themselves raised to an equality with the temporal thanes, called to the great council of the nation, and vested with rank and wealth, which rendered them respectable even in the eyes of those who still adhered to the idolatry of their fathers.[2]

---

[1] At vero nunc, cum gratia superna longe lateque profusius eniteceret, cœnobialia etiam loca sparsim virorum, sparsimque virginum Deo famulantium erigenda statuimus, ut ubi truculentus et nefandus prius draco errorum deceptionibus serviebat, nunc versa vice ordo in clero conversantium Domino protrocinante gaudens tripudiet. Quamobrem ego, &c. Cod. Diplom. p. 16.

[2] It has often been said that females of high rank, such as queens and abbesses, were members of the witenagemot, or national council. I see great reason to doubt it. The conference at Whitby, where Queen Eanfled, and the abbess Hild, were present, was not a council of the

I. The reader is aware that landed property among the Anglo-Saxons was divided into bocland and folcland. The lands bestowed on the church were of the former description. If the donation came from a subject, he could give no other, for his bocland alone was at his disposal : if from the sovereign, unless he chose to give a parcel out of his own bocland,[1] he was accustomed to convert, with the consent of the witan, a certain portion of the national folcland into an estate of perpetual inheritance.[2] But that which rendered the church lands of greater value was their frequent enfranchisement from the services and burthens to which the lands of other subjects were liable; burthens which may be divided into two classes: those which had for their object the public service and safety, and those which tended only to the emolument of the king, or of the king's officers, the ealdorman, and the reeve.

---

witan, but a meeting for the adjustment of differences between two religious parties. We find, indeed, a few subscriptions of queens to charters, but they may have been asked to subscribe out of compliment, because they were present with the king when the signatures to the instrument were collected. (Cod. Dip. 50, 95, 114, 146.) As to abbesses, I do not recollect ever to have met with them as present in a national council, except when they were parties to some suit, or solicitors for some favour. Cod. Dip. 177, 281.

[1] There can be no doubt that the Anglo-Saxon kings possessed family estates of inheritance. When Beda mentions the lands given to Bennet Biscop for the foundation of the monastery at Wearmouth, he is careful to add that the king gave them—de suo—out of his own property. (Bed. Op. Min. p. 143.) In the same sense I interpret the term, lands juris mei, proprii mei juris, in many charters.

[2] See the note (K).

The burthens or services of the first class were the bryge-bot, or contribution towards the repair of bridges and highways; the burgh-bot, or contributions towards the maintenance of the burghs or places of defence; and the fyrd, or contribution towards the military, and also, at a later period, the naval force of the kingdom. These were called the three-fold need, in Latin the trinoda necessitas, or communis labor : and, as they had for their object the public welfare and safety, might not inaptly be termed national services. With respect to them there exists no doubt : they are fully and expressly described in the laws and charters. But there were other, and probably far more onerous services, imposed for the personal emolument of the king, and of his officers ; which appear to have been originally incident to all folc-land, and to have been still reserved, on the conversion of the folcland into bocland. Being founded on custom only, they were not very accurately defined : and thence frequently became sources of arbitrary oppression on the part of the sovereign and his ealdormen and reeves.[1] Of such services we possess no correct list; but many are accidentally mentioned in scattered passages of deeds of enfranchisement : for example, payments in kind out of the produce of the land and the waters, probably as an acknowledgment to the king; contributions of provisions for the royal household, either when the king chanced to be in the neighbourhood, or at certain specified

---

[1] This I infer from the frequent use in enfranchisements of the clause—ab omnibus causis notis vel ignotis, and jussiones incognitæ (Ibid. 205); which seem to denote unknown claims set up by the royal officers.

times in the course of the year; the obligation of
finding board, lodging, and carriages for his officers,
or for messengers to him or from him ; of maintaining his horses, hounds, and hawks, as well as their
keepers ; of supplying pasturage to a certain number
of his swine; of furnishing workmen and timber
towards the building or the repair of his villa; and support to persons claiming it under his warrant, besides
the payment of yearly gafols or rents, and of the bots
or compensations arising out of the punishment of
offenders.[1] Nor were these services demanded by
the king only : the same, but probably to a smaller
amount, were claimed by the ealdorman, or ealdormen
of the district, who often in cases of enfranchisement
received a sum of money or a parcel of land as an

---

[1] For example, we find mention of the tributum quod
regibus datur; of payments ex fructibus sylvarum, agro-
rumque, et utilitatibus fluminum et captura piscium; and
of munuscula in sæculare convivium regis vel principis
exacta (Cod. Dipl. i. 120); opera regis vel principis (Ib.
204); constructio regalis villæ, and pastus regis et principum (Ib. 314); the felling of timber ad regis vel principis
ædificia (Ib. 313); pastus duodecim hominum (Ib. 254);
and pastus regum et principum, ducum et præfectorum, ex-
actorum, equorum et falconum, accipitrum et canum, et
illorum hominum quos festigmen appellamus refectio ; para-
frithi, et omnes difficultates regalis vel sæcularis servitii.
Ib. 288. See also 270, 272, 313, ii. 30, 60. From vol. ii.
p. 30, it appears that sometimes particular rights were
reserved. Bertulf of Mercia frees a monastery from Cum-
feorme and Eafore, the burthen of supplying board and
lodging to comers and goers on the king's service, but with
this exception, that if messengers to the king arrive from
beyond the sea, or from Wessex, or from Northumbria,
and chance to come between nine in the morning and three
in the afternoon, they and their suite shall be entitled to
dine at the abbey; if later in the day, to board and lodging
for the night, but must depart in the morning.

indemnity, in lieu of the accustomed services.[1] Hence it probably came that in later times the earl, the successor of the ealdormen, took as his perquisite the third penny of the royal income from the county. It is reasonable to infer from the language of Beda,[2] that at first the church lands were exempt from all secular burthens whatsoever. Such lands had been given to God himself; with what propriety could they be brought into a state of servitude to men? Their possessors were not of a worldly, but of a spiritual profession: what but spiritual services could be exacted from them? But as monasterial establishments multiplied, it became necessary to modify this doctrine. The distinction just explained was introduced ; and the services of the first class, the bryge-bot, the burgh-bot, and the fyrd, were declared so essential to the safety of the nation, and of course of the churches themselves, that from them no exemption on any pretext could be admitted. So we are informed about the middle of the eighth century by the kings of Mercia, Ethelbald and Offa ;[3]

---

[1] Thus, for the enfranchisement of the lands of Heanbury (anno 836), the ealdorman Sigrede received as indemnity 600 shillings in gold, and the ealdorman Muckle ten hides of land at Crockley. Cod. Dipl. i. 315. Humberct, prince of the Tonseti, surrendered to the monastery of Breodune, all the perquisites belonging to him and his successors for a sum of money presented in a beautiful drinking cup ornamented with gold. Ib. ii. 31, Anno 844. In 966, Ælfstan, bishop of Rochester, bought the freedom of Bromley, both of king Edgar, for eighty mancuses of gold and six pounds of silver, and of the king's prefect, Wulfstan, for thirty mancuses of gold. Ib. 411.

[2] Bed. Op. Min. ii. pp. 145, 217-8-9.

[3] In 749, Ethelbald calls them services quæ communiter

and such we afterwards find to have been the practice to the end of the Anglo-Saxon period. We
meet, indeed, occasionally with charters containing
such exemptions; but they are charters, which,
liable to suspicion on other accounts, are rendered
still less worthy of credit from the appearance in
them of a clause which is absent from every grant of
undoubted authenticity.

But with respect to the second class of services, it
was far otherwise. As they were rights personal to
the sovereign, and sources of profit to him, he was
at liberty to reserve them or transfer them at the
same time that he transferred the land, and with
such limitations as he chose to prescribe. By some

---

fruenda sunt, omnique populo edicto regis facienda jube11-
tur: id est, in structionibus pontium, et necessariis defen-
sionibus arcium contra hostes. Cod. Dipl. i. 120. So
Offa, about the year 790, frees some lands ab omni tributo
parvo aut majore publicalium rerum, et a cunctis operibus
regis vel principis in posterum præter expeditionalibus
causis, et pontium structionem, et arcium munimentum;
quod omni populo necesse est agere, atque ab eo opere
neminem excusatum esse. Ib. 204. I will add another
charter of Cœnulf of Mercia, in 811, because it not only
shews the distinction between the two classes of services,
but also between those claimed by the king and those by
his officers, and the confirmation of the grant by the witan.
Integram quoque libertatem his terrulis atque ruriculis rex
Cœnulf cum auctoritate *supradicti concilii* decreverat, ut
perpetuo sint liberatæ ab omnibus publicis tributis, et a
cunctis regalium rerum vel operum debitis, sive *principum
seu ducum vel procuratorum*, aut etiam ab omni sæcularium
causarum rerumve gravedine, exceptis his debitis, id est,
pontis instructionem, et contra paganos expeditionem,
atque arcis munitionem destructionemve, cum tamen hoc
universo populo opportunitas summa poposcerit, et necessitas eximia hoc agendum cunctos undecunque coherceret,
tunc et illi rite sua reddent. Ib. 243.

charters the land is wholly enfranchised : by others partially ; by some gratuitously, and in reward of services already performed : by others in return for an equivalent given at the time, in lands or money. The more ancient enfranchisements are termed grants of church right, or church freedom : an argument that they were confined exclusively to grants for religious purposes : they even retained that appellation for a long time after they became common to lay and church property ;. nor was the distinguishing adjunct of *church* totally dropped before the beginning of the ninth century.[1] It cannot, however, have been, as sometimes is stated, that enfranchisement was essential to the creation of boclands, or estates of inheritance : for we have numbers of charters creating such estates without a word of enfranchisement, and others granting enfranchisement to such estates long after they had been created.[2]

---

[1] See grants of jus ecclesiasticum to laymen, Cod. Dipl. i. 123, 154, 159, 169, 174, &c.; but after the year 800, we generally meet with the Latin word " libertas," or the Saxon "freodom," without the adjunct.

[2] See charters of bocland without enfranchisement (Cod. Dipl. i. 137, 152, 191, 211, 216). Cœnulf of Mercia had unjustly taken possession of lands belonging to the see of Canterbury. In 825, at Cloveshoe, the witan, under King Beornalf, decreed that Cwœndrythe, the daughter and heiress of Cœnulf, should restore those lands to Archbishop Wulfred. Cwœndrythe and her kinsfolk claimed the protection of the king, who prevailed with great difficulty on the archbishop to accept, in lieu of the original lands, four other parcels of land, the property of Cwœndrythe, amounting to 100 folclands ; and, as only one of these parcels had hitherto been enfranchised, granted the same benefit to the other three, that they might be worth the acceptance of Wulfred. Cum consilio ejusdem synodi illam terram, quæ non fuerat antea liberata hujus præ-

In 854 was passed a general measure of partial
enfranchisement for the kingdom of Wessex. In
that year, at Wilton, in the presence of the witan,
King Ethelwulf signed a charter, stating that, " for
the benefit of his soul, the prosperity of his kingdom,
and the safety of his people, he, with the advice of
his bishops, earls, and great men, had come to the
resolution of freeing for ever the tenth part of the
lands throughout the kingdom (not only those belonging to the churches, but also to his thanes) from all
secular services and burthens; and that in return for
this grant, Alstan, bishop of Sherborne, and Swithin,
bishop of Winchester, had engaged that certain religious services should be weekly performed on the
Saturday for the benefit of the king, and of the great
men, subscribers to the charter."[1] From the mention of the two West-Saxon bishops, we may infer
that this grant concerned the kingdom of Wessex
alone. But the next year, just before his pilgrimage
to Rome, on Nov. 5th, at Winchester, in the church

---

dictæ donationis, eadem libertate liberabat, sicut et altera
terra æt Hearge jamdudum liberata fuerat, et in altera
charta conscripta habetur. (Ib. i. 282.) In vol. ii. 256,
King Edmund, in 945, appears to enfranchise, in favour of
Bishop Alfred, an estate in land, which he and his predecessors had long possessed as belonging to the bishopric.
In the same volume, p. 111, Ethelred frees the abbey of
Berkley from some services of which it had formerly been
left ' unfreed.'

[1] Pro meæ remedio animæ et regni prosperitate, et
populi mihi collati salute, consilium salubre cum episcopis,
comitibus, et cunctis optimatibus meis perfeci, ut decimam
partem terrarum per regnum, non solum sanctis ecclesiis
darem, verum etiam ministris nostris in eodem constitutis
in perpetuam libertatem concederem, ita ut talis donatio
fixa incommutabilisque permaneat, ab omni regali servitio,
et sæcularium absoluta servitute. Cod. Dipl. ii. 51, 52.

of St. Peter, before the high altar, and in the presence of the kings of Mercia and East-Anglia,[1] and of the archbishops, bishops, abbots, abbesses, ealdormen, thanes, and lieges of the land, he subscribed a second charter of the same tenour, in which, having observed that they lived in times of alarm and peril,· from the repeated descent of the northern pirates, he states that it has been resolved by the witan to solicit the protection of God, and that, with that view, he has granted the immunities of holy church to a certain portion of the lands of inheritance in the possession of persons of all ranks, whether they be men or women, servants of God, or lay thanes; that is, to every tenth mansion, or, where there are not ten mansions, to the tenth part of the whole, so that they may be exempt from all secular services, all rents to the king, great or small, and all the taxations called witerden, in order that the holder may pray for him with less interruption, inasmuch as he has eased them of a part of their servitude.[2]

There can be no doubt that the owners of land would be careful to avail themselves of the benefits held out to them by this charter: and, from docu-

---

[1] This would justify the inference that by this charter the grant was extended to those kingdoms; but its accuracy may be doubted, as the presence of these kings is omitted in Malmesbury's copy. Malm. i. 170.

[2] Ut aliquam portionem terrarum hæredetariam, antea possidentibus omnibus gradibus, sive famulis et famulabus Dei Deo servientibus, sive laicis miseris (ministris, in the other copy), semper decimam mansionem, ubi minimum sit tamen partem decimam, in libertatem perpetuam donari dijudicavi, ut sit tuta et libera ab omnibus, &c. (Malms. i. 170; Cod. Dipl. ii. 56.) There are several copies in different writers, all incorrect by themselves, but easily corrected from each other.

ments which have descended to us, it would appear
that they procured from the king copies of the
original charter, with an additional clause containing
the metes and bounds of the lands in their possession to which its provisions extended.[1] It is manifest that this grant must have been a considerable
sacrifice on the part of the king. Still it applied
only to one-tenth part of the lands previously unen-
franchised : the other nine parts remained subject
to the same charges as before ; and the purchase of
charters of enfranchisement from the sovereign continued in full practice during the remainder of the
Saxon times.

---

[1] See a copy obtained by the thane Wiferth for the
enfranchisement of one Cassata, ibid. 51; another by the
monks of Malmesbury, ibid. 52 ; and a grant to the
thane Dunne pro decimatione agrorum, quam, Deo donante,
cæteris ministris meis facere decrevi, ibid. 57. I am aware
that this grant by Ethelwulf has been very differently
explained by several writers : but it is plainly a general
grant of immunity to actual possessors of bocland—
portionem hereditariam antea possidentibus—and every
reader accustomed to ancient charters will recognize in it
the language of charters of enfranchisement. I may add
that Asser, who wrote in the court of Ethelwulf's son
Alfred, describes it in the same sense, as a charter of
enfranchisement. " He freed the tenth part of his whole
kingdom from all rents and services to the king, and with
the signature of the cross of Christ offered it a sacrifice to
the Tri-une God for the redemption of his soul, and of the
souls of his ancestors." Decimam totius regni sui partem ab
omni regali tributo et servitio liberavit, sempiternoque
graphio in cruce Christi pro redemptione animæ suæ et antecessorum suorum uni et trino Deo immolavit. (Asser, 8.)
The only doubt, it appears to me, is, whether it extended
to the tenth of all lands not hitherto enfranchised, or was
confined to those whose enfranchised lands did not com-
prise one-tenth part of their property.

II. The exemption from these burthens led the
way to the possession of privileges still more honourable and profitable.   It was natural that the prince
who founded a church or monastery should seek to
display his munificence, and should look on the
benefits and distinctions which he lavished on its inmates as reflecting a lustre on their benefactor. The
superior, the representative of the body, was frequently invested by him with some of the rights of
royalty, such as that of receiving toll on the trans-
port of merchandize through his domain, of levying
bots or fines for every breach of the peace, of determining civil suits among his vassals, of pursuing the
thief beyond his boundary, and of trying a multitude
of offences within his own courts.[1]   That the principal spiritual thanes enjoyed these privileges no less
that the secular thanes, cannot be doubted : but in
what manner were they conveyed to the possessors?
Among the multitude of charters, which have reached
us, there are very few indeed to be found containing
any mention of such rights, or any transfer of them
from the crown to the grantee.[2]   To me the follow-

---

[1] Cod. Dip. i. 293, 298; ii. 79. Wilk. 157.
[2] So we are assured by Mr. Kemble in his valuable
remarks on the subject (Introd. to Cod. Dipl. i. p. xliii.).
We have, indeed, charters pretending to be of higher date
than the reign of Edward the Confessor, and conveying
those privileges under the well-known formula of Sac and
Soc, Grithbrice and Burhbrice, Toll and Team, &c.   But
they were manifestly fabricated after the conquest; not, I
conceive, for the purpose of establishing new and unfounded
claims, but of protecting old and undoubted rights against
the cavils of the Norman lawyers.   There is, however, a
direct grant of royal privileges in the charter of Alfred,
which he made to the church of Shaftesbury, when his
daughter Agelyve entered that convent; a grant of 100

ing seems the most probable explanation. Before
the grant by the king, certain powers were exercised,
and certain perquisites received by his officers, by
the ealdorman, and by the court of the hundred :
after the grant, their claim to the exercise of such
rights, and consequently to the receipt of such
perquisites, was extinguished : whence I think it
probable that from that moment all the authority
which they had possessed, civil, criminal, or fiscal,
became of course vested in the lord of the soil without any further grant.

III. The charter of Osric at the commencement
of this chapter has pointed out the motives which led
to the first monasterial establishments : as Christianity extended its conquests, other causes came into
operation tending constantly to augment the possessions of the church, partly by new religious foundations, partly by additions to the existing endowments. There was the general spirit of the age
which pointed out this as the most useful and
honourable purpose to which superfluous wealth
could be devoted. Many considered it their duty to
promote by their donations the celebration of the
public worship. Engaged themselves, by their
station and habits of life, in other and distracting
pursuits, they trusted that they might compensate

---

hides of land," with," he adds, " the same " (' the rights of
my crown ' in the old Latin translation) " that I myself had
—that is, with forsteal, and hamsocne, and mundbreche "
—or the right of exacting the lawful bot or compensation
for the three offences of assaulting a man on the highway,
or of entering or attempting to enter his house by force,
or of violating the protection granted to him by the king.
Cod. Dipl. ii. 106.

for their own deficiency by contributing to the support of a class of men, who, relieved from all worldly cares, should have for their chief occupation to offer daily the Christian sacrifice, and to chant daily the praises of the Almighty. 2nd, With others it was the desire of securing permanent relief for the poor: and these frequently, instead of relying on the doubtful fidelity of their heirs, made donations to the church accompanied with the obligation of constantly maintaining a certain number of paupers in a particular district, or of distributing charity to a certain amount on particular days.[1] 3rd, On the other hand, there were numbers who had acquired opulence by a course of successful crimes, and had deferred the duty of restitution till the victims of their injustice had disappeared.[2] These men were frequently induced, towards the decline of life, to confer, as a tardy atonement, some part of their property on the church : and when they neglected it, their neglect was frequently compensated by the piety of their children and descendants.[3] 4th, To such motives may be added, the want of heirs, the hope of obtaining spiritual aid from the prayers of the clergy, gratitude for the protection which the church always offered to the unfortunate, and a wish to defeat the rapacity of a powerful adversary ; all of which contributed in a greater or less degree to augment the possessions of religious establishments. It

---

[1] Cod. Dipl. i. 291, 293, 298.

[2] Cod. Dipl. i. 293, 298.

[3] This is often the meaning of the words pro remedio, salute, redemptione animæ meæ et priorum, antecessorum meorum; for unc bucu and ealle uncɲe elbɲum: for us both and all our elders, &c.

should, however, be remembered, that if many circumstances tended to enrich, there were also many
which tended to pauperize the church; and that
each list of benefactions may be nearly balanced by
an opposite catalogue of losses and privations. 1st,
The liberality of their friends was shackled, and
liable to be defeated, by the restraints of the law.
After the death of the donor or testator, the validity of his gift or bequest was often disputed, and
generally on the ground that he had no legal right to
alienate the property from his kindred. Many suits
of this description were brought before the assembly
of the witan, whose decisions appear, occasionally at
least, to have been given more in accordance with
might than justice. Thus, to please Offa of Mercia,
it was held that Egbert king of Kent, being a vassal
of the Mercian crown, had not the power to convey
or enfranchise bocland without the confirmation of
his superior; and on that principle a valuable estate
was wrested from the church of Canterbury, the
title to which was derived from a charter issued
by Egbert.[1]　2nd, The easy concessions of former
kings often appeared unreasonable to their successors, whose wants were more pressing, or whose
veneration for the church was less indulgent. Sensible of their power in this world, they despised the
threats of future vengeance denounced by their predecessors against those who should violate their

---

[1] Quasi non liceret Ecgberto agros hæreditario jure
scribere. (Cod. Dip. i. 240.) See also 138. Sæpe ex igno-
rantia, sæpe, quod est execrabilius, ex improbitate contingit
ut denegatio rerum vere et recte gestarum nascatur. (Ib.
189.) Also Gale, 322, 6, 7.

charters; and sometimes with, often without, the
pretext of justice, they seized the manors, or still
more frequently set aside the enfranchisements possessed by religious bodies. The two first, who
invaded the patrimony of the church in this manner, were Ceolred of Mercia, and Osred of Northumbria. The former perished suddenly; the latter
fell by the sword of his enemies; and in a letter
from St. Boniface in Germany their fate was held
forth as a warning to Ethelbald of Mercia, if he continued to follow their example.[1] The king, it would
seem, was alarmed : for before the close of the year
he subscribed a charter granting to every church in
his kingdom a general exemption from all secular
services.[2] But Offa, his successor, paid little respect
to this grant : that powerful and rapacious prince
seized the lands of some monasteries, and revoked
the enfranchisements of others, and found the
witan sufficiently obsequious to confirm his iniqui-
tous proceedings.[3] Some atonement was made
during the short reign of Egfrith, his son and successor:[4] but Cœnulf imitated the rapacity of Offa:[5]

---

[1] Spelm. Conc. 235, 241.

[2] Cod. Dipl. i. 119. Anno 747.

[3] He disputed the right of the Bishop of Worcester to
six large properties. That prelate was forced to compound
with him by giving up to him some lands with the ' most
celebrated monastery at Bath.' (Cod. Dip. i. 173.) Archbishop Æthelheard speaks of Offa's rapacity sine norma
justitiæ. Ibid. 231.   [4] Malm. i. 130.

[5] It was found by the testimony of the whole people
that Archbishop Wulfred had been despoiled omni domi-
natione propria in his liberis monasteriis at Suðmynꞃtꞃe æt
Ræculꝼe omnibus rebus ac possessionibus quæ ad illos
pertinebant cum violentia ac rapacitate ejusdem præfati
regis Cœnulfi. Cod. Dipl. i. 280.

and in each succeeding century the royal charters
bear testimony to the continued occurrence of such
usurpations by ordering the restoration to the church
of lands, of which it had been previously despoiled.[1]
3rd, The rapacity of the monarch often stimulated
that of the nobles, who viewed with a jealous eye
the wealth of the clergy, and considered the donations of their ancestors as so many injuries offered to
their families. Whenever the favour of the sovereign,
or the anarchy in which the Saxon governments were
frequently plunged, afforded a prospect of impunity,
they seldom failed to extort by threats, or seize by
violence, the lands which were the objects of their
avarice.[2] 4th, The prelates themselves often contributed to the spoliation of their sees. They assumed a right of granting to their friends and
retainers a portion of lands to be holden by them
and their heirs during a certain number of lives or

---

[1] Thus Edred restored to the church of Winchester
one hundred mansions, restituendo quod injuste a me vel a
predecessoribus meis possessum fuerat vel minutum.
Ib. ii. 287. Edwy restores also a rus injuste abstractum,
ib. 314; and again two others, jam nuper tyrannide
abstracta, 338. From these and many other instances, I
am led to suspect, but have no direct proof, that after
the year 800 our kings adopted the practice of the continental sovereigns, who often seized the lands of the church
and gave them as fieffs to individuals. It is certain that
they did so with respect to the monasteries destroyed by
the Danes. Thus Edred restored to Abingdon the lands,
which Alfred, after its demolition by the barbarians,
malorum præventus consilio in suos suorumque usus
redegerat. Malm. de Pont. l. ii. fol. 143 b.

[2] Several lawsuits of this description are mentioned in
the Codex Diplomaticus, and in the histories of Ramsey
and Ely. See particularly pp. 416, 483, 487, 512.

years, and after that period to revert to the church : but their successors often found it difficult to recover what had thus been alienated, and were compelled either to relinquish their claims, or to continue the original grant in the same family.[1] 5th, War was another source of misfortune to the church. Its property was indeed guarded by the most terrific excommunications: but in the tumult of arms, spiritual menaces were despised : and if some princes respected the lands of the clergy, others ravaged them without mercy, and reduced the defenceless incumbents to a state of absolute poverty. So exhausted was the see of Rochester by the devastations of Edilred, king of Mercia, that two successive bishops resigned their dignity, and sought from the charity of strangers that support which they could not obtain in their own diocese.[2] From the whole

---

[1] Several curious charters of this description are printed in Smith's Beda (app. xxi.) ; Kemble's Codex Diplom. (i. 109, 157, 177, et seq., ii. 33, 62, et seq.) ; and a catalogue of them is preserved by Wanley (Ant. litt. Septen. p. 255). The celebrated St. Oswald was compelled to defend himself before King Edgar against the charge of having dilapidated the revenues of his church of Worcester, by the number of these læns, or estates for lives, which he had granted. His defence is, that he had granted them on terms beneficial to the bishopric, as the holders were bound to attend the bishop on horseback as his vassals ; to pay all the dues of the church; to aid in the carriage of lime for the building of the tower and the bridge ; to give their assistance at the time of taking his venison ; to perform a multitude of other services; and to be always ready at his command or that of the king, and subject to the orders of the chief officer over the bishopric, in virtue of the benefice which has been granted them : propter beneficium quod illis præstitum est, secundum illius voluntatem, et terrarum quod quisque possidet quantitatem. Cod. Dipl. i. Introd. xxxv.   [2] Bed. Hist. iv. c. 2.

history of the Saxon kingdoms, it is evident that the temporal prosperity of the church depended on the character of the prince who swayed the sceptre. If he declared himself its patron, the stream of wealth flowed constantly into its coffers : if he were needy and rapacious, it presented the most easy and expeditious means to satisfy his avarice. During the revolutions of each century, it alternately experienced the fluctuations of fortune : and the clergy of the same monastery at one time possessed property as ample as the most wealthy of their neighbours ; at another were deprived of the conveniences, perhaps even of the necessaries of life.[1]

IV. Here it may not be amiss to notice the charges to which the donations of their friends have exposed the clergy of former times, from the prejudices of later writers ; charges of covetousness, fraud, and hypocrisy. The votaries of the cloister among our ancestors are frequently exhibited to us as men greedy of wealth, and adepts in the art of extracting it from the credulity of the people ; as seeking the acquisition of riches under the profession of poverty, and of honours and distinctions through the vow of humility and obedience.[2] But to investigate with accuracy the habits and characters of men who lived at a remote period is a task which requires a cool and cautious mind, emancipated from the control of religious antipathies and prepossessions : otherwise fictions of the imagination will take the place of real motives and facts ; and what may have been the guilt of an individual, will be attributed without

---

[1] See an extraordinary instance in Ingulf, p. 11.
[2] See note (L).

scruple to a whole body. If, as we are repeatedly told, in the theology of the monks—and under that name are included all the inmates of the ancient monasteries, whether monks or clergy—"to patronise the order was esteemed the first of virtues;" if they taught that "the foundation of a monastery was the secure road to heaven, and that a bountiful donation would, without repentance, efface the guilt of the most deadly sins,"[1] they were undoubtedly corrupters of morality, and enemies of mankind. But of these doctrines no vestige is to be found in their writings, and we have yet to learn from what source their accusers have derived the information. If they had consulted Beda, he would have taught them, that "no offering, though made to a monastery, could be pleasing to the Almighty, if it proceeded from an impure conscience;"[2] from the council of Calcuith, they might have learned, that "repentance was then only of avail, when it impelled the sinner to lament his past offences, and restrained him from committing them again;"[3] and in the acts of the synod of Cloveshoe they might have seen, how repugnant such interested morality was to the genuine doctrine of the Saxon church. "The man," say the prelates, "who indulges his passions, in the confidence that his charities will procure his salvation, instead of making an acceptable offering to God, throws himself into the arms of Satan."[4] Alms, in-

---

[1] Hume, Hist. pp. 42, 77; Sturges, Reflect. on Popery, p. 31; Hen. vol. iv. p. 299.   [2] Bed. ep. ad Egb. p. 312.
[3] Admissa deflere, et fleta in postmodum non admittere. Wilk. Con. p. 181.
[4] Sua Deo dare videntur, (sed) seipsos diabolo per flagitia dare non dubitantur. Id. p. 98, xxvi.

deed, were enumerated by the monks among the
most efficacious means of disarming the justice of
the Almighty: and in this opinion they were supported by the clearest testimonies of the inspired
writings.[1] But they did not point out their own
body as the sole, or the principal object of charity.
To the sinner, who was anxious to make his peace
with heaven, they proposed works of public utility.
They exhorted him to repair the roads and erect
bridges ; to purchase the freedom of slaves ; to exercise the duties of hospitality ; and to clothe and
support the distressed peasants, whom the broils of
their petty tyrants often reduced to the lowest state
of wretchedness.[2] If, among these different objects,
frequent donations were made to the religious houses,
the impartial reader will consider them as proofs
rather of merit than of avarice. For men, however vicious they may be, are seldom blind to the
vices of their teachers. The malignity of the human
heart is gratified with discovering the defects of those
who claim the reputation of superior virtue. Had
the monks been, as they are so frequently described,
an indolent, avaricious, and luxurious race, they would
never have commanded the confidence, nor have been
enriched by the benefactions of their countrymen.

V. If we read the history of these religious
societies in the only documents in which it has been
really preserved, we shall find that the Anglo-Saxon
monks of the seventh century were, many of them,
men who had abandoned the world through the
purest motives ; and whose great solicitude was to
practise the duties of their profession. They had

---

[1] Dan. iv. 24; Matt. xxiv. 35; Luke xi. 14.
[2] Wilk. pp. 140, 236.

embraced a life, in appearance at least, irksome and uninviting. Their devotions were long; their fasts frequent; their diet coarse and scanty. For more than a century wine and beer were, in the monastery of Lindisfarne, excluded from the beverage of the monks; and the first mitigation of this severity was introduced in favour of Ceolwulf, a royal novice.[1] The discipline, which St. Boniface prescribed to his disciples at Fulda, he had learned in England; and from it we may infer, that the Saxon monks, whose institute was less austere than that of the Scottish cœnobites, were men of the strictest abstinence. They refrained from the use of flesh, wine, and beer, refused the assistance of slaves, and with their own hands cultivated the deserts which surrounded them.[2] The voluntary professors of a life so severe and mortified ought certainly to be acquitted of the more sordid vices; and if they consented to accept the donations of their friends, we may safely ascribe such acceptance to lawful and honourable motives. The truth is, that to the church the Anglo-Saxons were indebted for every step which they advanced in civil as well as in religious improvement, and the donations which they made to religious bodies were in general amply repaid by the benefits which they derived from those bodies. Of this we have an admirable exemplification in that work of Beda, in which he relates in detail the origin of his monastery, and the travels, labours, and proceedings of its

---

[1] Hoved. anno 742, f. 240 b.
[2] Viros strictæ abstinentiæ; absque carne et vino, absque sicera et servis, proprio manuum suarum labore contentos. Ep. Bonif. p. 211.

first abbots. These men were descended from the noblest families in Northumbria, and their monastery was endowed with ample revenues. Yet they despised the vain distinctions of rank and wealth ; associated with their fellow-monks in the duties of the cloister and the labours of husbandry ; and in their diet, their dress, and their accommodations, descended to a level with the lowest of their disciples. Their riches were not spent in the encouragement of idleness, or the gratification of sensuality, but in promoting by every means in their power the improvement of their countrymen. By their liberality, foreign artists were invited to instruct the ignorance of the Anglo-Saxons ; paintings were purchased for the decoration of their churches ; and their library was enriched with the choicest volumes of profane and sacred literature. The last care of their founder was directed to these objects. He had a brother, whose avarice, he thought, would grasp at the government, and whose prodigality would quickly exhaust the treasury of the abbey. Him he conjured the monks to banish from their thoughts ; to permit nor age, nor authority, nor affection, to influence their suffrages ; and to elect for his successor the worthiest, though he might be the youngest and most ignoble, brother in the monastery.[1]

The conduct of the abbots of Wearmouth was the conduct of almost all the superiors of religious societies at this period. To erect edifices worthy of the God whom they adored, to imitate the solem-

[1] Beda, Vitæ Abbatum Wirem, passim. Homilia in Natal. Divi Benedicti. Op. tom. vii. col. 464.

nity of the worship which they had witnessed at
Rome, and to arrest by external splendour the attention of their untutored brethren, were the principal
objects of their ambition : and in the prosecution of
these objects, they necessarily accelerated the progress of civil as well as religious improvement.
1. The architecture of the Saxons, at the time of
their conversion, was rude and barbarous. They
lived, indeed, amid ruins, which attested the taste
of a more civilized people : but their ignorance be-
held them with indifference, and their indolence
was satisfied with the wretched hovels of their ancestors.[1] The first impulse was communicated by
the missionaries, who constructed churches for the
accommodation of their converts. Those built by
the Scots were of oaken planks, those by the
Romans, of unwrought stone. Both were covered
with reeds or straw.[2] But when the Saxons, in
their visits to the tombs of the apostles, had seen

---

[1] From the speech of the Thane consulted by Edwin
(c. 1, p. 23), we may infer, that the palace of the Northumbrian king was merely a large hall, with two opposite
openings for doors, and an aperture in the centre of the
roof, to emit the smoke of the fire which was kindled
under it. Beda, in his life of St. Cuthbert, has described
the habitation which the bishop built for himself in the isle
of Farne. It consisted of two separate rooms, surrounded
by a wall about two yards high. The latter was built with
stone and turf : the rooms were partly excavated in the
rock : so that their walls were composed of stone, and
clay, and wood. For roofs they had branches of trees
covered with straw. Bed. pp. 243, 263.

[2] The church of Lindisfarne was built, *more Scotorum*,
of split oak, and covered with reeds. Bed. l. iii. c. 25.
The first church by Edwin, at York, was of similar materials; but by the assistance of the missionary Paulinus, he
was soon enabled to erect a second of stone. Id. l. ii. c. 14.

the public buildings of other countries, they blushed at the inferiority of their own, and resolved to imitate, what they had learned to admire. The considerations of labour and expense were despised; and every art, which that age connected with the practice of architecture, was introduced or improved. Walls of polished masonry succeeded to the rough erections of their ancestors; the roofs of their churches were protected with sheets of lead;[1] lofty towers added to the size and appearance of the building: and, to the astonishment of the untravelled multitude, windows of glass admitted the light, at the same time that they excluded the wind and rain.[2] A century had not elapsed from the arrival of St. Augustine, before all these improvements were generally introduced under the patronage of prelates and princes. In the south, Egwin, bishop of Worcester, Aldhelm, abbot of Malmesbury, and Bugge, the daughter of Centwin, king of Wessex, are mentioned with peculiar praise; and in the north, the labours of St. Bennet and St. Wilfrid have been gratefully recorded by their respective biographers. Bennet, aware of the inferiority of the natives, passed into Gaul, and brought back with him a supply of experienced workmen to build his church at Wearmouth. The next year he sent to the same quarter, and procured the services of men skilled in the manufacture of glass. In a few years there was no want of foreign artists at Wearmouth, but native

---

[1] Eadberct, the seventh bishop of Lindisfarne, covered not only the roof, but also the walls of his church with lead. Id. l. iii. c. 25.

[2] Edd. Vit. Wilf. c. 14.

workmen from the banks of the Wear were employed to build a church of stone for Naiton, king of the Picts.[1] The attempts of Wilfrid were more numerous, and more widely diffused. His first attempt was to repair and beautify the cathedral church of York, which had been originally built by Edwin of Northumbria, and now, after the short interval of forty years, was hastening to decay. By his instructions the walls were strengthened, the timber of the roof was renewed, and a covering of lead opposed to the violence of the weather. From the windows he removed the lattices of wood, and curtains of linen, the rude contrivances of an unskilful age ; and substituted in their place the more elegant and useful invention of glass. The interior of the church he cleansed from its impurities, and washed the walls with lime, till they became, according to the expression of his biographer, whiter than the snow.[2] His success at York was a fresh stimulus to his industry, and at Ripon he raised a new church, which was built from the foundations according to his design. We are told that the masonry was finely polished, that rows of columns supported the roof, and that porticos adorned each of the principal entrances.[3] The monastery at Hexham was the last and the most admired of his works : in the erection of which (as perhaps was the case in the former instance), his plans were improved and executed by the skill of the masons and plasterers,

---

[1] Beda, Oper. Min. p. 143.   Hist. v. c. 21.

[2] Super nivem dealbavit.   Edd. Vit. Wilf. c. 16.   See also Malm. de Pont. l. iii.

[3] Edd. c. 17.

whom, at a considerable expense, he had procured from Rome.[1] The height and length of the walls, the beautiful polish of the stones, the number of the columns and porticos, and the spiral windings, which led to the top of each tower, have exercised the descriptive powers of Eddius, who, after two journeys to the apostolic see, boldly pronounced that there existed not, on this side of the Alps, a church to be compared with that of Hexham.[2] It is, indeed, probable that these buildings, which once excited raptures in the breasts of their beholders, would at the present day displease by the absence of symmetry and taste. But we should recollect, that they were the first essays of a people emerging from barbarism, the rudiments of an art which has been improved by the labours of succeeding generations. The men, by whose genius and under whose patronage they were constructed, were the benefactors of their countrymen, and might justly claim the gratitude not only of their contemporaries, but also of their posterity.

2. The interior of these edifices exhibited an equal spirit of improvement and a superior display of magnificence. Of the spoils which their barbarous ancestors had wrested from a more polished people, a considerable portion was now dedicated to the service of the Deity; and the plate and jewels, which their piety poured into the treasuries of the principal churches, are represented of such immense value,

---

[1] Arbitratu quidem multa proprio, sed et cæmentariorum, quos ex Roma spes munificentiæ attraxerat, magisterio. Malm. de Pont. f. 155.
[2] Id. c. 22.

that it is with reluctance we assent to the testimony
of contemporary and faithful historians. From them
we learn that, on the more solemn festivals, every
vessel employed in the sacred ministry was of gold
or silver ; that the altars sparkled with jewels and
ornaments of the precious metals ; that the vestments of the priest and his assistants were made of
silk, embroidered in the most gorgeous manner ; and
that the walls were hung with foreign paintings and
the richest tapestries.[1] In the church built by
Bugge, in Wessex, before the year 700, the principal altar was covered with curtains of cloth of gold;
the cross was of gold, with silver ornaments and gems;
the chalice and patene, ' which bore the sacred body
and blood of Christ,' were, a cup of gold chased with
precious stones, and a dish of silver of great magnitude.[2] In the church of York stood two altars,
entirely covered with plates of gold and silver. One
of them was also ornamented with a profusion of
gems, and supported a lofty cross of equal value.
Above were suspended three rows of nine lamps, in
a pharus of the largest dimensions.[3] Even the books

---

[1] Bed. pp. 295, 297, 299, 300; Edd. Vit. Wilf. c. 17;
Alc. de pont. v. 1224, 1266, 1488.

[2] Aurea contextis flavescunt pallia filis,
  Quæ sunt altaris sacri velamina pulchra.
  Aureus atque calix fulgescit gemmis opertus
  Sic lata argento constat fabricata patena,
  Quæ divina gerunt nostræ medicamina vitæ,
  Corpore nam Christi sacroque cruore nutrimur.
  Hic crucis ex auro splendescit lamina fulvo,
  Argentique simul gemmis ornata metalla.
                    Inter. Oper. Alcuini, ii. 550.

[3] Alc. ibid. v. 1488. The pharus was a contrivance for
the suspension of lights in the church. (Georgi de liturg.
Rom. pont. vol.i.p.lxxix.) Mr. Churton, unacquainted with

employed in the offices of religion were decorated
with similar magnificence. St. Wilfrid ordered the
four gospels to be written with letters of gold, on a
purple ground, and presented them to the church of
Ripon in a casket of gold, in which were enchased
a number of precious stones.[1] Of these ornaments
some had been purchased from foreign countries ;
many were executed by the industry of native artists.
In their convents the nuns were employed in elegant
works of embroidery : in the monasteries the monks
practised the different mechanical arts. The iron-
smith, the joiner, and the goldsmith, were raised, by
their utility, to a high degree of consequence among
their brethren ; their professions were ennobled by
the abbots and bishops, who occasionally exercised
them ; and these distinctions contributed to excite
emulation, and to accelerate improvement.[2]

Catholic rites, has fallen into several mistakes on this subject. He calls the altar a shrine ; the gold flagon, out of
which the priest poured the wine into the chalice preparatory to the consecration, is with him the sacramental cup
itself ; and he tells us that the use of the pharos was to
light up the altar by night, though its real use was to
light it up chiefly by day during the celebration of mass.
See Churton, 166.

[1] Edd. c. 17 ; Bed. l. v. c. 19. If the reader wish to
see other accounts of the magnificent furniture of their
churches, he may consult the Monasticon, vol. i. pp. 40,
104, 165, 222.

[2] Beda, p. 296. St. Dunstan worked in all the metals
(Ang. Sac. vol. ii. p. 94): he made organs (Gale, p. 324),
and bells (Monast. vol. i. p. 104). St. Ethelwold practised
the same trades as his instructor. (Ibid.) By a law published in the reign of Edgar, but probably transcribed from
a more ancient regulation, every priest was commanded
" to learn some handicraft in order to increase knowledge
—to eacan læpe." Wilk. p. 225.

3. While the mechanic trades thus flourished under the patronage of the richer ecclesiastics, the more important profession of agriculture acquired a due share of their attention. The estates of the lay proprietors were cultivated by the compulsory labour of bondmen and theowas, or slaves : but in every monastery the greater number of the brotherhood was devoted to the occupation of husbandry; and the superior cultivation of their farms quickly demonstrated the difference between the industry of those who worked through motives of duty, and of those whose only object was to escape the loss of their holdings, or the lash of the surveyor.[1] Of the lands bestowed on the monks, a considerable portion was originally wild and uncultivated, surrounded by marshes, or covered with forests. They preferred such situations for the sake of retirement and contemplation ; and as they were of less value, they were more freely bestowed by their benefactors.[2] But every obstacle of nature and soil was subdued by the unwearied industry of the monks. The forests were cleared, the waters drained, roads opened, bridges erected, and the waste lands reclaimed. Plentiful harvests waved on the coast of Northumbria, and luxuriant meadows started from the fens of

---

[1] From the Domesday survey, Mr. Turner observes, that the church lands were in a higher state of cultivation than those of any other order of society. Vol. iv. p. 205.

[2] Beda, pp. 128, 144, 156, 164. Several monasteries took their names from their situation, as Atbearwe, in the forest (Bed. p. 144); Ondyrawuda, in the wood of the Deiri (Bed. 183); Croyland, boggy land (Ing. f. i.); Thorney, the island of thorns (Hug. Cand. p. 3); Jarrow or Gyrvum, a fen (Id. p. 2).

the Girvii.[1] The superior cultivation of several counties in England is originally owing to the labours of the monks, who, at this early period, were the parents of agriculture as well as of the arts.

4. If the monastic bodies thus acquired opulence for themselves, they were not insensible to the wants of the unfortunate. The constant exercise of charity and hospitality had been indispensably enjoined by all their legislators. Within the precincts of the monastery stood an edifice, distinguished by the Greek name of Xenodochium, in which a certain number of paupers received their daily support, and which was gratuitously opened to every traveller, who solicited relief. The monks were divided into classes, of which each in rotation succeeded to the service of the hospital. The abbot alone was exempted. To confine his attendance to particular days was inconsistent with his other and more important occupations : but he was exhorted frequently to join his brethren in the performance of this humble and edifying duty. To the assistant monks it was recommended to shut their ears to the suggestions of pride and indolence.; to revere the Saviour of mankind in the persons of the poor, and to recollect that every good office rendered to them, he would reward as done to himself.[2] Moroseness and impatience were

---

[1] The coast of Northumbria was cultivated by the monks of Coldingham, Lindisfarne, Bambrough, Tinmouth, Jarrow, Weeamouth, Hartlepool, and Whitby : the marshes of the Girvii were drained and improved by the monks of Croyland, Thorney, Ely, Ramsey, and Medhamsted. This fenny region, the theatre of monastic industry, extended the space of 68 miles, from the borders of Suffolk to Wainfleet in Lincolnshire. (Camden's Cambridgeshire.)

[2] St. Matt. c. xxv. v. 40.

strictly forbidden : they were enjoined to speak with
kindness, and to serve with cheerfulness ; to instruct
the ignorance, console the sorrows, and alleviate the
pains, of their guests : to attach the highest importance to their employment ; and to prefer the
service of the indigent brethren of Christ, before that
of the wealthy children of the world.[1] The legislator
who framed these regulations must have been inspired with the true spirit of the gospel ; to execute
them with fidelity, required men actuated by motives
superior to those of mercenary attendants ; and
humanity will gratefully cherish the memory of
these asylums, erected for the relief of indigence and
misfortune.[2]

5. In all the ecclesiastical documents of the age,
the practice of almsgiving is inculcated as a duty of
the highest obligation ; and history bears testimony,
that, by many of the bishops and abbots, it was most
religiously performed. Some of them, as Eadberct
of Lindisfarne, and Tatberct of Ripon, made it a rule
to distribute to the poor the tithe of the annual income of their churches :[3] few of them ever made any

---

[1] Nec pauperibus æterni Christi vicarius tardus ac tepi-
dus ministrare differendo desistat, qui celer ac fervidus
divitibus caducis ministrando occurrere desiderat. Apost.
Bened. app. par. 3, p. 92.

[2] The same kind of charity was also kept up in the
clerical monasteries. "Consideret," says Alcuin to his
disciple, Archbishop Eanbald, "tua diligentissima in elee-
mosynis pietas ubi xenodochia, i.e. hospitalia fieri jubeas,
in quibus sit quotidiana pauperum et peregrinorum sus-
ceptio, ut ex nostris substantiis habeant solatia." Ep. l.
p. 65.

[3] Eadberct omnibus annis decimam non solum quadru-
pedum, verum etiam frugum omnium atque pomorum,

disposition of their property without appropriating a considerable portion to the same benevolent purpose. Of this practice I select the following instance from the life of St. Wilfrid, because it will prove instructive on other points. Some time before his death, the bishop led eight of his most trusty friends into his treasury, and superintended the division of its contents into four portions. Then, pointing to the most valuable, he said, " It has long been my intention, if God be willing, to go once more to the see of St. Peter, to which I am so much indebted; and to take with me that first portion, that I may have wherewith to make offerings in the churches on my way, and donations to the church of the holy Mary, mother of the Lord, and to that of the apostle Saint Paul. Should God, however, dispose of me otherwise, then I charge you to send the same portion, for the same purposes, to Rome. The second portion you shall distribute among the poor of my people for the benefit my soul; the third shall be given to the abbots of my monasteries of Ripon and Hexham, that they may have wherewith to secure by presents the protection of the kings and prelates; the last shall be given to those who have followed me in exile, and have not yet received from me donations in land. Divide it among them according to their rank, that each may have the means of support when I am gone." These orders were faithfully observed after his sepulture; and, in addition, a most munificent benefaction was yearly dis-

---

necnon et vestimentorum partem pauperibus dabat. (Bed. iv. c. 29.) For Tatberct, see Edd. Vit. Wilf. c. lx.

tributed among the poor of the district, on the anniversary of his death.[1]

But it was in the time of public distress, that the charity of the monks was displayed in all its lustre. In their mutual wars the Saxon princes ravaged each other's territories without mercy; and, after the establishment of the monarchy, the devastations of the Danes frequently reduced the natives to the extremity of want. Agriculture was yet, except among the monastic bodies, in its infancy. The most plentiful years could scarcely supply the general consumption, and as often as an unfavourable season stinted the growth, or a hostile invasion swept away the produce of the harvest, famine, with its inseparable attendant pestilence, was the necessary result. On such occasions the monks were eager to relieve the wants of their countrymen; and whoever is conversant with their writers, must have remarked the satisfaction with which they recount the charitable exertions of their most celebrated abbots. Among these, a distinguished place is due to Leofric, the tenth abbot of St. Alban's.[2] To erect a church, which in magnificence might equal the dignity of the abbey, had been the favourite project of his two immediate predecessors. The ruins of the ancient Verulam had been explored; the necessary materials had been prepared: the treasury was filled with the donations of their friends; and a profusion of gold and silver vases proved the extent of their resources. Leofric, in the vigour of manhood, succeeded to their riches and their projects; and his mind was gratified

---

[1] Eddius, ibid. p. 87.   [2] An. 1000.

with the prospect of erecting an edifice, which would transmit his name with honour to posterity. But the public calamity soon dissipated the illusion. The horrors of famine depopulated the country, and his heart melted at the distress of his brethren. He cheerfully resolved to sacrifice the object of his ambition; the granaries of the monastery were opened to the sufferers; the riches of the treasury were expended for their relief; the plate reserved for his table was melted down; and, as a last resource, he ventured to sell the valuable ornaments destined for the use and decoration of the church.[1] Of his monks, there were several who murmured at the liberality of their abbot, but were careful to conceal their avarice beneath the mask of piety. Whatever had been once consecrated to the service of God, could not, they observed, without impiety, be alienated to profane purposes. Leofric meekly, but truly replied, that the living were to be preferred to the inanimate temples of God: and that to support the former was a work of superior obligation to the decoration of the latter. His conduct was applauded: and his opponents were reduced to silence by the voice of the public.[2]

In the same rank with Leofric, we may place Godric, the abbot of Croyland, whose monastery, situated in the midst of deep and extensive marshes, offered a secure asylum to the crowds that fled from the exterminating swords of the Danes. Though his treasury had been lately pillaged by the officers of the

---

[1] Some jewels and cameos were excepted, for which he could find no purchaser. Mat. Paris, p. 995.
[2] Ibid.

crown; though Swein, the chieftain of the barbarians, threatened him with his resentment; Godric listened not to the suggestions of terror or of prudence, but received the fugitives with open arms, consoled them in their losses, and associated them to his own fortunes. During several months Croyland swarmed with strangers, who were accommodated and supported at his expense. The cloisters and the choir were reserved for his own monks, and those of the neighbouring monasteries: the fugitive clergy received for their residence the body of the church : the men were lodged in the other apartments of the abbey; and the women and children were placed in temporary buildings erected in the cemetery. Still Godric was aware that the maintenance of so great a multitude would soon exhaust the resources of the abbey; and his anxiety was daily increased by the suspicions of King Ethelred, and the menaces of Swein. In his anguish he was heard to envy the fate of those whom he had followed to the grave. A last expedient remained, to solicit the friendship of Norman, a powerful retainer of Duke Edric ; and the grant of a valuable manor for one hundred years secured the protection of that nobleman. While he lived, Croyland enjoyed tranquillity; but the estate was unjustly detained by his descendants, and never recovered by the abbey.[1]

VI. In the sequel of this chapter I shall notice another privilege granted by our kings to the churches of their own realm, and their valuable donations to foreign churches.

1. The privilege is that of sanctuary, one which,

---

[1] Ingulf. f. 507, an. 1010.

however inconsistent it may be with a more perfect
system of legislation and internal policy, was dear to
humanity in times of anarchy and barbarism: because, whilst it offered an asylum to the innocent
and powerless from the vengeance of a remorseless
enemy, it compelled the guilty to make to the
injured party legal compensation for the offence.
The origin of the institution is lost in remote antiquity. Among the Jews we find ' cities of refuge '
appointed, that the involuntary homicide might *flee
thither, and fleeing to one of them might live.*[1] Among
the pagans we behold the weak and defenceless continually seeking protection at the altars of the gods.
In the Roman empire, after the conversion of Constantine, the right of asylum was transferred by the
practice of the people from the pagan to the Christian temples : the silence of the emperors gradually
sanctioned the innovation; and by the Theodosian
code, the privilege was extended to every building
designed for the habitation, or the use of the clergy.[2]
To this decision of the imperial law the Saxon converts listened with respect, and their obedience was
rewarded by the numerous advantages which it procured.   Though religion had softened, it had not ex-
tirpated, the ancient ferocity of their character. They
continued to cherish that barbarous prejudice, which
places the sword of justice in the hand of the injured

---

[1] Deut. iv. 41—43.

[2] The motive of this extension was the indecency of
permitting the fugitive to remain for several days and
nights in the church.   Hanc autem spatii latitudinem ideo
indulgemus, ne in ipso Dei templo et sacrosanctis altaribus
confugientium quenquam mane vel vespere cubare vel
pernoctare liceat.   Cod. Theod. l. ix. tit. 45.

individual, and exhorts him to punish his enemy
without waiting for the more tardy vengeance of
the law.[1] As their passions frequently urged them
to deeds of violence, this system of retaliation was
productive of the most fatal consequences. The
friends of each party associated in his defence :
family was leagued against family ; and in the prosecution of these bitter and hereditary feuds, innocence
too often suffered the fate which was due to guilt.
On such occasions, the church offered her protection
to the weak and the unfortunate. Within her precincts they were secure from the resentment of their
enemies, till their friends had assembled, and either
proved their innocence, or paid the legal compensation for their offence.[2] It should however be
observed, that the right of asylum, though it retarded,
did not prevent the punishment of the guilty.[3]
After a certain time the privilege expired. The
three days allotted by the laws of Alfred were successively extended to a week, to nine days, and

---

[1] This prejudice was so inveterate among some of the
northern nations, that by the Salic law, every member of a
family who refused to join his brethren in the pursuit of
vengeance, was deprived of his right of inheritance.
Henault, Abreg. Chron. vol. i. p. 118.

[2] Wilk. Leg. Sax. p. 15, v. 35, ii. iii.   The first Anglo-
Saxon law on this subject was passed by Ine in 693 : " If
any one be guilty of death, and he flee to a church, let him
have his life, and make bot as the law may direct him. If
any one put his hide in peril, and flee to a church, be the
scourging forgiven to him." (Thorpe, i. 105; Wilk. 15, v.)
This law should be explained by others which follow, that
he was " to have his life for a certain time only, during
which he might find the means of making bot, or compensation."

[3] Templorum cautela, says Justinian, non nocentibus
sed læsis datur a lege.   Novel. 17, c. 7.

lastly to an indefinite period, which might be shortened or protracted at the discretion of the sovereign :
but when it was elapsed, the fugitive, unless he had
previously satisfied the legal demands of his adversaries, was delivered to the officers of justice.[1]
Neither were the churches open to criminals of
every description. The chance of protection was
wisely diminished in proportion to the enormity of
the offence. The thief who had repeatedly abused,
at last forfeited the benefit of the sanctuary : and
the man who had endangered the safety of the state,
or violated the sanctity of religion, might legally be
dragged from the foot of the altar to receive the
punishment of his crime.[2] There were, however, a
few churches which claimed a proud pre-eminence
above the others.[3] To them their benefactors had
accorded the extraordinary privilege of securing the
life of every fugitive, how enormous soever might
be his guilt, and of calling upon the prosecutor to
accept in lieu of his head a pecuniary compensation. Among these may be numbered the churches
of York, Beverley, Ripon, Ramsey, and Westminster ;[4] but none could boast of equal immu-

---

[1] Wilk. Leg. Sax. p. 35, ii. 36, v. 110.

[2] Ibid. p. 198, vi.

[3] That there were such churches is plain from the law
respecting murder committed within the walls of a church.
" Let the homicide be botless : and let every one of those
who are friends to God pursue him, unless it happen that
he escape thence, and seek so *awful* a sanctuary, that the
king through that grant him his life against full bot both
to God and to man." Thorpe, i. 341.

[4] Spelman's Gloss. voce Fridstol; Monast. Ang. vol. i.
pp. 60, 236. Thus at Beverley the right of sanctuary
reached from the church to certain stone crosses at the

nities with the abbey of Croyland. The monastery, the island, and the waters which surrounded it, enjoyed the right of sanctuary; and a line of demarcation, drawn at the distance of twenty feet from the opposite margin of the lake, arrested the pursuit of the officers, and insured the safety of the fugitive. Immediately he took the oath of fealty to the abbot, an dthe *man* of St. Guthlake might laugh in security at the impotent rage of his enemies. But if, without a written permission, he presumed to wander beyond the magic boundary, the charm was dissolved, justice resumed her rights, and his life was forfeited to the severity of the laws. When the monastery was rebuilt, after its destruction by the Danes, Edred offered to revive the ancient privilege in favour of his Chancellor Turketul; but if we may believe the historian of Croyland, it was declined by the hoary statesman, who considered the ordinary right of asylum, as equally beneficial to the public, and less liable to abuse.[1]

The *peace of the church* was an institution of a

---

distance of a league from the church, and the time allotted for the residence of the fugitive extended to thirty days, during which it was the duty of the canons to reconcile him with his enemy, or to convey him by land or water out of the country, under the protection of their officers, whose presence was sufficient to preserve him from capture or assault. See Libertates Eccl. Si. Johannis in the Sanctuar. Dunel. pp. 99, 100.

[1] Wilk. Con. pp. 176, 181; Cod. Dip. i. 301; ii. 37; Ingulf, f. 500.—It is manifest that the charters of Wiglaff and Bertulf, which we still have, were never composed in the time of those kings: yet I see no reason to suppose that they contain other privileges than were granted by the ancient charters, or might be collected from the ancient customs of the abbey.

similar nature, and adopted by the clergy, in order
to mitigate the ferocity of their countrymen. To
devote to the work of vengeance the days which
religion had consecrated to the worship of the
Almighty, they taught to be a profanation of the
blackest die. At their solicitation, peace was pro-
claimed on each Sunday and holiday, and during the
penitential times of Lent and Advent: every feud was
instantly suspended; and the bitterest enemies might
meet and converse without danger under the protection of the church. The same indulgence was
extended to the man who quitted his home to assist
at the public worship, to obey the summons of his
bishop, or to attend the episcopal synod or national
council. Covered by this invisible ægis, he might
pursue his journey in security; or if his enemy dared
to molest him, the presumption of the aggressor was
severely chastised by the resentment of the laws.[1]

VII. But England was not the only theatre on
which the Saxon kings and nobles displayed their
regard for the ministers of religion. In their frequent pilgrimages to the tombs of the apostles, they
were careful to visit the most celebrated churches
on the continent, and to leave behind them numerous evidences of their liberality. Before the close
of the eighth century, the monastery of St. Denis, in

---

[1] Leg. Sax. 109, 110, 197; Thorpe, 309, 443. — It
should be remembered that not only the churches, but also
the palaces of kings, and the houses of their officers, possessed the privilege of sanctuary. Moreover, the king's
peace, like that of the church, was granted to all who were
engaged in his service, or travelling on the four great
roads, or employed on the navigable rivers. Leg. Sax.
p. 199.

the neighbourhood of Paris, was possessed of extensive estates on the coast of Sussex ;[1] and to the presents of the Saxon princes several of the churches, originally established in Armorica by the fugitive Britons, were indebted for their support.[2] Of Alfred it is recorded by his biographer, that in the latter years of his life he distributed one-eighth part of his annual income in charity to religious establishments without the boundaries of Wessex, in Mercia, Northumbria, Wales, Cornwall, Gaul, Armorica, and Ireland; in addition to which, we often meet with messengers carrying his alms to Rome, and on one occasion to the Christians of St. Thomas, in the East Indies.[3] The charities of Canute have been celebrated by the canon of St. Omer's, who viewed with astonishment the offerings of the king on the altar of that church, and the amount of his alms to the people : and assures us, that he left similar memorials of his munificence in many cities of Flanders, Gaul, and Italy.[4] Rome, however, was the chief object of Anglo-Saxon liberality. The imperial city was no longer the mistress of the world. More than once she had been sacked by the barbarians : the provinces from which she formerly drew her subsistence, had submitted to their arms ; her walls were insulted

---

[1] Dublet Ant. St. Dion. apud Alf. tom. ii. pp. 650, 656.

[2] Malm. de Pont. l. v. p. 363.

[3] Asser, 66, 67; Malm. de Reg. i. 187; Chr. Sax. ann. 883, 7, 8, 9. To Fulk, archbishop of Rheims, he sent as a present a pack of hounds to extirpate the wolves that infested the neighbourhood. Misistis nobis generosos et optimos canes ad abigendam rabiem luporum quibus inter cætera flagella justo Dei judicio nobis inlata, plurimum abundat patria nostra. Ep. Ful. apud Wise, Asser. 126.

[4] Encomium Emmæ, p. 173.

by the frequent inroads of the Saracens ; and the popes, with the numerous people dependent on their paternal authority, were frequently reduced to the lowest distress. By the Saxon princes, the affection which Gregory the Great had testified for their fathers, was gratefully remembered. They esteemed it a disgrace that the head of their religion should suffer the inconveniences of want, and each succeeding king was careful, by valuable donations, to demonstrate his veneration for the successor of St. Peter, and to contribute a portion of his wealth to support the government of the universal church. The munificence of Ethelwulf is particularly described by Anastasius, an eye-witness. During the year of his residence in Rome,[1] he spread around him with pro-

---

[1] During Ethelwulf's stay in Rome, a conspiracy to dethrone him was formed in England, to which I may be allowed to refer, for the purpose of correcting certain erroneous statements. The original narrator is Asser; of modern writers, one tells us that it was caused by the jealousy of the elder brothers, who suspected the father of an intention to raise Alfred to the throne; another, that it sprung from the discontent of the thanes that he had not abdicated, like Ine, before he left the kingdom; a third, that it grew out of some infamous transaction which Asser does not choose to describe. Now, Asser must certainly have been misunderstood. His narrative is perfectly plain: that, according to some, this conspiracy was got up by the bishop of Sherborne and the ealdorman of Somerset, who suggested the plan to Ethelbald, the king's son; but that, according to others, it was entirely owing to the ambition of Ethelbald, whose headstrong character was displayed in this as well as in other unjustifiable deeds. " Interea quædam infamia contra morem omnium Christianorum in occidentali parte Selwuda orta est. *Nam* Æthelbald rex Æthelwulfi regis filius, et Ealhstan Shireburnensis ecclesiæ episcopus, Eanulf quoque Somertunensis pagæ comes conjurasse referuntur, ne unquam Æthelwulf rex a Roma

fusion the treasures which he had brought from England. To the pontiff, Benedict III., he gave a crown of pure gold weighing four pounds, two cups and two images of the same precious metal, a sword tied with pure gold, four Saxon dishes of silver-gilt, a rochet of silk with a clasp of gold, several albs of white silk with gold lace and clasps, and two large curtains of silk embroidered with gold. In the basilic of St. Peter he distributed presents of gold to the clergy and nobility of Rome; and gratified the people with a handsome donative in pieces of silver.[1] But these were occasional charities; the Romescot was perpetual. During a long period anterior to the Norman conquest, a silver penny was annually paid by every family possessed of land or cattle to the yearly value of thirty pence, and the general amount was carefully transmitted to the Roman pontiff. The origin of this tax is involved in considerable obscurity. If we may credit the narration of later historians, it was first established by Ine, king of Wessex, about the commencement of the eighth century; was afterwards extended by Offa of

revertens, iterum in regno reciperetur. Quod inauditum omnibus sæculis infortunium episcopo et comiti solummodo perplurimi reputant, ex quorum consilio hoc factum esse perhibetur. Multi quoque regali solummodo insolentiæ deputant: quia et ille rex in hac re et in multis aliis perversitatibus pertinax fuit." Asser, 8.

[1] Anast. Biblioth. de Vitis Pontif. tom. i. p. 403. For the names and destination of these and similar presents, see Domenico Georgi, de Liturgia Romani Pontificis, vol. i. The crown and images were probably suspended over the tomb of St. Peter (id. p. 243); the dishes (gabathæ) were used to receive the offerings at mass (id. p. 91); the curtains of silk embroidered with gold (vela de fundato, id. p. 372), were employed in the church on great festivals.

Mercia, to all the shires of that populous nation; and at last, by the command of Ethelwulf, was levied in all the provinces of the Saxons. But this fair and well-connected system will vanish at the approach of criticism. If Ine was the original author of the Romescot, it will be difficult to account for the silence of Beda, who particularly relates his devotion towards the Roman see, and of every other historian that wrote during the five following centuries. The claims of Offa and Ethelwulf are more plausible. Offa was accustomed to ascribe the success of his arms to the intercession of St. Peter; and gratitude induced him to promise from himself and his successors a yearly pension of three hundred and sixty mancuses to the church of the apostle; which promise was confirmed by a solemn oath in presence of the papal legates.[1] That he faithfully performed his engagement, we know from the best authority; but on the death of his son Egferth, the sceptre passed into the hands of Cœnulf, a prince of a distant and hostile branch of the royal family, who seems to have treated the grant of Offa as binding perhaps the heirs to the lands of Offa, but not the successors to his throne. After Cœnulf, we meet with no mention of any such payment before the pilgrimage of Ethel-

---

[1] See the letter of Leo III. in Anglia Sacra (vol. i. p. 461). The money was to be expended in relieving the poor, and furnishing lights for the church. The want of oil for this purpose was often lamented by the popes. Cum neque oleum sit nobis pro luminaribus ecclesiæ juxta debitum Dei honorem. (Ep. Steph. VI. Basil. Imper. apud Walker, p. 7.) A mancus was the eighth part of a pound, equal to thirty pence, if of silver; to about nine times that amount, if of gold.

wulf to Rome, where he is said by some writers to have renewed the grant originally made by Offa. But this is most probably a mistake. Ethelwulf, by a will made a little time before his death, charged the heirs to his lands of inheritance with the obligation of supplying with food, and drink, and clothing one poor man for every ten mansions, until the day of doom, and also of sending yearly to Rome three hundred mancuses; one for the personal use of the pontiff, one to supply oil for the lamps in St. Peter's at the evening and midnight service on Easter-eve, and a third for the same purpose in the church of St. Paul.[1] It is possible that Ethelwulf in making this bequest may have had the example of Offa before his eyes : but there plainly could be no resemblance between it and the Rome-feoh or Peterpence : which was not a legacy charged on the lands of a particular family, but a national tax levied after a fixed rate on every proprietor of lands in all the Anglo-Saxon kingdoms. It must then have been originally established by authority of the king with the consent of the whole legislature; but at what time this took place, it is impossible to discover from the imperfect records of the age. There is no reason to think that the Peter-pence was in existence before the reign of Alfred : and whether the

---

[1] It was left in an hæreditaria et commendatoria epistola (Asser, p. 13). But were they mancuses of gold or silver ? Asser does not say ; he calls it magnam pecuniam ; whence Malmesbury infers that they were mancuses of gold. (De Reg. p. 170.) Yet one hundred mancuses of gold—each the eighth part of a pound weight—must have been sufficient to purchase oil, not for one night only, but for a whole year. Hoveden, therefore, is probably correct, when he calls them mancuses of silver pennies—manculas denariorum. Hov. f. 238.

royal alms which that monarch sent yearly to Rome were the Rome-feoh, or the bequest of his father Ethelwulf, is uncertain. Under his son Edward the Rome-feoh is mentioned for the first time by name, and then it appears, not as new imposition, but as one of the accustomed dues of the church. In the laws of his successors it is the subject of many regulations. The time for payment is limited to the five weeks which intervene between the feast of St. Peter and the first of August; and the avarice of the man, who may attempt to elude the law, is ordered to be punished by fines of thirty pence to the bishop, and of one hundred and twenty shillings to the king.[1] The total amount appears to have been about two hundred pounds of Saxon money.[2]

---

[1] Thorpe, i. 244, 308, 342.   [2] Selden Analec. p. 72.

CHAPTER VII.

RELIGIOUS WORSHIP.

THE LITURGY—CELEBRATION OF THE MASS—GENERAL CONFORMITY OF
THE ROMAN AND SCOTTISH RITUAL—THE FORMER UNIVERSALLY
ADOPTED—THE COURSE AND CANONICAL HOURS OF PUBLIC PRAYER—
PSALMODY—OBSERVANCE OF THE SUNDAY—OF HOLIDAYS—PRIVATE
PRAYER FOR MORNING AND EVENING—BAPTISM OF ADULTS—OF INFANTS
—CONFIRMATION—COMMUNION—TIMES FOR COMMUNION—PENANCE—
CONFESSION—PENITENTIAL CANONS—COMMUTATION OF PENANCE—
PUBLIC AND PRIVATE PENANCE.

THE ecclesiastical history of the Northern, forms a remarkable contrast with that of the Oriental Christians. In the East, the zeal of the orthodox pastors was, during several centuries, employed in opposing the attempts of numerous, and often successful, innovators: in the North, the voice of religious discord was but seldom heard, and as speedily silenced.[1] Of this difference the cause may be traced to the opposition of their national character. The Eastern Christians were a polished people, whose natural penetration had been sharpened by the disputes of philosophers, and the logic of Aristotle. Not content with believing the truths, they attempted to explore the mysteries, of the gospel :

---

[1] The disputes between the Roman and Scottish missionaries in England prove, that though they differed in some points of discipline, they agreed in all the articles of their belief. See p. 49.

and from the monstrous union of the opinions of
philosophers with the tenets of Christianity, engen-
dered those errors, which so often disfigured the
beauty of the ancient church. But the converts
among the northern nations were more simple, and
less inquisitive : without suspicion they acquiesced
in the doctrines taught by their missionaries ; and
carefully transmitted them as a sacred deposit to the
veneration of their descendants. When Æthelheard,
archbishop of Canterbury, demanded from the prelates in the council of Cloveshoe, an exposition of
their belief, they unanimously answered: " Know,
that the faith, which we profess, is the same as was
taught by the holy and apostolic see, when Gregory
the Great sent missionaries to our fathers."[1]   I shall
not, therefore, fatigue the reader with a theological
investigation of the doctrines which formed the creed
of the Anglo-Saxons. The description of their
religious practices is better calculated to arrest
attention, and gratify curiosity: and from them their
belief may be deduced with less trouble, and with
equal accuracy.[2]

---

[1] Notum sit paternitati tuæ, quod sicut primitus a sancta
Romana, et apostolica sede, beatissimo papa Gregorio
dirigente, exarata est, ita credimus. Wilk. p. 162. Anno
800. The profession of faith which St. Swithin, bishop of
Winchester, made to Archbishop Ceolnoth, is drawn up
in the same manner. Ego Swithunus, humilis vernaculus
servorum Dei, confiteor tibi, Celnothe archiepiscope, con-
tinentiam meam. Illam rectam et orthodoxam fidem,
quam priores patres nostri devote servaverunt, cum omni
humilitate et sincera devotione, sicut prædecessores mei
ipsi sanctæ sedi Dorobernensis ecclesiæ subjuncti sunt,
semper servare velle humiliter per omnia profiteor. Textus
Roffen. p. 269.   Anno 852.
[2] Yet how shall I pursue this inquiry, without entang-

A spiritual worship, unincumbered with ritual
observances, has been often recommended by the-
orists as the most worthy of man, and the least unworthy of God: but experience has shewn that no
religious system can practically maintain its influence
over the mind, and withdraw it from the pursuit of
earthly goods in preference to those which are of
another world, unless it be aided by external ceremonies, which may seize the attention, elevate the

---

ling myself in the nets of controversy? It was once the
belief of Protestant writers, that the Anglo-Saxon church,
from its infancy was polluted with the damnable errors of
Popery. (Augustinus ad Anglo-Saxones papisticis tradi-
tionibus initiandos apostolus primus mittebatur: intro-
duxit altaria, vestes, missas, imagines, &c. &c. Bale,
cent. 13, c. 1.) Præter pontificum traditiones et humana
stercora (a very delicate expression!) nihil attulit. (Id.
cent. 8, c. 85.) Cæremoniarum profecto hic fuit, Romano-
rumque rituum non Christianæ fidei aut divini verbi apostolus Anglis, eosque Romanos ac pontificios potius quam
Christianos aut evangelicos agere docuit. (Parker, Ant.
Brit. p. 35.) But this opinion has been shaken by the
efforts of several eminent Saxon scholars, who have
ascribed to their favourite study the important discovery
that our forefathers were true and orthodox professors
of the Anglican creed, as it was established at the Reformation. (See Whelock's Beda, passim; Hicke's Letters
to a Roman priest, c. iii.; Elstob, Saxon Homily, pref.) It
must be acknowledged, that to their industry Saxon
literature is much indebted: but the ardour of discovery
seems to have improved their fancy at the expense of their
judgment: and a reader must be credulous indeed, to
believe with them, that a translation of the Pater-noster,
and of a few books of Scripture, an exposition of the
apostles' creed without any mention of purgatory, an
observation that God alone is to be adored, and that the
body of Christ is in the Eucharist after a ghostly manner
and not after the manner of a natural body, are proofs
sufficient to establish the identity of the Anglo-Saxon with
that of the present established church in this country.

hopes, and console the sorrows of its professors. It was on this principle that the ancient Christians, from the moment when they were relieved from the pressure of persecution, regulated their worship both in the East and the West: and the same religious rites which then prevailed among the old churches of the West, were established by the missionaries in the new church of the Anglo-Saxons. The following pages will describe these rites, as far as they can be traced from indigenous sources, divided into two classes: 1st, of those which appertain to the celebration of divine worship in public, and 2nd, of those which had for their object the ministration of spiritual aid to individuals, and the consecration of persons and things to the service of God.

1. In every Christian society which dates its origin from the more early ages, the eucharistic sacrifice, commonly called the sacrifice of the mass, has been considered the most solemn and sacred form of religious worship. Under other forms of devotion, the Christian might offer to God the feelings and aspirations of his own heart: but under this he was believed to offer the very body and blood of the Lamb, that took away the sins of the world ; of him who had promised that whatever was asked in his name, should be granted by his heavenly Father. Hence everywhere, both in the East and the West, we meet with the priest who officiates at the sacrifice, the altar on which the victim is offered, and the liturgy, or form of prayer with which that offering is accompanied. The Britons, before the arrival of the Saxons, had "their altars, the seats of the heavenly sacrifice," and "their

priests, who stretched out their hands over the most holy sacrifices of Christ:" and the Scots, in the remote isle of Icolmkille, "celebrated the sacred mysteries of the holy sacrifice, and consecrated according to custom the body of Christ."[1] It is, indeed, true that in the arrangement of the ceremonies and the composition of the prayers, distant churches, as was to be expected, frequently followed different models; but the variations were accidental and unimportant, and the form of the service was substantially the same both in the anaphora of the Greeks and the canon of the Latins, each carefully preserving the trisagion or ter sanctus, the invocation, the consecration of the elements, the commemorations of the living and the dead, the fraction of the host, and the communion of the faithful.[2] It was in the first portion of the service, that portion which was preparatory to the canon, that the principal diversities existed, and into this portion several pontiffs of the fifth and sixth centuries, Celestine, Gelasius, Leo, and Gregory, had introduced many improvements: whence it happened that ancient churches, which originally had received their

---

[1] See the contemporary native writers : for the Britons, Gildas, "cœlestis sacrificii sedes," p. 37. " Manus sacrosanctis Christi sacrificiis extensuri," p. 41 —and for the Scots, Cuminian, "sacrificale mysterium, sacra sancti sacrificii mysteria," Vit. S. Colum. pp. 29, 32; and Adamnan, " sacra consecrare mysteria. Christi corpus ex more conficere." (Vit. Colum. pp. 93, 172.) Edit. Pinkerton.

[2] The general conformity of the ancient Roman, Gallic, Gothic and other Western canons with the present Roman canon has been shewn by Georgi, De Liturg. Rom. Pont. iii. p. 31.

liturgy from Rome, but were unacquainted with these improvements, found themselves at a later period in the practice of rites different from those of their mother church.[1]

In the works of our native writers, we meet with numerous indications of the profound respect with which they had been taught to view this sacred institution. Whenever they speak of it, they appear to want language to express their notions and feelings. It is ' the celebration of the most sacred mysteries,' ' the celestial and mysterious sacrifice,' ' the offering of the victim of salvation,' ' the sacrifice of the mediator,' ' the sacrifice of the body and blood of Christ,' ' the memorial of Christ's great passion,' and ' the renewal of the passion and death of the Lamb.'[2] Thus it is termed, when they speak of it in general; but when they refer to that part of the canon called the consecration, they tell us that ' the elements of bread and wine are, through the ineffable hallowing of the spirit, made to pass into the mystery of Christ's flesh and blood;'[3] that ' the bread and wine are then consecrated into the substance of his body and

---

[1] Gelasianum codicem de missarum solemniis, multa subtrahens, pauca convertens, nonnulla vero adjiciens in unius libri volumine Gregorius coarctavit. Joan. Diac. in Vita S. Greg. l. ii. c. 17.

[2] Bed. l. ii. c. 5; l. iii. c. 2; l. iv. c. 14, 22, 28. Hist. Abb. Gyrven. inter Bedæ Oper. Minora, p. 331; Ep. Bug. ad Bonif. p. 45: Theod. Pœnit. apud Thorpe, ii. p. 62. Dæᵹꝧamlice bið hiꞃ þꞃopunᵹe ᵹeebnipeð þuꞃh ᵹeꞃinu þæꞃ halᵹan huꞃleꞃ æt þæꞃe halᵹan mæꞃꞃan. (Serm. de Sac. apud Whelock, p. 474.) Ꞃemýnðe hiꞃ mæꞃꞃan þꞃopunᵹe. Thorpe, ii. 376.

[3] Panis ac vini creatura in sacramentum carnis et sanguinis ejus, ineffabili spiritus sanctificatione transfertur. Bed. Hom. in Epiph. p. 175; Edit. Giles, 1843.

blood;'[1] that 'the angels hover around in respectful silence;'[2] and that 'the holy body and the precious blood of the Lamb, by whom we have been redeemed, are again immolated to God for the benefit of our salvation.'[3]

From this belief in the supernatural excellence of the sacrifice, proceeded the numerous canons and rubrics concerning the manner of its celebration. It was forbidden to offer it in any profane or unhallowed building, unless in the case of extreme sickness, and in time of war, when it might be offered under a tent:[4] at all times, three things were required that had previously been consecrated by a bishop—an altar,[5] a patene or dish, and a chalice or

---

[1] Eo tempore opportuno quo panem et vinum in *substantiam* corporis et sanguinis Christi consecraveris. Alcuini Epist. ad Paulinum, Oper. i. p. 49, epist. xxxvi.

[2] Enȝlaʃ þæn hpeanɲıaᷓ. (Thorpe, ii. 328.) Nec dubitare licet, ubi corporis at sanguinis mysteria geruntur, supernorum civium adesse conventus. (Bed. Hom. p. 428.) "Where the name of God is frequently invoked, and the holy mystery offered in the mass-service, there is no doubt that the presence of God's angels is there very near." Thorpe, ii. 409.

[3] Missarum solemnia celebrantes corpus sacrosanctum et pretiosum agni sanguinem quo a peccatis redempti sumus denuo Deo in profectum nostræ salutis immolamus. (Bed. Hom. in vig. Pasch. p. 31, et tom. vii. col. 6.) It must strike a modern reader, that whenever the Anglo-Saxon writers speak of the eucharistic service, they never fail to use the word sacrifice, or another of similar import, such as oblatio, immolatio, hostia, victima.

[4] Thorpe, ii. 250, 292, 392, 408.

[5] Ibid. 250, 292. Altars at first were of wood, afterwards of stone; but in many places the old altars continued till the eleventh century. Erant tunc temporis altaria lignea jam inde a priscis temporibus in Anglia. Vit. S. Wulstani; Ang. Sac. ii. 264.

cup, of some fusile material, gold, silver, glass, or
tin, and on no account of iron or wood ;[1] the offlete
or bread for the oblation was to be made of the
finest flour, without the admixture of any kind of
levain, and was to be kneaded and baked under the
eye of the priest, or of one in whom he could place
confidence; the wine was to be pure, and, on that
account, to be poured through a strainer into the
chalice, and was to be mixed, according to the practice of every Christian church, with a small quantity
of clear water.[2]   On solemn festivals, the clergy in
attendance were dressed in their richest apparel ; the
altar with its furniture presented the most gorgeous

---

[1] Thorpe, ii. 360, 384.

[2] The bread, cut into a circular shape, was called in
Latin oblata, whence was formed the Anglo-Saxon word
offlete, which was afterwards corrupted into *obley*, the
word used by our ancestors in the fifteenth and sixteenth
centuries. " We enjoin," says the canon, " that no priest
ever presume to celebrate mass, unless he have all that
belongeth to the mystery : that is, a clean offlete, clean
wine, and clean water. Woe to him that beginneth to
say mass, unless he have every of these." (Thorpe, ii. 252.)
" We command that the offletes which in the holy mystery ye offer unto God, ye bake yourselves, or your servants in your sight, so that you may know that they are
pure and unmixed ; and we command that the offletes, and
the wine, and the water, that are for the offering in the
mass, be minded, and kept in all cleanness, and with all
carefulness, and with the fear of God." (Ibid. 404.)
Panis qui in corpus Christi consecratur, absque *fermento*
ullius alterius infectionis, debet esse mundissimus, et aqua
absque omni sorde mundissima, et vinum absque omni
commixione nisi aquæ purgatissimum. Ex aqua et farina
panis fit, qui consecratur in corpus Christi, aqua et vinum
in sanguinem consecrabitur Christi. (Alcuini Oper. i.
p. 107 ; Ep. lxxv.) This passage must have escaped the
eye of Mr. Soames, who tells us that " nothing is said of
the offletes being unleavened." Supplement, p. 22, note.

appearance; the sanctuary, or space within the
chancel, was illuminated with a profusion of lamps
and wax lights;[1] the air was perfumed with clouds
of incense;[2] to the voices of a numerous choir was
added the harmony of the organ and of musical
instruments; and no labour, no cost, no ingenuity
was spared, to attest by outward magnificence the
deep feelings of awe and devotion with which the
Anglo-Saxon Christians were taught to contemplate
the "celebration of the most sacred mysteries."[3]

The Italian missionaries would of course establish
the Roman liturgy in the new church ; and it might,
perhaps, have been expected, that in conformity with
the pre-eminence claimed by the apostolic see, the
pontiff would forbid them to admit of any rites not
sanctioned by the practice of that see. But the
mind of Gregory was above such petty considerations. He had already introduced into the service
forms which he had noticed and admired in the
church of Constantinople ;[4] and in the same spirit

---

[1] "Let them put the sanctuary into the best order, and
let there be always lights burning in the church, when mass
is singing." (Thorpe, ii. 252, can. 42.) Ornatis studiosius
templi parietibus, et pluribus accensis luminaribus. Bed.
Hom. xlii. p. 315.

[2] In natali sanctorum incensum accendatur. (Theod. in
Thorpe, ii. 57.) Besides the accustomed use of incense at
certain parts of the mass, in some churches an incensory,
or metallic vessel, was suspended from the roof, and in it
aromatic gums were kept burning during the whole of the
service. Alc. ii. 550.
        Pendet de summo fumosa foramina pandens.
[3] Sacrosancta mysteria. Bed. Op. Min. p. 222.
[4] See his letter to John of Syracuse. His conduct excited the murmurs of some, who complained that by borrowing from the church of Constantinople, he treated that

he instructed Augustine and his companions not to confine themselves exclusively to the Roman ritual, but to adopt from the observances of other churches whatever they might conceive likely, in their circumstances, to promote the service of God. " You know, brother," he says to Augustine, " the customs of the church of Rome, in which you have been bred up. But my will is, that whatever practice you may discover which in your opinion will be more acceptable to God, you establish it in the new church of the Angles, without considering the place of its origin, whether it be the Roman, or Gallican, or any other church. For things are not to be loved on account of the places from which they come, but places are to be loved on account of the good things which they produce. Wherefore, whatever you find in any church, pious, religious, and proper, select it, and bind it up in one body, and deposit it among the Angles, for the customary observance of their church."[1] How far the missionary profited by this permission is uncertain ; but there is evidence that the three rogation days before the feast of the Ascen-

church as superior to the church of Rome. He replies, " Who can doubt that the church of Constantinople is subject to the apostolic see ? It is constantly admitted by our lord the emperor, and by my brother the bishop of that city. But am I on that account to reject what there is of good in that church ? As it is my duty to correct my inferiors when they err, so am I ready to imitate them when they do well. It would be a folly to make my superiority consist in disdaining to profit by the example of those beneath me. Stultus est enim qui in eo se primum existimat, ut bona quæ viderit, discere contemnat." S. Greg. Ep. l. ix. ep. 12.

[1] Bed. l. i. c. 27.

sion, a Gallic practice unknown at that time in Rome, were kept in England from the beginning;[1] and it is highly probable that the solemn rite of the episcopal benediction pronounced by the Anglo-Saxon prelates immediately after the fraction of the host, was derived from the practice of the Gallic prelates.[2]

Whether the sacrificial service of the Scottish missionaries varied from that of the Romans, we have no means of judging. That it would accord with the liturgy established by St. Patrick in Ireland, is evident; but from what church St. Patrick derived it, is uncertain; some writers contending that he must have brought with him the Gallic form, because he resided for a long time with St. Martin, at Tours; and others, that he had adopted the Roman form,

---

[1] This I infer from the sixteenth canon of the Council of Cloveshoe. The Litania major was a Roman institution, and kept on the 25th of April: the three rogation days a Gallic institution, not in use at that time in Rome. The Council in 747, ordains that the first should be kept juxta ritum Romanæ Ecclesiæ; and the other, secundum morem priorum nostrorum (Spelm. Con. p. 249): thus intimating that their ancestors had adopted the latter from some other church than the Roman.

[2] Then the bishop turning round, with all the clergy and people on their knees before him, pronounced over them three or more short prayers, begging on them the blessing of God in terms appropriate to the festival of the day, and ending with these words, " May *he* grant these petitions, whose kingdom and empire last through ages of ages without end." *Amen.* " May the blessing of God, the Father, and the Son, and the Holy Ghost, and the peace of our Lord be with you for ever." *And with thy spirit.* He then turned to the altar, and the kiss of peace passed through the congregation. See the Benedictional of St. Ethelwold, from the original illuminated manuscript in the library of his Grace the Duke of Devonshire, published by John Gage, Esq., 1832.

because he was sent on his mission by Pope Celestine from Rome.[1] One thing, however, cannot be denied : that, if there was any discrepance between the forms in use among the Roman and Scottish preachers, that discrepance must have been of no importance : otherwise it would have become a subject of controversy between the two parties, no less than the time of Easter, and the form of the ecclesiastical tonsure.

2. From the mass, the most solemn and sacred portion of the public worship, we pass to the *course* or order of daily prayer for the seven hours, called by the Anglo-Saxons the night song and uht-song, for the nocturnal service, and the prime-song, undern-song, midday-song, none-song and even-song, for that of the day.[2] At all these hours the clergy,

---

[1] It was from Pope Celestine that he received the commission to preach in Ireland. Ad sanctum Celestinum urbis Romæ papam per Segetium præsbyterum suum eum direxit Germanus, qui viro præstantissimo probitatis ecclesiasticæ testimonium apud sedem ferret apostolicam, cujus judicio approbatus, auctoritate fultus, benedictione denique roboratus, Hiberniæ partes expetiit. (Erric. Vit. Si. Germ. i. c. 12.) Hence, by the Council of Leighlinn (anno 630), Rome is called the fons baptismi nostri et sapientiæ; and when opposition was made to the decision of that Council, messengers were sent to Rome—velut natos ad matrem— as children to their mother, in obedience to the canon which ordered that cases of difficulty should be referred to the head of cities. In the canon itself, ad sedem apostolicam—to the apostolic see. Ware, Opusc. p. 41, can. 6 ; Ussher, Sylloge, ep. xi.

[2] Leg. Sax. 156, 166. The time for the night-song was, strictly speaking, midnight; but it was frequently joined with the uht song, so called from uht, the latter part of the night. The prime and even-songs were fixed at sunrise and sunset. The interval between these two points was divided in the church service after the Roman

as well in parochial as collegiate and conventual churches, were summoned to sing the praises of God in imitation of the psalmist, who had said, *seven times a day do I praise thee*.[1] The layman was advised, the ecclesiastic was commanded, to attend : and the reason assigned for this distinction was, that the clergy formed an order of men exclusively dedicated to the worship of God. If they had been liberated from the distraction of secular employments, and had been endowed with lands and the means of support, it was with this view, that they might daily, in the name of their lay brethren, discharge a duty, to the performance of which the latter, from their ignorance of letters and their worldly pursuits, were plainly incompetent.

The Book of Psalms, a book abounding with the sublimest effusions of religious feeling, formed the body of the course. In the nocturnal, the longest portion of this service, the tedium of monotony was relieved by the introduction of lessons from the Old and New Testaments, the acts of the martyrs, and the writings of the fathers: and to these were subsequently added hymns, anthems, and responsories. In the shorter hours brief passages from scripture, called capitula, were substituted for longer lessons ; and each portion of the course terminated with a prayer, pronounced by the bishop or officiant in the name of the congregation, and denominated a collect, because it was supposed to

---

manner, into twelve equal parts or hours, which of course were much longer in summer than in winter. The third of these hours was called undern or terce ; the sixth, midday ; and the ninth, none.   [1] Ps. cxviii. 164.

collect into a few words the aspirations of all. Of
these collects many are still retained in the service of
the Latin church, and are deservedly admired for
the spirit of devotion which they breathe, and the
simple yet nervous language in which they are expressed.

The service of the mass had been composed for a
particular purpose, the oblation of the sacrifice : the
course had in view a more general object, to supply
matter for prayer at the canonical hours, and was
therefore more susceptible of diversity of form and
arrangement. Hence it happened that not only in national churches, but even in neighbouring churches
of the same nation, considerable discrepancies
existed in the performance of the choral service.
In England, however, these discrepancies did not,
any more than those in the preparatory part of the
mass, lead to controversy among the missionaries.
But it was not long before the Roman liturgy in
both its branches began to supplant the Scottish,
even in churches belonging to those who had been
taught by monks from Iona. There was in favour
of the former its superior excellence, the veneration with which the Anglo-Saxons looked up
to Rome as to the mistress of churches, the partiality
of the pilgrims who had visited the eternal city, and,
as far as the province of Canterbury was concerned,
the authority of the canons, which enjoined that the
provincial churches should conform to the manner of
service followed in the metropolitan church. At
length, in 774, was held the Council of Cloveshoe,
under Archbishop Cuthbert, which confirmed the
ascendancy of the Roman, and effected the abolition

of the Scottish forms, by the following decree. " The great solemnities of our redemption shall be everywhere celebrated according to the written ritual which we have obtained from Rome, in the administration of baptism the solemnization of mass, and in all things thereunto pertaining ; moreover, the feasts of the saints through the course of the year shall be kept on the days fixed in the Roman martyrology, with the chant and psalmody appointed thereto ; and nothing shall be permitted to be read or chanted but what is taken from the authority of the Holy Scriptures, and allowed by the custom of the Roman church."[1] After this Council we hear nothing more of the Scottish forms in the Mercian churches, which formed part of the southern province : but in the north they appear to have kept their ground till a much later period. It is indeed true that in the seventh century St. Wilfrid, Bennet Biscop, and other pilgrims, had established the Roman liturgy in their respective monasteries, yet we find that even at the close of the eighth century, the Scottish liturgy was in daily, though not exclusive, use in the church of York. Charlemagne, by a capitulary issued from Aix-la-Chapelle, in 789, had ordered the Roman to be everywhere substituted in Gaul for the national ritual :[2] and in 796, Alcuin, from his residence in France, exhorted his former pupil, the archbishop Eanbald, to accomplish a similar improvement in the church of York, " to the end that the Divine worship might be performed

---

[1] Spelman, Con. 249, can. 13, 15.   Labbe, tom. vi. See note (M).

[2] Baluzii Capit. Aquisgran. c. 90.

there in a reverential and praiseworthy manner;" a high compliment to the Roman form from one who had been so long a master at York, and was so much attached to that church.[1] By whom such improvement was effected, by Eanbald or by one of his successors, we know not.

Still it cannot be said that exact uniformity was ever obtained. In the arrangement of the psalms for the several hours of prayer, the selection of lessons and capitula, the form of the responsories and collects, the order of the diocesan calendar, and the adaptation of epistles and gospels to votive masses and local festivals, numerous diversities continued to exist; for on these points bishops and abbots, the founders of churches and monasteries, and often the successors of the founders, looking upon themselves as legislators for their own subjects, assumed the liberty of making innovations and improvements, or of borrowing those already made by others; and, as if it were wished to multiply these diversities, while some in the chant of the psalms continued to use with the Romans the old translation from the Greek of the Septuagint, others adopted, with the Gallic churches, the new version from the Hebrew by St. Jerome.[2] A third source of discrepancy arose out

---

[1] Numquid non habes Romano more ordinatos libellos sacratorios abundanter? Habes quoque et veteris consuetudinis sufficienter sacramentaria majora. . . . Aliquid voluissem tuam auctoritatem incepisse Romani ordinis in clero tuo, ut exempla a te sumantur, et ecclesiastica officia venerabiliter et laudabiliter vobiscum agantur. Alcuini Op. i. p. 231. Ep. clxxi.

[2] Sciendum est, says Beda, translationes esse duas apud Latinos in usu atque honore, Romanam scilicet et Gallicam. Romana est qua utuntur Romani et plerique

of the monastic course which had been composed by
St. Benedict for his Italian disciples. This was
adopted, perhaps in several monasteries, certainly in
that of Lindisfarne, and retained by the clergy of St.
Cuthbert, after the cessation of the monastic order
in that establishment :[1] by St. Dunstan it was extended to all the houses of the Benedictine institute
in England ; and, after the Conquest, was retained,
by the order of Lanfranc.[2] I should, however, add
that such diversities were not understood to interfere
with the unity of religious worship. They were to
be found in England, till the Reformation, in the
breviaries of the churches of Sarum, York, and Hereford ; and even at the present day the English Benedictine monks make use of the monastic breviary
approved by Paul V., while the English Catholic
clergy use the breviary of the church of Rome.

4. Among the Anglo-Saxons, both at the celebration of the sacrifice, and during the canonical hours,
the whole service, with the exception of certain
prayers during the mass, was chanted by the choir.

Itali, quæ de Græco in Latinum a Symmacho et Aquila
sumpta est secundum septuaginta interpretes Ptolomæi
regis. Gallica est qua præcipue Galli utuntur. Hæc
autem præcipue sumpta est rogatu Damasi Papæ a beato
Hieronymo de Hebræo ad sententiam. Tom. viii. col. 423.

[1] Sim. Dunelm. ed. Bedford, p. 4; Reginal. Dunelm.
p. 28.

[2] St. Dunstan, however, out of veneration for St. Gregory,
ordered the monks to exchange the course of St. Benedict
for that of St. Gregory during the week of Easter. Septem
horæ canonicæ a monachis in ecclesia Dei more canoni-
corum propter auctoritatem S. Gregorii celebrandæ sunt.
(Concord. Monach. apud Reiner, par. iii. p. 899.) Lanfranc cared less for the apostle of the Saxons, and abolished
the custom. Wilk. Con. inter Constitut. Lanf. i. 339.

St. Paul had advised his disciples to sing in their
hearts to God in psalms and hymns and spiritual
canticles;[1] and we know that the primitive Christians
in their religious assemblies carefully practised what
he had so strongly recommended.[2] But centuries
passed before the improvement was introduced of
dividing the singers into two choirs, who should
alternately answer each other. The first essay
among the Greeks was made at Antioch, about the
year 350; the first among the Latins by St. Ambrose, at Milan, in 386; but the merit of the innovation was universally admitted, and the practice of
alternate chant spread in a few years to almost every
Christian people.[3] Whether it reached Britain, is
uncertain; for of the British chant we know nothing
but from a passage in Gildas, who praises its sweet-
ness and melody;[4] that it was not adopted in Ireland appears from the claim of St. Wilfrid to the
merit of introducing it among the monasteries
founded in the north by the Scottish missionaries.
In ancient churches the ecclesiastical music would,
of course, be modified by the national taste; but in
missionary churches 'the daughter would speak the
language of the mother,' and the service would be

---

[1] Eph. v. 18, 19; Col. iii. 15, 16.

[2] Soliti stato die ante lucem convenire, carmenque
Christo, quasi Deo, dicere secum invicem. Plinii, l. x.
ep. 97.

[3] Tunc hymni et psalmi ut canerentur secundum morem
orientalium partium, ne populus mœroris tædio contabes-
ceret, institutum est, et ex illo in hodiernum retentum,
multis jam et pene omnibus gregibus tuis, et per cætera
orbis, imitantibus. S. Aug. Conf. ix. c. 7.

[4] Dei laudes canora Christi tyronum voce suaviter
modulante. Gild. p. 44.

chanted as it was chanted where the teachers had been educated. Among the Anglo-Saxons, as the first teachers were Romans, the Roman chant, which had been reformed and improved by Pope Gregory, was introduced; and in proportion as the knowledge of the gospel was propagated, pupils from the recently converted churches resorted to the school of ecclesiastical music which had been opened at Canterbury.[1] Some years later, Bennet Biscop obtained from Pope Agatho the services of John, abbot of St. Martin's, and arch-cantor of St. Peter's. John accompanied the Anglo-Saxon to England, resided for twelve months in his monastery at Wearmouth, and gave lessons in the chant, not only to the monks of that abbey, but to deputies from most of the churches in Northumbria. Subsequently, schools were everywhere established; both clergy and monks strove to distinguish themselves by the excellence of their choirs; and of the importance attached to such excellence we may judge from the fact, that in many instances we find the office of head teacher actually discharged by the bishop or the abbot himself.[2]

---

[1] Bed. Hist. iv. c. 2 ; v. c. 20.

[2] If the pupil could not learn the chant, he was still obliged to learn the psalter, and to recite the service by heart. Qui id non est idoneus assequi, pronuntiantis modo simpliciter dicat atque recitet, quidquid instantis temporis ratio poscit. (Con. Clov. apud Spelm. p. 248.) We have sufficient proof of the pains taken by the Anglo-Saxons to excel in church music; of their success we know nothing but from their own testimony. It is very possible that, after all, they may have provoked the ridicule of their Roman masters as much as their neighbours the Gallic clergy; of whom we read that bibuli gutturis barbara

It may, perhaps, be thought that the daily recurrence of the choral service at the seven hours of prayer, would be felt by the monks and clergy as a grievous and insupportable burthen. It certainly occupied a considerable portion of their lives; but to men, animated with the true spirit of their profession, it proved, if we may credit their own statements, the chief charm of their existence.[1] It was a heavenly employment. It assimilated them to the angels, who are described in holy writ as constantly singing the praises of the Creator. They believed that these blessed spirits descended invisibly from above to join with their brethren upon earth in songs of adoration and praise.[2] Hence they would suffer no consideration, no pretence of business or of study, to withdraw them from the performance of this duty.[3] When they travelled, whether it was by sea

feritas, dum inflexionibus et repercussionibus mitem nititur edere cantilenam, naturali quodam fragore, quasi plaustra per gradus confuse sonantia, rigidas voces jactat, sicque audientium animos, quos mulcere debuerat, exasperando magis ac obstrependo conturbat. Joan. Diac. Vit. Greg. l. ii. c. 7.

[1] See Alcuin de Psalmorum usu, Oper. ii. 21; and the council of Cloveshoe, can. 27. Psalmodia opus divinum spiritu et mente agentibus magnum est et multiplex animarum medicamentum suarum. Spel. p. 253.

[2] Maxime angelici nobis spiritus adesse credendi sunt, ... cum psalmodiæ operam damus. (Bed. Hom. Op. v. p. 427.) Angelorum visitationes loca sacra frequentare non dubium est. Alc. Op. i. p. 282.

[3] A canonicis horis nullus fratrum se separet. (Alc. Op. i. p. 10; ii. p. 163.) Beda mentions his *quotidiana* cantandi in ecclesia cura (l. v. c. 25). Though it was one of the innumera monasticæ servitutis retinacula (In. epis. ad Accam), yet he sought no exception from it. He used to say, si angeli ibi non invenerint me inter fratres, nonne

or land, they chanted the daily service.[1] If indisposition confined them to their cells, some of their brethren were ready to sing or read the ' offices' with them or for them. For several months Bennet Biscop was too weak to move from his bed ; yet he never allowed a canonical hour to pass, either in the day or night, without sending for some of his monks, who, divided into two choirs, chanted at his bedside the appropriate service.[2]

Neither was psalmody confined to the choral duty. It offered the most approved form of private devotion ; and that for two reasons : 1, the psalter was of inspired origin, and therefore more perfect in itself, and more acceptable to God, than any prayer of human invention : 2, it had moreover been committed to memory by every monk or clergyman at his initiation in his profession, and was therefore always at hand, even when the eye-sight failed, or written forms were not to be procured. Hence 1. It was made to serve all the purposes of a miscellaneous prayer-book ; and selections were formed of passages from it expressive of praise and adoration,

---

dicere habent, Ubi est Beda ? Quare non venit ad adorationes statutas cum fratribus? Alc. Oper. i. p. 282, ep. ad Fratres S. Petri, ccxix.

[1] See the example of Aidan in Bed. iii. c. 5 ; of Ceolfrid in his life, inter Bed. Oper. Min. p. 161. Tecum clerici equitando psalmos dulci modulamine decantent. (Alc. Op. i. p. 65, ep. l. ad Eanb. Antist.) Quocumque vadis, clerici servitium Dei pleniter persolvant. Id. ii. 163.

[2] Per singulas diurnæ sive nocturnæ orationis horas, aliquos ad se fratrum vocabat, quibus psalmos consuetos duobus in choris resonantibus, et ipse cum eis quatenus poterat psallendo, quod per se solum nequiverat, eorum juvamine suppleret. Vit. S. Ben. int. Oper. Min. p. 152.

or of joy and gratitude, or of fear of God's judgments
and of hope in his mercies, or of the many other
devotional feelings which may arise in the mind of
man during his communings with his Creator. Beda
composed a psalter consisting solely of verses that
were obvious in meaning, or general in application,
or indicative of some great truth, or calculated to
excite and nourish certain pious affections.[1] Alcuin
followed a different method. He collected entire
psalms of a similar tendency in eight separate
fasciculi, prefixed to each fasciculus a title explanatory of its object, and thus supplied individuals
with forms of supplication applicable to their respective circumstances.[2] 2. Men were often solicited
to pray for their parents and relatives, their friends
and benefactors. For this purpose they were accustomed to chant a longer or shorter portion of the
psalter, and at the conclusion to fall on their knees,
and to say in Latin or English, if he, for whom they
prayed, was still living, " O Lord, have mercy upon
him : spare his sins, and convert him that he may do
thy holy will :" or, if he was already dead," according
to thy' great mercy, O Lord, give rest unto his soul,
and out of thy boundless goodness grant to him
the enjoyment of eternal light in the company of
thy saints."[3] 3. This practice of private psalmody

---

[1] Quem Beda collegit per versus dulces in laude Dei et
orationibus, per singulos psalmos juxta Hebraicam veritatem. (Alc. Oper. i. 169, ep. ad Arnon. cxvii.) It is
published among Alcuin's works, ii. p. 96, and those of
Beda by Giles, i. 221.

[2] Alc. Oper. ii. 21. See the same with additions in the
Durham Ritual, p. 183.

[3] Con. Clov. apud Spelm. 253.

was in high estimation among the aged and infirm, especially among those whose sight was impaired: for in those days, when the aids which we derive from the skill of the optician were unknown, the failure of eye-sight with men of letters crept on at a much earlier period than it does at present. Psalmody was generally found to offer relief from the tedium of gloom and loneliness, and to cheer the spirits in the hours of pain and languor.[1] It was the daily and favourite exercise of Beda and Alcuin; of Beda during the illness which preceded his death,[2] of Alcuin for years, during which the weakness of his eyes prevented him from reading or writing."[3] To both it proved a source of cheerful employment, tranquillizing to the mind, and incentive to devotion.

It cannot have escaped the notice of the reader that both the sacrificial service and the canonical hours were performed in the Latin language.[4] For the instruction of the people, the epistle and gospel were read, and the sermon was delivered in their

---

[1] Psalmodia, says Alcuin, cum magna delectatione peragenda. Cantus enim superelevat labores, et aufert animo tædium. Op. Alcuini, i. p. 366.

[2] See Cuthbert's Letter on the death of Beda. Sim. Dunelm. p. 72.

[3] Modo jam senex psalmorum decantatione saturari non poterat. Vit. Alc. c. viii. in Oper. Tom. i. p. lxv. Also chap. xxii. xxiv.

[4] It has been pretended that "in the daily service they chanted the Lord's prayer, the creed, and many portions of the psalms (probably from Aldhelm's version), in their own tongue." Churton, 141. From what source Mr. Churton derived his information I know not, nor can I persuade myself that there is any foundation for the statement.

native tongue, but God was publicly addressed by
the ministers of religion in the language of Rome.
Thus it had always been in the conversion of the
western nations, at whatever period the gospel was
preached to them, and from whatever country their
teachers came. At a more early age the Latin
liturgy had been established among the people of
Gaul, of Spain, of Britain, and of Ireland; in the
seventh century it was equally established among the
Anglo-Saxons at their conversion. It was the language to which the missionaries, Italians, Gauls, and
Scots, had been always accustomed in their own
countries : they would have deemed it a degradation
of the sacrifice and of the liturgy to subject them to
the variations and caprice of a barbarous idiom;
and their disciples, who never felt the thirst of
innovation, were content to tread in the footsteps of
their apostles. The practice has in later times been
severely condemned : it was, however, fortunate for
mankind that the teachers of the northern nations
were less wise than their modern critics. Had they
adopted in the liturgy the languages of their proselytes, the literature would probably have perished
with the empire of Rome. By preserving the use
of the Latin tongue, they imposed upon the clergy
the necessity of study, kept alive the spirit of
mental improvement, and transmitted to posterity
the writings of the classics, and the monuments of
profane and ecclesiastical history.

5. It has already been observed that the church
service was publicly performed on every day in the
year : but it was only on Sundays and festivals that
it was performed with full solemnity. By the pro-

mulgation of Christianity, the Jewish religion with
its rites had ceased to exist : the Sabbath had been
succeeded by the Sunday, the day of rest by a day of
worship, the seventh by the first day of the week :
and we are told by the most ancient writers that the
preference was given to the first day, because it was
on that day that God began to fashion the earth for
the habitation of man ; on the same that the Saviour
by his resurrection completed the great work of our
redemption, and on the same that the new law was
published to the world by the descent of the Holy
Ghost on the apostles. This institution was of
course introduced by the missionaries among the
converts, who were taught that the Sunday was a
day sacred to the service of God, and that to devote
it to secular employments incompatible with such
service was a profanation and sacrilege. Impressed
with this opinion, the Anglo-Saxon legislature came
to the aid of the church, and prohibited on the
Sunday not only all predial labour and every sort of
handicraft, by which men of low and servile condition were accustomed to earn their livelihood,[1]
but also the field-sports of hunting and hawking, the
dissipation of travelling, the sale or purchase of
merchandize, the prosecution of family feuds, the
holding of courts of justice and the execution of

---

[1] Archbishop Theodore divides works which come under
the denomination of ' servile,' into two classes : those
which were peculiar to men, and those peculiar to women.
The first class comprehends husbandry and garden work,
the felling of trees, the construction of houses, walls, &c.,
and the work which is done in quarries ; the second,
weaving, washing, sewing, the combing of wool, beating
of lin, and shearing of sheep. Theod. Pœnit. p. 45.

criminals. The transgressor under any of these
heads was liable to the punishments prescribed in the
doom-book. If a clerk was convicted of working
on a Sunday, he was adjudged to pay a fine of one
hundred and twenty shillings ; if a free servant, acting of his own will, to the loss of liberty, or a fine of
sixty shillings ; if a bondman acting in the same
manner, to be whipped, or to pay the price of his
hide, which was ten shillings. In like manner, the
lord who compelled others to labour paid a mulct
of thirty shillings, and forfeited the services of his
bondmen, who became free.[1] One exception, however, was allowed in favour of those who could
plead a reasonable excuse for travelling on that day.
" Sunday," says the lawgiver, " is very solemnly to
be reverenced : therefore we command that no
man dare on that holy day to apply to any
worldly work, unless for the preparing of his food :
except it happen that he must of necessity journey.
Then he may ride, or row, or journey by such
convenience as may be suitable to his way; on
the condition that he hear his mass, and neglect not
his prayers."[2]

From the exemption from labour thus granted to
the working classes, the Sunday itself was called
a freolsday, or day of freedom, and the manner of
keeping it in conformity with the preceding regulations, the freolsung or freedom of the Sunday. But
the day was not then comprised within the same
hours as it is now with us. Our ancestors, like the
Hebrews, made the evening precede the morning,

---

[1] Thorpe, i. pp. 38, 104, 170, 320, 368 ; ii. 45, 248, 308.
[2] Thorpe, ii. 420.

and reckoned the Sunday from sun-set on Saturday, to sun-set on the following day.[1] To these twenty-four hours the freolsung was at first confined;[2] but at a later period, some time before the reign of Edgar, though probably no change had taken place in the ecclesiastical computation, the freedom of the Sunday was enlarged in favour of the working population, beginning at the hour of none on Saturday, and lasting till the dawn of light on Monday morning.[3]

With respect to the religious duties of the Sunday, it was ordered by the council of Cloveshoe, that the clergy should " devote it to the worship of God exclusively ; that all abbots and priests should remain the whole day at their minsters and churches, and celebrate the solemnity of the mass; that they should shun all external engagements, all company of seculars, and all travelling not of absolute necessity, and should employ themselves in teaching their

---

[1] A vespera usque ad vesperam dies Dominica servetur. Theod. Pœnit. Thorpe, ii. 45.

[2] On ꞅunnan æꝼen eꝼꞇeꞃ hiꞃe ꞃeꞇl-ʒanʒe oð monan æꝼeneꞃ ꞃeꞇl-ʒanʒe. On sun-evening after her setting to the setting of the moon's evening. (Laws of Wihtred in 700.) The reader will observe, that by this method of computation, our Saturday evening was called Sunday evening by them.

[3] Healðe man ælceꞃ Sunnan-bæʒeꞃ ꝼꞃeolꞃunʒa ꝼꞃam non-ꞇiðe þæꞃ Sæꞇeꞃneꞃ bæʒeꞃ oþ þæꞃ Ꝿonan bæʒeꞃ lihꞇinʒe. Let men keep every Sunday's freedom from none-tide of Saturday till the dawn of light on Monday. (Laws of Edgar and of Canute; Thorpe, i. 264, 368, and Ælfric's canons, Thorpe, ii. 362.) The hour of none was the point exactly in the middle between mid-day and sun-set. It was, however, continually drawn backwards towards the mid-day, till at last it was in common conversation substituted for mid-day. This law points out to us the origin of the old custom of a half-holiday on Saturdays.

dependents the rules of a holy life, and of religious
conversation from the holy scriptures; and that they
should frequently exhort the people to repair again
and again to the church, to hear the word of God, to
receive instruction, and to be present at the mysterious service of the mass."[1]

The duties expected from the laity may be collected from the following injunction:—" It is most
right and proper that every Christian man, who has
it in his power to do so, should come on Saturday to
the church, and bring a light with him, and there
hear the vesper song, and after midnight the uht-
song, and come with his offering in the morning to
the solemn mass; and, when he is there, let there
be no dispute, or quarrel, or discord, but let him
with peaceful mind during the holy office intercede
with his prayers and his alms" (his offering) " both
for himself and all the people of God. And after
the holy service, let him return home, and regale
himself with his friends, and neighbours, and
strangers, but, at the same time, be careful that they
commit no excess either in eating or drinking."[2]   It

---

[1] Spel. Con. p. 249, can. xiv.
[2] Thorpe, ii. 420. The reason for this admonition was,
that at the hour of prime, the prime or chapter mass was
celebrated, after which particular priests, to satisfy their
own devotion, were accustomed to celebrate mass in
the different chapels within the church. Now it often
happened that laymen attended at one or other of these
masses, and then, as if they had fulfilled the obligation of
the day, spent the rest of it in feasting and drinking. To
put down this abuse, it was made the rule that all such
masses should be said in private; that the *public mass*
should be celebrated at mid-morning or terce; and that no
one should break his fast, " or taste any meat, before the
service of high mass was ended, but that all, both males

was in the "holy and ghostly kirk" (the parish
church, not any private chapel), "and at the high
and solemn mass," that they were summoned to
attend ; because there and at that time they would
hear the "commands of God's word" explained,
and receive instruction in their respective duties.
" Wherefore," it concludes, "we command all men,
whatever may be their rank, to attend at the high
mass, with the exception only of the hallowed
maidens, whose custom it is not to go out of their
minsters : these should continue within the inclo-
sures of their minsters, and there hear mass."[1]

The Sundays came round weekly : other holidays
came yearly, and were observed, some with greater,
some with less solemnity. They had been instituted
in honour of the principal events recorded in the
history of our redemption, and in memory of the
virgin mother of Christ, of his apostles, martyrs, and
saints : and were divided into two classes : holidays of inferior rank, which were kept only by the
clergy and monks in their different minsters and
churches, "with fuller service," that is, of nine lessons in the nocturnal song, and with additional or
better fare in the common refectory ; and holidays
of higher rank, which bound the laity as well as the
clergy, and were kept as national festivals with all
the solemnity of the Sunday. In the beginning of
the ninth century, such holidays were confined to
the festivals of Christmas and the Epiphany, the

---

and females, should assemble at the high mass, and in the
holy and ghostly church, and there hear the high mass and
the preaching of God's word." Thorpe, ii. 440-2.
    [1] Ibid. 442.

three days after Easter Sunday, the assumption of
the Virgin Mary, and the commemoration of the
apostles Peter and Paul, of St. Gregory, and of all
the saints.[1] Before the reign of Edgar, the calendar had been augmented with the addition of the
three other festivals of St. Mary, and the days kept in
honour of the apostles ; in the tenth year of Ethelred,
was added the eighteenth of March, the day on which
the king's brother Edward had been murdered ; and
in the reign of Canute, the nineteenth of May, the
anniversary of the death of St. Dunstan.[2]

---

[1] The freolsung or freedom of the festival was sometimes
extended to the days which preceded or followed it, as to
the whole space between Christmas and the Epiphany, to
the week before and the week after Easter, and to a whole
week before the Feast of the Assumption, "in harvest
time ;" but it appears to me to have differed from the freedom of the festival or the Sunday in this, that it prohibited
compulsory labour only, permitting those, who chose, to
work for themselves; and that it was granted by law to
freemen exclusively, though the lords were exhorted to
concede a similar indulgence to their slaves and bondmen.
(Thorpe, i. 92.) The same freolsung also belonged to the
Wednesday in each Ember week, and to "the day on
which Christ overcame the devil," an allusion to the temptation in the wilderness (Matt. iv. 1); which was read for
the gospel on the first Sunday in Lent. The day was probably Ash Wednesday.

[2] Thorpe, 1. 308, 370. In 1830, Mr. Fox published from
the Thesaurus of Hickes a short Anglo-Saxon poem, with a
translation, under the title of "The Poetical Calendar of
the Anglo-Saxons." It is plainly, from its contents, the
calendar of some monastery of Benedictine monks. It
concludes thus—" Now may ye find the times of the saints
that men should observe, as the command goeth through
Britain of the king of the Saxons at this same time." Now
this cannot mean that the king has ordered all the days
mentioned in the calendar to be kept holy, but is a notice
to the reader, that he may find in it the days of the month
on which occur the holidays, that the king has ordered to

6. Here, at the close of this first section of the present chapter, it may not be amiss to notice the practice of private prayer, as it was taught to the Saxon laity. It should be remembered that, with some exceptions in the higher classes towards the latter portion of their history, they were ignorant of the art of reading, and therefore could not acquire the knowledge of any set manner of vocal prayer, unless it were by committing it to memory from the frequent recitation of others. From men in such circumstances it would have been idle to expect an acquaintance with many different forms; and it was held sufficient to require from them a correct knowledge of the Apostles' creed, and of the Lord's prayer; of the former as a summary of their belief, of the latter as containing the several petitions which Christ himself recommended to his disciples. To this the parish priest was ordered to pay the strictest attention. It was his duty to see that all under his care were acquainted with these two forms, to inculcate the daily use of them every morning and evening, and not to allow any one ignorant of them to be sponsor for a child at baptism, or to receive him from the hands of the bishop, at confirmation.[1] " It is also," says an ancient Anglo-Saxon document, " to be made known to Christian laymen, that every one pray, at least, twice in the day—that is, in the morning, and in the evening." " In this wise ye shall teach them to pray : First, they shall sing the Creed : for that is most likely to open to them the

be kept with the usual freedom or freolsung. Several such orders occur in Thorpe, i. 92, 264, 308, 370.

[1] Thorpe, ii. 248, 424.

foundation of their true faith; and after he shall
have sung the Creed, let him say thrice, 'O God,
thou that madest me, have mercy upon me;' and
thrice, 'O God, have mercy upon me, a sinner:' and
after that let him sing the Lord's prayer." "And
this being done, and his Creator alone being worshipped, let him call upon God's saints, that they
intercede for him with God; first on Saint Mary, and
then on all God's saints." "And then let him arm
his forehead with the sign of the holy rood—that is,
let him sign himself, and then, with upraised hands
and eyes, let him in his heart thank God for all that
he has given to him, whether pleasant or unpleasant." "Let those who can attend the church, do
this in church; but let those who cannot, do it
wherever they may be, either in the morning, or the
evening, because the psalmist said, 'in every place is
God's power.'" "But, if he have not the leisure
that he can do it all thus, then let him at least do,
as we have before said—that is, say thrice, 'O God,
thou that madest me, have mercy upon me;' and
thrice, 'God, have mercy on me, a sinner;' and
after that, with inward heart, let him sing the Lord's
prayer."[1]

II.—1. Of the second class of religious rites, those
which had for their object the ministration of spiritual aid or the hallowing of persons and things, the
first in importance was the sacrament of baptism.

---

[1] Eccles. Institutes, Thorpe, ii. 418, 420, 424; xxii.
xxiii. xxix. The verb, to sing, when used of prayer, did
not necessarily imply any chant or particular sound, but
only the religious repetition of the words. Thus the
rubric—"Let them so end the service that each *sing* his
pater noster apart," means, let him recite it in silence to
himself.

With respect to its necessity and its spiritual effect
there was no difference of opinion among the different sets of missionaries.   They all taught that the
malediction which Adam had drawn upon himself by
his transgression had been inherited by his posterity;
that, unless this stain were washed away by the
water of baptism, no man could find admission
within the fold of Christ ; and that even the infant
born of Christian parents was, until it should be
regenerated by the sacrament, a 'heathen child,'[1]
without claim to the title or to any of the privileges
of a Christian.   There may perhaps have been some
diversity in the practice of the several ceremonies
which preceded or followed the baptism itself; but,
if there was, it was completely done away by the
council of Cloveshoe, which commanded that the
Roman ritual should be universally followed.[2]   The
regular manner of administering it was by immersion, the time the two eves of Easter and Pentecost, the place the baptistery, a small building
contiguous to the church, in which had been constructed a convenient bath called a font.   When an
adult solicited baptism, after a preparatory series of
instructions and examinations, he was called upon to
profess his belief in the true God by the repetition
of the Lord's prayer and the Apostles' creed ; and to
declare his intention of leading a life of piety by
making a threefold renunciation of the devil, his

---

[1] Hæðen cilb. ibid. 292, 390.—" The child was sinful
through Adam's transgression :" but after baptism " he
was God's man, and God's bearn."   Saxon Hom. in
Whelock, p. 64.
[2] Spelm. p. 149, xiii.

works, and his pomps.[1] He then descended into the
font; the priest depressed his head three times
below the surface, saying, I baptize thee in the name
of the Father, and of the Son, and of the Holy
Ghost; and he rose from the water, purified from sin,
a member of Christ's church, and heir to a heavenly
kingdom.[2] He was now anointed on the crown
with chrism in the form of the cross, and a white
linen cap called a chrismal was fastened over his
head.[3] If the bishop were present, he was first
confirmed; if not, he proceeded immediately to the
church, and attended at the mass, "that he might
communicate of the flesh and blood of the Redeemer,
and be consecrated by the victim without equal, the
saving victim of the body and blood of Christ."[4]

---

[1] All the preparatory ceremonies prescribed by the
Roman ritual at this day were then in use, not only in
Rome (see the Gelasian sacramentary, Murat. 1. 329), but
also in England, for most of them are accidentally mentioned in different national writers : the insufflation, by
Beda (Hist. l. v. c. 6); the unction on the breast and
between the shoulders, by Ælfric (Thorpe, ii. 390); the
ephpetha, and touching with saliva of the ears and nose,
by Beda (Hom. in Dom. 12, post Trinit. p. 281); the renunciation of Satan and the office of the sponsors, by the
council of Cloveshoe (Spelm. 148) and the Saxon homilist
(Whel. Hom. in Epiph. p. 180); and the whole process,
both before and after the immersion, by Alcuin, in his
epistle to Odwin. Oper. ii. p. 127.

[2] Peccator in fontem descendit, sed purificatus ascendit;
filius mortis descendit, sed filius resurrectionis ascendit;
filius prævaricationis descendit, sed filius reconciliationis
ascendit; filius iræ descendit, sed filius misericordiæ
ascendit; filius diaboli descendit, sed filius Dei ascendit.
Beda, Hom. in Dom. 1 post Epiph. p. 111.

[3] See Beda, l. ii. c. 14, v. c. 7; Hom. in Epiph. p. 275;
and Ælfric, in Thorpe, ii. 390.

[4] Beda has mentioned, in three places, this communion

The rites of the day were concluded by his partaking of a mixture of milk and honey, which was given to him to taste, as a token that he was now introduced into the congregation of Christ, the true land of promise, of which the land of Canaan had been only the figure.[1] Still it was expected that he should return to the church on each of the next seven days, to attend to daily instruction and to receive daily the communion. On the last the chrismal was removed, and the ceremony was concluded.

In the baptism of children the same rites were observed with a few necessary variations. The sponsors were examined whether they possessed the qualifications required for the charge which they had undertaken, and then made the profession of faith, and the three renunciations in the name of the child. At the time of baptism they ranged themselves on each side of the font, those bearing the male children on the right, and those with females on the left. The priest himself descended into the water, which reached to his knees. Each child was suc-

---

after baptism in the following terms :—Ubi redemptoris nostri carni et sanguine communicemus. Bed. Hom. in Nat. S. Andreæ, p. 256. Dominici corporis et sanguinis victima singulari consecrari. Hom. in Dom. 2 post Epiph. p. 131. Salutari hostia Dominici corporis et sanguinis consecrandus. Hom. in Purif. S. Mariæ, p. 175.

[1] This rite is as old as the time of Tertullian, by whom it is mentioned. E fonte suscepti, lactis et mellis concordiam prægustamus. De Coron. Milit. c. iii. The blessing pronounced over it may be found in most sacramentaries : but in the Durham ritual it is not only copied incorrectly, but is most unaccountably interpolated, from line 5 in p. 129, to line 3 in page 130, with other matter, which seems to belong to the ceremony of planting a cross.

cessively delivered undressed into his hands, and he plunged it thrice into the water, pronounced the mysterious words, and then restored it to its sponsors. The anointing with chrism, the confirmation, and the communion followed : but the last was administered under the sole form of wine by the priest, who dipped the tip of his finger into the chalice, and then introduced it into the mouth of the child.[1] This was repeated during seven days, at the end of which the chrismal was removed.[2]

Such were the canonical regulations with respect to the administration of baptism ; but regulations which were often made to yield to convenience or necessity. The missionaries did not wait for the construction of baptisteries and fonts, but baptized their proselytes in rivers and running waters :[3] and after the conversion of a nation, in the course of a generation or two the baptism of adults almost ceased, and none but infants, and those too of very recent birth, were brought to the font at the appointed times of Easter and Whitsuntide. The multitude of single baptisms continued to increase, the baptisteries were gradually neglected ; and it was found more convenient to place a font of wood

---

[1] Martene, i. 56. No. xv.

[2] " Ye shall housel (communicate) children when they are baptized, and let them be carried to mass, that they be houseled all the seven days, whilst they are unwashed." Thorpe ii. 392. That is, till the chrismal was removed, when the head was washed with salt and water.

[3] Quibus triginta sex diebus a mane usque ad vesperam nil aliud ageret quam confluentem eo de cunctis viculis ac locis plebem Christi verbo salutis instruere, atque instructam in fluvio Gleni (the Glen) qui proximus erat, lavacro remissionis abluere. Bed. l. ii. c. 14.

or stone in the parish church; for, on account of the great importance attached to this sacrament, laws to secure its due administration to all children soon after their birth were enacted by civil as well as ecclesiastical authority. The parish priest was ordered to be always ready, whenever his ministry might be required, in cases of sickness. It made no difference whether he were summoned during the night or the day; whether to a child within his own shriftshire, or to one belonging to another. If through his negligence the child died without baptism, a severe punishment awaited him, amounting even to the forfeiture of his benefice, and of the privileges of his order.[1] Parents in like manner were commanded to present their children for baptism, within thirty-seven days from the birth in the south, within nine days in Northumbria: their negligence, however, if the child died without the sacrament, was differently punished in different places; sometimes according to the regulations in the 'Penitential,' sometimes with an additional fine imposed by the civil power.[2]

---

[1] Thorpe, i. 38, 102, 168; ii. 25, 292, 352, 412. I may add that to baptize an infant in danger of death was the duty of any man or woman, who might be present. Omnibus fidelibus licet, ubi forte morituros invenerit non baptizatos, necessitate cogente, baptizare; imo præceptum est baptizare illos in nomine Patris, et Filii, et Spiritus Sancti, intinctos aut superfusos aqua. Theod. Pœnit. apud Thorpe, ii. 51.

[2] Ibid. ii. 82, 246. In Northumbria, 'if a child died a heathen' before he was nine days old, through neglect on the part of the parents, they were to submit to the penance enjoined in the book, and to pay no fine; if he were more than nine days old, they were not only to do penance, but to pay twelve ores for their presumption in allowing him to remain a heathen so long. Ibid. 292.

2. It is evident that the rubric, directing confirmation to follow immediately after baptism,[1] could not be observed, when it became customary to baptize children in the parish churches, and at all seasons of the year. Hence the confirmation of the newly baptized was made an important part of the bishop's duty in his annual visitation. We repeatedly read of journeys undertaken by St. Cuthbert chiefly with this object. On one occasion, departing from Hexham with his clerks, he travelled among the mountains till he came to the district called Alise, where there was neither church nor house to receive him. But his attendants fixed tents for the bishop, and with the branches of trees built huts for themselves around the tents. Thither children were brought to him for confirmation from the secluded hamlets in the country; and he remained among them two days, ministering to those who had been recently born again in Christ the grace of the Holy Spirit by the imposition of his hands, " placing his hand on the head of each, and anointing them with the chrism which he had blessed."[2] These pas-

---

[1] The antiquity of this rubric is shewn by St. Cyprian, from whom we learn the practice of his time, ut qui in ecclesia baptizantur, præpositis ecclesiæ offerantur, et per nostram orationem et manus impositionem Spiritum Sanctum consequantur, et signaculo Dominico consummantur. Ep. lxxiii. p. 184. This word consummentur explains Augustine's demand of the Britons, ut baptizandi ministerium compleatis. Bed. ii. c. 2. The Britons did not confirm after baptism.

[2] Parochiam suam visitans, ut monita salutis omnibus largiretur, necnon etiam *nuper* baptizatis ad accipendam Spiritus Sancti gratiam manum imponeret. Beda, Vit. Cuthb. c. xxix. p. 106. Devenit in montana et agrestia loca... tetenderunt ergo ei tentoria in via, et cæsis de

sages are worthy of notice: as they prove both the grace attributed to this sacrament, and the manner in which it was conferred before the year 700; and are in perfect accordance with the form described in the pontifical of Archbishop Egbert, who succeeded to the see of York about thirty years afterwards. According to that pontifical, the bishop prayed thus—"Almighty and Everlasting God, who hast granted to this thy servant to be born again of water and the Holy Ghost, and hast given to him remission of his sins, send down upon him thy sevenfold Holy Spirit, the paraclete from heaven. *Amen*. Give to him the spirit of wisdom and understanding, *Amen*—the spirit of counsel and fortitude, *Amen*— the spirit of knowledge and piety, *Amen*. Fill him with the spirit of the fear of God and our Lord Jesus Christ, and mercifully sign him with the sign of thy holy cross for life eternal." The bishop then marked his forehead with chrism, and proceeded thus—" Receive this sign of the holy cross with the chrism of salvation in Christ Jesus unto life eternal." The head was then bound with a fillet of new linen to be worn seven days, and the bishop resumed—" O God, who didst give thy Holy Spirit to thine apostles, that by them and their successors he might be given to the rest of the faithful, look down on the ministry of our lowliness, and grant

---

vicina silva ramusculis sibi quique tabernacula ad manendum, qualia potuere, fixerunt. . . dum Spiritus Sancti gratiam nuper baptizatis per manus impositionem ministraret. Id. c. xxxii. p. 109. . . In the older life, by a contemporary monk of Lindisfarne, from which Beda wrote, it is expressed thus : manum ponens supra caput singulorum, liniens unctione consecrata quam benedixerat. Bed. Oper. Min. p. 277.

that into the heart of him whose forehead we have
this day anointed, and confirmed with the sign of the
cross, thy Holy Spirit may descend; and that dwelling therein, he may make it the temple of his
glory, through Christ our Lord." The confirmed
then received the episcopal blessing, and communicated during the mass.[1]

Hence it will appear that confirmation was administered to children at a very early age, as soon
as might be after baptism. The reason was, that in
the theology of the period no man was considered a
perfect Christian, who had not enjoyed the three great
privileges of a Christian: purification from sin by
baptism, participation of the body and blood of
Christ by communion, and the infusion of the Holy
Spirit through confirmation. The two first he might
receive from the priest at his baptism: for the last
was required the ministry of a bishop.[2]

3. From the arrival of Augustine till the reformation, the English name for the eucharist was
the housel. To administer the eucharist was 'to
housel;' to receive it was 'to go to the housel, or to be
houselled.' Since the reformation, the word 'sacrament' has generally been substituted for it; but

---

[1] Martene, l. 1, c. 1, art. v. p. 92.   Bassoni, 1788.

[2] There is no canon of the Anglo-Saxon church which
prescribes the time for confirmation. One under king
Edgar, after ordering baptism within thirty-seven days
from the birth, adds, "and that no man remain unbishoped
too long." Thorpe, ii. 246. But we find in the diocesan
synod of Worcester in 1240, a threat of exclusion from
entrance into the church, against all parents who allow
their children to remain a full year without confirmation;
a strong argument that some similar regulation prevailed
in the Anglo-Saxon period.

'sacrament' does not adequately supply its place. Sacrament denotes a sacred sign : but housel implies a victim of sacrifice.[1] After their conversion the Anglo-Saxons knew no other sacrifice than that of Christ's body and blood in the mass, and of consequence had no other victim or housel but the same body and blood. Their Latin writers adopted the tone of their vernacular language. With Beda the housel is—the saving victim of the Lord's body and blood—the victim without an equal—a particle of the sacrifice of the Lord's offering—the victim of his blood, the body that was slain and the blood that

---

[1] It is plain that the word 'husel,' or 'husle,' was not imported by the missionaries, nor formed from any Anglo-Saxon root, in consequence of the new doctrine. It must then have belonged to their old vocabulary, for we find it under the form of hunsle in the Mæso-Gothic version of the gospels made by Ulphilas, about the year 370. In the few fragments which remain of that version it occurs thrice ; and, as the version was made from the Greek gospels, we can, from the comparison, discover the meaning of the word, without any danger of error. According to Junius (Gloss. Goth. 205), it is found in Matt. ix. 13 ; in Mark ix. 48 ; and in John xvi. 2 ; and, if we turn to the Greek text, we shall see that hunsle in the two first passages represents the Greek word θυσία, a sacrifice or victim ; and in the third, λατρεία, generally a worship of God, but in that particular instance the sacrifice of a living victim. Hence there can be little doubt that before their conversion the Anglo-Saxons used the word husle to denote a victim of sacrifice, and after their conversion transferred it to the Christian sacrifice of the mass. So deeply, indeed, was this idea impressed upon the mind of Beda, that he employs the word ' victim,' to denote the service itself. Precor vos, Pater charissime, ut in sanctarum vestrarum (forsan, sanctis vestris), victimis in conspectu altissimi pro me misero peccatore fideliter intercedatis. Ep. ad Herefrid. Oper. vi. p. 344 ; Edit. Giles.

was shed by the hands of unbelievers.[1] The writings of the Scottish missionaries, if they left any writings, have long since perished; but the works of Cummian and Cumineus and Adamnan, and the antiphonary of the monastery of Benchor, bear testimony that similar language was in constant use also in the Scottish church.[2]

The time appointed for partaking of the housel was towards the conclusion of the mass, immediately after the communion of the celebrant. During the whole of the Anglo-Saxon period, it was administered under both kinds, first to the clergy of the church, and then to the people, the priest ad-

---

[1] Salutaris hostia Dominici corporis et sanguinis. (Homil. p. 256.) De sacrificio Dominicæ oblationis particula. (Hist. iv. c. 14.) Dominici corporis victima singularis. (Hom. p. 131.) Hostiæ proprii sanguinis. (Hom. p. 290.) Corpus et sanguis illius non infidelium manibus ad perniciem ipsorum funditur, et occiditur, sed fidelium ore suam sumitur ad salutem. Hom. p. 275.

[2] Sacrificium Missæ—sacrificale mysterium—sacra sancti sacrificii mysteria. (Cummian. Pœnit. c. xi.; Vita S. Columb. pp. 29, 32; Vit. S. Columb. l. i. c. 40, ii. c. 1, iii. c. 12, 17.) In the Antiphonary of Benchor, now in the Ambrosian library at Milan, we have the hymn sung during the communion—

Sancti venite,
Christi corpus sumite,
Sanctum bibentes,
Quo redempti sanguinem. . . .
Pro universis
Immolatus Dominus,
Ipse sacerdos
Existit et hostia. . . .
Alpha et Omega,
Ipse Christus Dominus
Venit, venturus
Judicare homines.

ministering the offletes, and the deacon the cup. Originally, during the time of persecution, it was deemed the duty of all to communicate who were present at the sacrifice : afterwards, when Christianity became the religion of the people, this practice could not with propriety be retained ; frequency of communion began to decline, and became dependent on the choice of the individual. When our ancestors received the faith, the custom of general communion on the Sundays was still preserved in the church of Rome ; and it is but reasonable to suppose that the Roman missionaries established it in the Anglo-Saxon churches of their foundation. But in the north, the Scottish missionaries had appointed three days in the year for general communion, the feasts of Christmas, the Epiphany, and Easter ; and this arrangement, by directing the devotion of the people to those particular seasons, had led almost to the extinction of frequent communion, except among the inmates of monasteries.[1] Venerable Beda noticed the abuse, and in strong language exhorted Archbishop Egbert to reform it by his authority. There were, he maintained, among his countrymen, thousands in every department of life, whose religious conduct entitled them to the privilege of communicating at the heavenly mysteries on every Sunday and holiday, as was done in other

---

[1] Quod genus religionis et Deo devotæ sanctificationis tam longe a cunctis pene nostræ provinciæ laicis per incuriam docentium, et quasi prope peregrinum abest, ut hi, qui inter religiosiores esse videntur, non nisi in natali Domini et Epiphania et Pascha sacrosanctis mysteriis communicare presumant. Bed. ep. ad Egb. inter Oper. Min. p. 222.

churches, and as Egbert himself had seen practised in the church of Rome. The fault was in the clergy, who neglected to instruct the people in the spiritual benefits of this sacrament, and thus suffered them to remain in ignorance, and in indifference, the natural offspring of that ignorance.[1]

The sentiments of this pious monk were shared by the bishops at the council of Cloveshoe, in 747, who recommend to laymen the practice of frequent communion, that they may not be of the number of those who eat not the flesh of the son of man, and drink not his blood ; whence it must follow that they have not life in them.[2] Later we meet with repeated admonitions that men, in consideration of their spiritual wants, ought to receive the housel at least three times in the course of the year ; and of advice that, if they lead religious lives, they communicate on each Sunday in Lent, and each of the three days before, and on each day within, the octave of Easter.[3]

The conditions required of the communicant were, that he should come fasting[4]—a practice which remounts to the first ages of Christianity ; and that, if he had fallen into sin, he should have confessed it,

---

[1] Cum sint innumeri innocentes et castissimæ conversationis pueri et puellæ, juvenes et virgines, senes et anus qui absque ullo scrupulo controversiæ omni die Dominico, sive etiam in natalitiis sanctorum apostolorum sive martyrum, quomodo ipse in sancta Romana et Apostolica ecclesia fieri vidisti, mysteriis cœlestibus communicare valeant. Ibid.

[2] Syn. Clov. Wilk. p. 98, xxiii.

[3] Apud Thorpe, ii. 438.

[4] "We enjoin that no man take of the housel unfasting, unless it be for extreme sickness." Can. apud Thorpe, ii. 253.

have submitted to the penance enjoined, and have received the permission of his confessor.[1]

4. In baptism were forgiven the sins committed before baptism : how were sins committed after baptism to be forgiven ?   To this important question the scripture replied indirectly, that there remained no second baptism ;[2] a more explicit answer may be drawn from the practice of those who were taught by the apostles, that a longer and more laborious process was required ; that to the Christian who had made the shipwreck of his innocence, penance was the only plank which could save him from ruin. The reader of ancient ecclesiastical history must be well acquainted with the several classes into which penitents were divided in the earlier ages, and the penitential discipline to which each class was subjected.   But the severity of these regulations was compelled to bend to the change of circumstances ; after the conversion of the emperors and the admission of the multitude into the church, it gradually wore away; the classes of penitents began to disappear, and, as early as in the fifth century, we find that the time for public penance was confined, even in the church of Rome, to the forty days of Lent.[3] Still the principle on which it had been founded

---

[1] " Yet may not he, who is polluted with deadly sins, dare to partake of God's housel, unless he first atone for his sins ; if he do otherwise, he will partake of it to his injury." (Ælf. Hom. i. 266.)   " No one ought to receive it without his confessor's leave, to whom he shall previously have confessed all that he has wrought against God's will, as far as he can recollect, and have made atonement according to his sentence."   Apud Thorpe, ii. 440.

[2] Heb. vi. 4.

[3] Gerbert, Disquis. v. p. 458.

was retained as the doctrine of the apostles ; and the necessity of penance was taught by all the missionaries to the Anglo-Saxons, from whatever country they came,[1] and was most earnestly inculcated by the preachers and divines during the whole existence of the Anglo-Saxon church. " No man," says the homilist, " can be baptized twice ; but, if a man err after his baptism, we believe that he may be saved, if he sorrow (behrcowsiath) for his sins with tears, and do penance for them, as his teacher shall instruct him."[2]

Penance in their theology comprised four things :

---

[1] I make this assertion designedly, because Inett assures us that auricular confession, the first step towards the imposition of penance, was unknown to the Anglo-Saxons converted by the Scots, and a burthen laid upon them by Archbishop Theodore. (Inett, i. p. 85.) Had he, then, never read Adamnan's Life of St. Columba, in which it is mentioned in pp. 71, 75, 80, 89, 139 ; nor the penitential of St. Cummian (Mab. Anal. Vit. p. 17) ; nor Beda's testimony respecting St. Cuthbert (Hist. l. iv. c. 25, and Vit. Cuth. c. ix. xvi.) ; nor his testimony respecting the confession of the Scottish monk (Hist. l. iv. c. 25) ? From these authorities it is manifest, that confession was inculcated by the Scottish theologians ; and it is equally certain that Inett misunderstood the only authority to which he appealed, the testimony of Archbishop Egbert. That prelate does not state that the practice of confession was unknown in the north before it was introduced by Archbishop Theodore ; but that from the time of Vitalian and Theodore it had been the *custom* to spend the two weeks before Christmas in fasting, and to go to confession, and to give alms at the same time, that men might be the better prepared for communion on the feast of the Lord's nativity. Quatenus puriores Dominicæ communionis perceptionem in Natali Domini perciperent. (Deal. Egb. apud Thorpe, ii. 96.) The custom introduced by Theodore regarded the particular time of the year, not the practice of confession.

[2] Hom. i. p. 292. De fide catholica.

sorrow for sin, confession of sin, penitential works, and reconcilement or absolution.

1. *Sorrow.* Of these things, the first, the foundation on which the other three were made to rest, was real sorrow of heart for the offence committed. Without it the others were of no avail. " The man who will not sorrow for his sins in this life, will obtain no forgiveness from God in that to come."[1] " God is so merciful, that he will shew mercy to him who turns from sin, if with inward sorrow of heart he turn to penance." It was called behreowsung, from the verb 'hreowan,' which has come down to us in English under the form of 'to rue.'

2. *Confession.* To confess with sorrow was the next requisite. " We cannot be saved, unless we confess sorrowfully, what through our negligence we have done unrighteously. All hope of forgiveness is in confession. Confession, with true penance, (dædbote) is the angelic remedy of our sins." . . . . " No man will obtain forgiveness of his sins from God, unless he confess to some of the ministers of God, and do penance according to his judgment." " Without confession there is no pardon."[2] " The medicine of a sinful man is that he confess, and do penance, and sin no more."[3] Hence they looked

---

[1] Ib. 272.

[2] Whelock, pp. 341, 343, 423.

[3] Thorpe, ii. 330. To these passages I might have added many more of similar import; but they are sufficient to shew with how little reason Whelock maintained that in the Anglo-Saxon, as in the Protestant church of England, confession was advised only, and not commanded. (Hist. Bed. pp. 215, 216. Index, art. Confessio.) Mr. Soames is delighted to find in an old manuscript (Vesp. D. 15, f. 100), and in Petit's Capitula collecta ex fragmentis (Tom.

upon confession not merely as a pious ceremony
dependent on the devotion of the individual, but as
a matter of obligation on the sinner, and binding the
highest minister in the church as strictly as the
lowest layman.[1] The penitent, whosoever he might
be, was instructed to approach with humility and
compunction, to make in the presence of his confessor a profession of his faith, to bare before him
the secrets of his conscience, and to disclose faithfully the offences of his life, " which he had ever
committed, whether in word, or in work, or in
thought."[2]

3. *Penitential works.* " By confession," to use the
words of an Anglo-Saxon document, " the venom
had been extracted : it now remained for the leech
to prescribe the manner of cure."[3] He had the
penitential lying before him, the doom-book, which
was supposed to apportion the measure of punishment to the degree of guilt ; but he was admonished
not to abide implicitly by its directions. It seldom
happened in practice that two cases were exactly
similar ; and he was therefore ordered not to decide

---

i. p. 47), that according to Theodore, in a case of necessity
a man may make his confession to God alone—Confes-
sionem suam Deo soli, si necesse est licebit facere (Bamp-
ton's Lectures, p. 287); and in his history is highly amused
at the " embarrassment which this passage has afforded to
Romanism." (Hist. p. 87.) It is, however, difficult to
understand this cause for exultation ; for the doctrine of
Theodore then, is the doctrine of Catholic divines yet ; that
in cases of necessity confession to God alone is sufficient.
   [1] Thorpe, p. 77.
   [2] Id. 428. There are several forms of confession in
Alcuin,—De usu psalmorum. Tom. ii. p. 44.
   [3] Id. ii. p. 278.

till he had carefully weighed every aggravating or extenuating circumstance, the disposition of the penitent, his age, health, ability, and station in life, and then to qualify the rigour of the penalty prescribed in the doom-book accordingly to what he honestly believed to be the exigency of the case.[1] This was justly considered one of the most perplexing and most painful of his duties,—one in which he was most liable to err from want of judgment, or worldly consideration; and he was therefore constantly reminded that God would demand at his hands every soul that he should suffer to perish through favour, or negligence, or incapacity.[2]

4. *Reconcilement.* There still remained the prayer of reconciliation or absolution. It was believed that the power of binding and loosing, conferred by Christ on his apostles, had been inherited by his church, and it became a question with the confessor, as a minister of that church, at what time, and in what circumstances, he should exercise that power in favour of the penitent. In lighter and secret cases, he generally absolved him after his confession, and restored him to communion immediately; but, where the offence was more heinous, or called for public example, he deferred the absolution for a con-

---

[1] "We must moderate, and discretely distinguish between age and youth, wealthy and poor, healthly and sickly, and men of every degree. And if a man do aught amiss unwilfully, that is not like to him who willingly and wilfully doeth amiss of his own accord. And also he, who is an unwilling agent in that which he misdoeth, is always worthy of protection and of a milder sentence. Let every deed be cautiously distinguished before God and the world." Id. p. 262; also pp. 278, 280.

[2] Thorpe, ii. 402.

siderable time, and waited till a great part, or the
whole of the penance had been performed. He was
ordered by the canon " to watch attentively with
what compunction of heart, and with what exactitude of performance, the penance was fulfilled;
and to judge from that whether he ought to grant
him forgiveness or not."[1]

In the preceding page mention has been made of
the 'penitential.' By that word was understood a
set of regulations made for the guidance of confessors,
that in the imposition of penance they might act
according to the spirit of the ancient canons, when
they could no longer enforce them according to the
letter. With this view, compilations had been made
and preserved in the different churches; but they
were all subsequently thrown into the shade by the
penitential which Archbishop Theodore composed
for the use of the English church. His authority
was sufficient to ensure its adoption among the
bishops of his province; its merit or reputation led
to its introduction into the neighbouring churches

---

[1] Ꞑnƀ ꞃpa hun be þam ꞅoꞃꝣꞁꝼenniꝽꞃꞁe ƀon. (Thorpe,
ii. 266.) This, and the similar expression ' to give him
absolution,' are repeatedly used in the canons. (Ibid. ii.
178, 266.) By the Saxon homilist it is likened to the office
of unbinding Lazarus committed by Christ to the apostles.
After he has risen from the grave by confession, "then
shall the teacher unbind him from eternal punishment, as
the apostles unbound the body of Lazarus,"—þonne ꞅceol
ꞃe laꞃꞃeoꝼ hine unƀinƀan ꝼnam þam ecan pꞁꞇeꞅ ꞃpa ꞃpa þꞁ
Ꞻpoꞃꞇoh hichamhce Lazaꞃum ahꝝƀon. (Serm. apud
Whelock, p. 405.) Alcuin says, Sacerdotes a Deo Christo
cum sanctis apostolis ligandi solvendique potestatem ac-
cepisse credimus; and thence infers the necessity of confession. Quomado sacerdos reconciliat, quem peccare non
novit? Oper. i. 143, 5.

on the continent, where it long formed the groundwork of the penitential codes followed in most
dioceses.[1] The principal species of punishment which
it enjoined was fasting; but the manner and duration varied with the nature of the offence. The
more pardonable sins of frailty or surprise might be
expiated by a less rigorous fast of ten, twenty, or
thirty days; but when the offence was of a darker
die, when it argued deep and premeditated malice,
a longer course of austerity was required, and one,
five, seven years, or even a whole life of penance,
was deemed a cheap and easy compensation. So
dreary a prospect might have plunged the penitent
into despair or indifference: but his fervour was
daily animated by the hopes and fears of religion;
his past fidelity was rewarded by subsequent indulgences; and the yoke was prudently lightened the
longer it was worn. After a certain period, to the
severe regimen of bread and water, succeeded a more
nutritious diet, which excluded only the flesh of
quadrupeds and fowls: and the fasts, that originally

---

[1] Many copies of these penitential codes are still in
existence. It should, however, be remembered that, when
they were composed, it was generally held that the apostolic prohibition of eating blood and strangled animals, as
well as some of the Mosaic regulations respecting clean
and unclean meats, were still in force; which will explain
the occurrence of several passages which may otherwise
appear trifling and ridiculous; and also that the owners
and transcribers of penitentials did not conceive themselves
bound to adhere scrupulously to the original text, but
interpolated new decisions from other sources, whenever
they thought proper, which will serve to explain the dis-
agreement that often exists between separate copies, and
the inconsistency which may be sometimes observed in
passages of the same copy.

had comprised six, were gradually contracted to
three, or even fewer days in the week.[1]

Still the severity of this discipline naturally led
to its extinction. It interfered too much with the
ordinary occupations of life to allow of its being
generally enforced ; and few persons possessed sufficient strength of resolution to persevere through so
long a course of privation and austerity. Necessity
introduced some mitigations, and the ingenuity of
penitents discovered others. 1st. When the sinner
had delayed his conversion, till he was alarmed at
the near approach of death, it was idle to enjoin
many years of penance : and he was rather advised,
according to the command of the holy scriptures, to
redeem his sins with works of mercy, and to com-
mute the fasts of the canons for donations to the
church, and to the poor.[2] An idea so consonant to
the maxims of Saxon jurisprudence was eagerly
adopted, and insensibly improved into a perfect
system, which regulated with precision, according to
the rank and wealth of the penitent, the price at
which the fast of a day, a month, or a year, might
be lawfully redeemed. This indulgence, which had
originally been confined to the dying, was claimed
with an equal appearance of justice by the sick and
the infirm ; and was at last extended to all, whose
constitutions or employments were incompatible

---

[1] Ibid. passim.

[2] Besides donations to churches, he might " build bridges
over deep waters and over foul ways;" " help poor men,
widows, and step-children and foreigners ; free his own
slaves, and redeem to freedom the slaves of other men ;
feed the needy, and clothe, house and fire, bathe, and
bed them." Thorpe, ii. 282.

with the rigour of a long and severe fast.[1] By the rich it was accepted with gratitude; but to the poor it offered an illusory boon, which only aggravated the hardships of their condition. 2nd. To remove the invidious distinction, a new species of commutation was adopted. Archbishop Egbert, founding his decision on the authority of Theodore, intrusted it to the prudence of the confessor, to enjoin, when the penitent pleaded infirmity or inability, a real equivalent in prayers or money. Thus a new system of canonical arithmetic was established; and the fast of a day was taxed at the rate of a silver penny for the rich, or of fifty paternosters for the illiterate, and fifty psalms for the learned.[2] That these compensations would accelerate the decline of the primitive discipline, was foreseen and lamented by the bishops: and the fathers of the council of Cloveshoe made a vigorous but fruitless attempt to uphold the ancient discipline. "It is necessary," they observe to the Saxon clergy, "that the enjoyment of forbidden pleasures should be punished by the subtraction of lawful gratifications. Alms and prayers are undoubtedly useful, but they are designed to be the auxiliaries, not the substitutes, of fasting."[3] The torrent, however, was irresistible; and the condemned indulgences were gradually sanctioned, first by the silence, afterwards by the approbation of their successors.

3rd. There was another, and a more singular innovation, which equally provoked and equally survived

---

[1] Thorpe, ii. pp. 61, 284, 286.
[2] Id. ii. pp. 67, 70, 133, 220.
[3] Spelm. p. 253. Anno 747.

their censure. Among a powerful and turbulent
nobility, it was not difficult to discover men, whose
offences were so numerous, that to expiate them, according to the letter of the canons, would require a
greater number of years than could probably fall to
the lot of any individual. Sinners of this description
were admonished to distrust so precarious a resource;
to solicit the assistance of their friends, and to relieve
their own insolvency by the vicarious payments of
others. In obedience to this advice, they recommended themselves to the prayers of those who were
distinguished by the austerity and sanctity of their
lives ; endeavoured by numerous benefits to purchase
the gratitude of the monks and clergy; and by procuring their names to be enrolled among the members of the most celebrated monasteries, indulged
the hope of partaking in the merit of the good works
performed by those societies. But it was not long
before a system, which offered so much accommodation to human weakness, received considerable
improvements ; and men were willing to persuade
themselves that they might atone for their crimes
by substituting in the place of their own, the austerities of mercenary penitents.[1] It was in vain that
the council of Cloveshoe thundered its anathemas

---

[1] "Nuper," say the bishops assembled at Cloveshoe,
"quidam dives petens reconciliationem pro magno quodam
facinore suo citius sibi dari, affirmavit idem nefas juxta
aliorum promissa in tantum esse expiatum, ut si deinceps
vivere posset trecentorum annorum numerum, pro eo plane
his satisfactionum modis, per aliorum scilicet psalmodiam,
et jejunium, et eleemosynam persolutum esset, excepto
illius jejunio, et quamvis ipse utcumque vel parum jeju-
naret." Spelm. p. 253.

against their disobedience: the new doctrine was supported by the wishes and the practice of the opulent; and its toleration was at length extorted, on the condition, that the sinner should undergo, in person, a part at least of his penance. The thane who submitted to embrace this expedient was commanded to lay aside his arms, to clothe himself in woollen or sackcloth, to walk barefoot, to carry in his hand the staff of a pilgrim, to maintain a certain number of poor, to watch during the night in the church, and, when he slept, to repose on the ground. At his summons, his friends and dependents assembled at his castle: they also assumed the garb of penitence: their food was confined to bread, herbs, and water; and these austerities were continued till the aggregate amount of their fasts equalled the number specified by the canons. Thus, with the assistance of one hundred and twenty associates, an opulent sinner might, in the short space of three days, discharge the penance of a whole year. But he was admonished that it was a doubtful and dangerous experiment: and that, if he hoped to appease the anger of the Almighty, he must sanctify his repentance by true contrition of heart, by frequent donations to the poor, and by fervent prayer.[1] How long this practice was tolerated I am ignorant: but I have met with no instance of vicarious penance in the Anglo-Saxon church after the reign of Edgar.

Here I may be allowed to remark how greatly mistaken those writers have been, who maintain that the converts of the Scottish missionaries knew

---

[1] See the chapter, Be mihtizum mannum. Thorpe, ii. 286.

nothing of this penitential system till it was imported
by Theodore from Rome. Columba, the founder of
the monastery in the Isle of Iona, from which the
Scottish missionaries came, lived a century before
Theodore. Now we read in his life by Adomnan,
one of his more early successors, that one day a Scot
from Connaught, by name Ildran, landed on the
beach, and was received at the guest-house. The
next day he informed Columba that he was come to
do penance for his sins, then made his confession to
the abbot, and on his knees promised to observe
faithfully the ' laws of penance.'[1] Columba ordered
him to proceed to one of the Hebrides called Ethica
(probably Eig), and there to give himself up in
servitude for seven years to the small monastery,
which he would find in that islet. "After which
time," he added, " you will return to me again during
the feast of Lent, that at Easter you may go to the
altar and receive the eucharist."[2] On another occasion, a Scot, guilty of the crimes of fratricide and
incest, comes to Iona, and like Ildran, after his confession, promises on his knees to fulfil ' the laws of
penance.'[3] The confessor replies, " If, during twelve
years, thou wilt do penance in exile among the
Britons, and never more return to thy native country,
God may perhaps pardon thy sin."[4] Now these

---

[1] Quid plura? Eadem hora omnia sua confessus peccata, *leges pœnitentiæ* flexis genibus se impleturum pro-
misit. Vit. S. Colum. l. ii. c. xi. p. 139.

[2] Ibid.

[3] *Leges pœnitentiæ* expleturum; l. i. c. xxii. p. 75.

[4] Si duodecim annos inter Britones cum fletu et lacrymis
pœnitentiam egeris, nec ad Scotiam usque ad mortem
reversus fueris, forsan Deus peccato ignoscat tuo. Ibid.

penances prescribed by Columba perfectly accord
with the rules laid down by Theodore;[1] and shew
that the penitential canons were as strictly enforced
among the Scottish Christians before, as they were
among the Anglo-Saxon Christians after, the time of
that prelate.

To return to the practice of penance in the
English church—the time chiefly devoted to it was
the forty days' fast of Lent. The parish priest was
ordered to announce to the people on what day of
the month that fast began, and to admonish them to
confess their sins beforehand, and to learn in what
manner they were to prepare themselves for the due
celebration of the festival of Easter. " Now," says
the homilist, " is a pure and holy time drawing nigh,
in which we should atone for our neglects. Let,
therefore, every Christian man come to his confessor,
and confess his secret sins, and amend by the teaching of his confessor." [2]

In ordinary cases it was the duty of that minister
to reconcile each penitent in private, having previously
instructed him in what manner he ought to fast,
and on what day or days to receive the holy housel.

---

[1] Qui multa mala fecit in homicidio, &c., et postea con-
versus pœnitere cupit, relinquat terrena omnia, intrans in
monasterii servitium, et pœniteat quæ gesserit, ut sacerdos
judicaverit. Si autem in monasterii servitium intrare
noluerit, duriter in laico habitu exul, usque ad exitum
vitæ pœniteat. Theod. Pœnit. in Thorpe, ii. p. 6.

[2] Ælfric's Hom. i. p. 164.—Hence it was called Shrove,
or confession-tide. (Thorpe, ii. 224.) The first duty of the
confessor at this time was to inquire whether any man
was engaged in deadly feud with another, and insist on a
reconciliation as the first duty of Lent. Ibid. 434.

But with the public sinner the case was different.[1] Of him it was required that he should atone in the face of his neighbours for the scandal which he had given : that he should submit to join the class of public penitents, be excluded with them from the church on Ash-Wednesday, and be publicly reconciled with them by the bishop on the Thursday before Easter—which ceremony was conducted in the following manner.

On Ash-Wednesday the public penitents from all parts of the diocese collected at the porch of the cathedral, and at the command of the bishop were introduced into the church, where they lay prostrate in the nave, while four psalms were chanted in the choir. After the prayer, the bishop imposed his hands on them, placed sackcloth and ashes on their heads, and announced that, as Adam for his disobedience had been excluded from Paradise, so they for their transgressions would be excluded from the church. The anthem was then sung—" In the sweat of thy brow thou shalt eat thy bread, until thou return to the dust from which thou wert taken : for dust thou art, and into dust shalt thou return." In the mean while they walked slowly into the porch; the doors were closed against them; and they withdrew to their own homes, or, if they were strangers, to a contiguous building, in which they spent the Lent in the performance of the penance which had been enjoined.

---

[1] Thorpe, ii. 422. Tales nullo modo reconciliari oportet nisi in cœna Domini. Ibid. 48.

On the Thursday before Easter, immediately after the gospel, the doors of the church were thrown open to the penitents. They entered, lay prostrate in the nave, and were instructed to repeat to themselves, " O God, be merciful to me, a sinner," while four psalms with the litany were chanted. The bishop then, at the request of the archdeacon, ascended the pulpit, and pronounced over them the prayers of absolution. Several forms are contained in all the pontificals, out of which he probably selected one or more at pleasure. The following may serve as a specimen. " O God, who didst give the keys to thine apostles, and didst without any merit of mine intrust their office to me, do thou by thy power accomplish that which is the object of my ministry. Acknowledge once more for thine, most merciful father, these sheep redeemed by thee, loosen them at the prayer of thy church from the chains of sin, in which they have been bound ; restore the famished exiles to thy family; clothe them in the best robe, and admit them to thy paternal banquet. They were adopted by thee for thy children ; let them lose no part of that honour : they were made heirs to thy kingdom; let them forfeit no share of their inheritance, but grant that they may henceforth enjoy, without change and for ever, those privileges, which were first bestowed on them by thy grace, and are now confirmed to them by thy mercy, through Christ our Lord."[1] At the conclusion of the prayer, they rose with joy from the

---

[1] See Thorpe, ii. 178, 266, and the two Anglo-Saxon pontificals in Martene, par. ii. p. 41, et seq.

ground. They were now restored to the communion of their more innocent brethren. They went with them to the offertory; assisted with them at the sacrifice; and sealed their reconciliation by receiving with them the body and blood of Christ, the sacrament of salvation, and pledge of a blissful immortality.

APPENDIX.

NOTE A (p. 2).

ON THE CONVERSION OF BRITAIN.

IT is proposed in this note to review the chief authorities, on the credit of which it has been pretended that a Christian church was established in Britain, even during the lifetime of some of the apostles.

I. We meet in the work of Gildas, a British writer of the sixth century, with a long and tortuous sentence, in which he has been understood to state, that the Christian religion was preached to mankind at large about the end of the reign of the Emperor Tiberius, and to the natives of Britain at some period, which is not expressly named, but is darkly indicated by the loose and indefinite word *interea*, or *in the mean while*. *Interea*, galciali frigore rigenti insulæ et velut longiore terrarum secessu soli visibili non proximæ, verus ille sol, non de firmamento solum temporali, sed de summa etiam cœlorum arce cuncta tempora excedente, fulgidum sui coruscum ostentans,—tempore, ut scimus summo Tiberii Cæsaris, quo absque ullo impedimento ejus propagabatur religio, comminata, senatu nolente, a principe morte delatoribus militum ejusdem—radios suos primum indulget, id est, sua præcepta, Christus. Gild. p. 15. § 8.

To this testimony, written five hundred years after the
time to which it is supposed to allude, immense importance has been assigned, especially by the late Dr.
Burgess, then bishop of St. David's, in his several publi-
cations on the 'independence of the ancient British
church.' He is convinced that the word 'interea' refers to
the rebellion and defeat of the native queen Boadicea in
the year 61, and thence he concludes that a Christian
church was about that time established in Britain.

Now this appears to me a gratuitous and unfounded
supposition. There is no direct mention of Boadicea in
Gildas, nor does the passage in question immediately
follow the account of any rebellion. Gildas compresses
the whole history of Britain during the first three centuries within the short compass of a single page. He tells
us that the Britons were idolaters; that they were subdued
by the Romans with threats rather than the sword ; that
they rebelled, were again subdued, and severely punished
for their rebellion; that the conquerors then returned
home, leaving behind them governors, who applied the
lash to the backs of the natives, fixed the yoke on their
necks, and gave a foreign appellation to their country, so
that it was no longer looked upon as a British, but a
Roman island, and no money, whether gold, silver, or
brass, was allowed to circulate among the inhabitants,
unless it were stamped with the head of the emperor—
Italiam petunt, suorumque quosdam præpositos relin-
quentes indigenarum dorsis mastigias, cervicibus jugum,
solo nomen Romanæ servitutis hærere facturos. . . ita ut
non Britannia sed Romana insula censeretur, et quidquid
habere potuisset, æris, argenti, vel auri, imagine Cæsaris
notaretur. Gild. ibid.

It is not till the close of this description that the passage, beginning with *interea*, occurs. The writer had
already told us that the Britons were idolaters: he was

now about to describe the persecution of the Christians at the commencement of the fourth century, and therefore found himself compelled to mention the introduction of Christianity among them. Had he known at what time, or by whose labours, that introduction had been effected, he would undoubtedly have stated it. But instead of that, he tells us that, *interea*, or at some time or other, while Britain was reduced to that state of abject servitude which he had described, the doctrine of the gospel was preached in the island, and was retained faithfully by some, imperfectly by others, till the general persecution under the Emperor Diocletian. This is all that can legitimately be deduced from the testimony of Gildas. He neither states, nor pretends to state, the exact time when the event took place. His words are as applicable to any year before the fourth century, as to the year 61.

II. There are, however, two Greek writers, earlier in time than Gildas, but not of that high antiquity which is desirable on such a subject, Eusebius, bishop of Cæsarea, in the fourth century, and Theodoret, bishop of Cyrus, in the fifth, who may be thought at first sight to countenance the notion, that the gospel was preached by some of the apostles in Britain.

1. Eusebius, in his Evangelical Demonstration, (Book iii. and chapter five or seven of the Greek text, but three of the Latin version,) undertakes to prove the truth of Christianity from the manner of its diffusion through the world. He contends that its founders, ' the twelve apostles, and the seventy disciples '— δώδεκα ὄντας τὸν ἀριθμὸν τοὺς ἐκκρίτους, ἐβδομήκοντα δὲ τοὺς λοιπούς— formed too numerous a body to agree in originating, or to work together in upholding, an imposture. This reasoning he pursues through part of three pages; and then proceeds to a new argument drawn from the personal un-

fitness of the missionaries compared with the magnitude of their object and the success of their endeavours. How could it enter into the minds of men, illiterate as they were, barbarians, ignorant of any but their native tongue, to conceive the notion of bringing over all nations to the adoption of a new and unheard-of religion? It was indeed possible that they might flatter themselves with the hope of success among their own countrymen : but that they should aspire moreover to the conversion of the whole human race; that dividing the earth among them, they should have taken for their several portions, some the empire of Rome, and the great queen of cities herself, some the empire of the Persians, some that of the Armenians, others the nation of the Parthians, and then again that of the Scythians; moreover, that some individuals should have gone even to the very extremities of the earth, and have penetrated into the country of the Indians, and *others have passed over the ocean to those called the British Isles*—καὶ τοὺς μὲν αυτῶν τὴν Ῥωμαίων ἀρκὴν καὶ αὐτὴν τε τὴν βασιλικωτάτην πόλιν νείμασθαι· τοὺς δὲ τὴν Περσῶν, τοὺς δὲ τὴν Αρμενίων, ἑτέρους δὲ τὸ Πάρθων ἔθνος, καὶ, αὖ πάλιν τὸ Σκυθῶν· τινὰς δὲ ἤδη καὶ ἐπ᾽ αὐτὰ τῆς οἰκουμένης ἐλθεῖν τὰ ἄκρα, ἐπί τε τὴν Ἰνδῶν φθάσαι χώραν, καὶ ἑτέρους ὑπὲρ τὸν Ὠκεανὸν παρελθεῖν ἐπὶ τὰς καλουμένας βρεττανικὰς νήσους, ταῦτα ὀυκ᾽ ἔτ᾽ ἐγώ γε ἡγοῦμαι, κ. τ. λ.—that they should have done all this, is what appears to him far beyond any human power, particularly beyond the power of vulgar, uneducated men, and still more the power of men labouring to establish what they know to be an imposture.

It is contended that, according to Eusebius in this passage, some of the twelve apostles, or of the seventy disciples, preached in the British isles : for they alone are the persons previously mentioned by him, and to them therefore must be referred the τοὺς μὲν and τοὺς δὲ, the τινὰς and ἑτέρους, as the missionaries of the converted nations.

Whatever may be thought of the grammatical accuracy of this reasoning, it should be observed that it overturns at once the hypothesis of Dr. Burgess, that Britain was converted by St. Paul; for St. Paul was not one of the twelve, nor of the seventy. He could not then, according to such reasoning, be the missionary who preached to the Britons.

This interpretation leads also to a conclusion, which is false in fact; by confining the conversion of the Gentiles to the twelve and the seventy, it excludes St. Paul and his associates from any share in that great work. Yet both history and scripture testify that he was pre-eminently the teacher of the Gentiles, and *had laboured more abundantly than all.* 1 Cor. xv. 10.

Moreover, this interpretation is indirectly contradicted by the testimony of Eusebius himself in the first chapter of the third book of his Ecclesiastical History, where he treats of the places in which the apostles preached. There he states, on the faith of tradition, that Thomas carried the knowledge of the gospel to Parthia, Andrew to Scythia, John to Asia; and, on the authority of Origen, that Peter, having preached to the Jews of the dispersion, proceeded to Rome, where he was crucified. So much he had learned of the places in which these four apostles had preached; of the places where the others preached, it appears from his silence, that he knew nothing more than we do at the present day.

How then are we to explain the long enumeration of nations converted by the twelve and the seventy? By considering it as the language of rhetorical amplification, and not of historical testimony. Eusebius at first thought only of the twelve and the seventy: in the progress of his argument his enthusiasm kindled : with them he identified in his mind's eye all who were their colleagues and successors in the ministry of the word to infidel nations, and looking upon them all as one body, ascribed to them collectively the conversion of every nation which, up to his day, had been introduced into the church of Christ. But, if this be his real meaning, his testimony bears not on the present question.

2. There is another authority, of the same class, to which appeal has also been made, as if it prove that some of the apostles preached in Britain. It is taken from Theodoret's treatise (Tom. iv. par. ii. p. 928), Ἑλλήνικων θεραπευτικὴ παθημάτων (Diss. ix. Περὶ νόμων), and offers to us a similar instance of amplification, with a still more pompous enumeration of converted nations. " Our fishermen," says Theodoret, " and publicans and tent-makers brought the law of the gospel to all men : and persuaded, not the Romans only and the subjects of Rome, but the Scythians and Sauromatæ, and the Indians and the Seres, and the Hircanians and Bactrians, and the Britons and Cimbrians, and Germans, and, in a word, every nation and race of men, to adopt the laws of him who died on the cross." Οἱ δε ἡμέτεροι ἁλιεῖς καὶ οἱ τελῶναι, καὶ ὁ σκυτοτόμος ἅπασιν ἀνθρώποις τοὺς εὐαγγελικοὺς προσενηνόχασι νόμους · καὶ οὐ μόνον Ῥωμαίους καὶ ὑπὸ τούτοις τελοῦντας, ἀλλὰ καὶ τὰ Σκυθικὰ καὶ τὰ Σαυροματικὰ ἔθνη, καὶ Ἰνδοὺς καὶ Αἰθίοπας, καὶ Πέρσας καὶ Σῆρας, καὶ Ὑρκανοὺς, καὶ Βακτριανοὺς, καὶ βρεττανοὺς, καὶ Κίμβρους καὶ Γερμανοὺς, καὶ ἁπαξαπλῶς πᾶν ἔθνος καὶ γένος ἀνθρώπων δέξασθαι τοῦ σταυρωθέντος τοὺς νόμους ἀνέπεισαν. In this passage, St. Paul, under the denomination of the tent-maker, is admitted to a place among the apostles of the Gentiles, but then the seventy of Eusebius are excluded. Did Theodoret, however, look upon this as a correct description of the

plain fact?—undoubtedly not : and therefore he soon afterwards qualifies the hyperbole, by admitting that it was
after the death of the apostles themselves that the laws of
the gospel were established among ' the Persians, Scythians, and the other barbarous nations'—among whom
the Britons must certainly be numbered.—Πρὸς γαρ τοῦς
Πέρσας καὶ Σκύθας καὶ τὰ ἄλλα βάρβαρα ἔθνη μετὰ τὴν
ἐκείνων οἱ νόμοι διεβήσαν τελευτὴν.

III. We now then proceed to a third class of authorities—the authorities on which Dr. Burgess has built his
Pauline church of Britain. It was a singular fancy, the
utter improbability of which must strike every reader,
acquainted with the history of that age : but it was
entertained as a truth and a reality by the learned prelate, who had convinced himself that St. Paul visited at
an early period the natives of Britain, founded among
them a church, with its full complement of bishops, priests,
and inferior ministers, and at his departure left the
charge of the new establishment to a bishop named
Aristobulus. Thus he was enabled to give to this Pauline
church of his own creation the precedency in point of
antiquity before the church originally founded by St.
Peter in Rome.

1. The first of these authorities is a passage from a
letter written to the Christians in Corinth, by Clemens
of Rome, the third of the successors of St. Peter. In it
he exhorts his readers to imitate the example which had
been set to them by the blessed Peter and Paul, who had
lately suffered martyrdom in the imperial city. Of St.
Peter he says, that the apostle, "after suffering not one
but many afflictions, had borne his testimony, and was
gone to the place of glory, which he had merited:" of St.
Paul, that " he had borne chains seven times, had been
beaten with rods, had been stoned, had made himself a
herald (of salvation) in the East and the West, and had

also obtained the reward of his patience." To this, however, is appended, as part of the same sentence, that he had received the noble glory of his faith, having taught righteousness to the whole world, having come to the terma or boundary (*gone to the utmost bounds,* in the version by Dr. Burgess) of the West, and borne testimony before the governors; that thus he had departed this life, and had gone to the holy place, a splendid pattern of patient suffering—τὸ γενναῖον τῆς πίστεως αὐτοῦ κλεός ἔλαβεν, δικαιοσύνην διδάξας ὅλον τὸν κόσμον, καὶ ἐπὶ τὸ τέρμα τῆς δύσεως ἐλθὼν, καὶ μαρτυρήσας ἐπὶ τῶν ἡγουμένων, οὕτως ἀπηλλάγη τοῦ κόσμου, καὶ εἰς τὸν ἅγιον τόπον ἐπορεύθη ὑπομενῆς γενόμενος μέγιστος ἐπιγραμμύς. Coteller. i. 148; Antwerp, 1700.

Now of this passage it may be observed, that it has been thought to be an interpolation (ibid. not. 38); and not without reason: for it reads very like an explanatory note, which has slipped from the margin into the text, being in reality nothing else than a repetition and amplification of the passage immediately preceding. If you leave it in the text, the entire sentence is most confusedly and inartistically put together; remove it into the margin, and every thing is in perfect order.

2. But without questioning its authenticity, what do we learn from it respecting any new church in Britain? Britain is not so much as mentioned. We are told, indeed, that St. Paul came or went to the boundary of the West—ἐπὶ τὸ τέρμα τῆς δύσεως—but what country was meant by that term? We know that the Greeks gave the name of Hesperia to both Italy and Spain, because, with respect to Greece, they were the most distant lands lying to the West. Hence, some have supposed that Spain is here meant by the τέρμα τῆς δύσεως, because its western shore is washed by the waters of the Atlantic; but it is more probable that Rome itself was the place,

because Rome lies on the western coast of Italy, and because it was to Rome that St. Paul came, and at Rome that he bore testimony before the governors,—or, in other words, suffered martyrdom. Dr. Burgess, indeed, tells us that Britain was the spot; that τὸ τέρμα τῆς δύσεως—was the usual appellation of Britain; and that the apostle could not reach that τέρμα, unless he actually visited Britain. But for all this he does not advance the semblance of a proof. It is based on the fanciful notion which he entertains, that the Greek word can designate no other place than the most remote spot known at that time to exist, in what was called the western division of the earth.

3. From Clemens we are led to two testimonies collected from the writings of St. Jerome. That father, on the authority of 2 Tim. iv. 17, tells us, that the design of God in liberating St. Paul from the 'lion's mouth,' his captivity in Rome, was " that the gospel might be preached by him also in the western parts;—ut evangelium in occidentis quoque partibus prædicaretur (De Viris Illust. c. v. Edit. Fabric. p. 34 : and Op. S. Hieron. Edit. Vallarsii, ii. 838): and in another work, his commentary on Amos c. v., the same writer states that St. Paul was called by God, and sent forth to preach with the whole world before him; that he preached from Jerusalem to Illyricum; and that, wishing not to build on the foundation laid by others, he directed his route towards Spain, running in imitation of his Lord, the Sun of Righteousness, his course from the Red Sea, or rather from the Eastern to the Western ocean—Vocatus a Domino effusus est super faciem universæ terræ, ut prædicaret evangelium de Hierosolymis usque ad Illyricum, et ædificaret non super alterius fundamentum, ubi jam fuerat prædicatum, sed usque ad Hispanias tenderet, et a mari rubro,

imo ab oceano usque ad oceanum curreret, imitans dominum suum et solem justitiæ. Tom. vi. 290. It is not easy to conceive how either of these passages can apply to the present question. For certainly it was possible for the apostle to preach in the West, as he had done in the East, without preaching in Britain; and also possible for him to travel from the Red Sea to the western coast of Spain, without passing through Britain.

3. The next proof is equally irrelevant. St. Chrysostom in one of his homilies to the people of Antioch says, that the power of the gospel is known, and that churches and altars for sacrifice are built in the British Islands, islands lying out of that, the Mediterranean sea, and being in the ocean itself—Καὶ γὰρ αἱ Βρεττανικαὶ νῆσοι, αἱ τῆς θαλάττης ἐκτὸς κείμεναι ταύτης, καὶ ἐν αὐτῷ οὖσαι τῷ ὠκεανῷ τῆς δυνάμεως τοῦ ῥήματος ἤσθοντο· καὶ γὰρ κᾀκεῖ ἐκκλησίαι καὶ θυσιαστήρια πεπήγασι. Tom. vi. p. 635. Now, remarks Dr. Burgess, Theodoret, explaining the psalm cxvi. says that St. Paul brought Christianity to the islands lying in the sea—ταῖς ἐν τῷ πελάγει διακειμέναις νήσοις τὴν ὠφέλειαν προσήνεγκεν. But Theodoret means by πέλαγος the Mediterranean : for he specifies Crete as one of these islands on the authority of Titus i. 5 : *for this cause left I thee in Crete.* Does it then follow that, because St. Paul preached to the inhabitants of certain islands in the Mediterranean during the first century, the gospel could not be known in the British islands lying out of the Mediterranean in the fourth, unless the same apostle had also formerly preached in them? It is plain that the Right Reverend prelate has confounded the πέλαγος of Theodoret with the ὠκεανὸς of Chrysostom, and the isles in the Mediterranean with the British Islands.

4. There remains but one more testimony, that of Venantius Fortunatus, a poet of the sixth century, who

in the following lines is supposed to state that St. Paul actually visited Britain :—

> " Transit et oceanum, vel qua facit insula portum,
> Quasque Britannus habet terras, quasque ultima Thule."

But did Venantius say this of St. Paul ? If so, he must have believed that the apostle preached also in the Orkneys, or whatever northern spot he might understand by ultima Thule ; for he predicates the same thing of them both. Venantius, however, says nothing so extravagant. He is not speaking of St. Paul personally, but of St. Paul's epistles, which forming a considerable portion of the Christian Scriptures are known wherever Christianity has penetrated—

> Et qua sol radiis tendit, *stylus* ille cucurrit,
> Arctos meridies, hinc plenus vesper et ortus,
> Transit et oceanum, vel qua facit insula portum,
> Quasque Britannus habet terras, quasque ultima Thule.

It was the stylus ille, not the apostle but his writings, that had reached in the sixth century both Britain and Thule.

The reader is now in possession of the "indisputable proofs," on which Dr. Burgess built his Pauline church in Britain. I shall only remark, that not one of them all has in reality any connection with the question. Those which mention St. Paul, take no notice of Britain : that which mentions Britain, takes no notice of St. Paul. But

> Velut ægri somnia, vanæ
> Finguntur species.

I shall not trespass on the patience of the reader by directing his attention to two other imaginary facts, the missionary labours of Aristobulus in Britain, and the foundation of the church of Glastonbury, by Joseph of Arimathea. No one can examine the authorities, on which these statements are founded, without pronouncing them at once collections of fables.

2 A 2

NOTE B (p. 13).

GILDAS, THE BRITISH HISTORIAN.

1. It is something remarkable that of the ancient Welsh saints we have no ancient biographies. It is the same thing with respect to Gildas. We possess, indeed, two lives of that historian; but neither of them can boast of an earlier date than the tenth, probably than the eleventh century: and both present a mere farrago of traditionary tales, tacked together without regard to place or chronology—tales which appear to have originally referred to several different individuals of the same name, and to have been afterwards appropriated to the 'historiographer,' the most celebrated of them all. To such works no credit can be given; all that we know of the history of Gildas, is the little which may be extracted from his works; which amounts only to this, that he lived at a time when the Britons had been driven by the Saxons to the western coast of the island; that he was born in the year of the great victory gained by the Britons at Mount Badon, which is conjectured to have been the year 520; that at the age of thirty-four he was desired by his monastic brethren to write the history of his country; and that he was then deterred by the scenes of sin and wretchedness which the subject presented to his view; but ten years later complied with their request by writing two small works, which he called his historiola and admonitiuncula, "not through a spirit of pride, as if he were better than all the others, but with the feelings of one who wept over the misery of his country, and found consolation in suggesting the remedy of those evils"—non affectu cunctos spernentis, omnibusve melioris, sed condolentis patriæ incommoditatibus miseriisque ejus, ac remediis condelectantis. Præf. Gild. p. 1.

2. The historiola, as the name imports, is very brief, and on that account very unsatisfactory, written too in a declamatory instead of an historical style.   Gildas possessed, as he complains, no British documents; and if he consulted foreign writers, disfigured their narratives by mixing them up with the traditions of his countrymen. Towards the close he becomes more interesting, by unfolding to us the real state of the natives, after the departure of the Romans, and during their wars with the Picts and the Saxons.   Here in every page, he writes with the true spirit of a Briton.   If he blame his countrymen—and he often blames them most severely—it is yet in a tone of commiseration ; but when he speaks of their enemies, he is at a loss for words to express the utter detestation in which he holds them.   The Scots and Picts are " vermiculorum cunei, tetri Scotorum Pictorumque greges, moribus ex parte dissimiles sed una eademque sanguinis fundendi aviditate concordes, furciferosque magis vultus pilis, quam corporum pudenda, pudendisque proxima, vestibus tegentes (Gild. p. 24): the Saxons are in like manner nefandi nominis Saxones, Deo hominibusque invisi, ferocissimi prædones, sacrilegi, furciferi, germen iniquitatis, radix amaritudinis, virulenta plantatio in nostro cespite ferocibus palmitibus pampinisque pullulans.   Id. pp. 30, 31, 33.

3. The admonitiuncula is divided into two parts, the first of which is addressed to five of the petty kings of the Britons, all contemporary with the writer.   The first of these is Constantine (probably the Cystennyn of the bards), " the whelp of an impure lioness, and tyrant of Damnonia," that is, of the present counties of Devon and Cornwall.   Then comes Aurelius Conan, an old man, whose fathers and brothers have all fallen in their youth, and who now stands alone, the last of his family, like a withered oak in the midst of the desert.   The third

is Vortiper (Gwrthefyr), a panther spotted over with crime like Conan, but with crime of a different kind, the wicked son of a virtuous father, the tyrant of Demetia, that is, of the counties of Cardigan, Pembroke, and Carmarthen. Cuneglas follows, a name which means the tawny butcher; he is the charioteer of the bear's den, the man who braves God, and persecutes God's ministers. The catalogue concludes with the last in name, but the first in power and wickedness, Maglocune, who, if he be, as is probable, the same with Maelgwn, was the king of North Wales. Each of these is arraigned in succession before the reader, and charged with a long list of crimes. Constantine, that very year, having first bound himself by oath to God in the presence of the clergy, and of the mother of two royal children, that he would keep peace with all his subjects; had murdered both the children in the arms of their mother, and under the vestment of the abbot, together with their tutors, two warriors as brave as Wales had ever borne; and had murdered them too within the chancel of the church, so that the blood of his victims had covered, as with a crimson mantle, the altar, the seat of the heavenly sacrifice. Ep. Gildæ, pp. 37—41.

To Maglocune it is objected that he had obtained the throne by the massacre of his uncle, and his uncle's faithful guard; that then, urged by remorse, he had withdrawn into a desert, and bound himself with the vows of a monk : that next repenting of the change, he had reassumed the sceptre, married a wife—a marriage, says Gildas, unlawful on account of his former vow—and at last made away not only with her, but also with his own nephew, that he might take to his bed the widow of that nephew. (Id. pp. 42—44.) The other three are described as fellows in iniquity with these two; the scourges of their native country, for they are always engaged in war with one or other of their neighbours, and the disgrace of their religion, for they are defiled with incest, adultery, and murder. (Id. 38—42.) After these charges Gildas warns them of the fate, which awaits them in a future world, calls on them to reform while they have time, and presents to them a vast accumulation of texts from the different books of scripture, calculated to encourage the penitent, and to alarm the impenitent sinner.

4. The second part of the " admonition " is addressed to the clergy—for impartiality would not allow him to re-prove the laity for their vices, and at the same time screen those of his own order—Ne personarum arguar exceptionis. (Id. p. 72.) This part is modelled after the same plan as the former, but with one exception : no individual is now mentioned by name. The invective is general; and the whole body is charged with ambition, simony, avarice, indolence, and the several vices most opposite to the sanctity of the priesthood. Then follows another vast collection of texts from scripture and of examples from history, illustrative of the duties of the pastor, and predictive of the judgments of God on the transgressor. But are we then to believe that this character applies to the whole nation without exception? Even in the impetuosity of his zeal Gildas has the honesty to admit that it does not. There are still, he confesses, men among the Britons—few indeed, very few —but there are among them, men, " the holiness of whose lives he prizes above all the wealth of this world ; and to be numbered among whom will be the constant object of his prayers and endeavours."—Exceptis paucis et valde paucis. (Id. p. 34.) Quorum vitam non solum laudo, verum etiam cunctis mundi opibus præfero, cujusque me, si fieri possit, ante mortem esse aliquamdiu participem opto et sitio. P. 72.

5. The earliest mention of these writings by Gildas

occurs in the great work of Beda. Six chapters of Beda's
first book (the 12th, 13th, 14th, 15th, 16th, and 22nd) are
transcribed with a few immaterial alterations from the
'historiola:' and allusion is also made by Beda to the
'admonitiuncula,' where he says, that " among the many
sins of the Britons enumerated by Gildas, their historian,
one of great magnitude has been omitted, their neglect to
preach the gospel to the Saxons," who were settled
among them one hundred and fifty years before the
arrival of St. Augustine—Inter alia inerrabilium scelerum
facta, quæ historicus eorum Gildas *flebili* sermone de-
scribit, et hoc addebant, ut nunquam genti Saxonum sive
Anglorum secum Britanniam incolenti verbum fidei
prædicando committerent. Bed. i. c. 22.

The works of Gildas are also mentioned by Alcuin, who
zealously recommends them to the notice of his countrymen, in consequence of the depredations of the Danes on
the coast of Northumbria in 793. In them might be seen
what were the crimes that provoked God to send the
Anglo-Saxons to Britain as the ministers of his wrath ;
and thence his own countrymen might learn to fear, that
if they imitated the vices of the Britons, the Danes would
prove to them, what their fathers had proved to the
Britons. In a letter to the archbishop of Canterbury he
says : Legitur in libro Gildæ Brettonum sapientissimi,
quod iidem ipsi Brettones propter rapinas et avaritiam
principum, propter iniquitatem et injustitiam judicum,
propter desidiam et pigritiam prædicationis episcoporum,
propter luxuriam et malos mores populi patriam perdiderunt. Caveamus hæc eadem vitia nostris temporibus
inolescere. (Epist. ad Æthelhard. p. 17.) And in another
to the people of Kent :—Discite Gildam Brettonum
sapientissimum, et videte ex quibus causis parentes
Brettonum perdiderunt regnum et patriam, et considerate
vosmetipsos, et in vobis pene similia invenietis. Ep. ad

Gent. et Populum Cantuar, p. 78.) From these passages it is plain that the works now attributed to Gildas, were well known to literary men in the seventh and eighth centuries, and were taken by them for the genuine productions of the British writer, whose name they bear.

6. Very recently, however, the authenticity of the works of Gildas has been called in question, but on grounds which, as far as I can judge, will not bear examination. It is alleged by Mr. Rees that "they are not likely to have been written by one of British race, because their spirit is anti-national, and their design is obviously to depreciate the Britons." (Rees, Welsh Saints, p. 227.) " There is in them," says Mr. Wright in his Biographia Britannica Literaria, published under the superintendence of the council of the Royal Society of Literature, " more of the tone of a foreign enemy than of a native churchman, in the over-strained invective which is here directed against the British priesthood. The presumption that the book was forged by some Anglo-Saxon or foreign priest of the seventh century, in his zeal to uphold the Romish church as it had been introduced among the Anglo-Saxons, against the church of Britain, which was resisting its ordinances, is in a certain degree countenanced by Beda, citing it in a remarkable manner as a testimony against the British clergy, and again by the manner in which it is quoted by Alcuin, when the heat of the disputes had not long subsided." (Wright, p. 128.) But does it necessarily follow that the writer who bewails the evils which press upon his country, must be actuated by an anti-national spirit? Or that the preacher who holds up to his audience the picture of their vices to alarm their consciences, and draw them to repentance, has no other design but to depreciate their character? It is moreover difficult to believe that any Saxon priest, in the short interval between the

conversion of the Saxons and the time of Beda, could
have been capable of such a forgery, and of disseminating
it among his own countrymen. There is not in the work
a single word which seems to betray a Saxon origin:
every line bears testimony to the British descent of the
writer, so feelingly does he deplore the misery of his
country, so intimately does he prove himself acquainted
with the habits of the natives, and with the forms of
their church, a church of earlier date than that of the
Saxons; and so earnestly does he call upon them to
appease the anger of God by the reformation of their
conduct: for of the whole work two-thirds are filled with
exhortations to amendment. Moreover, the insinuation
that such a forgery might be suggested to some Saxon
priest by the ' hostilities between the Anglo-Saxon and
British churches, which exceeded in bitterness the natural enmity between the two people,' is utterly indefen-
sible. The bitterness which existed was wholly on the
part of the Britons, arising out of their antipathy to their
conquerors : nor is there a single expression which can
justly be charged with bitterness, against the British
clergy in any Anglo-Saxon writer ; not even in the
passages of Beda and Alcuin to which we are referred,
and which the reader will find in p. 360 of this note.

7. There is an ancient document, which appears to me
to afford strong corroboration to the testimony of Gildas,
by shewing that the crimes which he attributes to these
five princes were common among the Welsh chieftains of
that period. This is what is known by the name of the
book of Landaff, and contains a multitude of entries
respecting donations made to, or acquisitions made by, that
church ; which entries are generally prefaced with an
account of the events that led to such donations and
acquisitions. Of their authenticity it seems impossible to
doubt, though the present copy is of later date, and

the copyist has occasionally introduced a more modern forensic word in lieu of the older and less intelligible term of his ancestors. From these entries I shall therefore transcribe a few passages which remount almost to the days of Gildas, and which present to us instances of perjury, adultery, and murder, as atrocious and repulsive as any to be found in the pages of that writer.

1. " In the time of the bishop Oudoceus, Guædnerth, by instigation of the devil, killed his brother Merchion in a contest for the kingdom ; and, after the murder, the fratricide was excommunicated by the blessed Oudoceus in a synod at Landaff, gathered from the mouth of the Wye to the mouth of the Towy : and so he remained under excommunication for three years, with the crosses laid on the ground, and the bells inverted, and entirely without communion with Christians."—Lib. Land. p. 172.

2. " King Meurig and Cynfeddw met together at Landaff in presence of the bishop Oudoceus, and with the relics of the saints lying before them, swore to keep peace with each other. Some time after this oath, king Meurig deceitfully killed Cynfeddw; and afterwards the bishop Oudoceus called together all his clergy from the mouth of Taratyr in Wye to the Towy, and in full synod, excommunicated king Meurig, both on account of the murder committed by him, · and of his breach of the agreement made in presence of the bishop, and on the altar of the apostle Peter, and of the saints Dubricius and Teilo : and thus laying the crosses on the ground, he deprived the country of baptism and Christian communion, and cursed the king and his progeny, the synod confirming the curse, and saying, " *may his days be few, and his children become orphans, and his wife a widow.*" Ibid. 139.

3. " King Morgan and Ffrioc, his uncle, met St. Oudoceus and his congregation, and Cyrigen, abbot of St.

Cadoc, Sulien, abbot of Docunni, and Cyngen, abbot of Illtyd, and in their presence on the altar of St. Illtyd, and with the holy relics before them, king Morgan and Ffrioc swore to keep peace towards each other without deceit; and on this condition, that if either killed the other, or laid snares for him, the transgressor should not be allowed to redeem his crime with land or money, but should resign his kingdom, and spend in pilgrimage the remainder of his life. Long afterwards, king Morgan deceitfully killed his uncle Ffrioc, and then came to the bishop Oudoceus to beg pardon for his perjury and the murder. And the bishop summoned his synod, and the king with the elders of Glamorgan came, and the synod adjudged, on account of the distressed state of the kingdom, and that it might not be left without the protecting shield of its natural lord, that he should redeem his pilgrimage with fasting, prayer, and almsgiving, and so purge away his perjury and murder." Ibid. 143.

4. "The kings Tewdwr, son of Rhun, and Elgystyl, son of Awst, king of Brecknock, swore on the altar of St. Dubricius, by the holy of holies, with the sacred volumes and the relics placed before them, that neither would lay snares for the other, but would sincerely keep peace between them : and this in the presence of the bishop Gwrwan with his clergy, and under this condition, that, if either did seek to deceive the other, he should resign his whole inheritance, and go on pilgrimage, leaving his kingdom, and remaining in exile for ever. Afterwards king Tewdwr, breaking the peace, killed Elgystyl, son of Awst, committing at the same time murder and perjury. When this was known, the bishop excommunicated the perjured murderer, uncovered the altars of God, placing the crosses on the ground with the relics of the saints, and depriving him of all communion with Christians." (Ibid. 159. See also pp. 168—180.) Now let the reader

compare these instances with those narrated by Gildas, and he will see as great reason to maintain that they were entered in the book of Landaff for the purpose of depreciating the character of the Britons, as that the invective of Gildas was a forgery, given to the world under his name, for that purpose. The one confirms the authority of the other.

———

NOTE C (p. 16).

THE following references will point out the passages in Gildas, from which has been formed the account of the British church in p. 15. With regard to

Doctrine.—Gildas mentions the three Divine persons of the Trinity by their names, pp. 84, 115. Trinitatis sacramentum, p. 77. Trinitatis mysterium, p. 78. Toto corde Trinitati gratias egit, 84. Of Christ he says—Qui est benedictus supra omnia Deus in sæcula, p. 35. Coævus Patri et Spiritui Sancto, communis ejusdemque substantiæ, p. 84. Cœlum et terram cum omni eorum inæstimabili ornamento fecit, p. 84. Omnis mundi opprobria delevit. Ibid. Salvator mundi factorque—omnium salvator, pp. 100, 113. On rewards and punishments—Tam sceleratorum sunt perpetim immortales igni animæ, quam sanctorum lætitiæ.

The Hierarchy.—At ordination lessons were read out of almost every part of Scripture. Lectiones ex omni fere sanctarum scripturarum textu merito excerptæ sunt, p. 111. Some of them he mentions, one from 1 Peter, c. i. ii.—two from the epistles of St. Paul; the second of which was from Tim. iii. 1. The fifth lesson was from Acts i. 16. and the Gospel from Matt. xvi. 16. The hands of bishops and priests were anointed and blessed at their ordination. Benedictio qua initiantur sacerdotum vel ministrorum manus, p. 111. The bishops sat in the seat of St. Peter—

sedem Petri apostoli, p. 72, who was the first of the apostles, p. 111, and the key-bearer of the kingdom of heaven—clavicularius cœlorum regni, p. 82. To them as his successors (ibid.) was given the power of binding and loosing—potestas suppetit supra mundum alligandi cum in mundo reos alligaverint, et solvendi cum pœnitentes solverint, p. 41. It was their duty to offer sacrifice—sacrificantes, p. 72, with hands extended over the sacrifice —manus sacrosanctis Christi sacrificiis extensuri, p. 76.

Of monks.—They had monasteries, or collections of huts in the wilds and mountains; and monks who took perpetual vows of obedience and poverty—Te monachum perpetuo vovisti, regni, auri, argenti, et quod his majus est, propriæ voluntatis distinctionibus ruptis—ad sanctorum speluncas te rapuisti, p. 43; also of chastity, for post monachi votum nuptials were illicitæ et presumptivæ, p. 45. They had also widows who made vows of continency—perpetuam viduitatis castimoniam Deo promittens, p. 41.

Churches.—They had churches dedicated in honour of martyrs at the beginning of the fourth century—Basilicas sanctorum martyrum, p. 19. A single church had several altars—inter altaria, p. 72, inter ipsa sacrosancta altaria, p. 37. The altar was the seat of the heavenly sacrifice —sacrificii cœlestis sedes, ibid. The service was chanted in the churches—Dei laudes canora Christi tyronum voce suaviter modulante—ecclesiasticæ melodiæ, p. 44.

Scripture.—Great part of his epistle consists of quotations out of different books of Scripture, according to the version called Vetus Itala. Among these are the books of Wisdom and Ecclesiasticus, to the authors of which is given the title of prophets, pp. 69-71.

The third canon of the council of Nice is alluded to in p. 75—Religiosam forte matrem seu sorores domo pellentes, et externas, veluti secretiori ministerio familiares, indecenter levantes, vel potius, ut vera dicam licet inepta, non tam mihi quam talia agentibus, humiliantes.

Their *simony* is described in p. 74 ; and their travels into foreign parts, to obtain the object of their ambition, in the following passage ; which, though obscure to us, would be plain to those, who were acquainted with the practices, which he exposed : Etenim eos, si in parochia, resistentibus severe commessoribus, hujus modi margaritam invenire non possint, praemissis antea nuntiis transnavigare maria, terrasque spatiosas transmeare non tam piget quam delectat, ut omnino talis species inaequiparabilisque pulchritudo et, ut vera dicam, diabolica illusio, vel venditis omnibus copiis, comparetur (the allusion is to Matt. xiii. 44). Dein cum magno apparatu magnaque phantasia, repedantes ad patriam, ex erecto erectiorem incessum pingunt, et dudum summitates montium conspicantes, nunc recte ad æthera vel ad summa nubium vellera luminum semidormitantes acies librant, ac sese nova quædam phasmata, imo diabolica organa, ut quondam Novatus Romæ, Dominicæ conculcator margaritæ, porcus niger, patriæ ingerunt, violentes manus, non tam venerabilibus aris quam flammis inferni ultricibus dignas, in tali schema positi, sacrosanctis Christi sacrificiis extensuri, p. 76.

NOTE D (p. 64).

ORDINATION OF ST. AUGUSTINE.

IT was the intention of Pope Gregory that Augustine, if he met with a favourable reception from the Anglo-Saxons, should be ordained bishop—quem eis episcopum ordinandum, si ab Anglis susciperentur, disposuerat (Bed. i. c. 23). Accordingly, after the baptism of Ethelbert, Augustine went back to Gaul, received episcopal ordination at Arles, and returned to Britain. Id. c. 26, 27.

Wharton, however, most positively asserts—clarissime constat (Ang. Sac. i. 89), that Beda is in error; and that Augustine was ordained bishop during his journey through Gaul, before he came to Britain. His only argument deserving of notice is, that Gregory, in a letter written in October 597, thanks Brunechild, queen of the Franks, for the protection which she had afforded to his brother and fellow-bishop Augustine, when he was on his road to Britain. But the title of bishop, which is here given to Augustine, does not shew that he was bishop at the time of his passage through Gaul, but at the time when the letter was written. Now that time was not, as Wharton supposes, the year 597, but 598. Calculating by the imperial indiction, which began on the 24th of September, Wharton found that October in the first indiction was October in our year 597. But the pontiff used not the imperial, but the pontifical indiction, which did not begin till the 25th of December; and consequently with him October of the first indiction was the October of the following year 598. Thus, if the missionaries arrived about the end of 596, and Ethelbert was baptized, as is asserted, in the July following, there was certainly sufficient time for Augustine to go to Arles, and to return, before the date of the letter to Brunechild, and even before the feast of Christmas, at which Augustine baptized such numbers of the men of Kent.

2. There is, however, a palpable error in Beda, with respect to the name of the bishop of Arles. When Augustine undertook the mission to Britain, Vergilius was bishop of that city, and Ætherius bishop of Lyons. Yet Beda tells us that the bishop of Arles, to whom the missionary was recommended (Bed. i. c. 24),

and by whom he was consecrated (Id. c 27), was
Etherius : and that afterwards (c. 28), Etherius was succeeded at Arles by Vergilius. That this is an error, is
manifest; but it is not difficult to discover the source of
that error. Nothelm, a priest of the church of London,
and afterwards archbishop of Canterbury, obtained at
Rome permission from Gregory III. to search the papal
archives, and to copy from them documents for Beda.
(Bed. Prol. p. 3.) Now among the recommendatory letters
from Gregory to the Gallic prelates in favour of Augustine
was one to Vergilius, another to Etherius, and others to
other bishops, all the same in substance, and very similar
in language. It is probable that Nothelm thought the
transcript of one of these sufficient for his purpose—at
least it is plain from the language of Beda, that he
copied but one—and that one chanced to be the letter
to Etherius, which the historian introduced into his narrative. Again of the letters sent by Lawrence and
Mellitus in 601, Nothelm copied one to the bishop of
Arles, and that Beda also has introduced. Both have the
same address with the exception of the name. Reverentissimo et sanctissimo fratri Etherio coepiscopo—Reverentissimo et sanctissimo fratri Vergilio coepiscopo. (Id.
c. 28.) Had Beda seen Gregory's register, he could not
have made the mistake ; but, having only these two
letters before him, and writing under the notion that both
were written to the papal vicar, the bishop of Arles, he
concluded of course from the change of names, that
Etherius must have been the predecessor of Vergilius.
This supposition appears to me to solve the difficulty, and
to account for the mistake.

NOTE E (p. 67).

ON THE DEPENDENCE OR INDEPENDENCE OF THE ANCIENT BRITISH CHURCH.

THE result of the conference between Augustine and the Britons suggests the inquiry, whether the ancient British church owned any dependence on the church of Rome. It is my intention to collect in this note whatever may be reasonably alleged on either side of the question: and with that view for its better illustration, I shall divide the first six hundred years of our era into three periods, of which one will be limited by the persecution under Diocletian, the second by the separation of the island from the dominion of Rome, and the third by the mission of St. Augustine to the Anglo-Saxons.

THE FIRST PERIOD.

I. From the introduction of Christianity till the persecution under Diocletian we meet with no evidence bearing directly on this question, in any contemporary authority, either native or foreign, ecclesiastical or profane. From this dearth of ancient testimony we are left in absolute ignorance with respect to the state of the British Christians during the first period. The only conclusion, therefore, to which we can reasonably come, is, that Christianity existed here on the same footing as in the other western provinces of the empire. If the superiority of the Roman pontiff was admitted or rejected there, so it would also be admitted or rejected in Britain.

SECOND PERIOD.

During the second period, from the persecution of Diocletian to the cessation of the imperial authority in Britain, a space of 250 years, history records no fact, supplies no testimony to shew that the British church was independent of the see of Rome. As a substitute therefore for direct proof, Stillingfleet, in his Origines Britannicæ, objects that the bishop of Rome did not ordain, or more properly, is not known to have ordained, the British metropolitans. But what then? He did not ordain the Anglo-Saxon metropolitans afterwards; yet the Anglo-Saxon church most certainly acknowledged his superior authority. Stillingfleet's argument is based on the practice in the Eastern patriarchates, where the metropolitans were ordained by the patriarchs, to whom they were subject. But why must the same discipline necessarily obtain in the Western church? Let the reader cast his eyes on the map, and he will immediately see the difference. There were four minor patriarchates in the East: but the West formed only one vast patriarchate. The extent of the Eastern partriarchates was of necessity circumscribed, so that from every part there was comparatively easy access to the patriarchal city. In the West most churches lay at a great distance from Rome; and the bishop elect would often have had to navigate the sea, to cross the Alps or the Pyrenees, to traverse tribes of barbarians, before he could reach the apostolic see. Why then are we to believe that, in circumstances so different, the same customs must have prevailed? But in reality Stillingfleet's whole argument is an attempt at evasion by changing the state of the question. For that question is not, whether the successor of St. Peter exercised throughout the Latin church the same rights with respect to the ordination of metropolitans, which were exercised by the eastern patriarchs; but whether he possessed, in quality of supreme pastor, a right to superintend the conduct of other bishops, and to inquire into the state of religion in other provinces.

In the fourth century several councils were assembled,

2 B 2

and in three of these, bishops from Britain sat as colleagues of the bishops from other parts of Christendom ;
the council of Arles in 314, that of Sardica (now Sophia
in Bulgaria) in 347, and of Rimini in 359. From these
facts two conclusions will follow : 1st, that the British
church formed an integral part of the universal church,
agreeing in doctrine and discipline with the other Christian churches ; 2nd, that the acts and declarations of
these councils may be taken as acts and declarations of
the British bishops, and therefore as expressions of the
belief and practice of the British church.

Now in the acts and declarations of these councils
there is one document, and, I believe, one only, which
bears a direct relation to the present inquiry. At the conclusion of the council of Sardica, the fathers sent a messenger to give an account of their proceedings to Pope
Julius, who ' though absent in person, had been present
with them in spirit ;' and in a common letter assigned as
the reason of this message, that he being the successor
of St. Peter was their head. " It will be seen to be best
and most proper, if the bishops from each particular
province make reference (or send information) to their
head, that is, to the seat of Peter, the apostle "—
Optimum et congruentissimum esse videbitur, si ad caput,
hoc est, ad Petri apostoli sedem, de singulis quibusque
provinciis Domini referant sacerdotes (Labbe, Con. ii. 690.
Venet. 1728). Hence, whatever may be the meaning of
the word ' referant,' whether it be confined to the transactions at Sardica, or, as is more probable, be understood
in the larger sense of all matters which may happen of
importance in any part of the church, this at least is
certain, that the members of the council, and therefore the
British bishops, looked upon the bishop of Rome as
their head ; because he was the successor of Peter the
apostle. It will perhaps be alleged that this proves

nothing more than a primacy of rank, not of jurisdiction, but it will be difficult to understand, why the bishops of each individual province—de singulis quibusque provinciis —should make reference, or send information to a foreign and distant bishop as their head, if such bishop, in that capacity, possessed no real authority in their respective provinces.

About eighty years later, St. Germanus of Auxerre and Lupus of Troyes came to Britain as missionaries sent to refute the Pelagians. The reader will recollect what has been already stated respecting their mission. If we may believe Constantius, who wrote about sixty years afterwards, they were sent by a council of French bishops in consequence of a petition for spiritual aid forwarded from Britain. Ex Britanniis directa legatio Gallicanis episcopis nuntiavit Pelagianam perversitatem in locis suis late populos occupasse, et quamprimum fidei Catholicæ debere succurri (Const. l. i. c. 19). By whom was the message sent ? To whom was it addressed ? Who received the missionaries on their arrival ? Who accompanied them in their travels over the island ? On these subjects Constantius is silent. He does not so much as mention the existence of a British priest or bishop throughout his narrative, though it is of considerable extent. Yet this unsatisfactory notice by him has been frequently converted into a proof that the British church was independent of its ' head,' the bishop of Rome, because assistance was solicited by the Britons from the bishops of Gaul. But could there be no other reason for the application ? Was not the distance much less ? Might not the petitioners be personally acquainted with some of the Gallic bishops ? May they not have applied to the bishop of Arles, the papal vicar in Gaul, in place of the pope whose representative he was ? However these things may be, we have testimony of much higher authority, which informs us that the mission of Germanus was derived from Rome—the testimony of Prosper, who was a Gaul by birth, who lived at the time, and who, from his office of secretary to Pope Celestine, had the means of possessing correct information. From him we learn in his Chronicle, which is confined to brief notices of the principal events of each year, that in 429, Celestine, at the application of the deacon Palladius, sent Germanus 'in his own place,' (that is, as his legate,) that he might drive out the heretics, and guide the Britons to the Catholic faith—Ad actionem Palladii diaconi Papa Celestinus Germanum Antissidorensem episcopum *vice sua* mittit, ut deturbatis hæreticis, Britannos ad Catholicam fidem dirigat. Prosp. in Chron. ad ann. 429 vel 433. To this positive testimony of the secretary of Celestine I see not what can be reasonably opposed, and it should be remarked that Prosper does not make this statement once only, but repeats it equivalently in his controversial work against Cassian ; where, speaking of Britain and Ireland, he says that Celestine kept the Roman island Catholic, and made the barbarian island Christian ; the first by expelling certain native leaders of Pelagianism from their hiding-place in the ocean ; the other by ordaining a bishop (Palladius) to establish Christianity among the Scots. Nec segniore cura ab hoc eodem morbo Britannias liberavit, quando quosdam inimicos gratiæ, solum suæ originis occupantes, ab illo secreto exclusit oceani, et ordinato Scotis episcopo, dum Romanam insulam studet servare catholicam, fecit etiam barbaram Christianam. Cont. Cass. c. 41, p. 113.

The letter of the council of Sardica to Pope Julius, and this mission of St. Germanus against the Pelagians, are the only two acts, which directly affect this question during the time that the island remained under the dominion of Rome, and both undoubtedly tend to establish the fact, that the Papal authority was then admitted by the Christians of Britain. There is, however, another light in which the subject may be viewed. No one can doubt that a close connection existed between the Christians of Britain and Gaul. This followed from their proximity to each other, which for a long time made the Gauls the only Christian neighbours of the Britons; from the civil policy of the imperial government, which had placed both countries under the command of the same magistrate, the prefect of the Gauls; from the presence of the British with the Gallic prelates in ecclesiastical councils; and from the missionary visits of the Gallic bishops to Britain. Hence the conclusion is, that both churches would recognize the same form of Ecclesiastical superiority and government; and that if the Gallic church admitted or repudiated the superintending authority of the church of Rome, the British church would admit it or repudiate it also.

On this question we have, as early as the second century, the testimony of the venerable Irenæus, bishop of Lyons, in that celebrated passage: " To the church of Rome, on account of her more powerful chiefdom, it is necessary that every church, or the whole church, that is, the faithful from every quarter, should conform " (or perhaps, make resort). Ad hanc ecclesiam, propter potiorem principalitatem, necesse est omnem ecclesiam, hoc est, eos qui undique sunt fideles, convenire. Iren. l. iii. c. 3.

Now it should be remembered that Irenæus was the bishop of Lyons, the metropolis of Gaul; that to him all the Gallic bishops looked up as to their immediate head; that he had collected their opinion on the great question of Easter, and had sent it as their head to Pope Victor—τῶν κατὰ Γαλλίαν παροικιῶν ἃς Εἰρηναῖος ἐπεσκόπει, Euseb. l. v. c. 23—and yet Irenæus in this passage openly proclaims the superiority of the church of Rome over

every other church, and pronounces it the duty of all
Christians from every place, and consequently from Gaul
itself, to conform to that church. More decisive testimony than this cannot be required.

We have from St. Cyprian, testimony equally decisive
for the third century. Novatian, the heresiarch, had been
condemned and excommunicated by St. Cornelius in
Rome. He solicited the communion of St. Cyprian and
the African bishops, but was refused. Subsequently he
found a friend in Gaul, Marcian, bishop of Arles, who
joined his party, and openly propagated his doctrine.
Information of their proceedings was sent by Faustinus,
one of the successors of Irenæus at Lyons, both to
Stephen, the successor of Cornelius in Rome, and to
Cyprian at Carthage. What effect his representation had
with Stephen, is unknown. It rekindled the zeal of
Cyprian, whose proceedings now call for the attention of
the reader. Cyprian was the chief of the African bishops,
having all the churches of Numidia and of both Mauri-
tanias under his immediate care (S. Cypriani, c. xlv.); but
that gave him no authority in Gaul. Did he then write
to Faustinus and exhort him, as the chief prelate of an
independent church, to call together the provincial bishops
and summon Marcian before that tribunal? No : he had
recourse to the authority of the Roman pontiff. He wrote
to Stephen in the most urgent terms to do his duty, by
sending to the Gallic bishops full instructions to punish
the presumption of Marcian, and other instructions to the
province and the people of Arles to sever themselves from
the communion of their bishop, and to substitute another
prelate in his place—Quapropter facere te oportet plenis-
simas literas ad coepiscopos nostros in Galliis constitutos,
ne ultra Marcianum collegio nostro insultare patiantur
. . . . . Dirigantur in provinciam et ad plebem Arelate con-
sistentem a te literæ, quibus, abstento Marciano, alius in

locum ejus substituatur.   Epist. Div. Cyp. ep. lxvii. p.
163. Such are the particulars disclosed to us in Cyprian's
letter to Stephen; particulars which appear to me to form
a case exactly in point, and to shew plainly the para-
mount authority exercised in Gaul by the popes in the
third century.

I may be allowed to add two more instances for the
following centuries.   Prosper of Aquitaine, was a Gaul by
birth and education.   What he states of the authority of
the holy see, may reasonably be considered as the common opinion among his countrymen.   Speaking of the
first appearance of Pelagianism, he tells us that Rome,
as the seat of Peter, is the head of the episcopal order in
the whole world, and thus holds in subjection through the
influence of religion more nations than it ever subdued by
the force of arms.

> Pestem subeuntem prima recidit
> Roma sedes Petri, quæ pastoralis honoris
> Facta caput mundo, quidquid non possidet armis
> Relligione tenet.
>
> *Prosper, De Ingrat.*, p. 150.

In his prose works he repeatedly makes the same remark.   Per Apostolici sacerdotii principatum amplior
facta est arce religionis quam solio potestatis.   De Vocat.
Gentium, ii. c. xvi. p. 231.

Prosper wrote about the year 430.   Not long afterwards, Pope Leo, offended with Hilarius, bishop of Arles,
deprived him of the office of apostolic vicar in Gaul, and
conferred it on the Bishop of Vienne.   On the election of
Ravennius to the bishopric after the death of Hilarius,
nineteen prelates wrote to Leo, begging of him to restore
the vicarship to the new bishop of Arles, and complain-
ing that the bishop of Vienne had consecrated one of the
provincial bishops subject to that metropolis.   In this
letter, they acknowledge that " the holy Roman church,
through the prince of the apostles, holds the principality

or chiefdom over all the churches of the whole world"—
Per beatissimum apostolorum principem sacrosancta Romana ecclesia tenet supra omnes totius mundi ecclesias
principatum. Leo, by his answer, settled the dispute
between the two metropolitans, attaching four bishoprics to the metropolitical see of Vienne; but refused to
withdraw the vicarship from its present possessor, who
had done nothing to forfeit the confidence of the holy
see. It was afterwards given back to the bishop of Arles.
See Epist. Decret. Div. Leonis, pp. 182, 3.

These few passages have been selected, because it does
not seem possible to interpret them fairly of a mere
superiority of rank. They import, as fully as language
can be expected to import, when it is not used expressly for the purpose of controversy, that the church
of Gaul admitted during the whole of this period the
superior authority of the church of Rome: and, if such
was the doctrine of the Gallic church, we may reasonably
conclude that such also was the doctrine of the British
church, though from the absence of documents bearing
on the subject, it may not be so directly proved.

THE THIRD PERIOD.

III. The third period comprehends a century and a
half, from the extinction of the civil power of Rome in
Britain, to the arrival from Rome of Christian missionaries in the island; a period of woe and extermination
to the natives who were engaged in perpetual but unsuccessful contests with the invaders of their country. There
exists no writer, foreign or national, who has mentioned
the church of Britain during this period, if we except
Gildas, the British historiographer. The reader is already
acquainted with his complaints respecting the state of
Britain in his day; meaning by Britain the present principality of Wales, with the counties of Devon and Cornwall: and will have noticed that passage, in which he

inveighs against the ambition of the British clergymen, who, refusing to submit to the judgment of their fellows, seek that of a foreign authority—an authority that resides beyond the seas; and not beyond the seas only, but at a still greater distance, for after they have passed the seas, they have to traverse spacious regions before they can reach it. (See the quotation in note C, p. 367.) I do not see how this description can apply to any other place and authority but Rome and the bishop of Rome; and if that be the case, it will follow that the British church, even during this calamitous period, acknowledged, both in doctrine and practice, the superior authority of the Roman pontiff.

Hitherto then, during the six first centuries of the Christian era, we have not met with a single document to shew the independence of the British church; all the evidence which has come down to us, tends to support the opposite opinion. Towards the close of this period came Augustine with his associates, missionaries to the Saxons, and to him, soon after he had received episcopal consecration, Pope Gregory wrote a letter, containing a scheme for the future government of the new church, and concluding with these words: " Moreover your brotherhood will have subject to you all the bishops of Britain by authority of our God and Lord, Jesus Christ, that from your instructions they may learn to believe correctly, and from your example, to live religiously, and thus by the faithful discharge of their duty, obtain the heavenly kingdom — Tua vero fraternitas omnes Britanniæ sacerdotes habeat, Deo Domino nostro Jesu Christo auctore, subjectos, quatenus ex lingua et vita tuæ sanctitatis et recte credendi et bene vivendi formam percipiant, atque officium suum fide ac moribus exsequentes, ad cœlestia, cum Dominus voluerit, regna pertingant. Bed. i. c. 29. The same occurs in his answer to a question from Augustine respecting the Gallic and British prelates : " But we commit all the bishops of Britain to your brotherhood, that the unlearned may be taught, the weak may be strengthened by your counsels, and the obstinate be corrected by your authority." Britanniarum vero omnes episcopos tuæ fraternitati committimus, ut indocti doceantur, infirmi persuasione roborentur, perversi auctoritate corrigantur. Id. c. 27, § 65. Now let any one peruse with attention these two documents, and he will confess that they must have proceeded from one, who believed it to be his duty to watch over the conduct, and to correct the delinquencies of bishops, whether in Gaul or Britain ; and that he did not anticipate any objection on the part of the British bishops to the delegation of this power to Augustine, who was his representative here, in like manner as the bishop of Arles was his representative in Gaul. Most assuredly had this been, as it often is represented, an attempt to bring under subjection a church, which for so many centuries had maintained its independence, he would have adopted other language in his correspondence with his agent, and have furnished him with very different instructions.

But did not the Britons at the conference at Austcliffe reject the papal authority, and maintain their own independence ? So it is, indeed, asserted by modern writers, but not in the narrative of Beda, the only real authority which we possess. There we meet with no mention of these subjects, with no hint that they were ever taken into consideration. Augustine said to the seven bishops—who they were we know not, but probably chorepiscopi, with whom Wales abounded—" In many things you act contrary to our custom, or rather to the custom of the universal church ; but if you will yield to me in these three things, to celebrate Easter at the proper time, to conclude the service of baptism after the manner of the holy Roman and Apostolic Church, and to preach with us the word of God to the Angles"—a singular request to be made by Augustine if the Britons rejected the papal supremacy—" then we will cheerfully put up with other things, how contrary soever they may be to our customs." But they, muttering to each other, "He did not rise to us. How then will he trample us under foot hereafter, if we begin to submit to him now?" answered, that they would do none of these things, nor have him for archbishop. Bed. ii. c. 2. This the reader will observe was in strict conformity with the advice of the hermit, to submit to the demands of Augustine, if he rose from his seat, to reject them if he did not. Can we believe that, if submission to Augustine had been a surrender of the spiritual independence of their church, they would have risked it on so uncertain a contingency, or rather on one which it was most probable would be unfavourable to it? The tendency of the whole story is to shew that their opposition to the demands of the missionary, was prompted by their apprehension of giving to themselves a severe and imperious master.

Lastly, an argument in favour of the independence of the British Church has been drawn from the controversy between the Roman missionaries and the Britons, respecting the proper time for the celebration of Easter; an instance how hastily and illogically conclusions are formed, when the mind is engaged in the support of some favourite opinion. The time of Easter was not a theological question; it could be solved only by astronomical calculation; the errors of former computations had been corrected in every other part of the church, but the Britons and Scots " extra orbem positi," continued to employ the old cycles; and when they were called upon by the Roman missionaries to exchange them for new, pertinaciously refused to depart from the practice of their ancestors. Is

this a proof that they did not admit the Bishop of Rome
for the supreme pastor of the church? At least men,
more likely to understand that question than any one at
the present day, Honorius, Archbishop of Canterbury, and
Felix, Bishop of East-Anglia, thought otherwise. These
prelates looked upon it, indeed, as an error of judgment,
but not as a breach of communion. For, though Aidan and
his Scots were not less stubborn than the Britons, they did
not exclude them from their communion: on the contrary,
they cherished and loved them as fellow-labourers in the
conversion of the Saxons, and bore with patience their
obstinate adhesion to this custom of their country in consideration of their zeal and piety. Hæc autem dissonantia
Paschalis observantiæ, vivente Ædano, patienter ab omnibus tolerabatur . . . ab omnibus, etiam ab his, qui de
Paschate aliter sentiebant, merito diligebatur, nec solum
a mediocribus, verum ab ipsis quoque episcopis, Honorio
Cantuariorum, et Felice, Orientalium Anglorum, venerationi habitus est. Bed. iii. c. 25.—In fact, it should be
observed that this custom of the Britons was not opposed
to the custom of Rome only, but to the decree of the
council of Nice (Euseb. Vit. Cons. iii. c. 14-17), and to
the practice of all other Christians throughout the world.
If it prove then that they were independent of Rome, it
must prove also that they were independent of general
councils and of the universal church; in other words, that
they were in reality schismatics.

NOTE F (p. 89).

ANGLO-SAXON BISHOPRICS.

THE number of bishoprics in the Anglo-Saxon church
varied at different times. If new sees were occasionally
founded to supply the wants of an increasing population,

old sees were frequently abandoned or suppressed in consequence of the ascendancy gained by one nation over another, or of the devastation wrought by foreign invaders. Without entering into the chronological or chorological difficulties which the subject sometimes presents, I shall content myself with briefly enumerating the bishoprics known to belong to each separate kingdom.

1. Northumbria contained four,—York, Lindisfarne, Hexham, and Whitherne in Galloway. Egbert, the seventh bishop of York, obtained the pallium before the middle of the eighth century, and became metropolitan with the other three for his suffragans. But by the end of that century Witherne was rescued from the Northumbrian yoke by the men of Galloway ; and soon afterwards Hexham and its neighbourhood were depopulated, and held by the Danish invaders. There remained but one suffragan bishop to York, the bishop of Lindisfarne, whose see, after several removals, was at last fixed at Durham in 995.

2. Mercia at first contained but one bishopric, that of Lichfield. In 678, the Northumbrians took possession of Lindissy or the county of Lincoln, and Theodore immediately placed there a Northumbrian bishop. On the recovery of the country by the Mercians, the new bishop retired to Ripon ; and a Mercian was appointed in his place, who fixed his episcopal seat at Sidnacester, the situation of which is unknown. The diocese of Lichfield still remained of enormous extent; and in the course of twenty years was successively divided into four bishoprics,—Lichfield, Worcester, Hereford, and Leicester. Thus Mercia had five bishops, but about the close of the ninth century the succession of bishops in the churches of Sidnacester and Leicester terminated, probably on account of the Danish devastations. In the

reign, however, of Edred, a new bishop was appointed to take the charge of the two dioceses, with Dorchester in Oxfordshire, a place of greater security for his residence. This arrangement lasted till the conquest.

3. Among the East-Angles, Felix, their apostle, fixed his see at Dunwich, as did his three immediate successors. The kingdom was then divided into two bishoprics, those of Dunwich and Elmham, which continued till the Danes took possession of the country in 870. From that time till after the year 950, we meet with no bishop in East-Anglia. Then a single bishop was appointed, who, as did also his successors, resided at Elmham.

4, 5. With respect to the kingdoms of Kent and of the East Saxons, it will be sufficient to state that Canterbury, Rochester, and London were bishoprics from the time of St. Augustine.

6. The first Christian kings of Wessex had placed their apostle Birinus at Dorchester. Heddi, the fourth of his successors, probably because Dorchester was exposed to the hostilities of the Mercians, transferred the see to Winchester; and at his death about 705, the kingdom was divided into two dioceses, that of Winchester to consist of Hampshire, Surrey, and the Isle of Wight; and that of Sherborne comprehending all the Saxon territory to the West. This by a long succession of conquests made by different kings extended at length to the Land's-end; and in the reign of Edward the son of Alfred was divided by archbishop Plegmund in council, into four bishoprics,—Ramesbury or Wilton for Wiltshire, Sherborne for Dorsetshire, Wells for Somersetshire, and Crediton for Devonshire and Cornwall. From Crediton, Bishop Leofric migrated to Exeter a little before the conquest.

7. The kingdom of Sussex was soon subjugated by that of Wessex. At first, the West-Saxon bishop claimed the

charge of Sussex, but it soon had a bishop of its own, the Bishop of Selsey.

Thus then at the close of the Anglo-Saxon period, there were two ecclesiastical provinces in England, the southern comprising the archiepiscopal see of Canterbury, and the episcopal sees of Rochester, London, Selsey, Winchester, Wilton, Sherborne, Crediton or Exeter, Wells, Hereford, Worcester, Lichfield, Dorchester and Elmham; and the northern province, consisting of the metropolitan church of York, and the episcopal church of Durham, sixteen in all.

NOTE G (p. 125).

THE COUNCIL OF CLOVESHOE.

THE reader is already aware that the council of Cloveshoe was convoked in obedience to the command of Pope Zachary, and to prevent the sentence of excommunication, with which he had threatened the Anglo-Saxon prelates. It was hardly to be expected that the proceedings of such a council would furnish proof that the Anglo-Saxon church considered itself independent of the church of Rome. The paradox, however, was hazarded by Inett (Orig. Anglicanæ, i. 174), and has been often repeated by subsequent writers. The disciples have even improved on the statements of their master. For, what he put forth under the more modest title of probabilities, they have represented as indisputable facts.

In their hypothesis it is taken for granted, but without the slightest attempt at proof, that the Anglo-Saxon Boniface, archbishop of Mentz, having brought the neighbouring prelates into subjection to the bishop of Rome, formed the notion of subjecting the independent church of his own country to the same servitude; that

with this view he sent certain canons enacted iu a council
at Mentz to Archbishop Cuthbert of Canterbury, to be
adopted by the English prelates; and that a council was
held for that purpose at Cloveshoe, in which certain
canons were passed, for the most part taken from the
very canons sent by Boniface. The English prelates,
however—so they tell us—to preserve their own independence, in place of a declaration of obedience to
the successor of St. Peter, passed a resolution to live in
peace with all the clergy in the world without flattering
any one particular person; and instead of the canon
allowing appeals from provincial councils to Rome, substituted a decree that all difficult matters should be
finally determined here by the archbishop in the synod of
his province.

Now, if this statement could lay any claim to truth, it
would fully justify the praise of patriotism, which has
been so gratefully bestowed on the council of Cloveshoe
by Henry (Hist. iii. 5), by Mr. Churton (Early Eng.
Church, 157), and Mr. Soames (Hist. of Ang-Sax. Church,
113). But unfortunately the whole fabric is built in
the air. It will not bear examination. It is contradicted in every particular by the very documents, on
which it is supposed to be founded.

The synod of Mentz under Boniface was held in
January 747. Now a constant correspondence was kept
up at that time between the Anglo-Saxon clergy and
their countrymen, the missionaries in Germany; and it
happened that the deacon Cynebert, having been sent in
the beginning of the same year with a letter and
presents from Archbishop Cuthbert, to his brother metropolitan, returned to England, the bearer of an
answer and of presents from Boniface to Cuthbert. In
this answer, as was natural, Boniface acquainted his cor-
respondent with the result of a synod which had just

been concluded, and with the purport of eight canons which had been passed in it. Modern writers are positive that his object was to bring the Anglo-Saxon church into subjection, and that he copied the eight canons as patterns for the imitation of his countrymen. But Boniface states in his letter, that he sends this account of the council, because Cuthbert had requested to know how he and his fellow-bishops were employed; and adds the canons themselves, that the English metropolitan may amend and correct them according to his better judgment. Non quia prudentiæ vestræ opus sit rusticitatis nostræ statuta audire vel legere, sed propter bonam et humilem et sanctam voluntatem vestram putamus vos libentius scire quam nescire, quæ hic sacerdotes nobiscum servanda decreverunt, vobis emendanda et corrigenda destinamus. (Spelm. Con. 237.) Certainly in this explanation there is no appearance of the object, which has been attributed to Boniface. Let us then proceed to the council of Cloveshoe itself.

This was opened by the archbishop with the lecture of two writings received "from the apostolic lord, the pontiff held in reverence by the whole world, the Pope Zachary, which, as he by his apostolical authority had commanded, were first read openly in Latin, and then in an English translation. In these he admonished the Anglo-Saxon inhabitants of this island of Britain, expostulated with them, and conjured them; and then threatened to cut off from the communion of the church all who should despise his warning, and obstinately persist in their wickedness—Scripta toto orbe venerandi pontificis papæ Zachariæ in duabus chartis prolata sunt, et cum magna diligentia, juxta quod ipse apostolica sua auctoritate præcepit, et manifeste recitata, et in nostra quoque lingua apertius interpretata sunt.   Quibus

2 c 2

namque scriptis Britanniæ hujus insulæ nostri generis
accolas familiariter præmonebat, et veraciter conveniebat
et postremo amabiliter exorabat, et hæc omnia contemnentibus, et in su a pertinaci malitia permanentibus anathematis sententiam procul dubio proferendam insinuabat.
(Wilk. Con. 94. Spelm. Con. 245). Such is the proem of
the council which has been selected to prove the independence of the Anglo Saxon church : certainly a most
unpromising and chivalrous attempt. The members
declare that they assemble in obedience to the mandate of the Pope, and enact canons to avoid his displeasure : and yet we are called upon to believe that
they at the same time rejected his authority, and braved
his displeasure.

Inett was aware of the inconsistency, and therefore, to
lull the suspicion of his readers, adroitly suggests that
" most likely the writings in question were not sent to
Cuthbert, the English archbishop, but some which had
been sent by Zachary to Boniface." (Inett, p. 175;
Soames, 113, not. 2). Most likely? Why nothing could
be more unlikely than that writings ordered by the pope
to be translated into English, and read in an English
synod, should be addressed to the German in place of the
English metropolitan ; or that the persons here called
" the men of our race, inhabitants of this isle of Britain "—
Britanniæ hujus insulæ nostri generis accolas— should
have been in reality the Germans dwelling on the banks
of the Rhine, under the spiritual jurisdiction of Boniface !

This paradox is followed by several others.

1. We are told that the canons enacted at Cloveshoe
were framed after the pattern sent by Boniface. Now
the canons sent by Boniface were eight, those passed at
Cloveshoe were thirty in number, and in only two or
three instances did they touch upon the same subjects.
How could the eight serve as patterns for the thirty ?

2. Whence then did the English prelates derive their canons? They state that having heard the message from the pope, and the fearful threat of anathema with which it was accompanied, they had conferred among themselves on the reformation of their own order, which was set to teach all others; and, having for that purpose consulted the homilies of the blessed father Gregory, and the canonical decrees of the holy fathers, they had resolved that each bishop should henceforth abstain from the exercise of any secular office, and should confine himself entirely to his pastoral duties, instructing and correcting, both by his words and his works, the people committed to his charge. Spelm. Con. p. 246.

The above is the first canon passed by the English prelates. Now in the council of Mentz, the first canon is a profession of obedience to the holy see; and the absence of such profession from the canons of Cloveshoe, is very adroitly taken as a proof that the English prelates did not acknowledge any obedience to that see, while in fact they were acting in obedience to it. "The deliberators," writes Mr. Soames, "abstained from any submission to the Roman see. In several particulars, his countrymen consented to follow Boniface, but they patriotically disregarded his example, when it would have led them to compromise their dignity as a nation by professing submission to a foreign ecclesiastical authority." (Soames, Hist. p. 113.) But could any profession of obedience be more expressive of submission to the papal authority than the proem which the English bishops prefixed to their canons? It is said that they disregarded the example of Boniface: but it should be proved that they were called upon to follow it. There might be many reasons which made such a profession desirable in Germany. But who can prove that similar reasons existed in England?

3. It has, however, been discovered that the bishops at Cloveshoe atoned for their submission in the proem by the insertion of an indirect denial of the papal superiority in their second canon. "Cuthbert," says Mr. Churton, "a wise and prudent prelate, did not imitate the example of Boniface in binding himself to obey in all things the orders of St. Peter, as they called the pope's commands ; but he and the other bishops engaged to maintain their own laws against encroachment, keeping up a free correspondence with foreign churches and a union of affection, but not flattering any person because he held a station of higher dignity in the church." Churton, p. 157.

This remark is founded on a covenant subscribed by the prelates there present, who bind themselves thenceforth to keep among them at all times and in all places true peace and sincere charity ; to preserve concord among them all in their respective rights, deeds, words, and judgments, without the flattery of any particular person, as being the servants of one Lord, and fellow-labourers in one ministry, so that though they are separated in point of locality, they may still be united in spirit, &c.—Secundo loco sub testificatione quadam confirmaverunt, ut pacis intimæ et sinceræ charitatis devotio ubique inter eos perpetuo permaneat, atque ut una sit omnium concordia in viris (juribus) ecclesiasticæ religionis, in sermone, in opere, in judicio, sine cujusquam adulatione personæ, utpote unius domini ministri, uniusque ministerii conservi, ut licet sedibus sint divisi per diversa loca, tamen mentibus sint conjuncti in uno spiritu, &c. Spelm. 246— which is thus briefly explained by Malmesbury, ut (præfati præsules) pacifico animo viverent, quamvis locis discreti degerent. Malm. de Pent. f. 112.

If the reader be unacquainted with controversial tactics, he will probably wonder what connection there can be between [this covenant and the question of the papal supremacy. The following is the real solution of the mystery. Inett and his disciples assume that the English prelates did not admit the authority claimed by the pope, and therefore, to signify their rejection of it in the least offensive way, devised this covenant, binding themselves to live in peace and harmony with all the bishops *in the world* without yielding to the pretensions of superiority, which may be set up by any *particular person* among those bishops. To give this meaning to the words, the title of the canon, "on unity of peace," has been supposed to mean "on the unity of the universal church;" whence it follows that the words *inter eos,* which confined the object of the covenant to the bishops of the province of Canterbury—for no other bishops were present to subscribe—must be understood of all the bishops *in the world,* and therefore include the bishop of Rome. From such premises it was easy to leap at once to the desired conclusion. But let the reader revert to the original document, and he will see at one glance that the covenant regards only the bishops of the province of Canterbury. They belonged to different nations having different and opposite interests, and lived under kings and ealdormen generally at variance, frequently at war with each other; on which account the covenant bound them to look upon themselves as one body, to preserve religious peace and harmony among themselves, and to protect according to their power the rights of their several churches. The fact, that within a few years, the bishoprics of Mercia and East-Anglia were torn from the province of Canterbury, and subjected to a new metropolitan at Lichfield, will countenance the conjecture, that some such project was already in agitation, and that the covenant was devised by Cuthbert to protect the ancient superiority of his church.

4. Among the thirty canons of the English council

there are but two which correspond with those of the German council; one of which, ordering the bishops to make an annual visitation of their dioceses is of such frequent recurrence, that it requires no comment. The other, No. 25 in the English, and No. 8 in the German collection, prescribes that the bishops returning from the provincial council, shall explain its enactments to their own clergy in a diocesan synod; and that, if a bishop find himself unable to correct any abuse in his diocese, he shall report it to the metropolitan and his fellow-bishops in the provincial council, that with their aid it may be corrected. Statuimus ut episcopi a synodo venientes in propria parochia cum præsbyteris et abbatibus conventus habentes, præcepta synodi servare insinuando præcipiant, et unusquisque episcopus, si quid in sua diocesi corrigere vel emendare nequiverit, ibidem in synodo coram archiepiscopo, et palam omnibus ad corrigendum insinuet. (Labbe, Con. viii. 281 ; Spelm. 238.) This was the universal discipline of the age. As the parish priest, when he could not put down an abuse in his parish, was ordered to carry the case before his bishop in the diocesan synod; so the bishop, in similar circumstances, was ordered to have recourse to his metropolitan in the provincial council. Yet this canon has obtained for the English bishops the reputation of patriotism for their care in protecting the independence of their church from foreign encroachment. But how so ? Is there any question in it of ecclesiastical independence or foreign encroachment ? No. Does it differ in any important point from the canon sent by Boniface? No: the English enactment is verbatim the same with the German. Not a word is added, not a word substracted. How then can it be taken as a specimen of episcopal patriotism? Inett himself shall explain it, who tells us that the English canon purposely omits " what Boniface says of the bishop of Rome in the latter part of his canon, and what he immediately subjoins of appeals from metropolitans to the bishop of Rome . . . . for by saying that appeals might be made from the bishop of a province to the metropolitan and his synod, without mentioning any other person to whom an appeal lay, the English prelates did in effect determine (against the doctrine of Boniface) that there lay no appeal from the metropolitan and his synod to the bishop of Rome; but on the contrary, that all disputes on ecclesiastical affairs should be finally determined in the province in which they arose." Inett, p. 176.

Now all this reasoning of Inett is founded on two most singular mistakes. 1st, He takes it as a fact that the English canon has omitted the latter part of the German canon, and yet it has not omitted a single word; and 2nd, he represents it as regulating appeals, a subject with which it has not the remotest connection. An appeal is an application to a higher authority for protection against the presumed injustice of a sentence pronounced, or about to be pronounced, by a lower : but the canon orders bishops in the difficulties, which they may meet with in the administration of their dioceses, to seek advice and aid of the metropolitan and their fellow-bishops in the provincial council; undoubtedly a very different subject. The origin of the mistake appears to be partly this. Boniface in his letter to Cuthbert states that at his ordination in Rome he was bound by oath to inform the apostolic see, whenever he found himself unable to withdraw bishops or people from practices contrary to the law of God : for it was his opinion that, in such case, it was the duty of the bishop to have recourse to his metropolitan, and of the metropo.itan to have recourse to the vicar of St. Peter, otherwise he would be answerable for the souls lost through his negligence—Eodem modo quo Romana ecclesia nos ordinatos cum sacramento obstrinxit ut, si sacerdotes vel plebes a lege Dei deviasse viderim, et corrigere non potuerim, fideliter semper sedi apostolicæ et vicario St. Petri ad emendandum indicaverim. Sic enim, ni fallor, omnes episcopi debent metropolitano, et ipse Romano pontifici, si quid de corrigendis populis apud ipsos impossible est, notum facere, et sic alieni fient a sanguine ovium perditarum. (Labbe, 313 ; Spelm. 238.) Now as this passage in the letter is subjoined to the canon, it would appear that Inett took it for the concluding portion of the canon. That he should have made so gross a mistake is certainly singular, and equally singular it is that he should have understood this part also as relating to appeals, instead of applications for advice and assistance.

I will only add that Malmesbury was so far from discovering in this canon the wonderful secrets discovered of late years, that he describes it as merely a canon ordering the bishops to take care that the decrees issued by the council be properly executed—ut episcopi observent, ne ista decreta negligantur. Malm. de Pont. f. 112 b.

NOTE H (p. 145).

St. Wilfrid, by his earnest endeavours to introduce the canonical observances among his countrymen, and his successful appeals to the justice of the pontiffs, has earned the severest reproaches from the enemies of the church of Rome. Hence, to paint his character in odious colours, has been a favourite theme with several writers, among whom the first place is undoubtedly due to Carte. In the following columns I shall confront a few of his mis-statements with the original text of Eddius, and add to those mis-statements two or three others from Mr. Soames's more recent History of the Anglo-Saxon Church.

1. According to Carte, (p. 250), "Wilfrid's appeal appeared so new and singular, that it occasioned a general laughter, as a thing quite ridiculous." He refers to Eddius, c. 24. Henry thought this observation so important, that he was careful to copy it.

2. Carte accuses Eddius of misrepresentation, when he says, that Wilfrid was advised to appeal by his fellow-bishops (cum consilio coepiscoporum suorum. Ed. c. 24, p. 63); because no one but Winfrid, the deposed bishop of Mercia, could give such advice. Carte, p. 250.

3. Carte asserts that the king of Northumbria would not restore the deposed prelate, because he conceived the conduct of the pontiff to be derogatory to the rights of the crown (p.

1. Eddius (c. 24, p. 63) says not, that the appeal excited either surprise or ridicule, but that the flatterers of the king expressed their joy at the disgrace of Wilfrid, by laughter. Adulatoribus cum risu gaudentibus—Qui ridetis in meam condemnationem. Ibid.

2. The assertion of Eddius is confirmed by Wilfrid's petition to the pontiff, in which he observes, that though several bishops were present with Theodore, not one of them assented to his measures. In conventu Theodori, aliorumque tunc temporis antistitum . . . . . absque consensu *cujuslibet episcopi*. Ed. c. 29, p. 66.

3. According to Eddius, the real ground of objection was, that the papal decree had been purchased with money ; pretio redempta. Edd. c. 33, p. 69. Fridegode says the like—Furtivis

251); because the papal jurisdiction was unknown in Northumbria. Soames, p. 82.

4. According to Carte (p. 252), the king offered him a part of his former diocese, if he would renounce the *authority* of the papal mandate. He refers to Eddius, c. 35.

5. If we may believe Carte (p. 254), Wilfrid made his submission to Theodore, and employed the good offices of the bishop of London to procure a reconciliation. His authority is Eddius, c. 42.

6. To prove that this reconciliation was not owing to any respect which the metropolitan paid to the papal authority, but solely to his esteem for the personal merit of Wilfrid, Carte sends his reader to the letter of Theodore, to king Ethelred, p. 254. —Mr. Soames hints the same, quoting, as if it were Theodore's only reason, this passage, quia longo tempore propriis or-

rebus adeptas.   Act SS. Ben. iii. 169.

4. Eddius informs us that the king offered him a part of his former diocese, if he would acknowledge the papal mandate to be a *forgery.* Si denegaret vera esse. Ed. c. 35, p. 70.

5. If Eddius is to be credited, it was Theodore, who, actuated by remorse for his past injustice, sent for Wilfrid and the bishop of London, and solicited the forgiveness of the man whom he had injured. Ed. c. 42, p. 73.

6. Theodore, in his letter to king Ethelred, assigns the authority of the pontiff as the cause of his reconciliation. Idcirco ego Theodorus, humilis episcopus, decrepita ætate, hoc tuæ Beatitudini suggero, quia *Apostolica* hoc, sicut scis, commendat *auctoritas.* Ep. Theod. apud Wilk. p. 64; Ed. c. 42, p. 74. Pope John asserts the same. Ut ex ejus dictis apparuit, *decretis pontificalibus obse-*

batus substantiis inter Paganos in Domino multum laboravit, p. 87.

7. Carte informs us that, when the controversy was terminated at the synod of Nid, it was agreed, without conforming to the terms of the papal decree, that Wilfrid should be restored to his see of Hexham, and monastery of Ripon, p. 259. Mr. Soames hints the same, pp. 88, 89.

8. According to Carte, the Anglo-Saxon bishops, during this contest, were careful to oppose the introduction of appeals, and to preserve the independence of their church. According to Mr. Soames, the appeals of Wilfrid were treated uniformly with contempt, not only by the civil authorities, but also by the ecclesiastical. Soames, p. 89.

cutus erat. Ibid. c. 52, p. 82.

7. Yet the restoration of Hexham and Ripon was all that Wilfrid demanded from the pontiff. Ed. c. 49, p. 79. It was also as much as the papal decree required, which is thus explained by Archbishop Brithwald. Ut præsules ecclesiarum hujus provinciæ cum Wilfrido episcopo pacem plene perfecteque ineant, et partes ecclesiarum, quas olim ipse regebat, sicut sapientes mecum judicaverint, restituant. Ed. c. 58, p. 85.

8. It is evident, from the whole history of Eddius, that neither of the archbishops had any notion of the independence of his church. Instead of opposing the introduction of appeals, both of them acknowledged the lawfulness of the practice, and sent messengers to Rome to support their own decisions against the appeals of Wilfrid. Edd. c. xxix. p. 66; c. lii. p. 79.

NOTE I (p. 161 and 180-194).

PARISH CHURCHES AND TITHES.

THE irregular manner in which parish churches are entered in the ancient record of Domesday, is a constant source of disappointment and vexation to antiquaries. In the returns from some counties we scarcely meet with the name of a single church; while in the returns from other counties scarcely a church is omitted. The cause of this diversity may perhaps be discovered in the instructions issued to the commissioners. In the Inquisitio Eliensis, they are ordered to inquire the name of the mansion, of the owner, both in the time of King Edward and at the present time; the number of hides in the manor, of carrucates in the hands of the lord, and in the hands of his men; the number of villeins, of cottars, of slaves, of freemen, and of sokemen; the quantity of wood, meadow, and pasture land; the mills and fisheries, what had been added to the manor or separated from it; what were the receipts in King Edward's time, and what at the present time, and how much each freeman or sokeman possessed then, or possesses now. (Ellis, Gener. Introd. Domesd. iii. viii., and Inquis. Eliens. Domes. iv. 497.) The reader will observe that here there is no express mention of churches; whence, if this, as seems most likely, was the general form of the instructions, it will follow that the several sets of commissioners were left at liberty to return the parish churches or not, according to their pleasure or judgment. The consequence has been, that many omitted them partially, many almost entirely. Still the returns from others are sufficiently full to enable us to form a general notion of the state of the churches, both under the conqueror, and also during the latter part of the Anglo-Saxon period.

1. The churches are generally entered under the name of church, occasionally under that of the minster (Dom. i. 191, ii. 286). The incumbent is always denominated the priest. Sometimes we meet with two or three priests to a church, or a priest with two or three clerks (Ibid. i. 16 b, 17), or six or seven clerks (Ibid. i. 280). In one place we find a church with twelve monks, whether they were monks properly so called, or clerks to whom that name was given, because they belonged to the monastery or minster (Ibid. ii. 293). Where the clergy lived together, the land of the church was possessed by them in common, communis terra (Ibid. i. 17); where separately, it was divided into prebends. (Ibid. i. 1 b, 16 b.)

2. It seems to have been the general rule, that all these churches should, at their foundation, receive an endowment in land. There are, indeed, a few, but very few, entries of churches without land (Ecclesia sine terra. Domes. ii. 169, 169 b, 282, 409); but these may be accounted for on the supposition, that the land originally conveyed to the church had, in the course of centuries, been severed from it, by the violence of the lord, or the encroachment of some powerful neighbour.

3. The church lands, entered in Domesday, varied considerably in extent, from many hides to a single hide, from hundreds of acres to a single acre. In the time of Edward the church of Boseham, in Sussex, possessed one hundred and twelve hides, which under the conqueror had been reduced to sixty-five (Domes. i. 17); that of Loiton, in Bedfordshire, is returned in possession of five hides (Dom. i. 209); that of North Langale, in Norfolk, of one hundred acres (Dom. i. 260 b); that of St. Gregory at Tinghoe, in Suffolk, of fifty acres (Dom. ii. 286); that of Wilsham, in Sussex, of one yardland (Dom. i. 18 b); and that of Stanton, in Shropshire, of only one acre and a half (Dom. i. 260 b).

These lands appear generally to have been held on the same conditions, and subject to the same rents and services, with the lands held by the lay tenants of the manor. There were, however, three exceptions—lands given to the church in alms, and on that account exempt from all rents and services; lands not subject to the jurisdiction of the lord claiming sac and soc, and therefore called free lands; and some lands enjoying both these immunities together—Qui non pertineret mauerio nisi de scoto, quia libera terra erat (Dom. i. 45). Ecclesiæ hujus villæ (Bradfield in Suffolk), jacent decem acræ liberæ terræ in eleemosyna (Dom. ii. 362). Ecclesiæ hujus villæ (Berton in Suffolk), quinquaginta acræ liberæ terræ pertinent pro eleemosyna (Ibid. 361 b).

4. The lords of manors and all other owners of churches, whether clergymen or laymen, men or women, derived a profit from their churches. This is evident from the record. The object of the inquisition was to discover the real value of the manor; and on that account the yearly rent, received by the lord from the church, was often returned with the same precision as that received from mills, or mines, or fisheries. Thus we meet with seven priests, who pay annually seven pounds five shillings (Dom. i. 4); three churches at Dunwich, paying four pounds ten shillings (Ibid. 311); one priest paying forty shillings (Ibid. 9); another paying twenty (Ibid. 40 b); and a third paying sixty-four pennies (Ibid. 16). But often the amount of these payments is omitted, because it is included in the return of the gross yearly profit to the owner (Omnes ecclesiæ de tota terra Hermerii sunt appreciatæ cum maneriis. Dom. ii. 208—Omnes ecclesiæ sunt in pretio cum maneriis. ii. 265). Generally, the rent received from country churches does not amount to more than a few pence; though in several instances it rises to a much higher sum.

5. There are many entries in Domesday, which make it probable that the same abuses with respect to churches existed in England, which are known to have prevailed on the continent; that they were become matters of traffic and private property; that occasionally new churches were built on speculation, with a view to the profits from the offerings of the people and the fees of the priest; and that the income of the older churches was often seized and appropriated to himself by a powerful land-owner, who bestowed only a share of it, or perhaps a yearly stipend in lieu of it, on the minister. In numerous entries, the income from the lands is broadly distinguished from the income from the church, a distinction which shews that both were equally claimed by the owners. Godric, the son of Garewine, inherited from his mother "the church of All Hallows in Lincoln, and the land of the church, and whatever belonged to it." (Dom. 1,336.) St. Mary's de Cormeliis held the church " of Bromsais in Herefordshire, and the priest with his land, and the whole of the tithe." (Ibid. 1, 170 b.) "Thomas, Archbishop (of York), held of the king the church of the manor of Mortesfunde, in Hampshire, and six chapels in the neighbouring hamlets (which are mentioned), with all customs both of the living and the dead, offerings, fees, mortuaries, &c." He who held it before him, held it in like manner of King Edward. (Ibid. 1, 42.) Roger de Ramis held in Suffolk "the fourth part of the church of Codeham, and the fourth part of that which pertained to the church." (Ibid. 11, 422.) " Ralf Piperell claimed one half of the hide and eighteen acres of land belonging to the church of Borham in Essex, and one half of the church." Ibid. 11, 31.

6. Shares of churches are entered in great numbers, and in every variety from one-half to one-twelfth of a church. From the comparison of different entries respect-

ing the same manor, it will often appear that the manor
had at some time been divided among certain coparceners, and that the church, or income from the church, had
been divided among them in the same proportion. Two
entries of Sibestune, in Huntingdonshire, shew that the
lands were equally shared between the abbot of Thorney
and Wulf, the man of Earl Eustace; and that the priest
and half of the church belonged to the abbot's moiety—
ibi presbyter et dimidia ecclesia—and the other moiety to
Wulf—ibi dimidia ecclesia. (Domes. 1, 205 ; Sibest. bis.)
The church buildings and residence of the minister were
on the lands of the abbot; but the income from the
church was shared equally between the two lords.

In many cases, though we may trace the names of
several shareholders, there still remains one of whom no
mention is made. Thus with respect to the church of
Codeham noticed before, we are told (11, 422), that
Roger de Ramis held a fourth part of the church of Codeham, and we find from p. 338, that Garinger held one
half of the same church of Roger Bigot; which accounts
for three-fourths, but who held the remaining fourth?
Odo, the arbalist, was owner of Trickengham in Lincolnshire, and the bishop of Durham and Uliet were joint
owners of the inland in Trickengham, called Newton.
To Odo's share, belonged the third part of the church of
St. Mary, and the third part of half a carrucate of land
appertaining to the same church (Dom. 1, 365 b). To
the other two belonged a similar share, that is, to each the
sixth part of the church, and the sixth part of the four
bovates of land appertaining to St. Mary's (Ibid. 341,
370). Here we have owners for two-thirds of the church,
but no one for the remainder. My opinion is, that the
remaining portion is that which was reserved for the
maintenance of the incumbent.

7. We meet occasionally with entries of half priests—

In eadem unus presbyter integer, et duo dimidii tenent centum acras—One whole priest and two half priests hold one hundred acres (ii. 196). This sort of phrase was a useful form of abbreviation in the fiscal language of the time. We find it applied to free tenants, sokemen and others, as ibi duo dimidii liberi homines, et duo integri (11, 285). Sometimes the free-tenant by a new division of the manor found his holding divided between two lords, and consequently divided his suit and service between them, becoming a half-tenant to each. Sometimes his holding was by the descent of property in his family, shared between two heirs, each of whom became a half-tenant, owing to the lord one-half of the suit and service of the original holder. In like manner, if the holding allotted to the priest was divided between two priests, or became subject to two lords, the same language was adopted to describe the nature of the ecclesiastical holding.

8. Of the sale of churches in the Anglo-Saxon times we have plenty of evidence in Domesday. "The jurors of Huntingdon say, that the church of St. Mary in the borough, and the land appertaining to it, belonged to the abbey of Thorney, the abbot of which mortgaged it to the burgesses. But King Edward gave it to Vital and Bernard, his chaplains, and they *sold* it to Hugo, the chamberlain of King Edward, and Hugo *sold* it to two priests of Huntingdon, who have for it the king's seal" (Dom. 1, 208). "Peter de Valonges has in Hertford two churches with a house, which he *bought* of Ulwi of Hatfield. They pay all customary rents. Ulwi himself could give them or *sell* them." (Ibid. 132.) This last is noticed, because in some boroughs the owner could not transfer his church to any one who was not a burgess. Thus in the case of the church of All Hallows in Lincoln, already mentioned, Godric, the son of Garewine, who

possessed " it and every thing belonging to it," became a
monk at Burgh, " and the abbot took possession of the
church, but unjustly, as all the burgesses of Lincoln say ;
because neither Garewine, nor Godric her son, nor any
other person, could give away the church to any one out
of the city, or from among their own relatives, without
the grant of the king. This church therefore, and every
thing pertaining to it, is claimed by Ernwin the priest, as
heir to his cousin Godric. Ibid. 336.

II. On the subject of tithes Domesday affords but
little information. They are very seldom mentioned, even
by the commissioners who return the churches with their
endowments in land ; and, in the few cases where they
are mentioned, there generally appears some reason why
they should be particularly noticed. Thus the Conqueror
gave the churches of Adrington and Bovecome to Earl
Roger, and that of Cladford to the foreign monastery of
Lire. We are accordingly told that the *tithes* went with
those churches (Dom. 1. 38 b, 39 b, 52). The king gave
several other churches, and Roger de Laci gave one
church to St. Mary's de Cormeliis in Normandy; and of
these we are also told, that the priests (that is their dues)
and the *tithes* also made part of the gift (Ibid. 1. 164,
179, 180, 184 b.). The same is said of the church and
tithes of the castle of Monmouth given to the church of
Salmur in the Orleannois (Dom. 180 b). Again, it
would appear that in some places the king's officers had
claimed for his lands exemption from tithe; but that
judgment had been given in the hundred court in favour
of the church (Ibid. 1. 41 b, 377): and it is very possible
that two or three other entries may have been made in
consequence of disputed claims. The return for Wallope,
which manor was the property of the king, is curious,
stating that one half of the tithe of the parish belonged
to the church, and all the kirkshot, and forty-six pence

out of the tithe of the villeins : and that there was there also a small church, to which eight acres of tithe belonged—Cui ecclesiæ pertinet medietas decimæ manerii, et totum cirset, et de decima villanorum xlvi denarii: est et ibi adhuc ecclesiola cui pertinent viii acræ de decima. Hence it seems to follow that, before the conquest, a division had been made between the owner and the incumbent; the latter of whom received for his share one half of the tithe of the manor, a rent charge for the tithe of the land of the villeins, and a small portion of land in lieu of the claims of his ecclesiola.

In the returns for Lincolnshire, extending over seventy-two folio pages, there is not, I believe, a single notice of tithe. Yet in the list of claims heard and determined in the court of the Nesse Wapentack and of the whole Riding, we meet with the following entries. " They say that the tithes and church dues of the wapentacks of Winebruge and Treos, and of all the sokes and inlands which the king has there, belong to the church of Grantham—Dicunt pertinere ad ecclesiam de Grantham decimas de Winbruge Wapen. et de Treos Wapen. et omnibus socis et inlandis, quas Rex habet ibi." (Dom. 1. 377). They say that the tithe and the *other* church dues of the land of Thory (he is elsewhere described as a great land-owner in the time of king Edward), in Ropesley hundred, belong to the church of St. Peter " (in Peterborough). Dicunt quia decima et aliæ ecclesiæ consuetudines de terra Thori in Ropeslai hund. pertinent ad ecclesiam S. Petri. (Ibid. 377 b.) Hence we may conclude, 1st, that the absence of any mention of tithe in the return of a church is no proof of its non-existence; 2nd, that some of the old minsters, such as that of Grantham, still possessed the tithe of a large surrounding district, as that of the wapentacks of Treos and Winebruge; and 3rdly, that consecrations of tithes, as they were called, had already taken place among the Anglo-Saxons; since the tithes of Thory's lands in Ropeslai hundred had been consecrated to a distant church, the abbey of Peterborough.

On the continent this consecration of tithes had long been practised. It was with difficulty that men could be brought to pay tithes at all; and many still claimed the right of paying them wherever they pleased, and therefore conveyed them in legal form to some distant and favourite church, to be enjoyed by it in perpetuity. How far this practice prevailed among the Anglo-Saxons, it is difficult to ascertain. That it was known among them, is plain from the last paragraph; and in Domesday we are told of an Anglo-Saxon named Story, who could send the tithe of his lands in Nottinghamshire wheresoever he chose. But the entry is conceived in language which seems to shew that the rights claimed by him were an exception to the general rule. De Story antecessore Willelmi de Aincourt dicunt, quod sine alicujus licentia potuit facere sibi ecclesiam in sua terra et in sua soca, et decimam suam mittere quo vellet. (Dom. i. 280). He could *without leave* build a church for himself, and within his own jurisdiction, and send his tithe where he pleased. May we not thence infer that others could not do the same *without leave?* Story was succeeded in the possession of his land by William of Aincourt.

But whatever it may have been with the Anglo-Saxons, the consecration of tithes was frequently practised by the Normans. The reader has already met with several instances of the manner in which foreign churches were enriched with the tithes of the conquered by William and his barons: and Selden has proved that such donations were in constant use in England from the conquest to the end of the twelfth century (Seld. on Tithes, c. 6—10); when Innocent III., by a decretal epistle, authorized the

archbishop of Canterbury to put down the abuse with
the infliction of ecclesiastical censures, and in defiance of
contradiction or appeal. Auctoritate præsentium indulgemus, ut liceat tibi super hoc, non obstante contra-
dictione vel appellatione cujuslibet, seu consuetudine
hactenus observata, quod canonicum fuerit, ordinare, et
facere quod statueris per censuram ecclesiasticam firmiter
observari. Inno. 111. ep. Decret. p. 452.

<hr/>

NOTE K (pp. 226, 240).

BOCLAND AND FOLCLAND.

On occasion of these grants it may not be amiss to add
a few remarks on the Bocland and Folcland of the
Anglo-Saxons.

1. The language of the second doom of King Edward
on " the denial of right in bocland and folcland " (Thorpe,
i. 160), suggests the conclusion, that all landed property
among them was comprised under one or other of these
two denominations. Bocland, as the very name imports,
must have been land conveyed, and held by book or
charter ; and, as we possess a multitude of such books or
charters, we learn from them that boclands comprehended
estates in perpetuity, and estates for one or more lives,
subject to the limitations and burthens, if any, that might
be expressed in the original charters. On that point there
is no dispute, but much diversity of opinion has existed
with respect to the other division, that of folcland.

It appears from a great number of passages in Beda
(see l. iii. c. 24, bis; iv. c. 13, 16, 19 ; v. 19), that the
lands of the Anglo-Saxon tribes were parcelled out by
measurement or estimation into shares or allotments, each
of which was supposed to be capable of yielding a com-

petent support to the settler, his family, labourers, herds and flocks. By Beda these shares are uniformly called in the Latin language, " terræ familiarum," or family-lands. What were they called in the vernacular language ?

We have a version of Beda, which there is good reason to attribute to King Alfred. In this version, terra familiæ is generally rendered by the word " hide," as if the quantity of land known by that name were the usual amount of the family-land among the countrymen of the author. Thus, where Beda tells us that each parcel of land, given by Oswiu with his daughter Eanfled to the abbess Hilda, contained ten family-lands—singulæ possessiones decem erant familiarum, id est, simul omnes centum viginti, the translator says — Þær þær lanðer ealler hunð tpelptiȝ hiba (Bed. l. iv. c. 24)—but later, in the same chapter,where Beda writes that the Mercians, south of the river Trent, were said to amount to five thousand families, and that the lands of the northern Mercians amounted to seven thousand family-lands, quorum terra est familiarum septem millium (Ibid. § 224) ; we read in the version that the Southern Mercians were said to amount to five thousand *folcs*—fif þuyyenðo folcer—and the land of the North Mercians to that of seven thousand—þapa lanða iy yeopan þuyyenðo. Hence it seems to me fair to infer, that Beda's expression terra familiæ is the Latin translation of folcland, whence it will follow that the shares—folcsccaru—into which the lands of the tribe were originally divided, were called folclands, and were governed by folcriht, or the custom of the country, until they were taken out of the common stock, and converted by competent authority into boclands or estates in perpetuity, or for a term of lives with remainder to some other party for ever.

It appears to me, therefore, that folclands were considered as national property at the disposal of the king, to be distributed by him as læns (loans) or *benefices,* in return for which the holders were bound to render military or some other service. This will appear from the language of Beda. 1. Oswiu, on the occasion already mentioned, gave with his daughter twelve separate estates in land— donatis insuper duodecim possessiunculis terrarum—that these lands ceasing to support an earthly thaneship or service, might furnish a fit place and sufficient maintenance for a heavenly service—in quibus ablato studio militiæ terrestris, ad exercendam militiam cœlestem locus facultasque suppeteret. (Bed. iii. c. 24). This expression of the historian seems to imply that, had not these folclands, one hundred and twenty in number, been given as bocland to the convent, they would have continued to be, as they had been before, dealt out as benefices to the king's thanes; but that now, being devoted to religious purposes, they were liberated from earthly services for ever. The same is still more plainly shewn in the paraphrastic version of Alfred—he freed for her twelve boclands from earthly warfare and earthly service to be employed in the exercise of heavenly warfare. Ða ƿelƿ boclanð hım ᵹeꝼꞃeoðe eonþlıceꝛ camphaðeꝛ anð eonþlıceꝛ heꞃenyꞃꞃe to beᵹonᵹenne þone heoꝛonlıcan camphað.

2. Bennet, surnamed Biscop, the son of a noble Northumbrian, was in early youth a thane to King Oswiu, and received from him a parcel of land, such as was *due to his station*—possessionem terræ gradui suo competentem—but later, at the age of twenty-five, having resolved to embrace the monastic profession, he resigned his land into the hands of the king, " renouncing," says Beda, " the service of an earthly master with *the possession* of a perishable donative, that he might serve the true king and obtain an eternal kingdom in heaven above—Despiciens militiam cum corruptibili donativo terrestrem, ut vero

regi militaret, &c. (Vit. S. Ben. inter Oper. Min. p. 140). This incident, with the comment of Beda upon it, shews also the distribution of lœns or benefices among the Northumbrian thanes.

3. The same venerable writer, in his letter to Archbishop Egbert, declaims with great eloquence against the many grants of land to monasteries as boclands, on this ground, that boclands did not furnish thanes to fight against invaders in defence of their country—Quæ neque milites neque comites sœcularium potestatum, qui gentem nostram a barbaris defendant, possident. (Bed. Oper. Min. 217). He then proceeds to express his apprehension, that on this account the number of military men will gradually diminish, till the country will be left naked and defenceless against the incursions of the barbarians—ne, rarescente copia militiæ sæcularis, absint qui fines nostros a barbarica incursione tueantur (Ibid.); and complains that so few lands remain to be allotted to the sons of noble Angles and aged warriors, who are obliged on that account to abandon that country for which they ought to draw the sword, and to seek employment in foreign countries. Omnino deest locus, ubi filii nobilium vel emeritorum militum possessionem accipere possunt . . . ob hanc rem patriam pro qua militare debuerunt, trans mare abeuntes, relinquunt. Ib. p. 218.

These passages from Beda, coupled with the history of Bennet, lead to the conclusion that in Northumbria the folclands were national property, out of which lœns or benefices were distributed to the royal thanes and military men, as fees for their services. But this custom was not confined to the Northumbrians. The same system appears to have prevailed among the other tribes; of which we have a remarkable instance in the will of the ealdorman Alfred in Kent or Surrey, about the close of the ninth century. By this instrument he left to his son Ethelwald only three hides of bocland, with the hope that the king would bestow on him the folcland, which he (Alfred) had held during his own life. Anticipating, however, the possibility of a refusal, he gave to Ethelwald in that case as a compensation, the choice of one out of two estates of bocland, which he had previously devised to his daughter (Cod. Dipl. ii. 120). Plainly he had held the folcland as a benefice.

II. A second question is, by what authority were the folclands converted into bocland? The preceding instances shew that all such conversions were considered as grants made by the king: but then was the royal will sufficient, or was the consent of the witan also necessary? On that point much information may be derived from the same letter of Beda to Archbishop Egbert.

As monasteries and churches were intended for permanent establishments, it was natural that the lands for their support should be estates in perpetuity; and as the services required from their possessors were of a spiritual description, it was deemed incongruous to burthen them with secular services more than might be necessary. Hence the ealdormen and thanes viewed with envy the superior advantages attached to the lands of the bishoprics and monasteries: and Beda informs us that a Northumbrian nobleman devised the following plan of placing his lands on the same footing. Soon after the death of King Aldfrid in 705, he stated to the next king his desire of erecting a monastery, accompanied with a request that the property might be, as usual, converted into bocland for that purpose. The prince assented; and the ealdorman obtained the grant, but forgot to build the monastery. This was the first attempt; but its success and impunity stimulated the cupidity and hope of others: year after year similar petitions were presented by ealdormen and thanes and favourites at court; and year after year new

estates in perpetuity were created out of the common
stock. It was not possible that the real object of the
petitioners could be kept secret; it was sufficiently known
and loudly condemned by patriots and divines : but the
kings were needy and rapacious : their consent was purchased with sums of money; and the charters which they
granted, were confirmed with the subscriptions of the
prelates and principal lords. Data regibus pecunia emunt
sibi sub prætextu monasteriorum construendorum terri-
toria, in quibus suæ liberius vacent libidini : et hæc insuper *in jus sibi hæreditarium* edictis regalibus faciunt
ascribi, ipsasque quoque literas privilegiorum suorum
quasi veraciter Deo dignas, pontificum, abbatum, et
potestatum sæculi obtinent *subscriptione firmari.* Ibid.
p. 218.

The reader will notice the expression of Beda, which
he repeats twice in the following page—subscriptione
firmari. It proves that, either to establish the legality of
the grant, or to guard against the resumption of the
property by some subsequent monarch, it was requisite
to have the charter confirmed with the subscription of the
witan. We also learn from the same venerable testimony
that this was not always an easy task; that it was often
necessary to purchase such consent with presents; and
that occasionally the reluctance of the members was
proof against presents, or threats, or the commands of the
prince. He even hints at attempts to destroy or obliterate
the deed and the subscriptions—Qui vel subscriptioni
avari mercatus, rege licet imperante, manum subtrax-
erunt, vel ad eradendas inutiles scripturas ac subscrip-
tiones manum apposuerunt. Ibid. p. 224.

Not one of the Northumbrian charters to which Beda
alludes, has come down to us : but among the charters,
published in the Codex Diplomaticus by Mr. Kemble, are
several which coincide so exactly with the description given

by Beda, that there can be no doubt of their having been drawn after the same form. Thus Ethelbald, 'the most reverend king of Mercia,' gave, for the redemption of his soul, the land called Acton, of three families, to his ealdorman Bucan, in exchange for Bucan's money, to be to him a permanent inheritance; but on condition that there be thereon a perpetual dwelling for servants of God, and that the service of God be kept up in it. Cod. Dipl. 1. 90, Anno 727.   See also pp. 96, 100, 108, 152.

In corroboration of the conclusion drawn from the statement of Beda, that the subscriptions or signatures of the witan were thought necessary, I may refer to an instance pointed out by Mr. Kemble, where Ethelwulf, king of Wessex, *books* the lands of twenty families, not to a subject, but to himself; that is, converts twenty folclands into bocland, or an estate of inheritance for himself—id est, mi ad habendum et perfruendum. . . . . . et iterum qualicumque, prout mi placabilis sit, æternaliter relinquendum.   Still he does it not of his own authority alone, but with the consent and permission of the witan, whose grant he pronounces it to be—cum consensu et licentia episcoporum et principum.—Then follow the boundaries of the lands, which to Ethelwulf regioni homme (regi omnes) senatores *concesserunt.*   Cod. Dipl. ii. 28, Anno 847.

Beda also speaks of folclands purchased not from the king alone, but from the king *and his counsellors* or witan. Attulit et pallia duo oloserica incomparandi operis, quibus postea ab Aldfrido rege *ejusque consiliariis* terram trium familiarum ad austrum Uuiri fluminis juxta ostium, comparavit.   Vit. S. Ben. Op. Min. p. 149.

NOTE L (p. 256).

ST. ELOY ON THE GOOD CHRISTIAN.

In support of this charge against the clergy of former times, it is customary to refer to the definition of ' the good Christian,' attributed to St. Eloy, bishop of Noyon in the sixth century. The history of this definition may, perhaps, amuse the reader. Dachery, a Benedictine monk, had rescued from the moths and cobwebs an old manuscript, containing the life of the saint; he published it in the fifth volume of his spicilegium; where it was found by Maclaine, the English translator of Mosheim. With an eager eye this writer perused its contents, and selected from it a passage, which he appended, as a valuable ornament, to the text of the German historian. It was the character of the good Christian: and this character was made to consist in paying the dues of the church, and performing a few external practices of devotion: qualifications which, as he very justly observes, might fill the coffers of the clergy, but could not satisfy the demands of the gospel. (Mosh. cent. vii. part ii. c. 3.) The present of Maclaine was gratefully accepted by the prejudices of his readers; and Robertson not only copied it, but acknowledged his obligations to Maclaine for the perusal of so important a passage. (Hist. Charles V. vol. i. p. 218, octavo edit.) From that period, it has held a distinguished place in every invective which has been published against the clergy of former ages: and the definition of the good Christian has been echoed and re-echoed a thousand times by the credulity of writers and their readers. But had any one of them ever been at the trouble of consulting the original? If he had, he would have discovered that the bishop of Noyon has been foully calumniated; and that, instead of his real doctrine, a garbled extract has been palmed upon the public. That the good Christian should pay the dues of the church, he indeed requires; but he also requires, that the Christian should cultivate peace among his neighbours, forgive his enemies, love all mankind as himself, observe the precepts of the decalogue, and faithfully comply with the engagements which he contracted at his baptism—Non ergo vobis sufficit, charissimi, quod christianum nomen accepistis, si opera christiana non facitis. Illi enim prodest, quod christianus vocatur, qui semper Christi præcepta mente retinet, et opere perficit: qui furtum scilicet non facit, qui falsum testimonium non dicit, qui nec mentitur nec perjurat, qui adulterium non committit, qui nullum hominem odit, sed omnes sicut semetipsum diligit, qui inimicis suis malum non reddit, sed magis pro ipsis orat, qui lites non concitat, sed discordes ad concordiam revocat, &c. (Dach. Spicil. tom. v. p. 213.) On account of its similarity, I shall subjoin another description of the good Christian from an Anglo-Saxon prelate, Wulstan, archbishop of York. " Let us always profess one true faith, and love God with all our mind and might, and carefully keep all his commandments, and give to God that part (of our substance) which by his grace we are able to give, and earnestly avoid all evil, and act righteously to all others, that is, behave to others as we wish others to behave to us. He is a good Christian who observeth this." (Sermo Lupi Epis. apud Whel. p. 487.) It would be tedious to copy similar passages from other writers, but no man, who is conversant with the works of Beda, Boniface, Alcuin, the Saxon homilies, the Institutes of polity civil and ecclesiastical, and the Ecclesiastical Institutes (Thorpe, ii. 304, 394), can doubt that the observance of the commandments of God, and the practice of every moral duty, was

as strictly inculcated by the Anglo-Saxon divines, as
they ever were by the teachers of any age since the time
of the apostles.

NOTE M (p. 299).

THE CHURCH SERVICE.

THERE cannot be a doubt that, after the council of
Cloveshoe, the service for the canonical hours of prayer
was generally celebrated in the Anglo-Saxon church according to the model which the archbishop had received
from Rome. At the present day the Catholic clergy in
England perform the service for the same hours according to the abridged form in which it now stands in the
Roman Breviary. It may be a matter of interest to
some of my readers to compare, where it is possible, the
ancient with the modern form, and to examine how far
they agree with each other.

In 1715, Elstob published from a MS. of Junius in the
Bodleian library, and under the title of "a public office
of daily and nightly devotion for the seven hours of
prayer used in the Anglo-Saxon church," a treatise de
officiis diurnalium (et) nocturnalium horarum. The manuscript (No. 121) was known by the name of the Codex
Wigorniensis, from the description given of himself by
the writer—Hunc librum scripsit Wulfgeatus scriptor
Wigorniensis; ora, obsecro, pro ipsius nevis cosmicra-
torem. Amen. Et, qui me scripsit, semper sit felix.
Amen. fol. 101.—Of the author we know nothing. His
work is written in both Latin and Anglo-Saxon, the latter
being mostly a poetic paraphrase of certain portions of
the service. It was not his object to describe that service,
but to excite devotional feelings in those whose duty it was
to perform it. Hence, however, as he proceeds step by

step through the several "hours," we are enabled by
following him to form a pretty accurate notion of the
parts, of which it was composed. The first hour is that of Prime or sunrise—be ɼunnon
upȝanȝe—which begins with—Deus in adjutorium meum
intende—Gloria Patri—and the hymn—Jam lucis orto
sidere, Deum precemur supplices—exactly in the same
words, as we read in the Roman breviary at the present
day. The psalms should follow, but these he only indi-
cates by the first line of the first—Deus, in nomine tuo
salvum me fac. This, however, is the first also in the
breviary; whence it is reasonable to conclude that the
others which follow it are the same in both. After the
psalms the Worcester manuscript places the capitulum,
Regi sæculorum from 1 Tim. i. 17, and the short respon-
sory—Christe, fili Dei vivi, miserere nobis, with the addition of—cum sancto spiritu after Dei vivi; which addition
is the only difference between the Anglo-Saxon and the
modern form; the Preces follow, and in them it is that
the variations become more considerable; not that the
two forms appear to have been composed after different
models—the contrary is evident—but that the Preces in
the breviary have been, as the name of breviary imports,
abbreviated or shortened.

The Preces begin in both with the Kyrie eleison, Pater-
noster, and Creed; but the manuscript, both here and in
several other places, interposes two versets with their responses between the Pater and the Creed. *V.* Vivet
anima mea et laudabit te. *R.* Et judicia tua adjuvabunt
me. *V.* Erravi sicut ovis quæ perierat, require servum
tuum, Domine. *R.* Quia mandata tua non sum oblitus.
Between the Creed and the Confiteor the Codex contains
twenty-seven versets and responses, the breviary only six
for the dominical, and eighteen for the ferial office. But
as all these are among the twenty-seven in the Codex, it is

plain that before the abbreviation, the whole were originally in both forms. The omissions are of versets from the psalms, Verba mea—Ad te Domine, levavi—and Judica, Domine. The Confiteor is then indicated by the initial words—confiteor Deo cœli—to which are subjoined in the manuscript, the preces for the king and people, which are found in the breviary at Vespers and Lauds. Here the Prime-song properly ends with the prayer — Domine sancte, Pater omnipotens eterne Deus, qui ad principium hujus diei nos pervenire fecisti, as in the Breviary.

The prayers which follow belonged originally to the service in the chapter house. The martyrology is not mentioned in the Codex, but, that it was read is plain, for the next entry is the verset—Pretiosa in conspectu Domini mors sanctorum ejus, followed by the prayer,— Sancta Dei genetrix virgo Maria, et omnes sancti Dei intercedant pro nobis peccatoribus ad Dominum Dominorum, ut nos mereamur ab eo adjuvari et salvari, qui vivit et regnat, &c. The sequel is the same as in the Breviary, with two exceptions. 1. The short lesson at the breaking up of the chapter—ad absolutionem capituli—is omitted in the manuscript; and the blessing at the end is shorter, in this manner. Ask the blessing—God—the son of God vouchsafe to bless us. Amen. Benedicite—Deus—Dei filius nos benedicere dignetur. Amen.

With respect to the three hours of terce, sext, and none, I shall content myself with pointing out the only variations of any moment. 1. In the Codex the hours of terce and sext have different capitula. The chapter for terce is from Romans i. 7, Gratia vobis et pax a Deo Patre nostro et Domino Jesu Christo; and for Sext, from 1 Thess. v. 21, 22. Omnia autem probate, quod bonum est, tenete, ab omni specie mala abstinete vos—2. The collect or prayer at these three hours in the breviary is taken from the mass for the day or for the preceding

Sunday, but in the Anglo-Saxon form each hour has a collect appropriated to it. The collect at terce is—Domine Deus, qui hora tertia diei ad crucis pœnam pro salute mundi ductus es, te suppliciter deprecamur, ut de præteritis malis nostris semper apud te inveniamus veniam et de futuris jugiter habeamus custodiam—At sext— Domine Jesu Christe, qui sexta hora pro nobis in cruce ascendisti, et Adam de inferno eruisti, eumque in paradiso restituisti, quæsumus ut ab omnibus peccatis nostris eripi nos jubeas, et in operibus tuis sanctis semper custodias, Jesu Christe, qui &c. At none—Domine Jesu Christe, qui hora nona in crucis patibulo confitentem latronem intra mœnia paradisi transire jussisti, tibi, suppliciter confitentes, peccata nostra deprecamur deleas, et post obitum nostrum paradisi nobis gaudia introire concedas, salvator mundi, qui, &c.

At the evening service the only variations are that the capitulum is taken from 2 Cor. xiii. 14. Gratia Domini nostri Jesu Christi, et caritas Dei, et communicatio spiritus sancti sit semper cum omnibus vobis. The hymn is—O lux beata Trinitas, which is to be found assigned to the Saturday in all breviaries, that retain the hymns as they stood before the correction by Urban VIII. The prayer after the Magnificat runs thus—Majestatem tuam suppliciter exoramus ut, expulsis de cordibus nostris peccatorum tenebris, ad veram lucem, quæ Christus est, nos facias pervenire. Per &c.

At Complin the manuscript takes no other notice of the first part of the service than that it has the verset— Converte nos Deus salutaris noster before the Deus in adjutorium, with which the other hours begin. It mentions two hymns,—Te lucis ante terminum—which is in the Roman breviary, and Christe, lux lucis et dies—which is not in the Roman, but may be found in the Sarum breviary as the hymn for complin during the time of

Lent. In the capitulum, Preces and prayer there is no difference worthy of notice. The nocturnal service is not described, the writer contenting himself with exhorting his readers to attend at it with diligence and devotion.

In the collection, however, lately published under the name of the Durham Ritual, we have several fragments of the ancient choral service, some of which belong to that nocturnal service, and may, therefore, supply in part the deficiency in the Worcester Codex. In pp. 132—135, we find a huge mass of mutilated entries, which at first sight appear unintelligible, but which were meant to point out to the reader by the initial words the responsories and anthems which were sung, as the lessons from scripture were read during the nocturnal office. Now, if he will compare these with the corresponding portion of the Roman breviary, he will discover there the very lessons and responsories to which they refer, extending from the third week in September to the beginning of Advent. Again in pp. 185, 187 of the ritual, occurs another collection of similar entries, and in the service for the time of Advent in the breviary will be found at full length all the passages to which these entries belong. In p. 135—138 of the ritual are three hymns for Lent, passion week, and the time between Easter and Whitsuntide: the same hymns in the same words with the exception of the numerous errors of the ancient transcriber, are to be found in all editions of the breviary, in which the metrical corrections by Urban VIII. have not been adopted. The four hymns for the hours of prime, terce, sext, and none, and the first of the two for complin, of which the initial words only were entered in the Worcester Codex, are copied entirely in the ritual (p. 162, 180), and correspond exactly with the hymns for the same hours in the breviary. Lastly, we find in the ritual (pp. 166, 182), the Preces for the different hours, all of which have plainly the same origin

with those in the breviary. They are, indeed, more numerous than even those in the Worcester manuscript: but
contain most of the matter in it, and all that is in
the Roman form of the present time. In those for the
hour of prime occurs the prayer—Sanctus Deus, sanctus
fortis, sanctus immortalis, miserere nobis, which is
omitted in the Worcester copy, and also a form of the
Confiteor, which is different from the Worcester form, but
rendered in one part unintelligible from the fault of the
copyist. It runs thus—Confiteor Deo et tibi, frater, quia
peccavi nimis in cogitatione, et in locutione, et in opera-
tione. . . propterea, precor te, frater, ora pro me peccatore.
In the Preces for the evening service or vespers are a
multitude of prayers for different individuals, benefactors,
persons in distress, or on a journey, or at sea, for the sick
and for the dead, of which a few only are retained in
the breviary at the end of the preces at vespers and after
the litany.

The reader will recollect that the same order had been
made with respect to the liturgy for mass, as with respect
to the choral service. The council had directed that both
should be copied from the Roman model; and the few remains which we possess shew, that the decree was carried
into execution. In general the ritual at mass is the same;
on a few days in the year only are there any variations :
and it seems to have been customary for the bishops to
remind the parish priests of such variations at the
yearly distribution of the chrism, after it had been
blessed. We have two discourses composed by Ælfric
for this purpose, one in what are called his canons
(Thorpe, ii. 358), and another in a document recently
published by Mr. Soames in the supplement to his
History (p. 14). Now the directions in these papers
agree in every point of the least importance with the
rubrics in the present Roman missal. On Candlemas day

we have in both the blessing pronounced over the candles, and on Palm Sunday that over the palm-twigs, and then the procession before mass, with only this difference, that the candles and palms twigs are ordered by Ælfric to be offered *at* the part of the mass which is called the offertory: a ceremony which has been omitted in the missal, since the custom of offering at the mass has been abolished. On Ash-Wednesday the priest is ordered to sprinkle the ashes with blessed water, and to make with them the sign of the cross on his own head, and the heads of the people, as in the missal. On the Thursday before Easter we have the maundy or washing of the feet, and the denuding of the altars, and on Friday and Saturday the whole of the service, as it is arranged in the Roman missal at present, with this unimportant difference, that on the Friday two assistants, instead of the priest, carry the cross to the place appointed for it. Mr. Soames, indeed, would make a distinction when he comes to the kneeling before the cross, and very charitably acquits the Anglo-Saxons of idolatry on that occasion, by assuring us that they did not worship it, but only prayed *by* it or near to it, " for such is the only meaning which can be given the rubric in the Saxon language, and such prayer was not idolatrous though it led to idolatry" (Supplement, p. 19). Whether the worship paid to the cross was idolatrous or not, is not a question for these pages : but that the rubric ordered the persons present to pay worship to it, is certain—hι ᵹebιᴆᴆaᴆ æꞇ or ꞇo þæpe poᴆe—literally bid themselves to the cross— which can have no other meaning than worship the cross. To bid oneself is to worship : as when St. Alban in Beda speaking of God says—illum colo—the translator of Beda makes him say—Ic me ꞇo hιm ᵹebιᴆᴆe—I bid myself to him—I worship him. The same is more fully expressed in Ælfric's 36th canon—ᵹebιᴆᴆon hy ꞇo þæpe halᵹan roðe ꝥ hi ealle ᵹeᵹreton þa Lroðer roðe miб corre —"they worship the holy rood, so that they all greet God's rood with a kiss." Thorpe, ii. 358.

The conclusion which I draw from these remarks is, that the church service of the Anglo-Saxons, both at mass and at the canonical hours, was the same in every important point with that contained in the present Roman missal and breviary.

The reader, however, is aware that in the infancy of the Anglo-Saxon church the missionaries from Iona established their own, or what is called the Scottish, course, in Mercia and Northumbria. Was that course derived from Rome, or from some other country ?

From a manuscript in the Cotton Library, Spelman (Con. i. p. 176) published a short treatise, or perhaps fragment of a treatise, on the origin of the choral service in different churches. The character of the manuscript was, he tells us, very difficult to decipher : the language certainly defies all the rules of grammar ; and the matter will appear to every reader fanciful and fabulous. It is plain that the writer was a monk in one of the monasteries of St. Columban on the continent : and that he undertook to trace the genealogy of the different courses, with the view of shewing to his adversaries in Gaul, that the Scottish course was of as ancient and noble parentage as their own. According to him, the course first established in Gaul was that of Rome by missionaries from Rome ; but Irenæus, bishop of Lyons, had formerly learned from St. Polycarp the course which had been composed by St. John the evangelist, and by his authority substituted it in the place of the Roman course in Gaul. Thus the present Gallic course came from St. John. That, he adds, which is now called the Scottish course, was originally composed by St. Mark, the evangelist, at Alexandria — so the blessed Jerome teaches—and was sung by St. Gregory of Nazian-

zum, the master of Jerome, by the blessed Basil, the
brother of Gregory, and by Anthony, Paul, Macharius,
and the fathers of the desert of Thebais; whence Cassian
brought it to the isle of St. Honoré. In that island it
became known to Germanus and Lupus, who were afterwards bishops, and preached the gospel in the lands of
the Scots and the Britons. Now these prelates taught
the same course to St. Patrick, and appointed him archbishop to preach in their place to the Scots and the
Britons; and he continued to sing it till his death at the
age of one hundred and fifty-three years. After this it
was preserved by the blessed old man Wandelock, and by
Comgall, and by the blessed Columban, who came to
Gaul and preached there, being still the very course which
had been sung by St. Mark at Alexandria; and, adds he,
if any man refuse to believe this statement, let him read
the lives of the blessed Columban, and of Eustace (his
successor at Luxeu), and the sayings of the blessed
Attala, the abbot (of Bobbio). Spelm. Ibid.

The reader must excuse this long and tedious account of
the manuscript. It was necessary that he might form some
judgment of the learning and discernment of the writer,
who could not describe so recent an event as the preaching of the apostle of his own nation without betraying his
ignorance and credulity. He has, however, found favour
with Archbishop Ussher, and Bishop Stillingfleet; because
his statement appears to countenance the notion that St.
Patrick brought the Gallic course and liturgy with him to
Ireland. According to him, St. Patrick learned the course
from Germanus and Lupus; they were Gallic prelates, and
thence it seems to follow, that the Scottish course established by St. Patrick must have been the Gallic.

This reasoning, or the authority of Ussher and Stillingfleet, has satisfied most writers on this subject, who affirm
the identity of the two courses as universally admitted.

It should, however, be observed that the conclusion to which these prelates have come, is not that of the monk himself. His testimony is to the contrary. He wrote to shew that, if the Gallic course had one evangelist for its author, the Scottish had another, an object inconsistent with the notion of their identity—he moreover tells us that they were different courses—a point on which with all his ignorance and credulity he could not be ignorant; for he daily sung one course, and lived in a country, the clergy of which daily sung another. The only conclusion then, which can with any degree of certainty be drawn from his testimony, is that the Scottish was not the same with the Gallic course.

Of the Scottish course itself a few immaterial particulars may be gleaned from the rule of St. Columban, and from the Antiphonarium Benchorense, written in the sixth century, and deposited in the monastery of St Columban at Bobbio, whence it came with other MSS. to the Ambrosian library in Milan. From these sources we learn that in the Scottish course the same canonical hours of prayer were observed as in other courses; that to each hour certain psalms and a collect was assigned; that hymns were also sung; and that at the close of the psalms all fell on their knees, and prayed for a short space in private, a practice which might appear peculiar to the Scots, were it not equally enjoined by the English council of Cloveshoe (Can. xvii. Spel. p. 253); the same council which enjoined the strict observance of the Roman forms. Hence we have no sufficient data on which to form a judgment how far the Scottish did, or did not, depart from the course in use at Rome. The probability is that it retained much of the ancient Roman form, without any of the improvements which had been introduced into that form by the popes of the sixth century.

Mabillon discovered among the MSS. of Bobbio an

ancient missal, which he published at the end of the first
volume of his Museum Italicum, under the title of Sacra-
mentarium Gallicanum; and which Muratori republished
under the same name (Lit. Rom. Vet. ii. 371). There can
be no doubt that it was a Gallican missal, written in the
seventh century, and belonging to some church in the
kingdom of Burgundy. This is plain from internal
evidence. Some writers have, indeed, considered it a
Scottish missal (O'Conor, Ep. Nuncup. p. 130): but
there is nothing more to shew that it had any connection
with the Scottish church, than the mere fact that it was
found among the manuscripts of one of St. Columban's
monasteries about 1000 years after the foundation of that
monastery. It contains the Roman canon of the mass,
with the addition of the names of the confessors Hilary,
Martin, Ambrose, Augustine, Gregory, Jerome, and
Benedict, in the commemoration of the saints; whereas
the Roman admits no names besides those of apostles and
martyrs.

Before I conclude this note, I may allude to the British
course and liturgy, which has been also pronounced the
same with the Gallic; but, as far as I can discover, without
even the semblance of a proof. If we may judge from
the quotations in Gildas, it will follow that the Britons
in his time sang the psalms after the old version, which
is still followed in the Roman service; whereas the Gallic
church had adopted the new version from the Hebrew
by St. Jerome. In this particular the British must have
approached nearer to the Roman than to the Gallic form,
when the gospel was preached to the Saxons: in several
other respects it must have differed from the Roman, if
it were only on account of the numerous improvements
which had been lately introduced into the latter by
several pontiffs, especially by St. Gregory. We read,
however, of no controversy respecting such differences,
which slowly and silently disappeared by the gradual

adoption of the Roman course and liturgy in the several churches in Wales.

NOTE N (p. 314).

FASTS IN THE ANGLO-SAXON CHURCH.

THE fasts established in the Anglo-Saxon church were, 1st, the fast of Lent, which began on the seventh Wednesday before Easter; 2nd, the ember fasts, on Wednesday, Friday, and Saturday, four times in the year. They derived their name from ymbren, a going round, or a circuit: whence some writers have supposed that they were so called because they made the circuit of the year. But from the manner in which the word is used—as ' the gospel for the ymbrene in harvest time on the Saturday ' (Quat. Evang. p. 244)—it appears to denote some part of the service of the day, probably the circuit or public procession made at the time. 3rdly, every Wednesday and Friday was once kept a fast in all monasterial establishments after the example of St. Aidan. This we are told by Beda (l. iii. c. 5); after which we meet with no mention of these days till the time of Archbishop Odo (Spelm. 417), when they appear as general fasts for both clergy and laity. But immediately afterwards the Wednesday is dropped, and Friday alone remains (Thorpe i. 264). After the year 1000 we meet with fasts on the vigils of all St. Mary's ' solemn feast tides ' and of every apostle. But from this law were exempt the Fridays and vigils which might fall between Christmas-day and the octave day of the Epiphany, and between Easter and Whitsuntide. (Ibid. i. 320, 368.)

END OF VOL. I.

Printed by J. & H. COX, BROTHERS (LATE COX & SONS), 74 & 75, Great Queen-street, Lincoln's-Inn Fields.

1381738R0

Printed in Great Britain by
Amazon.co.uk, Ltd.,
Marston Gate.

Printed in Dunstable, United Kingdom

Daniel W. Hartley is a strategic systems thinker with a deep interest in patterns, probability, and the psychology of games. He has spent over a decade studying how structure and observation can influence chance-based outcomes — particularly in the context of the UK's National Lottery.

Driven by a belief that luck favours the prepared, Hartley has developed a range of lottery systems that prioritise intelligent design over random play. His work combines real-world data, practical templates, and mindset frameworks designed to help players approach the game with discipline and curiosity.

Outside of lottery systems, Daniel explores broader questions around how people make decisions under uncertainty. His writing reflects a balance between analytical thinking and accessible guidance — always with an eye toward empowering the reader to play smarter, not harder.

Some leave behind binders full of notes. Others share what they've learned with family members or fellow players. A few even create syndicates using these principles, giving their communities a better shot at winning together.

You're not just playing the lottery anymore. You're designing something. Something that reflects your mind, your observations, and your philosophy.

That's not just play — that's craft.

One Last Thought

There will always be randomness in life. Some things will always be out of our hands.

But what you've learned in this book is that luck is not something to be chased — it's something to be **positioned for**. You don't control the draw, but you *do* control how you approach it. You control how you think. You control how you play.

So take your knowledge. Refine it. Personalise it. Share it. And keep building systems that work for *you*.

Because in the end, the smartest lottery player isn't just hoping for a win.

They're *engineering* one.

and building something sustainable. Systems shine most not in a single week, but across months, even years.

Every ticket you play with strategy becomes a data point. Every draw becomes an opportunity to learn something. And every small win is proof that your system is evolving.

If you're consistent — even modestly so — you create the conditions for what most players never do: compounding advantage.

Risk, Reward, and Responsibility

It's worth restating: no system can *guarantee* a lottery win. The odds are steep, and they always will be. What this book does offer is the best possible approach to stacking those odds in your favour — incrementally, intelligently, and responsibly.

Be honest about your budget. Track your spending. Celebrate wins, but never chase losses. Lottery play should be a hobby with potential — not a desperate attempt to force an outcome.

The irony is that the more disciplined your system becomes, the more fun the game becomes. Because when you remove chaos, you make room for *real intrigue.*

The Legacy of a Smart Player

Here's a thought few lottery players consider: *What if your system outlives you?*

That may sound dramatic, but think of the players who develop highly refined pools, data archives, and methods over years — quietly testing, tweaking, learning.

We began this journey with a question: *Is there a better way to play the lottery?*

Now, several chapters later, you've learned that the answer is yes — not through shortcuts or secrets, but through systems. Systems based on logic, analysis, patience, and observation. Systems that work in harmony with probability rather than wishful thinking.

If you've followed along closely, you now have:

- A core understanding of how lottery number pools behave over time

- Strategies for building your own lines using balance, gaps, and frequency analysis

- Tools to track and refine your performance week by week

- Insights into game-specific behaviours across Lotto, Thunderball, EuroMillions, HotPicks, and Set For Life

- A mindset shift from blind play to *purposeful participation*

But here's the real prize: You're no longer just playing the lottery — you're building your own luck.

The Power of Consistency

One of the great myths in gambling is that "luck changes." But in truth, *habits* change, and when habits improve, outcomes often follow.

This book was never about chasing short-term jackpots. It's about the long-term game — the game of decision-making, trend-tracking,

3. Create a "reverse" set (your six *least played* numbers)

4. Combine pairs that have been drawn together three times

5. Use only prime numbers in one full line

6. Test a **spiral pattern** (e.g., 3-10-17-24-31-38)

7. Mirror a previous winning line (e.g., turn 12 into 21)

8. Run an "Odds Only" or "Evens Only" line for 5 weeks

9. Create a birthday-only set, but add 30 to each number

10. Track one lucky number across all games for 10 draws

- Avoid consecutive numbers or 1–2–3 patterns

G. Key Takeaways Checklist

✓ Have I defined my core number selection philosophy?
✓ Am I playing each game with a specific purpose?
✓ Do I track results weekly, monthly, and yearly?
✓ Is my budget clear, realistic, and segmented?
✓ Have I documented changes to my system over time?
✓ Could someone else understand and use my system from my notes?

H. Recommended Resources (UK-Focused)

- <u>National Lottery Official Site</u> — draw results, game rules

- <u>Lottery Stats UK</u> — historical data, frequency tables

- Excel/Google Sheets — tracking, archiving, visualisation

- Free random number generators — to shuffle pools or test randomness

- Community forums (Reddit, Lottery Syndicate groups) — for fresh strategy ideas

I. Bonus: 10 Quick System Prompts to Try

1. Try only numbers ending in **7** for one week

2. Build lines using only numbers from the **middle third** of the pool

2.0	Feb 2025	Added odd/even balancing	Increase in 2-number hits
3.1	Mar 2025	Removed cold + cold pairings	Lotto returns improved
4.0	April 2025	Introduced rollover multiplier play	Syndicate wins increased

F. Sample Line Strategies

1. Hot/Cold Hybrid (Lotto 6/59):

- 2 Hot numbers (recently frequent)

- 2 Cold numbers (rare in 30 draws)

- 2 Balanced numbers (appear every 10–15 draws)

2. Diagonal Leap (Set For Life):

- Numbers spaced diagonally across the ticket (e.g., 5, 13, 21, 29, 37)

- Use number intervals of 8 ±1

3. High-Tier Gap Pattern (EuroMillions):

- Choose 3 high numbers (30+) and 2 low (under 10)

- Aim for gap differences like 6, 11, 17

4. HotPicks Focused Win-Line:

- Pick 3 numbers from the 4 most drawn in past 20 draws

Print several copies and fill in after every draw.

D. Budget Planner

Keep your lottery budget healthy and strategic:

Category	Monthly Amount	Weekly Avg.	Notes
Base Play	*£30*	*£7.50*	Core lines, all games
Stretch Budget	*£20*	*£5.00*	For rollovers or hot streaks
Experiment Pool	*£5*	*£1.25*	Try unusual patterns or combos
Total Budget	*£55*	*£13.75*	Adjust per income or goals

E. System Version Log (Changelog Format)

Version	Date Started	Major Change(s)	Outcome/Notes
1.0	Jan 2025	Built 30-number pool using heat	Initial wins on HotPicks

Line	Number 1	Number 2	Number 3	Number 4	Number 5	Number 6	Game	Combo Type
1							Lotto	2 Hot + 2 Cold + 2 Balanced
2							EuroMillions	Spiral Pattern
3							Thunderball	Odd-Even Mix
4							Set For Life	Mirror + Diagonal
5							HotPicks	3-number High Tier

C. Weekly Tracker (Quick-Use Format)

Week #	Game	Lines Played	Wins	Notable Hits	Budget Spent	Notes/Adjustments
1	Lotto	3	£0	2-number match	£6	Rotate in cold pairings
1	Thunderball	4	£10	Matched main ball	£4	Cold ball appeared
2	Set For Life	2	£0	4-number near hit	£3	Retry diagonal combo

A. Master Pool Template

Use this table to build and refine your own number pools for each game.

Game	Hot Numbers	Cold Numbers	Balanced Picks	Notes
Lotto 6/59				Refresh monthly
EuroMillions				Consider Lucky Stars pattern
Thunderball				Watch main + Thunderball gap
Set For Life				Prime numbers often cluster
HotPicks				Pairs & triplets patterns

Tips:

- Hot = Drawn frequently in last 15–25 draws

- Cold = Drawn 0–2 times in last 30–40 draws

- Balanced = Evenly spread across decades (e.g., 10s, 20s, 30s)

B. Line Builder Grid

Use this grid when designing strategic lines.

- You've shaped a system that is more than luck — it's legacy

The National Lottery may be a game of chance.
But your approach no longer is.

Whether you win £10 or £10 million, the deeper reward is knowing you've played with *clarity, control,* and *curiosity.*

And that? That's winning — every single week.

9. Building the "Final System" — A True Signature Strategy

Eventually, you'll notice that your adjustments get smaller.
That your patterns get sharper.
That your results become more predictable.

At this point, you're nearing your **Final System** — the strategy that reflects:

- Your personal preferences

- Your tested combinations

- Your highest return vs. cost

- Your unique structure and routine

You may keep tweaking it forever. Or you may settle in. Either way, it becomes a part of your lifestyle.

This is the point where luck stops feeling random — and starts feeling guided.

10. Conclusion: From the First Draw to the Final Win

You began this journey curious.
You'll end it equipped.

- You now know how to build number pools that adapt with time

- You've mastered the structure of multiple games

- You've implemented tracking, versioning, and scaling

- Budgeting and timing routines

- Your changelog (system versions)

- Sample lines for each game

- FAQs or beliefs ("I never play 3 evens in a row")

This document becomes your **System Manual** — your strategic legacy.

You might even leave this behind for family, or hand it to a curious friend who's ready to play with purpose.

8. Psychological Resilience: Staying the Course

Legacy play requires long-term calm.

- **Don't chase losses.** Recovery is built into your system.

- **Don't get attached to any single number.** Attachment clouds decision-making.

- **Don't expect every version to improve performance.** Some iterations are just stepping stones.

- **Don't play every week if your energy is low.** A system rests better than it breaks.

You are not a gambler. You are a system builder, a strategist, a tracker of probabilities and momentum. The wins will come. Your job is to keep the framework ready to receive them.

This becomes your personal changelog — a living history of strategic improvement.

6. Archiving and Record-Keeping

A Legacy System depends on solid records. Set up simple folders or spreadsheets for:

- **Draw History:** Keep last 100 draws per game

- **Line History:** Record every ticket you play, per week

- **Hits/Misses:** Track which numbers are hitting, and how often

- **Combo Performance:** Record success rates of specific patterns (e.g., 2-hot + 1-cold)

- **Budget Log:** Every £ in and out

Back these up online (Google Drive, Dropbox, or even printed folders). This is the "memory" of your system.

7. Teaching the System: Making It Transferable

If you're thinking about passing this system on — or collaborating — it needs to be teachable.

Create a short **System Overview Document** with:

- Your Master Pool rules

- Game strategies and line examples

C. Syndicate Scaling

If you play with friends or work colleagues:

- Assign roles (e.g., number analyst, line designer, budget holder)

- Use cloud tools like Google Sheets for shared tracking

- Create group-specific line structures using everyone's favourite number logic

- Document *syndicate-only wins* to measure group performance over time

5. Versioning: Iterations of Your System

Like software or design, your system can go through **versions**.

Treat each version like a formal release:

- **Version 1.0:** The original method — your first attempt at structure

- **Version 2.0:** Adjusted with data, refined with weekly tracking

- **Version 3.0:** Post-budget optimisation and maintenance routines

- **Version 4.0+:** External input (syndicates, family testing, hybrid approaches)

Write short summaries for each version:

"Version 3.1: Removed 2-number cold combos. Added spiral line pattern.
Set Thunderball lines to focus on primes and gaps of 3+."

D. Annual Deep Review

- Compare your total annual spend vs. total return

- Identify best-performing lines, worst patterns, and most frequent near-hits

- Rebuild your system from scratch if it feels stale — it's a design, not a religion

4. System Scalability: From Solo Play to Syndicates

As your system matures, you may wish to scale it:

A. Personal Scaling

- **When income rises:** Increase the number of lines, not the riskiness of play

- **When time drops:** Focus only on one or two games, using tighter pools

- **When you need a break:** Automate with pre-selected combinations and revisit after 10–15 draws

B. Family Systems

Many players teach their system to a family member:

- Give them a game (e.g., Thunderball) to manage

- Share pool updates and draw review

- Rotate game roles each month — treat it like a shared project

This creates a **supportive structure** and turns play into connection.

3. Maintenance Cycles: Keeping the Engine Tuned

No system survives untouched.

Maintenance is about checking what's working, what's drifting, and where small tweaks can revive performance.

A. Weekly Maintenance (5–10 mins)

- Log wins/losses

- Update hit/miss patterns for each number

- Note any personal hunches or visual anomalies (e.g., patterns forming on your tracker)

B. Monthly Maintenance

- Rebalance your Master Pool (swap out underperforming numbers)

- Review budget performance — did your return justify your cost?

- Rotate in fresh number patterns (e.g., mirrored pairs, diagonals, prime clusters)

C. Quarterly or Seasonal Maintenance

- Recheck each game's role — do you still enjoy it? Does it serve your system's goals?

- Archive older data and start fresh if needed (keep records but lighten the load)

- Adjust your combo structures based on the last 40–50 draws of performance

This becomes your **signature logic** — the mental fingerprint of your system.

B. Game Tiers and Roles

Clarify which games serve which purposes. For example:

- **Lotto & EuroMillions:** Combo experiments, rollovers, syndicate sharing

- **Set For Life & Thunderball:** Frequent small wins, budget stability

- **HotPicks:** Controlled high-reward testing

Define entry patterns, line structures, and frequency per game.

C. Budget Structure

A good legacy system has flexible, resilient budgeting.
Break your budget into:

- **Base Budget** (minimum weekly play)

- **Stretch Budget** (for rollovers or confidence patterns)

- **Test Budget** (experimental systems or cold streak recovery)

Example:

"I play a base of £15/week, stretch to £25 during triple rollovers, and set aside £5/month for experimental 3-number HotPicks."

This prevents overspending and builds emotional neutrality into your system.

- **Documented methods** for number selection and line building

- **Recorded performance data** and adjustments based on outcomes

- **Clear budgeting and play cycles** that adapt with your financial situation

- **Transferable knowledge** that could be used by a family member, partner, or group

In the same way that a chess player refines their opening over years or an investor adapts their portfolio, you will shape your lottery system across *draws, decades, and data.*

This is about *sustainable, strategic play* — not flashes of inspiration.

2. The Core Framework: Your System's Skeleton

Every legacy system has a core framework that rarely changes, even as the numbers evolve. Here are the pillars to build yours on:

A. Your Number Philosophy

Define and document:

- How you select Hot, Cold, and Balanced numbers

- How often you rotate and refresh your pools

- Whether you use historical data, gap analysis, frequency tables, or other signals

- Any superstitions, hunches, or patterns you consider valid

You've built the system. You've learned the games. You've mastered the tools. Now it's time to think even bigger — **beyond the next draw**, beyond the next jackpot, beyond even your own lifetime of playing.

This chapter explores the *long-term dimension* of strategic lottery play:

- Maintaining your system over months and years

- Using data to refine performance continuously

- Building scalable routines that survive burnout or budget shifts

- Creating a legacy that can be taught, adapted, and passed on

If the previous chapters turned you into a strategist, this one makes you an architect. Because every enduring system needs strong foundations, periodic maintenance, and a blueprint that others can follow.

Let's futureproof your strategy.

1. The Concept of a "Legacy Lottery System"

A **Legacy System** is more than a set of rules or number pools. It's a personal playbook that evolves with time.

It has:

With a unified system in place, you've shifted into a new role:

✅ You're no longer chasing luck — you're managing it.
✅ You're no longer reacting — you're tracking, adapting, predicting.
✅ You're no longer hoping — you're building.

And now, you're ready for the final step.

In the next and final chapter, we'll talk about **system maintenance, refinement, and how to build your own legacy strategy**—a living, breathing lottery method that evolves as you do.

Welcome to the real game.

- **Lotto:** Legacy — play combo systems and track rollovers

- **EuroMillions:** Dream — one shot at the big time, low cost

Together, they support each other like pillars:

- Wins in Thunderball or Set For Life can **fund** larger entries for EuroMillions or Lotto

- Patterns from Lotto can **inform** HotPicks strategies

- Cold numbers from EuroMillions may appear in Thunderball later

The synergy between games creates a **rolling momentum** — no longer playing in isolation, but **systematically connected.**

9. Common Mistakes in Multi-Game Play

Mistake #1: Using random numbers across all games

Fix: Anchor everything to your Master Pool

Mistake #2: Ignoring tracking and performance

Fix: Simple spreadsheet or notebook, updated weekly

Mistake #3: Playing too many games with no structure

Fix: Budget layering + game roles = sustainable play

Mistake #4: Treating each draw as a new story

Fix: Think in 10-draw cycles, not single tickets

10. Summary: From Player to Planner

7. Evolution: Scaling and Improving Over Time

The unified system isn't static. It's a **living framework**. Here's how to keep it sharp:

- **Every 15–20 draws:** Update your Master Pool using new frequency data

- **Every 5 weeks:** Rebalance sub-pools for each game

- **Every 10 draws:** Review prize hits and adjust line structures accordingly

- **Monthly:** Rotate Thunderballs, Life Balls, and Lucky Stars if not performing

Track how your total budget converts to **return on investment**. Even small wins add up when systemised.

Over time, your system becomes smarter than random chance. Not because you're beating the odds—but because you're **working with them.**

8. System Synergy: How Games Can Support Each Other

Each game in your weekly routine serves a **different role**:

- **Thunderball:** Prize frequency — wins almost every other week if played well

- **Set For Life:** Stability — medium prizes, good odds, long-term goals

- **HotPicks:** Control — test sharp combinations of 2–4 picks

- Lotto = **legacy value**, especially for combo systems

Keep one **"Wildcard Line"** each week: a line made from *entirely new logic* — this keeps creativity flowing.

6. Tracking: The Control Panel of Your System

The only way to *improve* a system is to **measure** it.

Use a spreadsheet (or a journal) to track:

Week	Game	Line	Hits (main)	Bonus/Extra Ball	Prize	Notes
15	Thunderball	#3	*3*	Miss	*£10*	—
15	Lotto	#1	*2*	Bonus Hit	*£0*	—
15	EuroMillions	#1	*1*	1 Lucky Star	*£0*	—

Update every week. Highlight:

- Which numbers consistently appear in wins

- Which number patterns are dormant

- Which Thunderballs or Life Balls are underperforming

- Which line structures hit more often

After 10 weeks of data, patterns start emerging. You'll see which **sub-pools** yield results, and where to refine.

This approach saves you **planning time** and ensures consistency in strategy.

5. Budget Layering: Building a Sustainable Play Routine

Your time and money are finite. A unified system has to work **within your budget**, not beyond it.

Example Weekly Budget: £20

Game	Lines	Cost
Lotto	3 lines	£6.00
Thunderball	4 lines	£4.00
Set For Life	2 lines	£3.00
EuroMillions	1 line	£2.50
HotPicks	2 lines	£4.00
Total	—	**£19.50**

Layer your entries based on **expected value** and **odds**:

- Thunderball and Set For Life = **better odds**, more frequent wins

- EuroMillions = **jackpot potential**, but lower odds

- HotPicks = **custom control**, especially 3 or 4-pick plays

This is where **you fine-tune the system** for each instrument in the orchestra.

4. Entry Design Across Games

Using your sub-pools, you'll now generate actual lines. But here's the key:

Never build lines in isolation.

Each line you build should come from the **same design language**.

Example: Lotto Line Blueprint (from 35-number Master Pool)

- 2 hot

- 2 cold

- 1 recent

- 1 wildcard

- Avoid 3+ consecutive numbers

- Mix odd/even and high/low

Now apply similar logic to:

- **EuroMillions:** 5 main numbers + 2 Lucky Stars

- **Thunderball:** 5 numbers + 1 Thunderball

- **Set For Life:** 5 numbers + 1 Life Ball

- **HotPicks:** Choose the number of HotPicks and base them on the Lotto pool

- **10 Cold Numbers** (longest overdue)

- **5 Recent Repeats** (drawn 2–3 times in the last 10 draws)

- **5 Balanced Picks** (mid-frequency)

Use visual tools (charts, frequency tables, graphs) to build this list. Update it **every 15–20 draws**.

3. Game-Specific Sub-Pools: Tailoring the Master Set

Once your Master Pool is built, divide it into **Sub-Pools** for each game, matched to their draw ranges:

Game	Use From Master Pool
Thunderball	Only numbers 1–39
Set For Life	Use numbers 1–47
Lotto & HotPicks	Use 1–59 as needed
EuroMillions	Use 1–50

Each sub-pool should contain:

- 10–15 numbers from the Master Pool that fit that game's range

- A balanced mix of hot, cold, and mid-frequency numbers

- Specific patterns tailored to that game's ideal play (see Chapters 1–7)

Think of it like this:

- Your **Core Pool** is your orchestra.

- Each **Game Strategy** is an instrument section.

- Your **Tracking Sheet** is the conductor.

Now let's build your symphony.

2. The Master Pool: One Set of Numbers, Many Applications

The foundation of the unified system is your **Master Pool** — a carefully crafted group of numbers that feed into all your games.

▶ Step 1: Define the Boundaries

Your master pool must be broad enough to cover all number ranges:

- **EuroMillions:** 1–50

- **Lotto & HotPicks:** 1–59

- **Thunderball:** 1–39

- **Set For Life:** 1–47

☞ So your Master Pool should span from **1 to 59**, the maximum required.

But you won't use all 59 numbers. That would be too unfocused.

Instead, create a curated **Master Pool of 30–35 numbers**, selected from:

- **10 Hot Numbers** (top drawn over last 50–100 draws)

The systems you've built so far are strong on their own. Each game—whether it's Lotto, EuroMillions, HotPicks, Thunderball, or Set For Life—has its own logic, its own quirks, its own ideal strategy. But no lottery player truly evolves until they begin to think in *systems*—not isolated plays.

This chapter is the heart of strategic play.
This is where you graduate from lottery *player* to lottery *strategist*.

You'll learn how to:

• Unify your number pools for efficient coverage

• Manage multiple games from a single, central system

• Reduce duplication and cost

• Monitor performance across all games with minimal effort

• Build routines that scale with time, budget, and data

Let's step into the control room of your entire lottery operation.

1. Why a Unified System Matters

Many casual players spread themselves thin: they dabble in multiple games, using random numbers, half-baked hunches, or autopicks. There's no rhythm. No structure. No long-term tracking. Every draw is isolated.

A unified system changes all of that.

It lets you play *across multiple games* using one central pool of numbers, one logic system, and one tracking process.

It's Not Just Luck, It's Structure

Thunderball and Set For Life reward **structure** more than spectacle. They're not headline games, but they are **system-friendly, budget-friendly, and rich with opportunity**.

By treating them seriously — building core pools, rotating balls, and tracking your performance — you develop a system not just of play, but of *habit*. The kind that can turn even modest games into consistent wins.

In the next chapter, we'll explore how to bring everything together. You'll learn how to run a complete, unified system across multiple games — and how to adapt it week after week, no matter what the odds throw at you.

Mistake 2: Ignoring the Life Ball

Fix: Rotating Life Balls gives consistent access to mid-tier prizes.

Mistake 3: Copying other people's numbers

Fix: Every system should reflect *your data*, not someone else's.

Mistake 4: Overcommitting budget in one game

Fix: Diversify with systems that cover both games without exceeding your budget.

8. Summary: The Smart Player's Weekly Setup

Game	Focus	Entry Type	Notes
Thunderball	Frequency play	10 lines + 5 TBs	Best for regular small wins
Set For Life	Stability	5 lines + 4 LBs	Better odds, fixed prizes
Add-on	EuroMillions	1 line if budget allows	Adds variety and jackpot chance

Maintain a tracking spreadsheet:

- Wins per week

- Thunderball/Life Ball accuracy

- Number pool updates every 10 draws

- ROI per system

Total	15 lines	*£17.50*

Alternative: Add a £2 EuroMillions Lucky Dip if you want full UK coverage for under £20.

6. Strategic Stack Play: Combining the Two Games

Want to play both games using the same system logic? Here's how:

*   Use overlapping number pools (Thunderball 1–39, Set For Life 1–47)

*   Base your systems on the *lowest common range* (1–39)

*   Use a central core pool of 20 numbers to feed into both games

*   Adjust line counts to balance cost

*   Assign different frequency priorities to each game (e.g., hot for Thunderball, cold for Set For Life)

This makes your system **leaner and more efficient**, especially for multi-game players.

7. Pitfalls to Avoid

Mistake 1: Treating Thunderball like Lotto

Fix: Thunderball needs smaller pools and more frequent refresh cycles.

- Rotate these across your main lines

- Every 10 draws, review performance

This gives you **40% Life Ball coverage** per cycle with minimal cost.

Step 3: Entry Structures and Line Design

From your 20-number pool:

- Create 12–15 combinations of 5 numbers

- Avoid reusing the same line

- Mix hot/cold/mid numbers in each line

Sample structure for a 10-line entry:

- 3 lines with 3 hot, 2 cold

- 3 lines with 2 hot, 2 cold, 1 recent

- 4 lines with all mid/low frequency picks

Each line should carry one of the Life Balls from your chosen 4.

5. Budget-Conscious Weekly Play

Here's a **smart plan** for consistent weekly play:

Game	Lines	Cost
Thunderball	10 lines @ £1	£10
Set For Life	5 lines @ £1.50	£7.50

Key Difference:
Prizes are fixed, not jackpot-based. Odds are better than EuroMillions and Lotto.

4. System Play for Set For Life

Step 1: Pool of 20 Numbers

Build a pool using:

- 6 frequent numbers

- 6 cold numbers

- 4 mid-frequency

- 4 most recently drawn

This provides both history-driven and recency-driven logic.

Ensure:

- At least 9 numbers below 24, 11 above

- Odd/even balance

- Avoid three or more consecutive numbers

Step 2: Life Ball Strategies

With only 10 options and just 1 drawn, you can afford **targeted rotation**.

- Choose 4 Life Balls

    ◦ 2 hot, 1 cold, 1 wildcard

3. Set For Life: System Play for Stability

Set For Life offers something no other game in the UK does — **a fixed monthly income prize.**

► How it Works:

- Choose **5 numbers from 1 to 47**
- Choose **1 Life Ball from 1 to 10**

Draws take place **every Monday and Thursday**.

► Prizes:

Match	Prize	Odds (1 in...)
5 + Life Ball	£10,000/month for 30 years (£3.6M)	15,339,390
5	£10,000/month for 1 year (£120,000)	1,704,377
4 + Life Ball	£250	73,045
4	£50	8,116
3 + Life Ball	£30	1,782
3	£20	198
2 + Life Ball	£10	134
2	£5	15

- Drop any Thunderball that misses more than 20 draws without a hit

This ensures you're always **circulating fresh, viable picks**.

Step 3: Reduced Wheeling for 5-Number Lines

From your 15-number pool, generate **combinations of 5-number lines** using reduced wheeling logic. Here's a structure:

- From 15 numbers, create **10–15 combinations**, ensuring:

    ◦ No exact number line repeats

    ◦ Each line includes a mix of hot, cold, and mid picks

    ◦ Each line plays with a different Thunderball

This produces a diversified entry set without overextending your budget.

Step 4: Focused Frequency Play

Because Thunderball draws four times a week, **tracking frequency pays off fast**. After every 10 draws:

- Rebuild your core pool

- Reevaluate your Thunderball set

- Look for 3-number or 4-number hits and build new lines from those combos

This approach gives you a **responsive system** that adapts to changing number behaviours.

- 5 numbers from the most frequently drawn in the last 100 draws

- 5 numbers not drawn in the last 15 draws (cold)

- 5 numbers drawn exactly **once or twice** in the past 10 draws (mild-hot)

Ensure balance:

- At least 7 numbers below 20, and 8 above

- A near even split between odd/even

- Avoid consecutive number clusters (e.g., 11, 12, 13)

This creates a dynamic, balanced pool that covers **hot, cold, and overdue patterns**.

Step 2: Thunderball Pairing System

The Thunderball (1–14) has **only one number drawn** each game. Here's how to maximise your odds:

- Select **5 Thunderballs**:

    ◦ 2 from the hottest

    ◦ 2 from the coldest

    ◦ 1 wildcard (a mid-range frequency)

Now build **Thunderball pairings**:

- Play 3–5 main number lines with each Thunderball

- Track each Thunderball's performance every week

▸ Prizes (Fixed):

Match	Prize	Odds (1 in…)
5 + Thunderball	£500,000	8,060,598
5	£5,000	620,046
4 + Thunderball	£250	47,415
4	£100	3,648
3 + Thunderball	£20	1,437
3	£10	111
2 + Thunderball	£10	135
1 + Thunderball	£5	35
0 + Thunderball	£3	29

Key Insight: You only need the Thunderball to win a prize. That means *every* ticket you buy has a chance at something.

2. Systemising Thunderball: Turning Structure into Strategy

Step 1: Core Pool Selection (Main Numbers)

Build a **15-number core pool** using the following criteria:

Among the loud glamour of EuroMillions and Lotto, two games sit quietly in the background — underestimated, under-discussed, and **full of untapped potential**.

These games are **Thunderball** and **Set For Life**, and while they don't offer nine-figure jackpots, they *do* offer something far more interesting to the system player:

Fixed prizes. Better odds. And the opportunity for structured, repeatable wins.

In this chapter, we're going to explore how these two games work — not just how they're played, but how they can be *mastered*. We'll build systems designed for frequent payouts, long-term tracking, and strategic number coverage.

If EuroMillions is a long-range missile, then Thunderball and Set For Life are **precision tools** — and it's time to add them to your toolbox.

1. Thunderball: A Strategic Treasure

Thunderball is **the most underrated draw game** in the UK.

► How it Works:

- Choose **5 numbers from 1 to 39**

- Choose **1 Thunderball from 1 to 14**

Draws take place **four times a week** — Tuesday, Wednesday, Friday, and Saturday — making it ideal for regular system play.

Coming Up: Beyond the Big Names — Exploring Thunderball and Set For Life

Now that you've tackled the giants of UK and European lottery play, it's time to turn to the overlooked contenders.

In the next chapter, we explore **Thunderball and Set For Life** — games with better odds, fixed prizes, and unique structures. And for system players? They offer some of the most reliable ways to build regular wins.

Let's uncover what the public misses — and where strategic play shines brightest.

Fix: Rotate 5–6 different pairs over 10+ lines.

Mistake 2: Choosing birthday numbers

Fix: Use statistical ranges — 1–50, not 1–31.

Mistake 3: Too many lines with the same numbers

Fix: Build variety into your core set. Use wheels.

Mistake 4: Playing only when the jackpot is high

Fix: Play small and consistent, but scale smart during rollovers.

Final Template: EuroMillions System Play (Summary)

Weekly Budget: £15

- 10 lines from a 10-number core pool (balanced, odd/even, low/high)

- 5 rotating Lucky Star pairs across lines

- Optional: 5 lines of HotPicks Pick 3 from same pool (£5 total)

Track every draw

- Rotate core numbers every 5–10 draws

- Review Lucky Star performance

- Watch for common 3-number or 4-number hits

This system won't guarantee the jackpot — but it **increases your chance of consistent wins**, keeps you playing smarter, and allows you to play with **structure, purpose, and control.**

- Also, statistically, rollovers lead to unusual combinations — so variety pays

7. Second-Chance Systems: EuroMillions Hot Picks (UK Only)

Many UK players don't know this exists.

EuroMillions HotPicks is like Lotto HotPicks — **but based on the EuroMillions draw**. It uses **only the 5 main numbers** and lets you choose how many to match (Pick 1 to Pick 5).

It has better odds for certain prizes than the main game.

Combine your EuroMillions system with HotPicks by:

- Selecting Pick 3 or Pick 4 from your existing number sets

- Playing one or two lines on rollover weeks

- Using main numbers only (Lucky Stars not required)

This gives you:

- A second way to win on the same numbers

- Higher odds on fixed prizes

- A budget-friendly backup

8. Common Pitfalls — and How to Avoid Them

Mistake 1: Always using the same Lucky Stars

- Prize per line

- ROI per draw

This helps you:

- Spot overplayed numbers

- Identify successful star pairings

- Retire cold lines and introduce fresh ones

Make changes every **5–10 draws**. Think of it like tending a garden. Systems must evolve to stay sharp.

6. Jackpot Events — When to Play Aggressively

Jackpot over £100 million? Here's how to go big **without overspending**:

Add-on plan for rollover weeks:

- Add 5 new lines with completely **different Lucky Star pairings**

- Introduce **5 new main numbers** from recent draws (fresh set)

- Play for **2–3 rollover draws**, then revert

Why this works:

- Jackpot rollovers increase player volume — meaning **more winners will share**

- But if you win lower tiers, they often pay more due to boosted prize funds

4. Budget-Conscious Tiered Play

You don't need to spend hundreds to run a smart EuroMillions system. Let's build a system on **a £15 weekly budget**:

Component	Entries	Cost
Main System	10 lines w/ mixed Lucky Stars	£10
Lucky Star Focus	5 lines with fixed 5-number set & rotating stars	£5

What this gives you:

- Full coverage of your 10-number core

- Rotating Lucky Star match potential

- Systematic visibility into what's working

5. Tracking and Adjustment

Here's where many system players fail: **they don't adapt**.

Use a simple spreadsheet with:

- Draw date

- Your lines

- Winning numbers

- Matches per line

- Choose 10 main numbers

- Create **15 lines**, each containing a unique mix of 5 numbers

- Ensure no line repeats a full 5-number set

- Avoid placing all 5 low or high numbers in any single line

Why this works:
This approach **covers all combinations of your 10 numbers,** without exploding your line count. If 3 or more of your core 10 appear in a draw, you have a high chance of catching a tiered prize.

Step 3: Rotate Lucky Stars Efficiently

The Lucky Star field is only **12 numbers**, and only **2 are drawn**.

This is where many players go wrong — they over-randomise.

Here's the fix:

1. Identify the **top 5 most frequently drawn Lucky Stars** in the past 50 draws

2. Select **3 Lucky Stars** from this group

3. Pick **2 cold Lucky Stars** (not drawn in 15+ draws)

Then:

- Create **6 pairings** using these 5 numbers (e.g., 2 & 3, 2 & 10, etc.)

- Apply these pairs across your 15 main number lines

💡 **Important:** Don't use the same Lucky Star pair in every line. It limits your coverage. Use **at least 5–6 different pairings** across your ticket set.

3. Building a EuroMillions System from the Ground Up

Let's now construct a repeatable, affordable, and intelligent way to play EuroMillions regularly.

Step 1: Build a Balanced Number Pool

From the 1–50 main number range, select **15 to 20 core numbers**. Use these principles:

- Include **5 numbers** from the top 10 most frequently drawn (past 100 draws)

- Include **5 numbers** that have **not appeared in the last 10–15 draws**

- Ensure **at least 7 low numbers (1–25)** and **8–10 high numbers (26–50)**

- Use a 50/50 split of **odd and even numbers**

These principles ensure **coverage of statistical tendencies**, not just random picks.

💡 **Pro Tip:** Use a spreadsheet to log draw results and build frequency charts. Free tools exist online for this purpose.

Step 2: Construct Main Number Lines Using Wheel Design

From your pool of 15–20 numbers, we'll use a **reduced wheeling system**.

You don't need to cover every combination. Instead:

Minimum jackpot: £14 million
Max jackpot cap: ~£200 million (rolls over until capped)

So, what does this mean for the system player?

It means that *your odds of winning the jackpot are slim* — but your odds of winning **something** are not. And that's the foothold we'll use.

2. Why Most EuroMillions Players Are Set Up to Fail

The typical EuroMillions player picks one or two lines, maybe Quick Picks, and crosses their fingers.

Here's the problem:

- Random Quick Picks don't take probability into account

- There's no coverage planning (Lucky Star duplication, number balance)

- There's no tracking of draw patterns or hot/cold behaviour

- There's no system structure — just hope

This is fine for occasional players. But for someone who wants **frequent smaller wins with a chance at higher-tier prizes**, this approach simply doesn't hold up.

That's where systems come in.

That's **7 numbers per ticket**. The main numbers are drawn from a different pool than the Lucky Stars, so it's not possible to double-pick (e.g., a Lucky Star cannot also be a main number).

▶ Prize Tiers

There are **13 prize tiers**, with winnings starting at matching **2 main numbers**:

Match	Approximate Prize	Odds (1 in...)
5 + 2	Jackpot (variable)	139,838,160
5 + 1	~£130,000+	6,991,908
5 + 0	~£13,000	3,107,515
4 + 2	~£850	621,503
4 + 1	~£80	31,076
3 + 2	~£50	14,126
4 + 0	~£35	13,812
2 + 2	~£10	986
3 + 1	~£8	707
3 + 0	~£6	314
1 + 2	~£6	188
2 + 1	~£4.50	50
2 + 0	~£2.50	22

When the jackpot grows into the hundreds of millions, the excitement becomes almost gravitational. **EuroMillions isn't just a lottery — it's an event.** It unites players across nine European countries with the promise of changing lives in an instant.

But that excitement also masks a sobering truth:

The odds are enormous. The field is crowded. And most players don't stand a chance.

In this chapter, we'll move beyond the spectacle and look beneath the surface of EuroMillions. We'll study its structure, dissect the probabilities, and — most importantly — **build systems that increase your practical chances of winning something, not just anything.**

This isn't about blind luck. This is about stacking the odds, line by line.

1. Understanding EuroMillions: Structure and Odds

Before you can build an effective system, you must know the landscape.

▶ Game Format

- **Choose 5 main numbers from 1–50**

- **Choose 2 Lucky Stars from 1–12**

Coming Up: EuroMillions Under the Microscope — When Odds Go Big, So Must Your System

Now that you've mastered the precision approach of Lotto HotPicks, we're going wide again. EuroMillions brings bigger pools, bigger prizes — and far more complexity. But with the right strategic toolkit, you'll be equipped to navigate it like a pro.

Let's explore what happens when the jackpot goes continental.

- Only play Pick 5 when jackpot rollover occurs (higher reward = higher risk tolerance)

5. The Discipline of Small Wins

Most players chase £350,000 with a single Pick 5 ticket and no plan.

System players build:

- A weekly structure

- Predictable costs

- Frequent small wins

- A self-funding strategy

Hitting Pick 2 once every 20 draws can fund dozens of future lines. Hitting Pick 3 once every 40 can give a major bump. Everything else is upside.

Final System Template

Weekly Budget: £10

- Pick 2: 4 lines = £4

- Pick 3: 4 lines = £4

- Pick 4 or Pick 5: 2 lines (alternate weekly) = £2

- Use a **12-number rotating pool**

- Change 3–4 numbers every 5 draws

- Track performance per line

- Game type (Pick 2, 3, 4, 5)

- Your chosen numbers

- Winning numbers

- Matches

- Profit/loss

Over time, you'll start seeing patterns:

- Which pairings are recurring

- Which pick types yield ROI

- When to rotate numbers out

4. When to Play — Timing is a System Too

Sometimes, **not playing** is the best move.

System players often skip draws intentionally when:

- Multiple "cold" numbers haven't appeared for 15+ draws (high volatility)

- A recent draw had **multiple hot numbers** (reversal often follows)

- The jackpot has just reset (lower incentive, higher duplication)

Conversely, smart players:

- Increase Pick 3/4 lines after 2–3 low-frequency draws

- Play hot triplets after 2 of 3 just appeared in recent draws

- At least 4 numbers that haven't hit in 10+ draws

- 50/50 balance of low/high (1–29 / 30–59)

- 3–5 odd numbers

Update this pool every 5–7 draws.

Step 2: Use Historical Pairs and Triplets

Numbers often appear together. Use this to your advantage.

Example:
If 14 and 36 have been drawn together 4 times in 20 draws, they're **a viable Pick 2**.

Likewise, if 12, 27, and 42 have appeared in any 3 draws together, they become a **Pick 3 anchor set**.

✅ Use online HotPicks tools or check past results manually.

Step 3: Create Targeted Combinations

From your 10–12-number pool:

- Generate 5–10 lines of 2–3-number combinations

- Ensure **no duplicated combinations** across tickets

- Use a spreadsheet or play slip app to avoid overlap

This gives you **maximum coverage** across your pool without wasting entries.

Step 4: Track Your Results Religiously

Log:

- Date of draw

Now we enter big money territory.

- Pick 4: £13,000

- Pick 5: £350,000

- But: no partial wins

- And much harder odds

So why include them?

Because with the right system, these become **affordable side-channels** for skilled players.

Let's say you're already playing Lotto. You've got a 12-number pool. Out of those, you generate:

- 4 lines of 4-number picks

- 2 lines of 5-number picks

You don't play them *every week*. You play them **only after specific draw conditions** are met (see Section 6).

In these high-payout picks, the goal isn't frequency — it's **timing**.

3. Designing a HotPicks System

Here's a step-by-step framework for building your own Lotto HotPicks system.

Step 1: Build Your Core Number Pool

Start with 10–12 numbers, selected using:

- Recent frequency (last 20 draws)

This is where Lotto HotPicks becomes a serious contender.

To win:

- You must correctly identify **3 of the 6 drawn numbers**

- And have **all three in your selection**

Many players try this casually — but those who use it as part of a structured system often find it more profitable than standard Lotto.

Let's break it down:

Say you create a **10-number pool** of historically active numbers. From this, you generate 10 three-number combinations using **balanced pairing**:

- Mix low/high

- Mix odd/even

- Use at least one number from the last 5 draws

If even one of those lines lands all three numbers — you win **£800 on a £1 line**.

That's an 80x return — better than Lotto's 5-number match in many cases.

✅ Use Pick 3 for:

- Focused wheeling (e.g. 10 lines from a 10-number pool)

- Testing historical triplet frequency

- Risk/reward balancing

▶ Pick 4 & Pick 5 — The High-Risk Arsenal

▶ Pick 2 — Consistency Mode

- Odds: 1 in 1,032

- Prize: £60

Pick 2 is a hidden gem. The odds are **far better than matching 3 on Lotto**, and the prize is more than double a traditional £30 match.

This makes it ideal for:

- Small bankroll players

- Daily systems

- Long-term consistent strategy

Let's say you play Pick 2 with the same two-number combinations over 50 draws. If you're using **high-frequency pairs** (more on this later), your chances of hitting go up — not because of probability, but because of *targeted design*.

✅ Strategy:

- Choose 5–7 pairs of numbers that appear together historically

- Track results across 10–20 draws

- Rotate only if the pair hasn't hit in 20 draws

☐ **Tip:** Use Hot Number Pairs — see Section 4.

▶ Pick 3 — The Strike Zone

- Odds: 1 in 3,386

- Prize: £800

This isn't just theory — data from the National Lottery reveals that HotPicks players tend to:

- Play fewer lines

- Spend less overall

- But earn **more in mid-tier prizes** when played strategically

In short: HotPicks players play tighter and smarter. That's your edge.

2. Choosing the Right Pick Strategy

Not all pick types are created equal. Let's walk through each.

► Pick 1 — The Training Ground

- Odds: 1 in 59

- Prize: £6

This is simple. Choose a single number, hope it appears.
But it's not profitable. You'd need to win **every 6th time** just to break even.

✅ Use this mode to:

- Practice number prediction

- Track "hot" numbers in current circulation

- Test your instincts

Not ideal for serious returns — but useful as a warm-up tool.

Pick 5	5	£350,000	1 in 834,398

Cost per play: £1 (regardless of pick type)

The key distinction? **You must match *all* your numbers to win.** There are no partial prizes. If you choose to Pick 4 and only three of your numbers appear, you win nothing.

So why play it at all?

Because when played strategically, HotPicks offers **better odds for certain prize tiers than Lotto itself** — especially in Pick 3 and Pick 4. It also rewards focused play styles that many Lotto players avoid.

Let's explore how.

1. The Psychology of Precision

The typical lottery player is conditioned to think in scatter — to choose 6 numbers, cross their fingers, and hope for overlap.

HotPicks rewires that instinct.

It forces the question:

"Which numbers do I *truly* believe will be drawn?"

And that leads to smarter habits:

- Players research frequency data

- They study number balance

- They engage with previous draw patterns

- They treat their picks more seriously

If Lotto is the general's battlefield, **Lotto HotPicks** is the sniper's perch.

It's not about broad coverage. It's not about hoping that three of your numbers land somewhere in the draw. **It's about precision. Accuracy. Hitting your mark.** And when you do, the rewards can be substantial — far greater than traditional Lotto for the same price.

In this chapter, we'll unpack exactly how Lotto HotPicks works, why most players ignore its potential, and how a few focused systems can turn this specialist game into a **secret weapon** in your lottery strategy arsenal.

What Is Lotto HotPicks?

Lotto HotPicks is based on the same draw as the UK National Lottery's main Lotto game (6/59 format), but instead of playing for matched sets across a 6-number ticket, **you choose how many numbers you want to play — and how many of them you aim to match**.

Here's how it breaks down:

Game Type	Pick	Prize (if all matched)	Odds of Winning
Pick 1	1	£6	1 in 59
Pick 2	2	£60	1 in 1,032
Pick 3	3	£800	1 in 3,386
Pick 4	4	£13,000	1 in 30,342

It's controlled. It's strategic. It's sustainable.

And best of all — **it's entirely within your control.**

Coming Up: Mastering Lotto HotPicks — When Precision Pays Off

Now that you've built your first system, we're ready for something a little more specialised. In the next chapter, we'll explore **Lotto HotPicks** — a game that rewards accuracy, not coverage. Fewer numbers, higher rewards, and a completely different mindset.

You're about to learn the art of surgical strikes.

Most players obsess over matching 6.
System players aim to match **3s, 4s, and 5s — repeatedly**.

Why?

Because:

- Matching 3 wins your money back (£30)

- Matching 4 earns a **profit**

- Matching 5 can return **hundreds or thousands**

- These hits are more common and more **statistically reachable** when wheeling smartly

Over time, frequent small wins can fund more plays — giving you a **longer runway** for that rare big hit.

Summary: Your First System, in Practice

Here's what a full system-based Lotto approach looks like for a modest player:

- **Budget:** £10/week (5 lines)

- **Number Pool:** 12 carefully selected numbers with a balance of high/low, odd/even

- **Wheel:** 5-line abbreviated system

- **Tracking:** Manual or spreadsheet-based log

- **Rotation:** Every 4–6 weeks, change 3–4 numbers in the pool

- **Mindset:** Targeting 3–5 number matches, not jackpot miracles

If your budget is £10 per week, focus on **5 smart lines**, not 10 random ones.

Tracking

Keep a **Lotto Play Log**:

- Date

- Draw numbers

- Your selections

- Wins/losses

- Number matches

Over time, this helps you:

- Spot frequently appearing numbers in your own pool

- Rotate out stale numbers

- Adjust wheeling strategy

Ticket Rotation

Don't play the exact same numbers forever. Systems aren't set in stone — they're **alive**. Rotate part of your number pool every 10–12 draws. Keep the frequent flyers, replace the sleepers.

Step 4: Don't Chase the Jackpot — Chase Frequency

This is the final shift in mindset:

A **smaller, manageable subset** of all possible combinations. You cover fewer lines, but with intelligent overlap — meaning if several of your chosen numbers hit, you still win.

Example:
Let's say you choose a 12-number pool:
3, 7, 14, 21, 25, 31, 36, 42, 45, 50, 54, 58

Using a 10-line abbreviated wheel, you might get combinations like:

- 3, 7, 14, 25, 36, 42

- 14, 21, 25, 36, 45, 50

- 3, 21, 31, 36, 42, 58

- …and 7 more

Now, if **any 5 or 6 numbers** from your pool are drawn, you are more likely to match 3 or more on at least one line — potentially winning **multiple prize tiers** in one draw.

Abbreviated wheels strike a balance between cost and coverage. Even with a small budget, they can **significantly increase your odds** of hitting a lower-tier prize — which is where consistent returns are found.

Step 3: Add Game Sense

This is where your decisions become personal — where system meets psychology.

Budget Discipline

Pick a number of lines you can afford to play consistently, week after week. Consistency is key. One-off bursts rarely produce results.

- Numbers that haven't appeared in the last 30 draws (known as **sleepers**)

- Numbers that appear frequently over a long period (known as **frequent flyers**)

Include a few of each in your pool — this creates **dynamic coverage**.

d. Eliminate Common Patterns

Avoid:

- Consecutive strings (e.g., 34, 35, 36)

- Same-ending digits (e.g., 7, 17, 27, 37)

- All single digits or all numbers under 31

These look neat, but they're **too popular**.

Step 2: Wheel Your Numbers

A **wheeling system** is a structured way of creating multiple tickets from your chosen number pool — ensuring every combination covers different subsets without repeating the same lines.

There are two main types of wheeling:

✅ Full Wheeling

Every possible 6-number combination from your selected pool. If you choose 12 numbers, that's **924 combinations** — too expensive for most players.

✅ Abbreviated Wheeling

Step 1: Build a Smarter Number Pool

The full Lotto pool contains numbers from 1 to 59 — but playing all 59 in one system is too costly and inefficient. A better way is to **build a pool of 12–20 numbers** from which you'll generate multiple combinations.

Here's how to construct your pool with purpose:

a. Include a Mix of Low and High Numbers

Split the 59-number field in half:

- Low: 1–29

- High: 30–59

A common error is playing only low numbers (especially birthdates). But balanced tickets — e.g. 3 numbers below 30, 3 above — occur **more frequently** in winning combinations.

✓ Rule: Always include at least 2 high numbers over 30 in your pool.

b. Avoid All-Even or All-Odd

Draws that are all even or all odd are **extremely rare**. Most winning combinations contain a mixture.

✓ Rule: Aim for 2–4 even numbers per line — not all 6. Do the same with odds.

c. Use Historical Frequency Wisely

While past results don't predict future draws, they can reveal **patterns of underuse and overuse**.

Find:

- Every Wednesday and Saturday, **six main numbers** are drawn, along with a **Bonus Ball** (drawn from the same pool but used only for certain prize levels)

- To win the jackpot, your six numbers must **match all six drawn numbers**

- Prize tiers exist for 3, 4, 5, and 5 + Bonus Ball matches, with 2 numbers earning a free Lucky Dip

Cost per play: £2
Top prize: Rollover jackpot (starts around £2 million and can climb)
Biggest problem: Odds of jackpot = 1 in 45 million

If this sounds like terrible value, that's because it is — *unless* you play it differently.

Why Quick Picks Aren't Enough

Quick Picks (Lucky Dips) are a system of their own — a system of **pure randomness**. Every ticket is computer-generated, and while this avoids common human biases, it also removes **intentionality**. You're giving up all control.

More importantly, you're giving up the opportunity to avoid **duplicate selections** — combinations that are statistically more likely to appear on other players' tickets.

In 2016, the National Lottery revealed that over **10,000 players** had chosen the combination 1, 2, 3, 4, 5, 6 at one time or another. If that combination ever hit, each winner would receive a **tiny fraction of the jackpot**.

System players don't leave that kind of thing to chance. They take the wheel.

The UK Lotto is the flagship game of the National Lottery — it's the one most players know, the one that commands the headlines, and the one most commonly misunderstood. With two draws per week and a minimum jackpot in the millions, Lotto attracts a vast pool of players. But with a 1 in 45,057,474 chance of winning the jackpot, it's also where most people quietly burn through money.

So why focus on Lotto at all?

Because it provides a perfect foundation for **system play**. It offers structure, repetition, and just enough numerical room to apply intelligent design. It's where bad habits flourish — but also where **strategic habits shine**.

This chapter will take you step-by-step through the logic of smarter Lotto play:

- How to break the 6/59 matrix into usable chunks

- How to avoid common traps

- How to build number pools

- How to use balance, distribution, and wheeling to play wider and smarter

- How to do more with less

The Fundamentals: What is 6/59 Lotto?

Let's start with the mechanics.

- You select **six numbers** from a pool of numbers ranging from **1 to 59**

- How to **track, analyse, and improve** your systems over time

In a game where randomness is guaranteed, **discipline and strategy are your tools**. And almost no one is using them.

So Why Do People Keep Playing?

Because hope is powerful.

Because the idea of changing your life with one ticket is compelling.

And because most people *want* the fantasy more than they want a method. But you're different. If you've made it this far, you're not here for fantasy — you're here for structure, insight, and action.

You're here to give yourself the **best possible version of luck**.

Coming Up: Lotto Logic — Building Smarter Tickets for the 6/59 Draw

Now that you know what *not* to do, we're ready to move into the heart of the system.

In the next chapter, we'll break down the UK's flagship game — **Lotto** — and show you how to use number pools, balance, and simple wheeling methods to transform six numbers into a disciplined approach.

Let's build your first system.

6. They Chase Losses

Let's say you've played the same 6 numbers every week for ten years. You've spent over £1,000 on tickets, and won maybe £60 total. You feel committed. You can't stop now — what if *next week* is the week?

This is the **gambler's trap**: the belief that the longer you've played, the closer you are to a win. But lotteries **don't work like that**. Every draw is independent. Your numbers are no "closer" now than they were the day you chose them.

Smart players know when to **change tactics**, take breaks, or reset. Systems are designed to be tested, adapted, and — when necessary — retired.

7. They Don't Use Systems At All

The vast majority of players go in blind. They don't know what a number wheel is. They've never heard of a pool strategy. They've never adjusted a ticket based on frequency, balance, or historical draws.

This gives you an advantage.

By the time you've finished this book, you'll know:

- How to create **abbreviated wheeling systems**

- How to build **strategic number pools**

- How to choose tickets that **reduce the odds of splitting a prize**

- How to match your budget to the right game and play style

But tracking is one of the easiest habits to adopt. It helps you:

- Avoid repeating poor combinations

- Identify patterns in your own behaviour

- Spot overlaps across games

- Fine-tune your systems over time

In Chapter 14, we'll include a **Lottery Logbook** system you can use to record every ticket, win, and pattern you play — helping you become a more reflective, more consistent player.

5. They Don't Understand Prize Splitting

Many players think that if they win, the prize is theirs — simple as that.

But **prize splitting** is real, and it's brutal.

In Lotto and EuroMillions, the jackpot is divided equally among all winners. If you share a combination with hundreds of others, you may only get a fraction of what you'd expected.

That's why system players deliberately:

- Avoid common number patterns

- Mix high and low numbers

- Use less popular games or draws

- Play combinations that are unique and unappealing to most people

Sometimes the **ugliest tickets** are the smartest ones. No birthdays. No sequences. Just quiet statistical edge.

Your goal isn't just to pick winning numbers. It's to pick **unique winning numbers** — combinations that **other people are unlikely to choose**. That alone gives your win a bigger impact if it happens.

3. They Rely on Emotional Picks

- Birthdays

- Anniversaries

- House numbers

- "Lucky" numbers from childhood

- Sequences they've dreamt about

These are emotionally satisfying — but often strategically poor. Why?

Birthdays restrict your number range. No one is born on the 32nd of anything, so birthday players tend to pick numbers between 1 and 31. But Lotto numbers go up to 59. That means higher numbers are statistically **underused** — and therefore more likely to result in a **solo win** if drawn.

Playing emotionally keeps you in a **small, crowded pool**. Playing systematically lets you **swim alone**.

4. They Don't Track What They Play

Ask most players what numbers they played last month, or whether they've ever repeated combinations accidentally, and you'll get a blank look. Most players forget — or worse, throw tickets away without checking them properly.

thunderstorm holding a metal rod — *once a week* — and hoping lightning will strike you.

But does that mean you shouldn't play? Not at all. It simply means that **your expectations should match the math**. And it also means we need to **reframe the goal**.

Most lottery success stories didn't begin with someone aiming for the jackpot. They began with someone playing **consistently, intelligently, and strategically** — often with the aim of winning *smaller prizes more often*, rather than everything at once.

2. They Choose Predictable Patterns

Take a moment to think about these combinations:

- 1, 2, 3, 4, 5, 6

- 7, 14, 21, 28, 35, 42

- 5, 10, 15, 20, 25, 30

- 3, 13, 23, 33, 43, 49

These are **not random picks**. They're highly structured, and because of that, **thousands of players use them**.

If one of these combinations ever won, you'd be sharing the jackpot with *potentially tens of thousands* of people — reducing your prize to a sliver of what it could have been.

In 1995, the Lotto numbers drawn were 7, 17, 23, 32, 38, 42. It wasn't a particularly special sequence — but **133 people** had chosen it. Each winner walked away with just over **£120,000**, instead of the several millions a solo winner would expect.

Ask a typical player how they choose their lottery numbers, and you'll usually hear one of three answers:

"They're my lucky numbers."
"It's my birthday, my partner's, and the kids'."
"I just go with a Lucky Dip — it's all random anyway."

These answers aren't wrong — but they reveal something critical: **most people play the lottery emotionally, not strategically**.

They play the way they've always played, with no real reflection on how that affects their chances. They stick to the same routines. They hope for a miracle. But here's the truth: **hope is not a system**.

If you want to play differently — and win differently — you have to first understand why most players lose.

1. They Underestimate the Odds

The first and most common reason players lose is simple: they don't realise just *how unlikely* a jackpot actually is.

Let's break it down:

- The odds of winning the **Lotto jackpot** are 1 in **45 million**

- The odds of being **struck by lightning in the UK** are around 1 in **1.2 million**

- The odds of finding a **four-leaf clover** on your first try? About 1 in **10,000**

So if you're playing Lotto every week, hoping to win the jackpot with a single line, you're essentially stepping outside during a

- **Lotto** rewards jackpot hunters with deep pockets or syndicate backing.

- **HotPicks** suits players with focused number-picking skills.

- **Thunderball** offers strong value for those targeting smaller, fixed wins.

- **Set For Life** is ideal for players looking for long-term financial comfort rather than windfalls.

- **EuroMillions** is a high-risk, high-reward game — best played strategically or as a group.

By knowing how each works, you can choose games that match your goals, budget, and preferred style of play.

Coming Next: Why Most Players Lose

In the next chapter, we'll look at the behaviours and habits that lead to poor lottery outcomes — and how you can avoid them. From overused number patterns to emotional decision-making, we'll uncover the subtle ways in which luck is often misused.

And from there? We'll start building systems — one game at a time.

- Small prizes can be under £5; jackpots reach astronomical levels

- UK-specific raffles and "Millionaire Maker" draw often included

Complexity: Higher than other games, but offers **syndicate potential** due to scale.

Comparing the Odds at a Glance

Game	Top Prize	Odds of Winning Jackpot
Lotto	Variable (rollover)	1 in 45,057,474
Lotto HotPicks	£350,000 (Pick 5)	1 in 1,906,884
Thunderball	£500,000	1 in 8,060,598
Set For Life	£10k/month x 30 yrs	1 in 15,339,390
EuroMillions	£14m to £180m+	1 in 139,838,160

You'll notice that Lotto has far worse odds than Thunderball — yet both cost the same. This is where **strategy begins**: understanding where your money has the best chance of returning value.

Why Game Choice Matters

Each game appeals to a different kind of player:

- Fixed jackpot (doesn't roll over)

- Better overall odds (1 in 13 of any win)

- You can win the top prize even if someone else also wins — no splits

4. Set For Life

Draw Days: Monday & Thursday
Format: Pick 5 numbers from 1–47 and 1 "Life Ball" from 1–10
Top Prize: £10,000/month for 30 years
Odds of Winning Top Prize: 1 in 15,339,390

Other Prizes:

- £10,000/month for 1 year (Match 5)

- £250 (Match 4 + Life Ball)

- Smaller prizes down to £5

Notable Feature: Prize is paid in **monthly instalments**, not a lump sum.

5. EuroMillions

Draw Days: Tuesday & Friday
Format: Pick 5 numbers from 1–50 and 2 Lucky Stars from 1–12
Jackpot: Starts at approx. £14 million, can exceed £180 million
Odds of Winning Jackpot: 1 in 139,838,160

Prize Tiers:

- 13 prize levels

Prize Structure:

- Match 6: Jackpot (odds 1 in 45,057,474)

- Match 5 + Bonus Ball: Approx. £1 million

- Match 5: £1,750

- Match 4: £140

- Match 3: £30

- Match 2: Free Lotto Lucky Dip

Key Feature: No partial matches (e.g. 3 + Bonus) except for 5 + Bonus.

2. Lotto HotPicks

Draw Days: Same draw as Lotto
Format: Pick 1 to 5 numbers from the same 6 drawn in Lotto
Jackpot (Pick 5): £350,000

Key Difference: You must match **all** the numbers you select — no partial wins. Odds improve with fewer numbers picked, and payout increases with higher picks.

3. Thunderball

Draw Days: Tuesday, Wednesday, Friday & Saturday
Format: Pick 5 numbers from 1–39 and 1 Thunderball from 1–14
Top Prize: £500,000
Odds of Winning Top Prize: 1 in 8,060,598

Why It's Unique:

Before we can apply systems, we need to understand the terrain. Every game offered by The National Lottery follows a distinct structure, with specific odds, prize tiers, and draw mechanics. This chapter will guide you through each game — not just in terms of how it's played, but in terms of how it's **strategically different**.

The Structure of the UK Lottery System

The UK National Lottery is run by **Allwyn Entertainment**, under license from the government. It offers several games, each with different draw days, prize models, and odds. These games fall into two main categories:

1. **Main Draw Games** – where players select numbers from a range and await a scheduled draw.

2. **Instant Win & Scratchcards** – which are not covered in this book, as they are not system-based and offer limited strategic depth.

We'll focus exclusively on **draw-based games**, where your ability to apply a system can influence your odds of success.

Game Overview: The Core Line-Up

1. Lotto

Draw Days: Wednesday & Saturday
Format: Pick 6 numbers from 1 to 59
Jackpot: Variable, rolls over up to a capped limit

- Systems you can apply to improve your chances

- Common pitfalls to avoid

Whether you play casually or regularly, whether you favour single lines or syndicates, this book is designed to sharpen your thinking and elevate your game.

The Mindset of a System Player

Luck plays a role in every draw. But systems are about **discipline**, not desperation. You don't chase a win. You build a method, you follow it consistently, and you learn from the results.

In short, this book will teach you how to **play like a strategist**, not a dreamer. Because luck — while never guaranteed — tends to show up more often for those who prepare.

Ready to explore what's possible when you stop guessing and start playing smart? Let's begin.

- Chooses birthdates, anniversaries, or "lucky" numbers

- Plays a quick pick and hopes for the best

These habits are convenient — but not strategic. They often lead to **limited number ranges**, poor coverage, and duplicate combinations used by thousands of others. Even if those numbers do win, the prize is diluted.

A system player takes a different approach. They study. They test. They track. And over time, they give themselves **a fighting chance at consistent results**.

The Games We'll Explore

Throughout this book, we'll cover the core games offered by The National Lottery in the UK:

- **Lotto (6/59):** The classic game, drawn every Wednesday and Saturday.

- **Lotto HotPicks:** A high-stakes twist on Lotto that rewards precision.

- **Thunderball:** With a top prize of £500,000 and better odds than Lotto.

- **Set For Life:** A unique game offering £10,000 per month for 30 years.

- **EuroMillions:** The transnational behemoth with massive jackpots and complex odds.

For each, you'll learn:

- How the game works (in detail)

- What the odds look like at each prize level

Whether it's Lotto, HotPicks, EuroMillions, Thunderball, or Set For Life, the National Lottery offers more than just a jackpot chase. With the right system — and the right mindset — you can tilt the odds slightly more in your favour. Not to break the system, but to **play it more intelligently**.

What Makes a "System"?

A system, as used in this book, is any repeatable structure that helps you:

- Choose numbers in a strategic way

- Cover a wider or smarter set of combinations

- Play within a set budget

- Track and adjust your play over time

Some systems use **number wheeling**, where you create multiple tickets from a small pool of chosen numbers. Others focus on **balanced ticket design**, avoiding overly common combinations that result in split prizes. Some systems are built around **data tracking**, watching which numbers appear most frequently, and which are long overdue.

None of these systems change the draw. But they change **how you engage** with it.

Why Most Players Lose

The typical lottery player does one of the following:

- Picks the same six numbers every week

Every week, millions of people across the UK enter their numbers into the same ritual — a hopeful sequence of digits inked onto a ticket or tapped into a phone screen. For some, it's tradition. For others, it's entertainment. And for a smaller group still, it's a calculated effort to find **an edge in a game of chance**.

This book is for that last group.

But let's be clear from the start: there is no secret formula that guarantees a jackpot. There's no hack, no hidden code, no government algorithm waiting to be reverse-engineered. The National Lottery games are **built on randomness**, and the odds — as advertised — are steep.

So why write a book about systems? Why explore patterns, strategies, and approaches if the numbers are truly random?

Because even in a random environment, **how you play can make a meaningful difference**.

The Purpose of This Book

This book isn't about false hope or superstition. It's about understanding the structure of lottery games and exploring **smart, mathematically grounded ways** to:

- Increase your chances of **winning smaller prizes more often**

- **Maximise the value** of every pound you spend

- **Reduce the risk** of sharing your prize with thousands of other winners

- Play with **discipline, consistency, and purpose**

If you've ever felt the thrill of checking your numbers —
only to end the night with a shrug —
you're not alone.

Most people play the lottery the same way: quick picks, birth dates, favourite numbers, or gut feelings. It's exciting. It's casual. But over time, it's also unreliable.

This book isn't about magic formulas. It's not a guarantee of riches. It's a guide to *playing with intention* — built specifically for the games of the UK's National Lottery.

Inside, you'll learn how to build smart number pools, spot real patterns, and apply strategies that give your lines the best possible statistical footing. You'll design systems tailored to your style, your budget, and your goals — whether you're chasing big jackpots, steady wins, or long-term refinement.

Most of all, you'll start to feel **in control**. Because luck, contrary to popular belief, can be cultivated — if you know how to prepare for it.

Table of Contents

Epigraph

"Luck is what happens when preparation meets opportunity."
— Seneca

Dedication

For the curious, the optimists, and the quietly determined —
those who look at odds and see possibilities.

System Luck:
Smarter with the National Lottery

How to Increase Your Odds, Build Strategic Lines, and Play the Long Game

By Daniel W. Hartley